To David.
On his

S.

Hymns
Ancient & Modern
New Standard

Hymns
Ancient & Modern
New Standard

Melody Edition

HYMNS ANCIENT & MODERN LIMITED

MELODY EDITION

ISBN 0 907547 38 9

First published October 1983
Second impression November 1983
Third impression February 1984
Fourth impression October 1984

Filmset by Eta Services (Typesetters) Ltd, Beccles, Suffolk
Printed and Bound in Great Britain by
William Clowes Ltd, Beccles and London

PREFACE

Christians have in their hearts a song, and hymns have been vehicles of the instinct for praise and worship by the congregation. They belong by nature to the people of God, and more to the laity in the nave than to the clerks in the choir. At times ecclesiastical authority has been anxious about the words and the popular doctrines they may convey. Musical authority has been anxious that among the melodies enjoyed by congregations some have not been the noblest to offer to either God or man. Yet not every great Christian poem makes a good hymn, and not every chorale by J. S. Bach can be safely enjoyed by a lay congregation. A good hymn-book is necessarily an endeavour in high democracy. The lifetime of a hymn is one which congregations decide by an unconscious process. But a fine melody must have shape, and a good hymn's rhythm need not invariably be four square to be taken to heart.

Hymns Ancient and Modern was first published, in a full music edition, in 1861, and rapidly achieved a success which astonished its first editors. The book has received various supplements and new editions since that time. To the first revision of 1875 a supplement was added in 1889. A new edition of 1904 did not oust the earlier revision, which in 1916 was enlarged with a second supplement. The Standard edition of 1922 did better but has been replaced since 1950 by the far-reaching revision in the now generally used *Hymns Ancient and Modern Revised.* This 1950 edition introduced twentieth century matter in both words and music, and cut out many hymns which had not been used much or were losing favour. In both words and music the 1950 revision remains a strong hymnbook. Nevertheless after three more decades there is again need for reappraisal.

Two supplements to the 1950 book have appeared: *100 Hymns for Today* (1969) and *More Hymns for Today* (1980). Both books have been widely used in English-speaking churches. They make available a selection of the modern hymns written during the past thirty years, during which there has been a lively flourishing of the art of hymn-writing. These supplements have also tried to fill gaps in *Ancient and Modern Revised.*

The classical hymns that constitute the core of *Hymns Ancient and Modern* and its Supplements are presented in this volume. When the first edition of 1861 appeared, a few critics disliked the modern part of that book; but some of the best hymns which were modern in 1861 have achieved a permanent position, and they are here now. But the 1950 volume retained many hymns that have been shown, by a careful survey, to be used today little or not at all. These are omitted. Some tunes which are seldom used have been replaced, and some alternatives have been added. A few revisions in the words and music are made, but so far as possible the present book is designed to be usable side by side with the 1950 revision. Hence each hymn has not only its number in the natural sequence of this book, but also a bracketed number which is that in

Preface

Hymns Ancient and Modern Revised and its Supplements. The music of several hymns has been printed in a lower key to facilitate congregational use.

English liturgies of the 1980s provide prayers using both the 'Thou' and the 'You' form in address to God or Christ. It has seemed unnecessary to rewrite classical hymns to conform to the 'You' form. Experience suggests that congregations make the adjustment to 'Thou' without difficulty. The feminist movement has also affected attitudes to some hymns. Feminine authors of the Victorian age liked to use 'brothers' where we today would normally say 'brothers and sisters'. The poverty of English vocabulary makes for difficulty. Unlike many other languages, English has only the one word 'man' to carry three distinct meanings: (a) the human race as a whole, (b) an individual human being, (c) an adult male as opposed to a woman or a boy. Some voices of feminine emancipation have come to object to the first two meanings, not to the third. But we have not thought it right to alter the words of hymns to meet this objection.

The Council of Hymns Ancient and Modern place on record their gratitude to expert advisers who have assisted in making the selection.

We believe that in this new form a book which has long been highly valued in the life and worship of Christians will continue to strengthen the life of the Church.

CONTENTS

Contents

ACKNOWLEDGEMENTS

The Council of Hymns Ancient & Modern Ltd thank the owners or controllers of copyright for permission to use the hymns and tunes listed below. An asterisk denotes that the text has been altered by permission.

WORDS

AUTHOR	PERMISSION GRANTED BY	NO. OF HYMN
Alington, C. A.	Lady Mynors	492
Ambrose, G.	The Society of the Sacred Mission	430
Appleford, P.	Josef Weinberger Ltd (from *20th Century Hymn Book Supplement*)	379*, 382, 391
,,	USPG	355
Arlott, J.	Author	370
Bayly, A. F.	Oxford University Press	393, 397, 411*, 415, 432*, 493, 494
Bell, G. K. A.	Oxford University Press (from *Enlarged Songs of Praise*)	345*
Bowers, J. E.	Author	444, 445, 446, 447, 462, 513
,,	Free Church Choir Union	479
Bowie, W. Russell	Abingdon Press, Nashville, USA (from *Lift up your Hearts*)	387
,,	Harper & Brothers, New York (from *Hymns of The Kingdom of God*)	409
Bridge, B. E.	Free Church Choir Union	427
,,	Author	466, 475
Briggs, G. W.	Oxford University Press (from *Enlarged Songs of Praise*)	346, 349
,,	Oxford University Press	383, 402, 420, 469
Brooks, R. T.	Agape, Carol Stream, Il. 60187, USA	423
Burkitt, F. C.	SPCK	91
Burns, E. J.	Author	431
Caird, G. B.	The Exors of the late G. B. Caird	401
,,	Independent Press Ltd	338
Carter, S.	Essex Music Ltd	400
,,	Galliard Ltd (from *Songs of Sydney Carter in the Present Tense, Book 3*)	354, 433
,,	Galliard Ltd (from *Songs of Sydney Carter in the Present Tense, Book 2*)	375
von Christierson, F.	The Hymn Society of America	377*
Clare, T. C. H.	The Exors of the late T. C. H. Clare	504
Cosnett, Elizabeth	Author	438
Cross, S.	Author	356
Crum, J. M. C.	Mrs Mary Wright	364
,,	Oxford University Press (from *The Oxford Book of Carols*)	501

Acknowledgements

AUTHOR	PERMISSION GRANTED BY	NO. OF HYMN
Dearmer, G.	Author	339
Dearmer, P.	Oxford University Press (from *Enlarged Songs of Praise*)	341, 384
,,	Oxford University Press (from *The English Hymnal*)	378
,, and Humphreys, C. W. (trans.)	Oxford University Press (from *The English Hymnal*)	421
Dobbie, R.	Author	452
Dudley-Smith, Timothy	Author	422, 453
Edge, D.	Author	399
Foley, B.	Faber Music Ltd (from *New Catholic Hymnal*)	471, 485, 531
Fosdick, H. E.	The Exors of the late H. E. Fosdick	367
Franzmann, Martin	Concordia Publishing House	474
Fraser, I. M.	Stainer & Bell Ltd (from *New Songs for the Church*)	450
Gaunt, Alan	John Paul, the Preacher's Press	487
Gaunt, H. C. A.	Oxford University Press	348, 352, 363, 392, 406, 416, 476, 495, 509
Green, F. Pratt	Stainer & Bell Ltd	424, 434, 440, 457, 478, 484, 503, 508, 517, 524, 526
,,	Stainer & Bell Ltd (from *Partners in Praise*)	464
Greenwood, H.	The Society of the Sacred Mission	518
Gregory, J. K.	Author	451
Grieve, N.	T. & T. Clark Ltd.	206
Hardy, H. E.	A. R. Mowbray & Co. Ltd.	71
Herklots, Rosamond	Oxford University Press	362
Hoyle, R. B. (trans.)	World Student Christian Federation Geneva (from *Cantate Domino*)	428
Hughes, D. W.	J. R. Hughes	351, 390*
Hull, Eleanor	Chatto & Windus Ltd	343
"Icarus, Peter"	Mayhew-McCrimmon Ltd, Great Wakering, Essex	507
Jones, R. G.	Author	366, 369, 425
Kaan, F. H.	Stainer & Bell Ltd	358, 361, 385, 403, 419
,,	Agape, Carol Stream, Il. 60187, USA	481
,,	B. Feldman & Co. Ltd, 138–40 Charing Cross Road, London, WC2H 0LD	522
,,	Stainer & Bell Ltd (from *Partners in Praise*)	468, 500
Martin, H.	The Hymn Society of America (from *13 New Marriage and Family Life Hymns*)	407*
Martin, Marcella	Stanbrook Abbey	488
Merrill, W. P.	The Presbyterian Outlook, Richmond, Virginia, USA	418
Micklem, C.	Author	454
Milner-White, E.	SPCK (from *My God my Glory*)	398
Nicholson, N.	Author	350

Acknowledgements

AUTHOR	PERMISSION GRANTED BY	NO. OF HYMN
Oakley, C. E.	Oxford University Press (from *English Praise*)	470
O'Driscoll, T. H.	Author	467, 529
O'Neill, Judith	Author	521
Oxenham, J.	D. Dunkerley	376
Parsons, R. G.	Cannot trace copyright owner	266
Peacey, J. R.	Mrs J. R. Peacey	342, 359, 360, 389, 412
Preston, G.	Novello & Co. Ltd	528
Quinn, J.	Geoffrey Chapman, a division of Cassell Ltd	458, 465, 516
Rees, B. A.	The Exors of B. A. Rees	372
Rees, T.	A. R. Mowbray & Co. Ltd	365*
,,	Community of the Resurrection	368, 404, 439
Reid, W. W. (Jr)	The Hymn Society of America (from *15 New Christian Education Hymns*)	373
Riley, Athelstan	Oxford University Press (from *The English Hymnal*)	532
Riley, H.	Author	463
Routley, E.	Agape, Carol Stream, Il. 60187, USA	498
,,	Hinshaw Music Inc., PO Box 470, Chapel Hill, NC 27514, USA	514
Scott, R. B. Y.	Author	405
Sedgwick, S. N.	Cannot trace copyright owner	417
Shillito, E.	Oxford University Press	437
Struther, Jan	Oxford University Press (from *Enlarged Songs of Praise*)	394
Thompson, C. P.	Author	443
Tomlinson, G. A.	St. Martin's Publications, Ltd	410
Tucker, F. Bland	The Church Pension Fund, New York	337
,, (trans.)	The Church Pension Fund, New York	357
,,	The Church Hymnal Corporation, New York	442, 505, 511
Vanstone, W. H.	J. W. Shore	496
Westendorf, O.	World Library Publications, Inc.	510
Willis, R.	Author	512
Winslow, J. C.	The Exors of the late J. C. Winslow	395*, 396*
Woodward, G. R.	E. M. S. Wood	269
Wren, B. A.	Author	386
,,	Oxford University Press	441, 473, 482, 489, 515, 519, 525
Wright, R.	The Ampleforth Abbey Trustees	502
Yardley, H. F. and Whiteley, F. J.	Authors	506
Young, A.	The Exors of the late Andrew Young	486

MUSIC

COMPOSER	PERMISSION GRANTED BY	NO. OF HYMN
Ainslie, J.	Geoffrey Chapman, a division of Cassell Ltd	507
Allen, Hugh	The Exors of the late Lady Allen	423

Acknowledgements

COMPOSER	PERMISSION GRANTED BY	NO. OF HYMN
Appleford, P.	Josef Weinberger Ltd (from *20th Century Hymn Book Supplement*)	382, 391
Bell, M. F.	Oxford University Press (from *The English Hymnal*)	273(i)
Blake, Leonard	Composer	192
Buck, Percy	Oxford University Press	58(ii), 388
,,	Stainer & Bell Ltd.	188
Carter, S.	Essex Music Ltd	400
,,	Galliard Ltd (from *Songs of Sydney Carter in the Present Tense, Book 3*)	354, 433
,,	Galliard Ltd (from *Songs of Sydney Carter in the Present Tense, Book 2*)	375
Clarke, F. R. C.	Composer	467
Cocker, N.	Oxford University Press	489, 503
Cooke, G.	Composer	501(ii)
Copley, I. A.	Composer	509(ii)
Cutts, P.	Oxford University Press	340, 349, 386, 482
Douglas, W. (har.).	The Church Pension Fund, New York	409(ii)
Dykes Bower, John	The Exors of the late John Dykes Bower	480, 511, 528
,,	The Royal School of Church Music	146(ii), 478
Etherton, J. M.	The Royal School of Church Music	485
Evans, D. (har.).	Oxford University Press (from *The Revised Church Hymnary*)	383, 404
Ferguson, W. H.	Oxford University Press	235, 512
,,	The Royal School of Church Music	140(ii)
Finlay, K. G.	The Exors of the late K. G. Finlay	278
Fleming, Michael	The Royal School of Church Music	115, 193(ii), 533
Gibbs, A.	J. Curwen & Sons Ltd	396(i)
Gray, A.	Cambridge University Press	101, 121, 298
Greatorex, W.	Oxford University Press	241, 422
Griffiths, V.	Composer	460
Harris, W. H.	Oxford University Press	156(ii), 215(i), 306(i)
Harwood, B.	The Exors of the late B. Harwood	106, 171, 202
Holst, G. T.	Oxford University Press	42, 276
,,	J. Curwen & Sons Ltd	295
Howells, H.	Novello & Co. Ltd	336, 409(i)
Ireland, J.	The Exors of the late Mrs N. K. Kirby	63, 317, 363
Jackson, F.	Composer	457
Jagger, A. T. I.	Cannot trace copyright owner	451
Knight, G. H.	The Exors of the late G. H. Knight	315, 435, 459, 463, 476(ii), 484, 510, 513, 518
Laycock, G.	Faber Music Ltd (from *New Catholic Hymnal*)	500
Llewellyn, W.	Oxford University Press	475(ii)

Acknowledgements

COMPOSER	PERMISSION GRANTED BY	NO. OF HYMN
McCarthy, D.	Stainer & Bell Ltd	468
McKie, Sir William (har.)	Composer	426
Micklem, C.	Composer	454
Murray, A. Gregory	Composer	455, 465
Murrill, H.	Mrs Frith	368
Nicholson, Sydney (arr.)	The Royal School of Church Music	51, 104, 377
Potter, Doreen	Agape, Carol Stream, Il. 60187, USA	481
Routley, E.	Hope Publishing Co., Carol Stream, Il. 60188, USA	385
,,	Oxford University Press	432, 487, 488
,,	Hinshaw Music Inc., PO Box 470, Chapel Hill, NC 27514, USA	504
,, (har.)	Oxford University Press	343, 395
Rowlands, William P.	G. A. Gabe, Langland, Swansea	464
Shaw, G.	Oxford University Press	450
,, (har.)	Oxford University Press (from *Enlarged Songs of Praise*)	306(ii), 388
Shaw, M.	J. Curwen & Sons Ltd	113, 116(i), 470
,,	Oxford University Press (from *Enlarged Songs of Praise*)	438, 502
,,	Oxford University Press (from *The Oxford Book of Carols*)	501(i)
Shaw, Watkins	Composer	531
Slater, G.	Oxford University Press	473
,,	Oxford University Press (from *Songs of Praise for Boys and Girls*)	360
Somervell, Arthur	The Trustees of the late Arthur Somervell	477
,,	The Abbot of Downside	117(ii)
Stanford, Charles	Stainer & Bell Ltd	337
Stanton, W. K.	Oxford University Press (from *The BBC Hymn Book*)	371
Taylor, C. V.	Oxford University Press	254(ii), 366, 392, 399(i), 476(i), 516, 522(ii), 527(i)
,,	Oxford University Press (from *The BBC Hymn Book*)	172(i), 356, 394, 486
Terry, R. R.	Oxford University Press	462
,,	Search Press Ltd	490
Thiman, E.	Independent Press Ltd	344
Vaughan Williams, R.	Oxford University Press (from *The English Hymnal*)	40(i), 54, 70(i), 98(i), 105(i), 156(ii), 170(ii), 212(i), 247(ii), 305, 311, 321, 329, 339, 378, 385, 399(ii), 413, 444, 445, 446, 506, 509(i), 525, 532
,,	Oxford University Press (from *Enlarged Songs of Praise*)	393
,,	Stainer & Bell Ltd	410
Walford Davies, H.	Oxford University Press	40(ii), 158(ii), 164, 236
Watson, S.	Composer	389, 492(i)
Wedd, P.	Composer	529
Westbrook, F. B.	Oxford University Press	414, 461, 523

Acknowledgements

	PERMISSION GRANTED BY	NO. OF HYMN
Williams, D.	Composer	324(ii), 493(i)
Wilson, J.	Oxford University Press	172(i), 434, 472, 497, 515, 517(ii), 519
Wood, Thomas . . .	Oxford University Press (from *Enlarged Songs of Praise*)	411

The following copyrights belong to Hymns Ancient & Modern Ltd:

WORDS – 54, 62, 72, 85, 106, 175, 265, 273, 278, 284, 309, 315, 321, 371, 414, 533.
TUNES – 72, 87(ii), 91, 138, 158(i), 196, 268, 277, 348(i), 398, 441.
ARRANGEMENTS – 5(i), 6, 12, 23(i), 35(i), 56(i), 58(i), 59(i), 93, 94, 136, 166(ii), 220(i) & (ii), 240, 252(i) & (ii), 253(i), 254, 256, 262, 270(ii), 273(ii), 286, 297(i), 302(i), 303(i) & (ii), 309(i), 320, 332, 334, 341, 342, 351, 357, 373, 387, 390, 403, 415, 443, 479, 514.
DESCANTS – 1, 34, 96, 99, 126, 145, 198, 211(ii), 326.

The organ arrangements of tunes 354, 375, 382, 391, 400 and 433 are by John Birch.

COPYRIGHT

GRANTS

Liberal grants of Hymns Ancient and Modern are made by the Council to help parishes in the introduction of the book or in the renewal of existing supplies. An application form for a grant can be obtained from Hymns Ancient and Modern Limited, St Mary's Works, St Mary's Plain, Norwich, Norfolk NR3 3BH.

New Standard Edition
Part One

Hymns Ancient and Modern Abridged
1–333

EXPLANATION

AMR = Hymns Ancient and Modern Revised (1950).

HHT = 100 Hymns for Today (1969).

MHT = More Hymns for Today (1980).

NS = Hymns Ancient and Modern New Standard Edition (1983).

Refrains are printed in *italics*.

⋆ after an author's name denotes alteration of the original.

⋆ before a verse number denotes that the verse may be omitted if desired.

‿ at the end of a line indicates that there should be no break between it and the following line.

1 (AMR 3)
Morning Hymn L.M. F. H. Barthélémon (1741–1808)

The descant may be sung for the Doxology

Awake, my soul, and with the sun
thy daily stage of duty run;
shake off dull sloth, and joyful rise
to pay thy morning sacrifice.

2

Redeem thy mis-spent time that's past,
and live this day as if thy last;
improve thy talent with due care;
for the great day thyself prepare.

3

Let all thy converse be sincere,
thy conscience as the noon-day clear;
think how all-seeing God thy ways
and all thy secret thoughts surveys.

4

Wake, and lift up thyself, my heart,
and with the angels bear thy part,
who all night long unwearied sing‿
high praise to the eternal King.

PART 2

5

Glory to thee, who safe hast kept
and hast refreshed me whilst I slept;
grant, Lord, when I from death shall wake,
I may of endless light partake.

6

Lord, I my vows to thee renew;
disperse my sins as morning dew;
guard my first springs of thought and will,
and with thyself my spirit fill.

7

Direct, control, suggest, this day,
all I design or do or say;
that all my powers, with all their might,
in thy sole glory may unite.

This Doxology is sung after either part

8

Praise God, from whom all blessings flow,
praise him, all creatures here below,
praise him above, angelic host,
praise Father, Son, and Holy Ghost.

THOMAS KEN* (1637–1711)

2 (AMR 4)
Melcombe L.M. S. Webbe the elder (1740–1816)

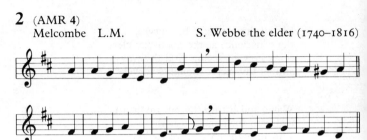

New every morning is the love
our wakening and uprising prove;
through sleep and darkness safely brought,
restored to life and power and thought.

2

New mercies, each returning day,
hover around us while we pray;
new perils past, new sins forgiven,
new thoughts of God, new hopes of heaven.

3

If on our daily course our mind‿
be set to hallow all we find,
new treasures still, of countless price,
God will provide for sacrifice.

4

The trivial round, the common task,
will furnish all we need to ask,
room to deny ourselves, a road‿
to bring us daily nearer God.

5

Only, O Lord, in thy dear love
fit us for perfect rest above;
and help us, this and every day,
to live more nearly as we pray.

JOHN KEBLE* (1792–1866)

3 (AMR 5)
St. Timothy C.M. H. W. Baker (1821–77)

My Father, for another night‿
of quiet sleep and rest,
for all the joy of morning light,
thy holy name be blest.

2

Now with the new-born day I give‿
myself anew to thee,
that as thou willest I may live,
and what thou willest be.

3

Whate'er I do, things great or small,
whate'er I speak or frame,
thy glory may I seek in all,
do all in Jesus' name.

4

My Father, for his sake, I pray,
thy child accept and bless;
and lead me by thy grace to-day
in paths of righteousness.

H. W. BAKER (1821–77)

4 (AMR 7)
Ratisbon 77.77.77. Melody from Werner's *Choralbuch* (Leipzig, 1815)

Morning

Christ, whose glory fills the skies,
  Christ, the true, the only light,
Sun of Righteousness, arise,
  triumph o'er the shades of night;
Dayspring from on high, be near;
Daystar, in my heart appear.

2

Dark and cheerless is the morn
  unaccompanied by thee;
joyless is the day's return,
  till thy mercy's beams I see,
till they inward light impart,
glad my eyes, and warm my heart.

3

Visit then this soul of mine,
  pierce the gloom of sin and grief;
fill me, radiancy divine,
  scatter all my unbelief;
more and more thyself display,
shining to the perfect day.

CHARLES WESLEY (1707–88)

5 (AMR 15) FIRST TUNE

O Lux beata Trinitas L.M. Mode viii

1 O Tri - ni-ty, most bles-sèd light, O Un - i-ty
2 To thee our morning song of praise, to thee our eve-
3 All praise to God the Fa-ther be, all praise, e-ter-

of sove-reign might, as now the fie-ry sun de -
-ning prayer we raise; thee may our souls for ev - er -
-nal Son, to thee, whom with the Spi-rit we a -

parts, shed thou thy beams within our hearts.
-more in low - ly rev - er-ence a - dore.
-dore, for ev - er and for ev - er -more. A - men.

SECOND TUNE

Westminster L.M. adapted from B. Cooke (1734–93)

O Trinity, most blessèd light,
O Unity of sovereign might,
as now the fiery sun departs,
shed thou thy beams within our hearts.

2

To thee our morning song of praise,
to thee our evening prayer we raise;
thee may our souls for evermore
in lowly reverence adore.

3

All praise to God the Father be,
all praise, eternal Son, to thee,
whom with the Spirit we adore,
for ever and for evermore. Amen.

St. Ambrose (c. 340–97)
tr. J. M. Neale* (1818–66)

6 (AMR **16**)
Te Lucis L.M. Mode viii

Before the ending of the day,
Creator of the world, we pray,
that with thy wonted favour thou‿
wouldst be our guard and keeper now.

2

From all ill dreams defend our eyes,
from nightly fears and fantasies;
tread under foot our ghostly foe,
that no pollution we may know.

3

O Father, that we ask be done,
through Jesus Christ thine only Son,
who, with the Holy Ghost and thee,
doth live and reign eternally. Amen.

Latin, tr. J. M. NEALE (1818–66)

7 (AMR **17**)
Strength and Stay   11 10.11 10.   J. B. Dykes (1823–76)

O strength and stay upholding all creation,
  who ever dost thyself unmoved abide,
yet day by day the light in due gradation
  from hour to hour through all its changes guide;

2

grant to life's day a calm unclouded ending,
  an eve untouched by shadows of decay,
the brightness of a holy death-bed blending‿
  with dawning glories of the eternal day.

3

Hear us, O Father, gracious and forgiving,
  through Jesus Christ thy co-eternal Word,
who with the Holy Ghost by all things living
  now and to endless ages art adored.

St. Ambrose (c. 340–97)
tr. J. Ellerton (1826–93) and F. J. A. Hort (1828–92)

8 (AMR **18**)

Sebaste Irregular John Stainer (1840–1901)

1. Hail, gladdening Light, of his pure glo - ry poured
who is the immortal Fa - ther, heaven - ly, blest,
ho - li-est of ho-lies, Je-sus Christ our Lord.
2. Now we are come to the sun's hour of rest,
the lights of eve - ning round us shine,
we hymn the Fa-ther, Son, and Ho-ly Spi - rit di-vine.
3. Worthiest art thou at all times to be sung with un-de-fil-èd
tongue, Son of our God, gi-ver of life, a - lone:
there - fore in all the world thy glo-ries, Lord, they own.

Evening

At the lighting of the lamps

Hail, gladdening Light, of his pure glory poured
who is the immortal Father, heavenly, blest,
holiest of holies, Jesus Christ our Lord.

2

Now we are come to the sun's hour of rest,
the lights of evening round us shine,
we hymn the Father, Son, and Holy Spirit divine.

3

Worthiest art thou at all times to be sung
with undefilèd tongue,
Son of our God, giver of life, alone:
therefore in all the world thy glories, Lord, they own.

Greek, 3rd cent. or earlier
tr. JOHN KEBLE (1792–1866)

9 (AMR **20**)
Angelus L.M. Adapted from G. Joseph (1657)

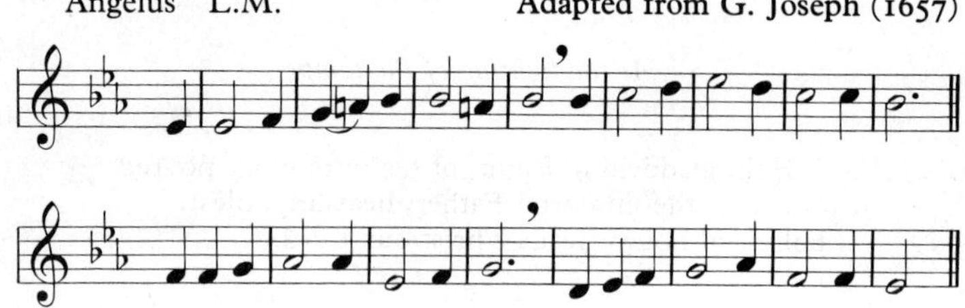

At even, ere the sun was set,
  the sick, O Lord, around thee lay;
O in what divers pains they met!
  O with what joy they went away!

2

Once more 'tis eventide, and we‿
  oppressed with various ills draw near;
what if thy form we cannot see?
  we know and feel that thou art here.

3

O Saviour Christ, our woes dispel;
  for some are sick, and some are sad,
and some have never loved thee well,
  and some have lost the love they had;

*4

and some have found the world is vain,
  yet from the world they break not free;
and some have friends who give them pain,
  yet have not sought a friend in thee;

*5

and none, O Lord, have perfect rest,
  for none are wholly free from sin;
and they who fain would serve thee best
  are conscious most of wrong within.

6

O Saviour Christ, thou too art man;
  thou has been troubled, tempted, tried;
thy kind but searching glance can scan‿
  the very wounds that shame would hide.

7

Thy touch has still its ancient power;
  no word from thee can fruitless fall:
hear, in this solemn evening hour,
  and in thy mercy heal us all.

H. TWELLS (1823–1900)

10 (AMR 23)
Tallis's Canon L.M. Thomas Tallis (*c.* 1505–85)
as shortened by T. Ravenscroft (1621)

Glory to thee, my God, this night
for all the blessings of the light;
keep me, O keep me, King of kings,
beneath thy own almighty wings.

2

Forgive me, Lord, for thy dear Son,
the ill that I this day have done,
that with the world, myself, and thee,
I, ere I sleep, at peace may be.

3

Teach me to live, that I may dread‿
the grave as little as my bed;
teach me to die, that so I may‿
rise glorious at the aweful day.

4

O may my soul on thee repose,
and may sweet sleep mine eyelids close,
sleep that may me more vigorous make
to serve my God when I awake.

5

When in the night I sleepless lie,
my soul with heavenly thoughts supply;
let no ill dreams disturb my rest,
no powers of darkness me molest.

6

Praise God, from whom all blessings flow,
praise him, all creatures here below,
praise him above, angelic host,
praise Father, Son, and Holy Ghost.

THOMAS KEN (1637–1711)

The descant may be sung for verse 6

Evening

Sun of my soul, thou Saviour dear,
it is not night if thou be near:
O may no earth-born cloud arise
to hide thee from thy servant's eyes.

2

When the soft dews of kindly sleep
my wearied eyelids gently steep,
be my last thought, how sweet to rest
for ever on my Saviour's breast.

3

Abide with me from morn till eve,
for without thee I cannot live;
abide with me when night is nigh,
for without thee I dare not die.

4

If some poor wandering child of thine
have spurned to-day the voice divine,
now, Lord, the gracious work begin;
let him no more lie down in sin.

5

Watch by the sick; enrich the poor
with blessings from thy boundless store;
be every mourner's sleep to-night
like infant's slumbers, pure and light.

6

Come near and bless us when we wake,
ere through the world our way we take;
till in the ocean of thy love
we lose ourselves in heaven above.

JOHN KEBLE (1792–1866)

12 (AMR **26**)
Ar hyd y nos 8 4.8 4.8 8.8 4.
(All through the night) Welsh Traditional Melody

God, that madest earth and heaven,
    darkness and light;
who the day for toil hast given,
    for rest the night;
may thine angel-guards defend us,
slumber sweet thy mercy send us,
holy dreams and hopes attend us,
    this livelong night.

2

Guard us waking, guard us sleeping,
    and, when we die,
may we in thy mighty keeping
    all peaceful lie:
when the last dread call shall wake us,
do not thou our God forsake us,
but to reign in glory take us
    with thee on high.

1 Reginald Heber (1783–1826)
2 Richard Whately (1787–1863)

13 (AMR 27)
Eventide 10 10.10 10. W. H. Monk (1823–89)

Evening

The evening of life

Abide with me; fast falls the eventide:
the darkness deepens; Lord, with me abide:
when other helpers fail, and comforts flee,
help of the helpless, O abide with me.

2

Swift to its close ebbs out life's little day;
earth's joys grow dim, its glories pass away;
change and decay in all around I see:
O thou who changest not, abide with me.

3

I need thy presence every passing hour;
what but thy grace can foil the tempter's power?
Who like thyself my guide and stay can be?
Through cloud and sunshine, Lord, abide with me.

4

I fear no foe with thee at hand to bless;
ills have no weight, and tears no bitterness.
Where is death's sting? Where, grave, thy victory?
I triumph still, if thou abide with me.

5

Hold thou thy cross before my closing eyes;
shine through the gloom, and point me to the skies:
heaven's morning breaks, and earth's vain shadows flee;
in life, in death, O Lord, abide with me.

H. F. LYTE (1793–1847)

14 (AMR **30**)

St. Columba 6 4.6 6. H. S. Irons (1834–1905)

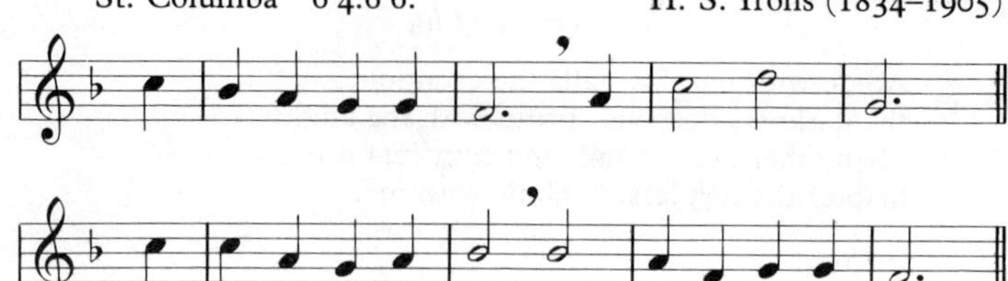

The will of God

The sun is sinking fast,
the daylight dies;
let love awake, and pay‿
her evening sacrifice.

2

As Christ upon the cross
his head inclined,
and to his Father's hands
his parting soul resigned,

3

so now herself my soul
would wholly give‿
into his sacred charge,
in whom all spirits live;

4

so now beneath his eye
would calmly rest,
without a wish or thought
abiding in the breast,

5

save that his will be done,
whate'er betide,
dead to herself, and dead‿
in him to all beside.

6

Thus would I live; yet now‿
not I, but he,
in all his power and love
henceforth alive in me.

7

One sacred Trinity,
one Lord divine,
may I be ever his,
and he for ever mine.

Latin, c. 18th cent.
tr. E. Caswall (1814–78)

15 (AMR **31**)
Ellers 10 10.10 10. E. J. Hopkins (1818–1901)

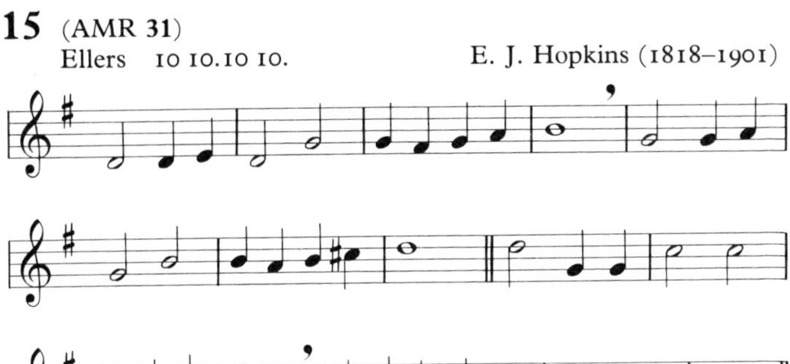

Saviour, again to thy dear name we raise
with one accord our parting hymn of praise;
we stand to bless thee ere our worship cease;
then, lowly kneeling, wait thy word of peace.

2

Grant us thy peace upon our homeward way;
with thee began, with thee shall end, the day:
guard thou the lips from sin, the hearts from shame,
that in this house have called upon thy name.

3

Grant us thy peace, Lord, through the coming night;
turn thou for us its darkness into light;
from harm and danger keep thy children free,
for dark and light are both alike to thee.

4

Grant us thy peace throughout our earthly life,
our balm in sorrow, and our stay in strife;
then, when thy voice shall bid our conflict cease,
call us, O Lord, to thine eternal peace.

J. Ellerton (1826–93)

16 (AMR **33**)
St. Clement 9 8.9 8. C. C. Scholefield (1839–1904)

Evening

The World Church

The day thou gavest, Lord, is ended,
  the darkness falls at thy behest;
to thee our morning hymns ascended,
  thy praise shall sanctify our rest.

2

We thank thee that thy Church unsleeping,
  while earth rolls onward into light,
through all the world her watch is keeping,
  and rests not now by day or night.

3

As o'er each continent and island
  the dawn leads on another day,
the voice of prayer is never silent,
  nor dies the strain of praise away.

4

The sun that bids us rest is waking‿
  our brethren 'neath the western sky,
and hour by hour fresh lips are making‿
  thy wondrous doings heard on high.

5

So be it, Lord; thy throne shall never,
  like earth's proud empires, pass away;
thy kingdom stands, and grows for ever,
  till all thy creatures own thy sway.

J. Ellerton (1826–93)

17 (AMR **34**)

Innsbruck 7 7 6.7 7 8. German Folk Song

ANOTHER VERSION

Set by J. S. Bach
in the *St. Matthew Passion* (1729)

Evening

The duteous day now closeth,
each flower and tree reposeth,
  shade creeps o'er wild and wood:
let us, as night is falling,
on God our maker calling,
  give thanks to him, the giver good.

2

Now all the heavenly splendour
breaks forth in starlight tender
  from myriad worlds unknown;
and man, the marvel seeing,
forgets his selfish being,
  for joy of beauty not his own.

*3

His care he drowneth yonder,
lost in the abyss of wonder;
  to heaven his soul doth steal:
this life he disesteemeth,
the day it is that dreameth,
  that doth from truth his vision seal.

4

Awhile his mortal blindness
may miss God's loving-kindness,
  and grope in faithless strife:
but when life's day is over
shall death's fair night discover
  the fields of everlasting life.

ROBERT BRIDGES (1844–1930)
based on *Nun ruhen alle Wälder*, P. GERHARDT (1607–76)

18 (AMR 35)
Seelenbräutigam (Thuringia) A. Drese (1620–1701)
5 5.8 8.5 5.

Round me falls the night;
Saviour, be my light;
through the hours in darkness shrouded
let me see thy face unclouded;
let thy glory shine
in this heart of mine.

2

Earthly work is done,
earthly sounds are none;
rest in sleep and silence seeking,
let me hear thee softly speaking;
in my spirit's ear
whisper, 'I am near.'

3

Blessèd, heavenly Light,
shining through earth's night;
voice, that oft of love hast told me;
arms, so strong to clasp and hold me,
thou thy watch wilt keep,
Saviour, o'er my sleep.

W. Romanis (1824–99)

19 (AMR 431)

Eudoxia 6 5.6 5. S. Baring-Gould (1834–1924)

1

Now the day is over,
  night is drawing nigh,
shadows of the evening
  steal across the sky.

*2

Now the darkness gathers,
  stars begin to peep,
birds and beasts and flowers
  soon will be asleep.

3

Jesu, give the weary
  calm and sweet repose;
with thy tenderest blessing
  may mine eyelids close.

*4

Grant to little children
  visions bright of thee;
guard the sailors tossing
  on the deep blue sea.

5

Comfort every sufferer
  watching late in pain;
those who plan some evil
  from their sin restrain.

*6

Through the long night watches
  may thine angels spread‿
their white wings above me,
  watching round my bed.

7

When the morning wakens,
  then may I arise
pure and fresh and sinless
  in thy holy eyes.

8

Glory to the Father,
  glory to the Son,
and to thee, blest Spirit,
  whilst all ages run.

S. Baring-Gould (1834–1924)

20 (AMR **40**)
Church Triumphant L.M. J. W. Elliott (1833–1915)

Again the Lord's own day is here
the day to Christian people dear,
as, week by week, it bids them tell
how Jesus rose from death and hell.

2

For by his flock their Lord declared
his resurrection should be shared;
and we who trust in him to save
with him are risen from the grave.

*3

We, one and all, of him possessed,
are with exceeding treasures blessed;
for all he did, and all he bare,
he gives us as our own to share.

*4

Eternal glory, rest on high,
a blessèd immortality,
true peace and gladness, and a throne,
are all his gifts, and all our own.

5

And therefore unto thee we sing,
O Lord of peace, eternal King;
thy love we praise, thy name adore,
both on this day and evermore.

Ascribed to THOMAS À KEMPIS (c. 1380–1471)
Latin, tr. J. M. NEALE* (1818–66)

21 (AMR 42)

Dominica S.M. H. S. Oakeley (1830–1903)

This is the day of light:
let there be light to-day;
O Dayspring, rise upon our night,
and chase its gloom away.

2

This is the day of rest:
our failing strength renew;
on weary brain and troubled breast‿
shed thou thy freshening dew.

3

This is the day of peace:
thy peace our spirits fill;
bid thou the blasts of discord cease,
the waves of strife be still.

4

This is the day of prayer:
let earth to heaven draw near;
lift up our hearts to seek thee there,
come down to meet us here.

5

This is the first of days:
send forth thy quickening breath,
and wake dead souls to love and praise,
O vanquisher of death.

J. Ellerton (1826–93)

22 (AMR **43**)

Bishopthorpe C.M.

Select Portions of the Psalms (H. Gardner, c. 1786)

Sunday

Day of Resurrection

This is the day the Lord hath made,
he calls the hours his own;
let heaven rejoice, let earth be glad,
and praise surround the throne.

2

To-day he rose and left the dead,
and Satan's empire fell;
to-day the saints his triumphs spread,
and all his wonders tell.

3

Hosanna to the anointed King,
to David's holy Son.
O help us, Lord, descend and bring
salvation from thy throne.

4

Blest be the Lord, who comes to men
with messages of grace;
who comes, in God his Father's name,
to save our sinful race.

5

Hosanna in the highest strains
the Church on earth can raise;
the highest heavens in which he reigns
shall give him nobler praise.

Isaac Watts (1674–1748)
Psalm 118. 24–6

23 (AMR 45) FIRST TUNE

Conditor alme L.M. Mode iv

SECOND TUNE

Brockham L.M. Jeremiah Clarke (*c.* 1673–1707)

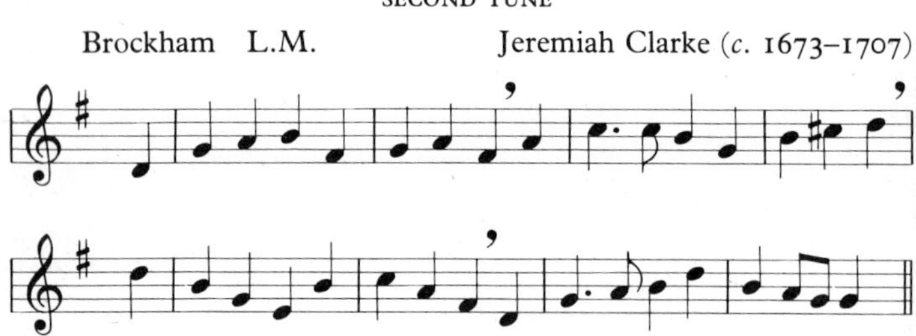

Creator of the starry height,
thy people's everlasting light,
Jesu, redeemer of us all,
hear thou thy servants when they call.

2

Thou, sorrowing at the helpless cry‿
of all creation doomed to die,
didst come to save our fallen race
by healing gifts of heavenly grace.

3

When earth was near its evening hour,
thou didst, in love's redeeming power,
like bridegroom from his chamber, come‿
forth from a Virgin-mother's womb.

4

At thy great name, exalted now,
all knees in lowly homage bow;
all things in heaven and earth adore,
and own thee King for evermore.

5

To thee, O Holy One, we pray,
our judge in that tremendous day,
ward off, while yet we dwell below,
the weapons of our crafty foe.

6

To God the Father, God the Son,
and God the Spirit, Three in One,
praise, honour, might, and glory be
from age to age eternally. Amen.

Latin, tr. J. M. NEALE* (1818–66)

24 (AMR **47**)
Merton 8 7.8 7. W. H. Monk (1823–89)

Hark, a thrilling voice is sounding;
'Christ is nigh,' it seems to say;
'cast away the dreams of darkness,
O ye children of the day.'

2

Wakened by the solemn warning,
let the earth-bound soul arise;
Christ, her Sun, all ill dispelling,
shines upon the morning skies.

3

Lo, the Lamb, so long expected,
comes with pardon down from heaven;
let us haste, with tears of sorrow,
one and all to be forgiven;

4

that when next he comes with glory,
and the world is wrapped in fear,
with his mercy he may shield us,
and with words of love draw near.

5

Honour, glory, might, and blessing
to the Father and the Son,
with the everlasting Spirit,
while eternal ages run.

Latin, tr. E. Caswall* (1814–78)

25 (AMR **48**)

Franconia S.M. *Harmonischer Liederschatz* (1738)
adapted by W. H. Havergal (1793–1870)

The advent of our King
our prayers must now employ,
and we must hymns of welcome sing
in strains of holy joy.

2

The everlasting Son
incarnate deigns to be;
himself a servant's form puts on,
to set his servants free.

3

Daughter of Sion, rise‿
to meet thy lowly King;
nor let thy faithless heart despise‿
the peace he comes to bring.

4

As Judge, on clouds of light,
he soon will come again,
and his true members all unite
with him in heaven to reign.

5

All glory to the Son
who comes to set us free,
with Father, Spirit, ever One,
through all eternity.

C. Coffin (1676–1749)
tr. J. Chandler* (1806–76)

26 (AMR **49**)

Veni Emmanuel 8 8.8 8.8 8. *Hymnal Noted*, 1856 (from a French Missal)

Unison

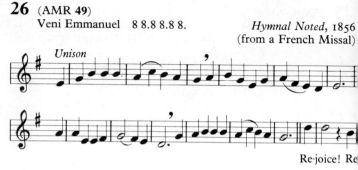

Re-joice! Re

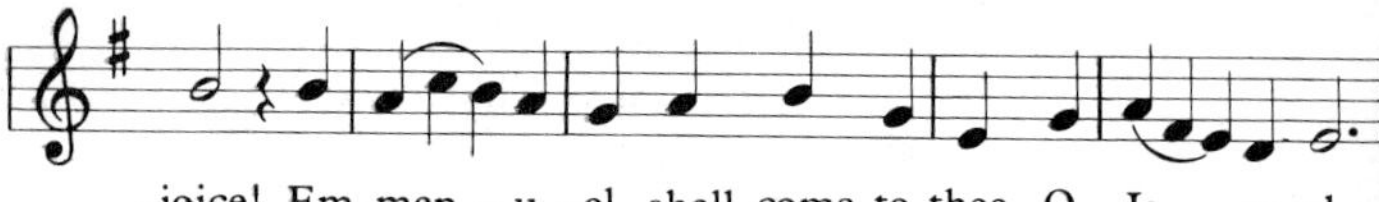

-joice! Em-man - u - el‿shall come to thee, O Is - ra-el.

Advent

O come, O come, Emmanuel,
and ransom captive Israel,
that mourns in lonely exile here,
until the Son of God appear:
Rejoice! Rejoice! Emmanuel‿
shall come to thee, O Israel.

2

O come, thou Rod of Jesse, free‿
thine own from Satan's tyranny;
from depths of hell thy people save,
and give them victory o'er the grave:

3

O come, thou Dayspring, come and cheer‿
our spirits by thine advent here;
disperse the gloomy clouds of night,
and death's dark shadows put to flight:

4

O come, thou Key of David, come,
and open wide our heavenly home;
make safe the way that leads on high,
and close the path to misery:

5

O come, O come, thou Lord of Might,
who to thy tribes, on Sinai's height,
in ancient times didst give the law
in cloud and majesty and awe:
Rejoice! Rejoice! Emmanuel‿
shall come to thee, O Israel.

Latin Advent Antiphons
tr. J. M. NEALE* (1818–66)

27 (AMR 50)
Winchester New L.M.

Adapted from *Musicalisches Hand-Buch* (Hamburg, 1690)

On Jordan's bank the Baptist's cry‿
announces that the Lord is nigh;
awake, and hearken, for he brings‿
glad tidings of the King of kings.

2

Then cleansed be every breast from sin;
make straight the way for God within;
prepare we in our hearts a home,
where such a mighty guest may come.

3

For thou art our salvation, Lord,
our refuge, and our great reward;
without thy grace we waste away,
like flowers that wither and decay.

4

To heal the sick stretch out thine hand,
and bid the fallen sinner stand;
shine forth, and let thy light restore‿
earth's own true loveliness once more.

5

All praise, eternal Son, to thee
whose advent doth thy people free,
whom with the Father we adore
and Holy Ghost for evermore.

C. Coffin (1676–1749)
tr. J. Chandler* (1806–76)

28 (AMR **51**)
Helmsley
8 7.8 7.8 7.

Later form of melody in J. Wesley's *Select Hymns with Tunes Annext* (1765)

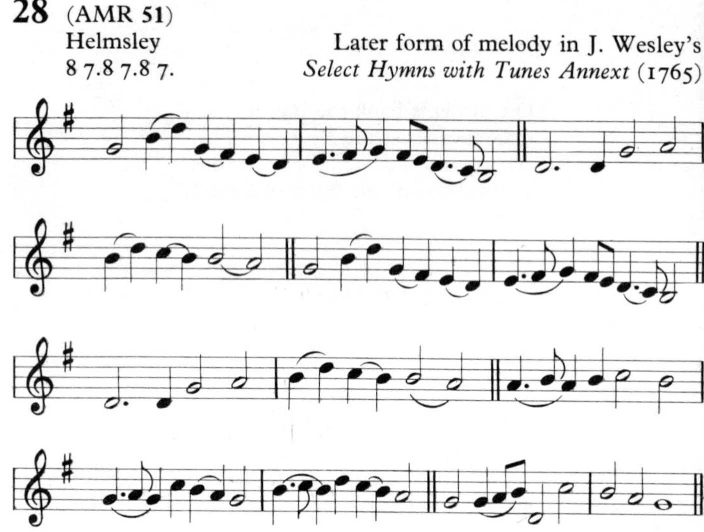

Advent

Thy kingdom come

Lo, he comes with clouds descending,
  once for favoured sinners slain;
thousand thousand saints attending
  swell the triumph of his train:
      Alleluia!
  Christ appears on earth to reign.

2

Every eye shall now behold him
  robed in dreadful majesty;
those who set at naught and sold him,
  pierced and nailed him to the Tree,
    deeply wailing,
  shall the true Messiah see.

3

Those dear tokens of his passion
  still his dazzling body bears,
cause of endless exultation
  to his ransomed worshippers:
    with what rapture
  gaze we on those glorious scars!

4

Yea, Amen, let all adore thee,
  high on thine eternal throne;
Saviour, take the power and glory,
  claim the kingdom for thine own:
      Alleluia!
  thou shalt reign, and thou alone.

Charles Wesley (1707–88)
and John Cennick (1718–55)

29 (AMR 52)
St. Stephen C.M. W. Jones (1726–1800).

The Lord will come and not be slow,
his footsteps cannot err;
before him righteousness shall go,
his royal harbinger.

2

Truth from the earth, like to a flower,
shall bud and blossom then;
and justice, from her heavenly bower,
look down on mortal men.

3

Rise, God, judge thou the earth in might,
this wicked earth redress;
for thou art he who shalt by right
the nations all possess.

4

The nations all whom thou hast made
shall come, and all shall frame
to bow them low before thee, Lord,
and glorify thy name.

5

For great thou art, and wonders great
by thy strong hand are done:
thou in thy everlasting seat
remainest God alone.

JOHN MILTON (1608–74)
Psalms 82, 85, 86

30 (AMR 53)
Bristol C.M. T. Ravenscroft (*Psalms*, 1621)

Hark the glad sound! the Saviour comes,
the Saviour promised long:
let every heart prepare a throne,
and every voice a song.

2

He comes, the prisoners to release
in Satan's bondage held;
the gates of brass before him burst,
the iron fetters yield.

3

He comes, the broken heart to bind,
the bleeding soul to cure,
and with the treasures of his grace
to bless the humble poor.

4

Our glad hosannas, Prince of Peace,
thy welcome shall proclaim;
and heaven's eternal arches ring
with thy belovèd name.

PHILIP DODDRIDGE* (1702–51)
Luke 4. 18–19

31 (AMR 54)
Cross of Jesus 8 7.8 7. John Stainer (1840–1901)

Come, thou long-expected Jesus,
born to set thy people free;
from our fears and sins release us;
let us find our rest in thee.

2

Israel's strength and consolation,
hope of all the earth thou art;
dear desire of every nation,
joy of every longing heart.

3

Born thy people to deliver;
born a child and yet a king;
born to reign in us for ever;
now thy gracious kingdom bring.

4

By thy own eternal Spirit,
rule in all our hearts alone:
by thy all-sufficient merit,
raise us to thy glorious throne.

CHARLES WESLEY* (1707–88)

32 (AMR 55)
Wachet auf 8 9 8. D. 6 6 4.8 8. P. Nicolai (1556–1608)
(Sleepers, wake)

Sleepers, wake! the watch-cry pealeth,
while slumber deep each eyelid sealeth:
awake, Jerusalem, awake!
Midnight's solemn hour is tolling,
and seraph-notes are onward rolling;
they call on us our part to take.
Come forth, ye virgins wise:
the Bridegroom comes, arise.
Alleluia!
Each lamp be bright
with ready light
to grace the marriage feast to-night.

2

Zion hears the voice that singeth,
with sudden joy her glad heart springeth,
  at once she wakes, she stands arrayed.
*Sec her Light, her Star ascending,
lo, girt with truth, with mercy blending,
  her Bridegroom there, so long delayed.
    All hail, God's glorious Son,
    all hail, our joy and crown,
      Alleluia!
    The joyful call
    we answer all,
  and follow to the bridal hall.

*3

Praise to him who goes before us,
let men and angels join in chorus,
  let harp and cymbal add their sound.
Twelve the gates, a pearl each portal –
we haste to join the choir immortal
  within the Holy City's bound.
    Ear ne'er heard aught like this,
    nor heart conceived such bliss.
      Alleluia!
    We raise the song,
    we swell the throng,
  to praise thee ages all along.

P. NICOLAI (1556–1608)
tr. FRANCES E. COX (1812–97)

**Miss Cox's original. AMR has* 'Her light is come'

33 (AMR **58**).
Corde natus 8 7.8 7.8 7.7.
(Divinum Mysterium)

Later form of melody
in *Piae Cantiones*
(Nyland, 1582)

Of the Father's love begotten
  ere the worlds began to be,
he is Alpha and Omega,
  he the source, the ending he,
of the things that are, that have been,
  and that future years shall see,
    evermore and evermore.

2

O that birth for ever blessèd,
  when the Virgin, full of grace,
by the Holy Ghost conceiving,
  bare the Saviour of our race,
and the babe, the world's Redeemer,
  first revealed his sacred face,
    evermore and evermore.

3

O ye heights of heaven, adore him;
  angel hosts, his praises sing;
powers, dominions bow before him,
  and extol our God and King;
let no tongue on earth be silent,
  every voice in concert ring,
    evermore and evermore.

PRUDENTIUS (348–c. 413)
tr. J. M. NEALE (1818–66)

A longer version is at 325

34 (AMR **59**)

Adeste Fideles Irregular

Probably by J. F. Wade (*c.* 1711–86)

DESCANT
4 Yea, Lord, we greet thee, born this hap - py
morn - ing; Je - su, to thee be
glo - ry given; Word of the Fa - ther,
now in flesh ap - pear - ing: O come,
O come, let us a -
O come, O
-dore him, O come let us a - dore him, O

come, let us a - dore him, Christ the Lord.
come, let us a - dore him, Christ the Lord.

The descant may be sung for verse 4

O come, all ye faithful,
joyful and triumphant,
O come ye, O come ye to Bethlehem;
come and behold him‿
born, the King of angels:
O come, let us adore him . . .

2

God of God,
Light of Light,
o, he abhors not the Virgin's womb;
very God,
begotten, not created:
O come, let us adore him . . .

3

Sing, choirs of angels,
sing in exultation,
sing, all ye citizens of heaven above:
'Glory to God
in the highest:'
O come, let us adore him . . .

4

Yea, Lord, we greet thee,
born this happy morning;
Jesu, to thee be glory given;
Word of the Father,
now in flesh appearing:
O come, let us adore him,
O come, let us adore him,
O come, let us adore him, Christ the Lord.

Latin, 18th cent.,
tr. F. Oakeley (1802–80)

A longer version is at 326

35 (AMR **60**)
Mendelssohn
7 7 7 7.D. 77.

Adapted from
F. Mendelssohn-Bartholdy (1809–47)
by W. H. Cummings (1855)

Christmas

Hark, the herald-angels sing
glory to the new-born King,
peace on earth, and mercy mild,
God and sinners reconciled.
Joyful, all ye nations, rise,
join the triumph of the skies;
with the angelic host proclaim,
'Christ is born in Bethlehem.'
    Hark, the herald-angels sing
    glory to the new-born King.

2

Christ, by highest heaven adored,
Christ, the everlasting Lord,
late in time behold him come,
offspring of a Virgin's womb.
Veiled in flesh the Godhead see:
hail, the incarnate Deity,
pleased as Man with man to dwell,
Jesus, our Emmanuel.
    Hark, the herald-angels sing
    glory to the new-born King.

3

Hail, the heaven-born Prince of Peace:
hail, the Sun of Righteousness.
Light and life to all he brings,
risen with healing in his wings.
Mild he lays his glory by,
born that man no more may die,
born to raise the sons of earth,
born to give them second birth.
    Hark, the herald-angels sing
    glory to the new-born King.

CHARLES WESLEY (1707–88) and others

36 (AMR **61**)
Yorkshire 10 10.10 10.10 10. J. Wainwright (1723–68)

Christians, awake! salute the happy morn,
whereon the Saviour of the world was born;
rise to adore the mystery of love,
which hosts of angels chanted from above:
with them the joyful tidings first begun
of God incarnate and the Virgin's Son.

2

Then to the watchful shepherds it was told,
who heard the angelic herald's voice, 'Behold,
I bring good tidings of a Saviour's birth
to you and all the nations upon earth:
this day hath God fulfilled his promised word,
this day is born a Saviour, Christ the Lord.'

*3

He spake; and straightway the celestial choir
in hymns of joy, unknown before, conspire;
the praises of redeeming love they sang,
and heaven's whole orb with alleluias rang:
God's highest glory was their anthem still,
peace upon earth, and unto men good will.

4

To Bethl'em straight the enlightened shepherds ran,
to see the wonder God had wrought for man,
and found, with Joseph and the blessèd Maid,
her Son, the Saviour, in a manger laid:
then to their flocks, still praising God, return,
and their glad hearts with holy rapture burn.

5

O may we keep and ponder in our mind
God's wondrous love in saving lost mankind;
trace we the babe, who hath retrieved our loss,
from his poor manger to his bitter cross;
tread in his steps, assisted by his grace,
till man's first heavenly state again takes place.

*6

Then may we hope, the angelic hosts among,
to sing, redeemed, a glad triumphal song:
he that was born upon this joyful day
around us all his glory shall display;
saved by his love, incessant we shall sing
eternal praise to heaven's almighty King.

J. BYROM* (1692–1763)

37 (AMR **62**)
Winchester Old C.M. T. Este (*Psalms*, 1592)

ALTERNATIVE VERSION

T. Ravenscroft (1621)

Christmas

While shepherds watched their flocks by night,
all seated on the ground,
the angel of the Lord came down,
and glory shone around.

2

'Fear not,' said he (for mighty dread‿
had seized their troubled mind);
'glad tidings of great joy I bring
to you and all mankind.

3

'To you in David's town this day
is born of David's line
a Saviour, who is Christ the Lord;
and this shall be the sign:

4

'the heavenly babe you there shall find
to human view displayed,
all meanly wrapped in swathing bands,
and in a manger laid.'

5

Thus spake the seraph; and forthwith‿
appeared a shining throng‿
of angels praising God, who thus‿
addressed their joyful song:

6

'All glory be to God on high,
and to the earth be peace;
good will henceforth from heaven to men
begin and never cease.'

Nahum Tate (1652–1715)

38 (AMR **63**)
St. George S.M. H. J. Gauntlett (1805–76)

God from on high hath heard:
let sighs and sorrows cease.
Lo, from the opening heaven descends‿
to man the promised peace.

2

Hark, through the silent night
angelic voices swell;
their joyful songs proclaim that God‿
is born on earth to dwell.

3

See how the shepherd-band
speed on with eager feet;
come to the hallowed cave with them
the holy babe to greet.

4

But O what sight appears
within that lowly door:
a manger, stall, and swaddling clothes,
a child, and mother poor.

5

Art thou the Christ? the Son?
the Father's image bright?
and see we him whose arm upholds‿
earth and the starry height?

6

Yea, faith can pierce the cloud
which veils thy glory now;
we hail thee God, before whose throne‿
the angels prostrate bow.

7

Our sinful pride to cure
with that pure love of thine,
O be thou born within our hearts,
most holy Child divine.

C. Coffin (1676–1749)
tr. J. R. Woodford* (1820–85)

39 (AMR **64**)

Iris 8 7.8 7.47. French or Flemish Melody

(Shepherds in the field)

Come
and wor - ship Christ, the new-born King:
Come and
wor - ship, wor-ship Christ, the new - born King.

Angels, from the realms of glory,
  wing your flight o'er all the earth;
ye who sang creation's story,
  now proclaim Messiah's birth:
come and worship
Christ, the new-born King:
come and worship,
worship Christ, the new-born King.

2

Shepherds, in the field abiding,
  watching o'er your flocks by night,
God with man is now residing,
  yonder shines the infant Light:

3

Sages, leave your contemplations;
  brighter visions beam afar:
seek the great Desire of Nations;
  ye have seen his natal star:

*4

Saints before the altar bending,
  watching long in hope and fear,
suddenly the Lord, descending,
  in his temple shall appear:

5

Though an infant now we view him,
  he shall fill his Father's throne,
gather all the nations to him;
  every knee shall then bow down:
come and worship
Christ, the new-born King:
come and worship,
worship Christ, the new-born King.

JAMES MONTGOMERY (1771–1854)

40 (AMR 65)

FIRST TUNE

Forest Green D.C.M. English Traditional Melody

SECOND TUNE

Christmas Carol D.C.M. Walford Davies (1869–1941)

Christmas

O little town of Bethlehem,
how still we see thee lie!
Above thy deep and dreamless sleep
the silent stars go by:
yet in thy dark streets shineth
the everlasting Light;
the hopes and fears of all the years
are met in thee to-night.

2

For Christ is born of Mary;
and, gathered all above,
while mortals sleep, the angels keep‿
their watch of wondering love.
O morning stars, together
proclaim the holy birth,
and praises sing to God the King,
and peace to men on earth.

3

How silently, how silently,
the wondrous gift is given!
So God imparts to human hearts
the blessings of his heaven.
No ear may hear his coming;
but in this world of sin,
where meek souls will receive him still,
the dear Christ enters in.

4

O holy Child of Bethlehem,
descend to us, we pray;
cast out our sin, and enter in:
be born in us to-day.
We hear the Christmas angels‿
the great glad tidings tell:
O come to us, abide with us,
our Lord Emmanuel.

PHILLIPS BROOKS (1835–93)

41 (AMR **66**)
Noel D.C.M. English Traditional Melody
adapted by Arthur Sullivan (1842–1900)

It came upon the midnight clear,
  that glorious song of old,
from angels bending near the earth
  to touch their harps of gold:
'Peace on the earth, good will to men,
  from heaven's all-gracious King!'
The world in solemn stillness lay
  to hear the angels sing.

2

Still through the cloven skies they come,
  with peaceful wings unfurled;
and still their heavenly music floats
  o'er all the weary world:
above its sad and lowly plains
  they bend on hovering wing;
and ever o'er its Babel-sounds
  the blessèd angels sing.

3

Yet with the woes of sin and strife
  the world has suffered long;
beneath the angel-strain have rolled
  two thousand years of wrong;
and man, at war with man, hears not‿
  the love-song which they bring:
O hush the noise, ye men of strife,
  and hear the angels sing.

*4

And ye, beneath life's crushing load,
  whose forms are bending low,
who toil along the climbing way
  with painful steps and slow,
look, now! for glad and golden hours‿
  come swiftly on the wing;
O rest beside the weary road,
  and hear the angels sing.

*5

For lo, the days are hastening on,
  by prophet-bards foretold,
when, with the ever-circling years,
  comes round the age of gold;
when peace shall over all the earth
  its ancient splendours fling,
and the whole world give back the song
  which now the angels sing.

E. H. Sears (1810–76)

42 (AMR 67)

Cranham Irregular — Gustav Holst (1874–1934)

1 In the bleak mid - win - ter
2 Our God, heaven can - not hold him
3 E - nough for him, whom cher - u - bim
4 An - gels and arch - an - gels
5 What can I give him,
frost - ty wind made moan, earth stood hard as
nor earth sus - tain; heaven and earth shall
wor - ship night and day, a breast - ful of
may have ga-thered there, cher - u - bim and
poor as I am? if I were a
i - ron, wa - ter like a stone:
flee a - way when he comes to reign:
milk, and a man - ger - ful of hay: e -
ser - a - phim thronged the air - but
shep - herd I would bring a lamb;

snow had fall - en, snow on snow,
in the bleak mid - win - ter a
- nough for him, whom an - gels
on - - ly his mo - ther
if I were a wise man
snow on snow, in the bleak mid -
sta - ble - place suf - ficed the Lord God Al -
fall down be - fore, the ox and ass and
in her mai - den bliss wor-shipped the Be -
I would do my part; yet what I can I
- win - ter, long a - go.
- migh - ty, Je - sus Christ.
ca - mel which a - dore.
- lov - èd with a kiss.
give him give my heart.

CHRISTINA ROSSETTI (1830–94)

43 (AMR **68**)

Es ist ein' Ros' 7 6.7 6.6 7 6. German Carol Melody

A great and mighty wonder,
  a full and holy cure!
the Virgin bears the Infant
  with virgin-honour pure:
    Repeat the hymn again
      'To God on high be glory,
    and peace on earth to men.'

2

The Word becomes incarnate,
  and yet remains on high;
and cherubim sing anthems
  to shepherds from the sky:

3

While thus they sing your Monarch,
  those bright angelic bands,
rejoice, ye vales and mountains,
  ye oceans, clap your hands:

4

Since all he comes to ransom,
  by all be he adored,
the infant born in Bethl'em,
  the Saviour and the Lord:
    Repeat the hymn again
      'To God on high be glory,
    and peace on earth to men.'

St. Germanus (c. 634–c. 734)
tr. J. M. Neale (1818–66)

44 (AMR **69**)

Kilmarnock C.M. Neil Dougall (1776–1862)

Behold, the great Creator makes‿
  himself a house of clay,
a robe of virgin flesh he takes
  which he will wear for ay.

2

Hark, hark! the wise eternal Word
  like a weak infant cries;
in form of servant is the Lord,
  and God in cradle lies.

3

This wonder struck the world amazed,
  it shook the starry frame;
squadrons of spirits stood and gazed,
  then down in troops they came.

4

Glad shepherds ran to view this sight;
  a choir of angels sings,
and eastern sages with delight
  adore this King of kings.

5

Join then, all hearts that are not stone,
  and all our voices prove,
to celebrate this Holy One,
  the God of peace and love.

T. Pestel (1585–1659)

45 (AMR 71)

Invitation (Devonshire) L.M. J. F. Lampe (1703–51)

To us a Child of royal birth,
heir of the promises, is given;
th' invisible appears on earth,
the Son of Man, the God of Heaven.

2

A Saviour born, in love supreme,
he comes our fallen souls to raise;
he comes his people to redeem,
with all the fulness of his grace.

3

The Christ, by raptured seers foretold,
filled with th' eternal Spirit's power,
Prophet, and Priest, and King behold,
and Lord of all the worlds adore.

4

The Lord of Hosts, the God most high,
who quits his throne on earth to live,
with joy we welcome from the sky,
with faith into our hearts receive.

Charles Wesley (1707–88)

46 (AMR **432**)
Irby 8 7.8 7.7 7. H. J. Gauntlett (1805–76)

**in verses 2 and 4 sung as two crotchets*

Once in royal David's city
  stood a lowly cattle shed,
where a mother laid her baby
  in a manger for his bed:
Mary was that mother mild,
Jesus Christ her little child.

2

He came down to earth from heaven
  who is God and Lord of all,
and his shelter was a stable,
  and his cradle was a stall;
with the poor and mean and lowly
lived on earth our Saviour holy.

*3

And through all his wondrous childhood
  he would honour and obey,
love and watch the lowly Maiden,
  in whose gentle arms he lay:
Christian children all must be‿
mild, obedient, good as he.

*4

For he is our childhood's pattern,
  day by day like us he grew,
he was little, weak, and helpless,
  tears and smiles like us he knew;
and he feeleth for our sadness,
and he shareth in our gladness.

5

And our eyes at last shall see him,
  through his own redeeming love,
for that child so dear and gentle
  is our Lord in heaven above;
and he leads his children on
to the place where he is gone.

6

Not in that poor lowly stable,
  with the oxen standing by,
we shall see him; but in heaven,
  set at God's right hand on high;
where like stars his children crowned
all in white shall wait around.

CECIL FRANCES ALEXANDER (1818–95)

47 (AMR 75) FIRST TUNE

Bede 11 10.11 10. Adapted from Handel's *Athalia* (1733) by John Goss (1800–80)

SECOND TUNE

Epiphany 11 10.11 10. J. F. Thrupp (1827–67)

Epiphany

Brightest and best of the sons of the morning,
  dawn on our darkness, and lend us thine aid;
star of the east, the horizon adorning,
  guide where our infant Redeemer is laid.

2

Cold on his cradle the dew-drops are shining;
  low lies his head with the beasts of the stall;
angels adore him in slumber reclining,
  Maker and Monarch and Saviour of all.

3

Say, shall we yield him, in costly devotion,
  odours of Edom, and offerings divine,
gems of the mountain, and pearls of the ocean,
  myrrh from the forest, or gold from the mine?

4

Vainly we offer each ample oblation,
  vainly with gifts would his favour secure:
richer by far is the heart's adoration,
  dearer to God are the prayers of the poor.

REGINALD HEBER (1783–1826)

The first verse may be repeated at the end

48 (AMR **76**)
Stuttgart 8 7.8 7.

Adapted from a melody by
C. F. Witt (1660–1716)

1 Earth has many a noble city;
   Bethl'em, thou dost all excel:
out of thee the Lord from heaven
   came to rule his Israel.

2 Fairer than the sun at morning
   was the star that told his birth,
to the world its God announcing
   seen in fleshly form on earth.

3 Eastern sages at his cradle
   make oblations rich and rare;
see them give in deep devotion
   gold and frankincense and myrrh.

4 Sacred gifts of mystic meaning:
   incense doth their God disclose,
gold the King of kings proclaimeth,
   myrrh his sepulchre foreshows.

5 Jesu, whom the Gentiles worshipped
   at thy glad Epiphany,
unto thee with God the Father
   and the Spirit glory be.

PRUDENTIUS (348–c. 413)
tr. E. CASWALL* (1814–78)

49 (AMR 77)

Was Lebet   13 10.13 10.   *Rheinhardt MS* (Üttingen, 1754)

1 O worship the Lord in the beauty of holiness;
bow down before him, his glory proclaim;
with gold of obedience, and incense of lowliness,
kneel and adore him: the Lord is his name.

2 Low at his feet lay thy burden of carefulness:
high on his heart he will bear it for thee,
comfort thy sorrows, and answer thy prayerfulness,
guiding thy steps as may best for thee be.

3 Fear not to enter his courts in the slenderness
of the poor wealth thou wouldst reckon as thine:
truth in its beauty, and love in its tenderness,
these are the offerings to lay on his shrine.

4 These, though we bring them in trembling and fearfulness,
he will accept for the name that is dear;
mornings of joy give for evenings of tearfulness,
trust for our trembling and hope for our fear.

J. S. B. Monsell (1811–75)

The first verse may be repeated at the end

50 (AMR **78**)

Tallis's Ordinal C.M. Thomas Tallis (*c.* 1505–85)

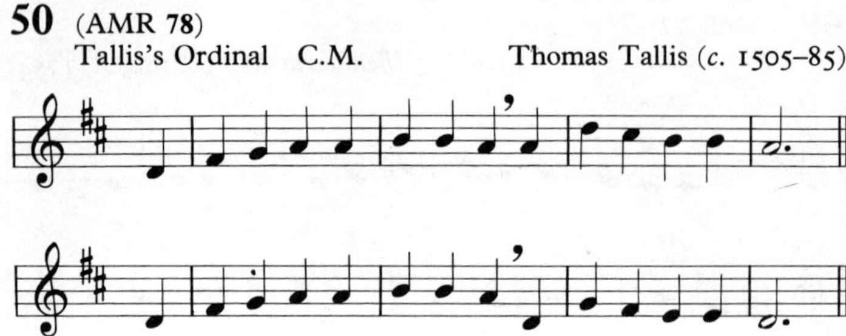

The heavenly Child in stature grows,
  and, growing, learns to die;
and still his early training shows‿
  his coming agony.

2

The Son of God his glory hides
  to dwell with parents poor;
and he who made the heavens abides‿
  in dwelling-place obscure.

3

Those mighty hands that rule the sky
  no earthly toil refuse;
the maker of the stars on high
  an humble trade pursues.

4

He whom the choirs of angels praise,
  bearing each dread decree,
his earthly parents now obeys
  in glad humility.

5

For this thy lowliness revealed,
  Jesu, we thee adore,
and praise to God the Father yield
  and Spirit evermore.

J. B. de Santeuil (1630–97)
tr. J. Chandler* (1806–76)

51 (AMR 79)
Dix 77.77.77.

Adapted from C. Kocher (1786–1872)
by W. H. Monk (1823–89)

The descant may be sung for verses 3 and 5

Epiphany

As with gladness men of old
did the guiding star behold,
as with joy they hailed its light,
leading onward, beaming bright;
so, most gracious Lord, may we‿
evermore be led to thee.

2

As with joyful steps they sped,
Saviour, to thy lowly bed,
there to bend the knee before‿
thee whom heaven and earth adore;
so may we with willing feet
ever seek thy mercy-seat.

3

As they offered gifts most rare
at thy cradle rude and bare,
so may we with holy joy,
pure and free from sin's alloy,
all our costliest treasures bring,
Christ, to thee our heavenly King.

4

Holy Jesus, every day‿
keep us in the narrow way,
and, when earthly things are past,
bring our ransomed souls at last
where they need no star to guide,
where no clouds thy glory hide.

5

In the heavenly country bright
need they no created light;
thou its light, its joy, its crown,
thou its sun which goes not down;
there for ever may we sing
alleluias to our King.

W. CHATTERTON DIX (1837–98)

52 (AMR **80**)

Dundee C.M. *Psalms* (Edinburgh, 1615)

ALTERNATIVE VERSION

T. Ravenscroft (1621)

The people that in darkness sat
  a glorious light have seen;
the light has shined on them who long‿
  in shades of death have been.

*2

To hail thee, Sun of Righteousness,
  the gathering nations come;
they joy as when the reapers bear‿
  their harvest treasures home.

*3

For thou their burden dost remove,
and break the tyrant's rod,
as in the day when Midian fell
before the sword of God.

4

For unto us a Child is born,
to us a Son is given,
and on his shoulder ever rests‿
all power in earth and heaven.

5

His name shall be the Prince of Peace,
the everlasting Lord,
the Wonderful, the Counsellor,
the God by all adored.

6

His righteous government and power‿
shall over all extend;
on judgement and on justice based,
his reign shall have no end.

*7

Lord Jesus, reign in us, we pray,
and make us thine alone,
who with the Father ever art
and Holy Spirit One.

J. MORISON* (1750–98)
Isaiah 9. 2–7

53 (AMR **81**)

St. Edmund 7 7.7 7. D. C. Steggall (1826–1905)

Songs of thankfulness and praise,
Jesu, Lord, to thee we raise,
manifested by the star
to the sages from afar;
branch of royal David's stem
in thy birth at Bethlehem:
anthems be to thee addrest,
God in Man made manifest.

2

Manifest at Jordan's stream,
Prophet, Priest, and King supreme;
and at Cana wedding-guest
in thy Godhead manifest;
manifest in power divine,
changing water into wine:
anthems be to thee addrest,
God in Man made manifest.

3

Manifest in making whole
palsied limbs and fainting soul;
manifest in valiant fight;
quelling all the devil's might;
manifest in gracious will,
ever bringing good from ill:
anthems be to thee addrest,
God in Man made manifest.

*4

Sun and moon shall darkened be,
stars shall fall, the heavens shall flee;
Christ will then like lightning shine,
all will see his glorious sign;
all will then the trumpet hear,
all will see the Judge appear:
thou by all wilt be confest,
God in Man made manifest.

5

Grant us grace to see thee, Lord,
mirrored in thy holy word;
may we imitate thee now,
and be pure, as pure art thou;
that we like to thee may be
at thy great Epiphany;
and may praise thee, ever blest,
God in Man made manifest.

CHRISTOPHER WORDSWORTH (1807–85)

54 (AMR 596)

Quem pastores 8 8 8.7. German Mediaeval Melody

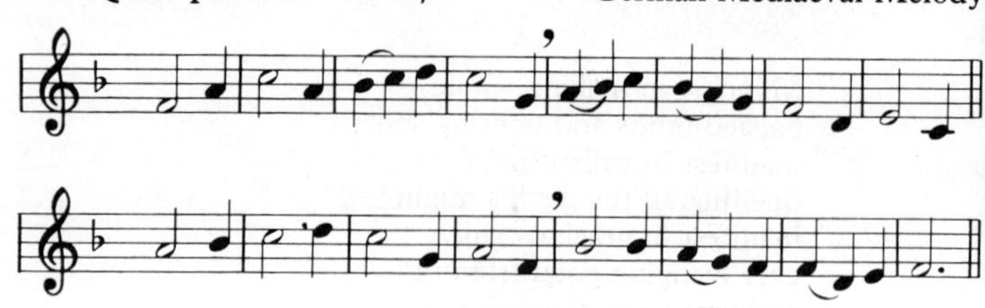

Thou whom shepherds worshipped, hearing
angels tell their tidings cheering,
'Sirs, away with doubt and fearing!
Christ the King is born for all;'

2

thou to whom came wise men faring,
gold and myrrh and incense bearing,
heartfelt homage thus declaring
to the King that's born for all:

3

bending low in adoration
thee we greet, for our salvation
given by wondrous incarnation,
King of Glory born for all.

Latin, tr. C. S. PHILLIPS (1883–1949)

55 (AMR **91**)

St. Andrew of Crete 6 5.6 5. D. J. B. Dykes (1823–76)

1

Christian, dost thou see them
  on the holy ground,
how the troops of Midian‿
  prowl and prowl around?
Christian, up and smite them,
  counting gain but loss;
smite them by the merit‿
  of the holy Cross.

2

Christian, dost thou feel them,
  how they work within,
striving, tempting, luring,
  goading into sin?
Christian, never tremble;
  never be down-cast;
smite them by the virtue‿
  of the Lenten fast.

3

Christian, dost thou hear them,
  how they speak thee fair?
'Always fast and vigil?
  Always watch and prayer?'
Christian, answer boldly,
  'While I breathe I pray:'
peace shall follow battle,
  night shall end in day.

4

'Well I know thy trouble,
  O my servant true;
thou art very weary,
  I was weary too;
but that toil shall make thee‿
  some day all mine own,
and the end of sorrow‿
  shall be near my throne.'

J. M. Neale* (1818–66)

56 (AMR **92**)
Aus der Tiefe 7 7.7 7. *Nürnbergisches Gesangbuch* (1676)
(Heinlein)

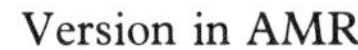

Version in AMR

I

Forty days and forty nights
thou wast fasting in the wild;
forty days and forty nights
tempted, and yet undefiled:

2

sunbeams scorching all the day;
chilly dew-drops nightly shed;
prowling beasts about thy way;
stones thy pillow, earth thy bed.

3

Shall not we thy sorrows share,
and from earthly joys abstain,
fasting with unceasing prayer,
glad with thee to suffer pain?

4

And if Satan, vexing sore,
flesh or spirit should assail,
thou, his vanquisher before,
grant we may not faint nor fa

5

So shall we have peace divine;
holier gladness ours shall be;
round us too shall angels shine,
such as ministered to thee.

6

Keep, O keep us, Saviour dear,
ever constant by thy side;
that with thee we may appear
at the eternal Eastertide.

G. H. Smyttan (1822–70)
and F. Pott (1832–1909)

57 (AMR **89**)

FIRST TUNE

Quam dilecta 66.66. H. L. Jenner (1820–98)

SECOND TUNE

Eccles 66.66. B. Luard Selby (1853–1918)

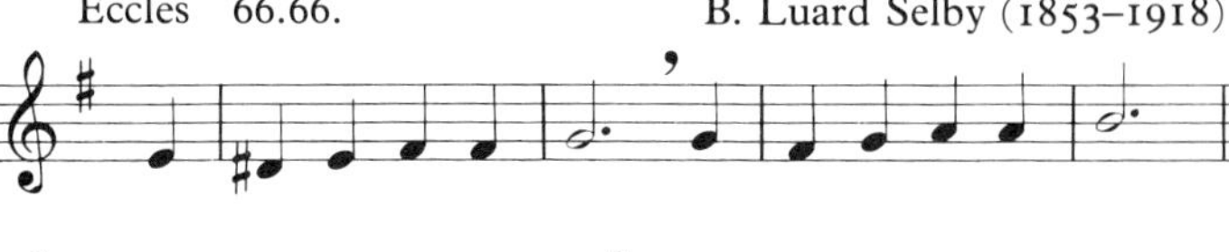

1

My spirit longs for thee
within my troubled breast,
though I unworthy be
of so divine a guest.

2

Of so divine a guest
unworthy though I be,
yet has my heart no rest
unless it come from thee.

3

Unless it come from thee,
in vain I look around;
in all that I can see
no rest is to be found.

4

No rest is to be found
but in thy blessèd love:
O let my wish be crowned,
and send it from above!

J. BYROM (1692–1763)

58 (AMR **96**) FIRST TUNE

Vexilla Regis L.M. Mode i

1 The roy - al ban - ners for - ward go,
2 There whilst he hung, his sa - cred side
3 Ful - filled is now what Da - vid told
4 O Tree of glo - ry, Tree most fair,
5 Up - on its arms, like bal - ance true,
6 To thee, e - ter - nal Three in One,
the Cross shines forth in mys - tic glow;
by sol - dier's spear was o - pened wide,
in true pro - phe - tic song of old,
or - dained those ho - ly limbs to bear,
he weighed the price for sin - ners due,
let hom - age meet by all be done:
where he in flesh, our flesh who made,
to cleanse us in the pre - cious flood
how God the hea - then's King should be;
how bright in pur - ple robe it stood,
the price which none but he could pay,
as by the Cross thou dost re - store,
our sen - tence bore, our ran - som paid.
of wa - ter min-gled with his blood.
for God is reign-ing from the Tree.
the pur - ple of a Sa - viour's blood!
and spoiled the spoil-er of his prey.
so rule and guide us ev - er - more. A - men.

SECOND TUNE

Gonfalon Royal L.M. P. C. Buck (1871–1947)

1

e royal banners forward go,
e Cross shines forth in mystic glow;
ere he in flesh, our flesh who made,
r sentence bore, our ransom paid.

2

ere whilst he hung, his sacred side‿
soldier's spear was opened wide,
cleanse us in the precious flood‿
water mingled with his blood.

3

Fulfilled is now what David told
in true prophetic song of old,
how God the heathen's King should be;
for God is reigning from the Tree.

4

O Tree of glory, Tree most fair,
ordained those holy limbs to bear,
how bright in purple robe it stood,
the purple of a Saviour's blood!

5

Upon its arms, like balance true,
he weighed the price for sinners due,
the price which none but he could pay,
and spoiled the spoiler of his prey.

6

To thee, eternal Three in One,
let homage meet by all be done:
as by the Cross thou dost restore,
so rule and guide us evermore Amen.

VENANTIUS FORTUNATUS (c. 530–c. 600)
tr. J. M. NEALE* (1818–66)

59 (AMR **97**) FIRST TUNE

Pange Lingua 8 7.8 7.8 7. Mode i

PART I

1 Sing, my tongue, the glorious battle,
sing the last, the dread affray;
o'er the Cross, the victor's trophy,
sound the high triumphal lay,
how, the pains of death enduring,
earth's Redeemer won the day.

2 When at length the appointed fulness‿
of the sacred time was come,
he was sent, the world's creator,
from the Father's heavenly home,
and was found in human fashion,
offspring of the Virgin's womb.

3 Now the thirty years are ended
which on earth he willed to see,
willingly he meets his Passion,
born to set his people free;
on the Cross the Lamb is lifted,
there the sacrifice to be.

4 There the nails and spear he suffers,
vinegar and gall and reed;
from his sacred body piercèd
blood and water both proceed:
precious flood, which all creation
from the stain of sin hath freed.

PART 2

5 Faithful Cross, above all other,
one and only noble tree,
none in foliage, none in blossom,
none in fruit thy peer may be;
sweet the wood, and sweet the iron,
and thy load, most sweet is he.

6 Bend, O lofty tree, thy branches,
thy too rigid sinews bend;
and awhile the stubborn hardness,
which thy birth bestowed, suspend;
and the limbs of heaven's high Monarch
gently on thine arms extend.

7 Thou alone wast counted worthy
this world's ransom to sustain,
that a shipwrecked race for ever
might a port of refuge gain,
with the sacred blood anointed
of the Lamb for sinners slain.

This Doxology is sung after either part

8 Praise and honour to the Father,
praise and honour to the Son,
praise and honour to the Spirit,
ever Three and ever One:
One in might, and One in glory,
while eternal ages run.

VENANTIUS FORTUNATUS (c. 530–c. 600)
tr. J. M. NEALE* (1818–66)

59 (AMR 97) SECOND TUNE

St. Thomas 8 7.8 7.8 7. Traditional Melody (18th cent.)

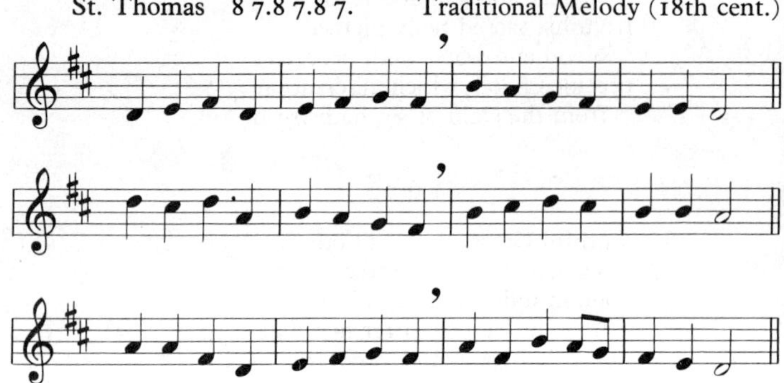

PART I

1 Sing, my tongue, the glorious battle,
sing the last, the dread affray;
o'er the Cross, the victor's trophy,
sound the high triumphal lay,
how, the pains of death enduring,
earth's Redeemer won the day.

2 When at length the appointed fulness‿
of the sacred time was come,
he was sent, the world's creator,
from the Father's heavenly home,
and was found in human fashion,
offspring of the Virgin's womb.

3 Now the thirty years are ended
which on earth he willed to see,
willingly he meets his Passion,
born to set his people free;
on the Cross the Lamb is lifted,
there the sacrifice to be.

4 There the nails and spear he suffers,
vinegar and gall and reed;
from his sacred body piercèd
blood and water both proceed:
precious flood, which all creation
from the stain of sin hath freed.

PART 2

5 Faithful Cross, above all other,
one and only noble tree,
none in foliage, none in blossom,
none in fruit thy peer may be;
sweet the wood, and sweet the iron,
and thy load, most sweet is he.

6 Bend, O lofty tree, thy branches,
thy too rigid sinews bend;
and awhile the stubborn hardness,
which thy birth bestowed, suspend;
and the limbs of heaven's high Monarch
gently on thine arms extend.

7 Thou alone wast counted worthy
this world's ransom to sustain,
that a shipwrecked race for ever
might a port of refuge gain,
with the sacred blood anointed
of the Lamb for sinners slain.

This Doxology is sung after either part

8 Praise and honour to the Father,
praise and honour to the Son,
praise and honour to the Spirit,
ever Three and ever One:
One in might, and One in glory,
while eternal ages run.

VENANTIUS FORTUNATUS (c. 530–c. 600)
tr. J. M. NEALE* (1818–66)

60 (AMR **98**)

St. Theodulph 7 6.7 6. D. Adapted from M. Teschner (1615)

Fine

D.C.

ANOTHER VERSION

arr. J. S. Bach (1685–1750)

1 *All glory, laud, and honour*
to thee, Redeemer, King,
to whom the lips of children
made sweet hosannas ring.

2 Thou art the King of Israel,
thou David's royal Son,
who in the Lord's name comest,
the King and blessèd one:

*3 The company of angels
are praising thee on high,
and mortal men and all things‿
created make reply:

4 The people of the Hebrews
with palms before thee went:
our praise and prayer and anthems
before thee we present:

5 To thee before thy passion
they sang their hymns of praise:
to thee now high exalted
our melody we raise:

*6 Thou didst accept their praises:
accept the prayers we bring,
who in all good delightest,
thou good and gracious King:

7 *All glory, laud, and honour*
to thee, Redeemer, King,
to whom the lips of children
made sweet hosannas ring.

THEODULPH OF ORLEANS (d. 821)
tr. J. M. NEALE (1818–66)

A longer version is at 328

61 (AMR **99**) FIRST TUNE

St. Drostane L.M. J. B. Dykes (1823–76)

SECOND TUNE

Winchester New L.M. Adapted from *Musicalisches Hand-Buch* (Hamburg, 1690)

Ride on, ride on in majesty!
Hark, all the tribes hosanna cry.
O Saviour meek, pursue thy road
with palms and scattered garments strowed.

2

Ride on, ride on in majesty!
In lowly pomp ride on to die:
O Christ, thy triumphs now begin
o'er captive death and conquered sin.

3

Ride on, ride on in majesty!
The wingèd squadrons of the sky‿
look down with sad and wondering eyes
to see the approaching sacrifice.

4

Ride on, ride on in majesty!
The last and fiercest strife is nigh:
the Father on his sapphire throne
awaits his own anointed Son.

5

Ride on, ride on in majesty!
In lowly pomp ride on to die;
bow thy meek head to mortal pain,
then take, O God, thy power, and reign.

H. H. MILMAN* (1791–1868)

62 (AMR **599**)
Farley Castle 10 10.10 10. Henry Lawes (1596–1662)

Ride on triumphantly! Behold, we lay‿
our lusts and sins and proud wills in thy way:
thy road is ready, and thy paths made straight
with longing expectation seem to wait.

2

Hosanna! Welcome to our hearts! for here‿
thou hast a temple too, as Sion dear:
enter, O Lord, and cleanse that holy place
where thou dost choose to set thy beauteous face.

Adapted from JEREMY TAYLOR (1613–67)

63 (AMR **102**)

Love Unknown 6 6.6 6.4 4.4 4. John Ireland (1879–1962)

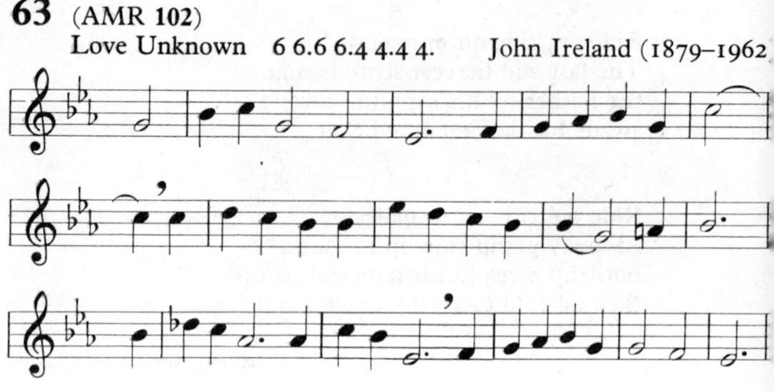

My song is love unknown,
my Saviour's love to me,
love to the loveless shown,
that they might lovely be.
O who am I,
that for my sake
my Lord should take‿
frail flesh, and die?

2

He came from his blest throne,
salvation to bestow;
but men made strange, and none‿
the longed-for Christ would know.
But O, my Friend,
my Friend indeed,
who at my need‿
his life did spend!

3

Sometimes they strew his way,
and his sweet praises sing;
resounding all the day
hosannas to their King.
Then 'Crucify!'‿
is all their breath,
and for his death‿
they thirst and cry.

*4

Why, what hath my Lord done?
  what makes this rage and spite?
he made the lame to run,
  he gave the blind their sight.
    Sweet injuries!
      yet they at these‿
      themselves displease,
    and 'gainst him rise.

5

They rise, and needs will have‿
  my dear Lord made away;
a murderer they save,
  the Prince of Life they slay.
    Yet cheerful he‿
      to suffering goes,
      that he his foes‿
    from thence might free.

*6

In life, no house, no home
  my Lord on earth might have;
in death, no friendly tomb
  but what a stranger gave.
    What may I say?
      Heaven was his home;
      but mine the tomb‿
    wherein he lay.

7

Here might I stay and sing:
  no story so divine;
never was love, dear King,
  never was grief like thine!
    This is my Friend,
      in whose sweet praise
      I all my days‿
    could gladly spend.

Samuel Crossman (1624–83)

64 (AMR **104**)

St. Bernard C.M. *Tochter Sion* (Cologne, 1741)

All ye who seek for sure relief
in trouble and distress,
whatever sorrow vex the mind,
or guilt the soul oppress,

2

Jesus, who gave himself for you
upon the cross to die,
opens to you his sacred heart:
O to that heart draw nigh.

3

Ye hear how kindly he invites;
ye hear his words so blest:
'All ye that labour come to me,
and I will give you rest.'

4

O Jesus, joy of saints on high,
thou hope of inners here,
attracted by those loving words
to thee we lift our prayer.

5

Wash thou our wounds in that dear blood
which from thy heart doth flow;
a new and contrite heart on all‿
who cry to thee bestow.

Latin, 18th cent.
tr. E. CASWALL (1814–78)

65 (AMR **106**)

St. Francis Xavier C.M. John Stainer (1840–1901)

1 My God, I love thee; not because‿
  I hope for heaven thereby,
nor yet because who love thee not
  are lost eternally.

2 Thou, O my Jesus, thou didst me‿
  upon the cross embrace;
for me didst bear the nails and spear,
  and manifold disgrace,

3 and griefs and torments numberless,
  and sweat of agony;
yea, death itself – and all for me
  who was thine enemy.

4 Then why, O blessèd Jesu Christ,
  should I not love thee well?
not for the sake of winning heaven,
  nor of escaping hell;

5 not from the hope of gaining aught,
  not seeking a reward;
but as thyself hast lovèd me,
  O ever-loving Lord.

6 So would I love thee, dearest Lord,
  and in thy praise will sing;
solely because thou art my God,
  and my most loving King.

Latin, 17th cent.
tr. E. Caswall (1814–78)

66 (AMR **107**)
Caswall 6 5.6 5. F. Filitz (1804–76)

Glory be to Jesus,
who, in bitter pains,
poured for me the life-blood
from his sacred veins.

2

Grace and life eternal
in that blood I find;
blest be his compassion
infinitely kind.

3

Blest through endless ages
be the precious stream,
which from endless torments
did the world redeem.

4

Abel's blood for vengeance
pleaded to the skies;
but the blood of Jesus
for our pardon cries.

5

Oft as it is sprinkled
on our guilty hearts,
Satan in confusion
terror-struck departs;

6

oft as earth exulting
wafts its praise on high,
angel-hosts rejoicing
make their glad reply.

7

Lift ye then your voices;
swell the mighty flood;
louder still and louder
praise the precious blood.

Italian, tr. E. CASWALL (1814–78)

67 (AMR **108**)

Rockingham L.M. Adapted by E. Miller (1735—1807

The descant may be used for verse 4

Crucifixion to the world by the Cross of Christ

When I survey the wondrous Cross
  on which the Prince of Glory died,
my richest gain I count but loss,
  and pour contempt on all my pride.

2

Forbid it, Lord, that I should boast
  save in the Cross of Christ my God;
all the vain things that charm me most,
  I sacrifice them to his blood.

3

See from his head, his hands, his feet,
  sorrow and love flow mingling down;
did e'er such love and sorrow meet,
  or thorns compose so rich a crown?

4

Were the whole realm of nature mine,
  that were an offering far too small;
love so amazing, so divine,
  demands my soul, my life, my all.

ISAAC WATTS (1674–1748)
Galatians 6. 14

68 (AMR **111**)

Passion Chorale 7 6 7 6. D. H. L. Hassler (1564–1612)

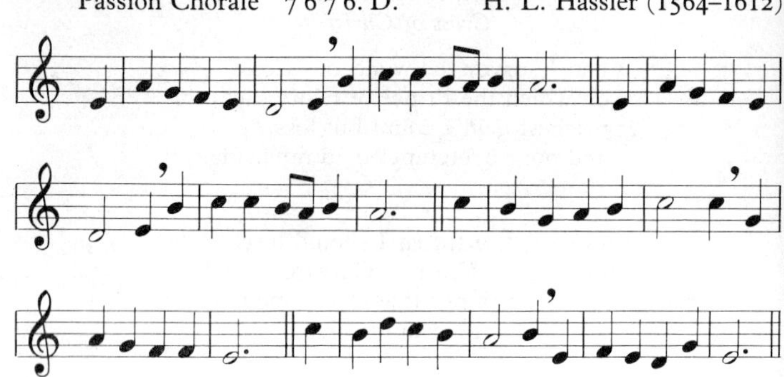

O sacred head, surrounded
by crown of piercing thorn!
O bleeding head, so wounded,
so shamed and put to scorn!
Death's pallid hue comes o'er thee,
the glow of life decays;
yet angel-hosts adore thee,
and tremble as they gaze.

2

Thy comeliness and vigour
is withered up and gone,
and in thy wasted figure
I see death drawing on.
O agony and dying!
O love to sinners free!
Jesu, all grace supplying,
turn thou thy face on me.

3

In this thy bitter passion,
good Shepherd, think of me
with thy most sweet compassion,
unworthy though I be:
beneath thy Cross abiding
for ever would I rest,
in thy dear love confiding,
and with thy presence blest.

P. Gerhardt (1607–76)
based on *Salve caput cruentatum*
tr. H. W. Baker (1821–77)

69 (AMR **118**)

Stabat Mater 8 8 7. D. *Maintzisch Gesangbuch* (1661)

'Woman, behold thy son . . . behold thy mother.'

1

At the cross her station keeping
stood the mournful Mother weeping,
  where he hung, the dying Lord;
for her soul, of joy bereavèd,
bowed with anguish, deeply grievèd,
  felt the sharp and piercing sword.

2

O how sad and sore distressèd
now was she, that Mother blessèd
  of the sole-begotten one!
Deep the woe of her affliction,
when she saw the crucifixion
  of her ever-glorious Son.

3

Who, on Christ's dear Mother gazing
pierced by anguish so amazing,
  born of woman, would not weep?
who, on Christ's dear Mother thinking
such a cup of sorrow drinking,
  would not share her sorrows deep?

4

For his people's sins chastisèd,
she beheld her Son despisèd,
  scourged, and crowned with thorns entwined;
saw him then from judgement taken,
and in death by all forsaken,
  till his spirit he resigned.

5

O good Jesu, let me borrow‿
something of thy Mother's sorrow,
  fount of love, Redeemer kind,
that my heart fresh ardour gaining,
and a purer love attaining,
  may with thee acceptance find.

Ascribed to JACOPONE DA TODI (d. 1306)
tr. E. CASWALL* (1814–78)

70 (AMR 435) FIRST TUNE

Herongate L.M. English Traditional Melody

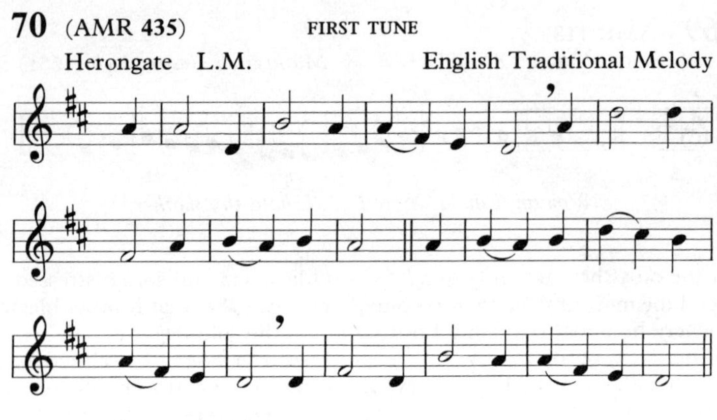

SECOND TUNE

Alstone L.M. C. E. Willing (1830–1904)

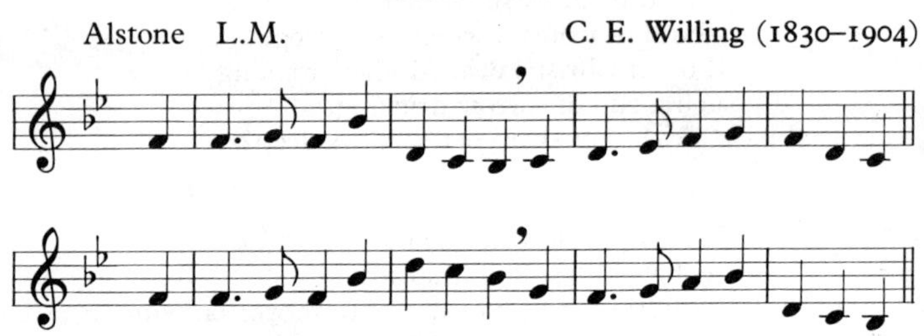

It is a thing most wonderful,
almost too wonderful to be,
that God's own Son should come from heaven,
and die to save a child like me.

2

And yet I know that it is true:
he chose a poor and humble lot,
and wept and toiled and mourned and died
for love of those who loved him not.

*3

I cannot tell how he could love
a child so weak and full of sin;
his love must be most wonderful,
if he could die my love to win.

*4

I sometimes think about the Cross,
and shut my eyes, and try to see‿
the cruel nails and crown of thorns,
and Jesus crucified for me.

*5

But even could I see him die,
I could but see a little part
of that great love which, like a fire,
is always burning in his heart.

6

It is most wonderful to know
his love for me so free and sure;
but 'tis more wonderful to see
my love for him so faint and poor.

7

And yet I want to love thee, Lord;
O light the flame within my heart,
and I will love thee more and more,
until I see thee as thou art.

W. Walsham How (1823–97)

71 (AMR **436**)
Albano C.M. Vincent Novello (1781–1861)

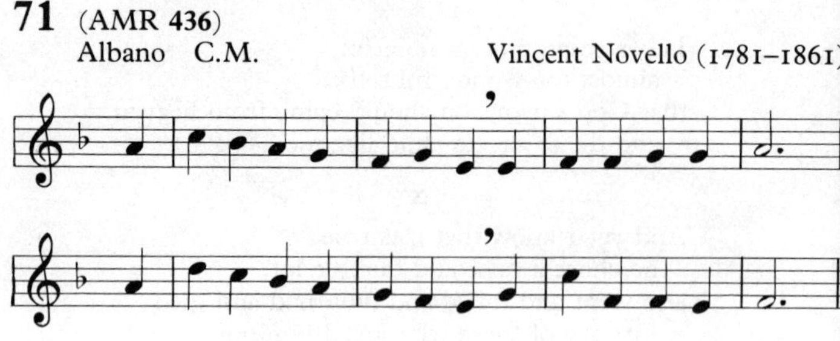

O dearest Lord, thy sacred head
with thorns was pierced for me;
O pour thy blessing on my head
that I may think for thee.

2

O dearest Lord, thy sacred hands
with nails were pierced for me;
O shed thy blessing on my hands
that they may work for thee.

3

O dearest Lord, thy sacred feet
with nails were pierced for me;
O pour thy blessing on my feet
that they may follow thee.

4

O dearest Lord, thy sacred heart
with spear was pierced for me;
O pour thy Spirit in my heart
that I may live for thee.

H. E. HARDY (Father Andrew) (1869–1946)

72 (AMR 633)

Crucifer 10 10. and refrain S. H. Nicholson (1875–1947)

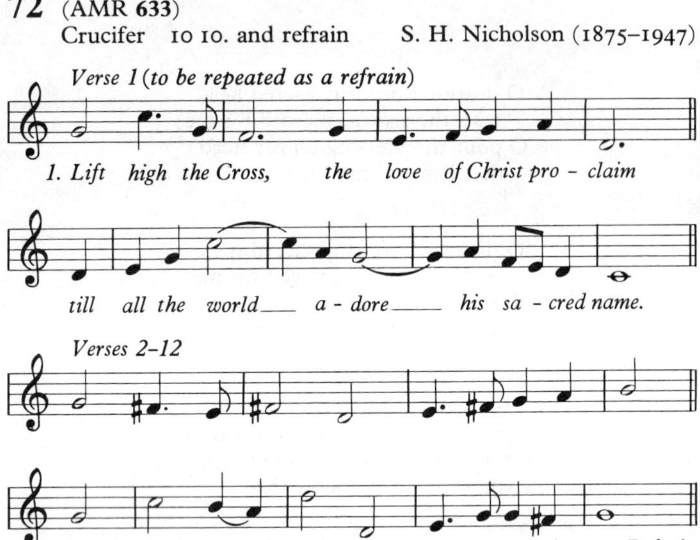
Verse 1 (to be repeated as a refrain)
1. Lift high the Cross, the love of Christ pro - claim
till all the world a - dore his sa - cred name.
Verses 2–12
Refrain

Lift high the Cross, the love of Christ proclaim
till all the world adore his sacred name.

2

Come, brethren, follow where our Captain trod,
our King victorious, Christ the Son of God:

*3

Led on their way by this triumphant sign,
the hosts of God in conquering ranks combine:

*4

Each new-born soldier of the Crucified
bears on his brow the seal of him who died:

*5

This is the sign which Satan's legions fear
and angels veil their faces to revere:

*6

Saved by this Cross whereon their Lord was slain,
the sons of Adam their lost home regain:

*7

From north and south, from east and west they raise
in growing unison their song of praise:

8

O Lord, once lifted on the glorious Tree,
as thou hast promised, draw men unto thee:

9

Let every race and every language tell
of him who saves our souls from death and hell:

10

From farthest regions let them homage bring,
and on his Cross adore their Saviour King:

11

Set up thy throne, that earth's despair may cease
beneath the shadow of its healing peace:

12

For thy blest Cross which doth for all atone
creation's praises rise before thy throne:

Lift high the Cross, the love of Christ proclaim
till all the world adore his sacred name.

G. W. Kitchin (1827–1912)
and M. R. Newbolt (1874–1956)

73 (AMR **128**)

St. Fulbert C.M. H. J. Gauntlett (1805–76)

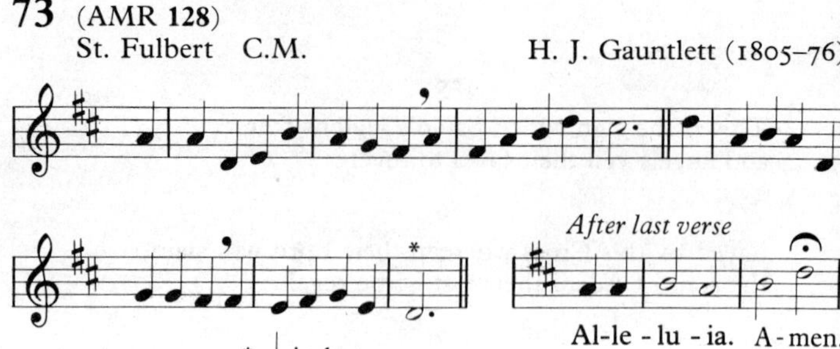
After last verse
Al-le - lu - ia. A-men.

* 𝅗𝅥 in last verse

Ye choirs of new Jerusalem,
your sweetest notes employ,
the paschal victory to hymn
in strains of holy joy.

2

For Judah's Lion bursts his chains,
crushing the serpent's head;
and cries aloud through death's domains
to wake the imprisoned dead.

3

Devouring depths of hell their prey‿
at his command restore;
his ransomed hosts pursue their way
where Jesus goes before.

4

Triumphant in his glory now
to him all power is given;
to him in one communion bow
all saints in earth and heaven.

5

While we his soldiers praise our King,
his mercy we implore,
within his palace bright to bring
and keep us evermore.

6

All glory to the Father be,
all glory to the Son,
all glory, Holy Ghost, to thee,
while endless ages run.
Alleluia. Amen.

St. Fulbert of Chartres (d. 1028)
tr. R. Campbell* (1814–68)

In verse 2, *lines* 1–2, *Christ*, '*the Lion that is of the tribe of Judah*' (*Rev.* 5. 5), *is portrayed as fulfilling the promise of redemption in Gen.* 3. 15

74 (AMR **130**)

O filii et filiae 8 8 8. with Alleluia French Melody (17th cent.)

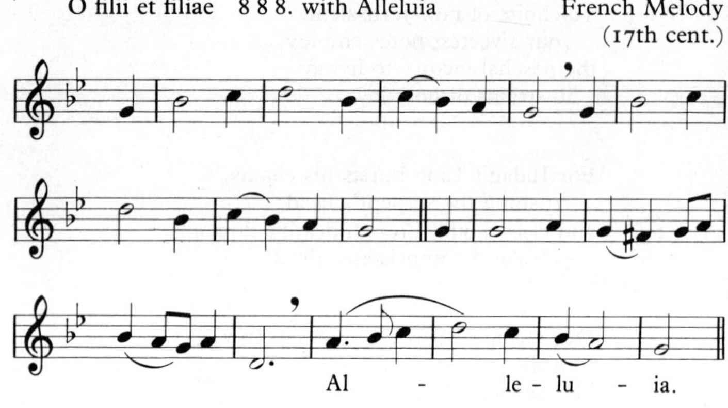

O sons and daughters, let us sing!
The King of heaven, the glorious King,
o'er death to-day rose triumphing.
Alleluia.

2

That Easter morn, at break of day,
the faithful women went their way
to seek the tomb where Jesus lay.
Alleluia.

3

An angel clad in white they see,
who sat, and spake unto the three,
'Your Lord doth go to Galilee.'
Alleluia.

*4

That night the apostles met in fear;
amidst them came their Lord most dear,
and said, 'My peace be on all here.'
Alleluia.

*5

When Thomas first the tidings heard,
how they had seen the risen Lord,
he doubted the disciples' word.
Alleluia.

*6

'My piercèd side, O Thomas, see;
my hands, my feet I show to thee;
not faithless, but believing be.'
Alleluia.

*7

No longer Thomas then denied;
he saw the feet, the hands, the side;
'Thou art my Lord and God,' he cried.
Alleluia.

8

How blest are they who have not seen,
and yet whose faith hath constant been,
for they eternal life shall win.
Alleluia.

9

On this most holy day of days,
to God your hearts and voices raise
in laud and jubilee and praise.
Alleluia.

J. TISSERAND (d. 1419)
tr. J. M. NEALE* (1818–66)

75 (AMR 132)

Ellacombe 76.76. D. *Württemberg Gesangbuch*, 1784

1

The day of resurrection!
  earth, tell it out abroad;
the Passover of gladness,
  the Passover of God;
from death to life eternal,
  from earth unto the sky,
our God hath brought us over
  with hymns of victory.

2

Our hearts be pure from evil,
  that we may see aright‿
the Lord in rays eternal
  of resurrection-light;
and, listening to his accents,
  may hear so calm and plain‿
his own 'All hail,' and, hearing,
  may raise the victor strain.

3

Now let the heavens be joyful,
  and earth her song begin,
the round world keep high triumph,
  and all that is therein;
let all things seen and unseen
  their notes of gladness blend,
for Christ the Lord is risen,
  our joy that hath no end.

St. John of Damascus (d. c. 754)
tr. J. M. Neale* (1818–66)

76 (AMR 133)

St. John Damascene 7 6.7 6. D. A. H. Brown (1830–1926)

Alternative Tune: *Ave virgo virginum* (NS 443, MHT 110)

1

Come, ye faithful, raise the strain
  of triumphant gladness!
God hath brought his Israel
  into joy from sadness;
Loosed from Paraoh's bitter yoke
  Jacob's sons and daughters;
Led them with unmoistened foot
  through the Red Sea waters.

2

'Tis the spring of souls to-day;
  Christ hath burst his prison,
And from three days' sleep in death
  as a sun hath risen:
All the winter of our sins,
  long and dark, is flying
From his light, to whom we give
  laud and praise undying.

3

Now the queen of seasons, bright
  with the day of splendour,
with the royal feast of feasts,
  comes its joy to render;
comes to glad Jerusalem,
  who with true affection
welcomes in unwearied strains
  Jesu's resurrection.

4

Alleluia now we cry
  to our King immortal,
who triumphant burst the bars
  of the tomb's dark portal;
Alleluia, with the Son
  God the Father praising;
Alleluia yet again
  to the Spirit raising.

St. John of Damascus (d. c. 754)
tr. J. M. Neale* (1816–66)

77 (AMR 134)

Easter Hymn 77.77. with Alleluias *Lyra Davidica*, 170
(later versio

DESCANT
Al - le - lu - ia.
Al - le - lu - ia.
Al - le - lu - ia.
Al - le - lu - ia.
Al - le - lu - ia.
Al - le - lu - ia.
Al - le - lu - ia.
Al - le - lu - ia.

The descant may be sung for verse 3

Easter

Jesus Christ is risen to-day, *Alleluia.*
our triumphant holy day, *Alleluia.*
who did once, upon the cross, *Alleluia.*
suffer to redeem our loss. *Alleluia.*

2

Hymns of praise then let us sing
unto Christ, our heavenly King,
who endured the Cross and grave,
sinners to redeem and save.

3

But the pains that he endured
our salvation have procured;
now above the sky he's King,
where the angels ever sing.

Lyra Davidica (1708)
and others

78 (AMR **135**) FIRST TUNE

Gelobt sei Gott
8 8 8. with Alleluias

M. Vulpius (*Gesangbuch*, 1609

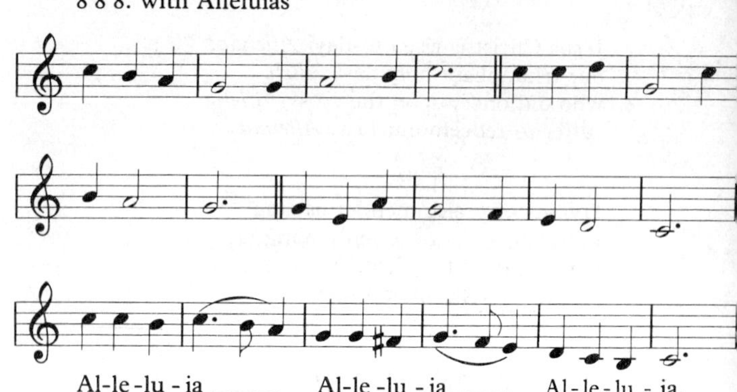
Al-le-lu-ia
Al-le-lu-ia
Al-le-lu-ia.

SECOND TUNE

Victory
8 8 8. with Alleluia

From a *Magnificat* by Palestrina (1591
adapted by W. H. Monk (1823–89

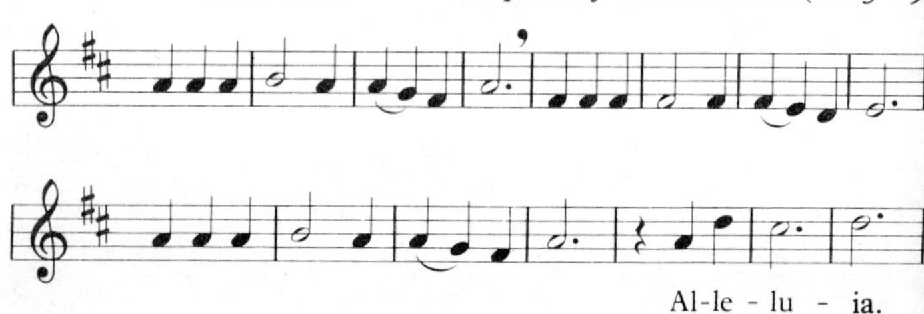
Al-le-lu-ia.

The strife is o'er, the battle done;
now is the Victor's triumph won;
O let the song of praise be sung:
Alleluia.

2

Death's mightiest powers have done their worst,
and Jesus hath his foes dispersed;
let shouts of praise and joy outburst:
Alleluia.

3

On the third morn he rose again
glorious in majesty to reign;
O let us swell the joyful strain:
Alleluia.

4

Lord, by the stripes which wounded thee
from death's dread sting thy servants free,
that we may live, and sing to thee
Alleluia.

Latin, ? 17th cent.
tr. F. POTT (1832–1909)

Another translation of these words is at 455

79 (AMR **136**)
Württemberg
7 7.7 7. with Alleluia

Hundert Arien
(Dresden, 1694)

Christ the Lord is risen again,
Christ hath broken every chain.
Hark, angelic voices cry,
singing evermore on high,
Alleluia.

2

He who gave for us his life,
who for us endured the strife,
is our paschal Lamb to-day;
we too sing for joy, and say‿
Alleluia.

3

He who bore all pain and loss
comfortless upon the Cross,
lives in glory now on high,
pleads for us, and hears our cry:
Alleluia.

*4

He whose path no records tell,
who descended into hell,
who the strong man armed hath bound,
now in highest heaven is crowned.
Alleluia.

5

He who slumbered in the grave
is exalted now to save;
now through Christendom it rings
that the Lamb is King of kings.
Alleluia.

6

Now he bids us tell abroad
how the lost may be restored,
how the penitent forgiven,
how we too may enter heaven.
Alleluia.

7

Thou, our paschal Lamb indeed,
Christ, thy ransomed people feed;
take our sins and guilt away:
let us sing by night and day
Alleluia.

M. WEISSE (c. 1480–1534)
tr. CATHERINE WINKWORTH (1827–78)

80 (AMR **137**)

Lux Eoi 8 7.8 7. D. Arthur Sullivan (1842–1900)

Alternative Tune: *Blaenwern* (NS 464, MHT 131)

Alleluia, Alleluia,
  hearts to heaven and voices raise;
sing to God a hymn of gladness,
  sing to God a hymn of praise:
he who on the Cross a victim
  for the world's salvation bled,
Jesus Christ, the King of Glory,
  now is risen from the dead.

2

Christ is risen, Christ the first-fruits‿
  of the holy harvest field,
which will all its full abundance
  at his second coming yield;
then the golden ears of harvest
  will their heads before him wave,
ripened by his glorious sunshine,
  from the furrows of the grave.

3

Christ is risen, we are risen;
  shed upon us heavenly grace,
rain, and dew, and gleams of glory‿
  from the brightness of thy face;
that we, with our hearts in heaven,
  here on earth may fruitful be,
and by angel-hands be gathered,
  and be ever, Lord, with thee.

4

Alleluia, Alleluia,
  glory be to God on high;
Alleluia to the Saviour,
  who has gained the victory;
Alleluia to the Spirit,
  fount of love and sanctity;
Alleluia, Alleluia,
  to the Triune Majesty.

Christopher Wordsworth (1807–85)

81 (AMR **139**)
Salzburg 7 7.7 7. D. J. Hintze (1622–1702)

At the Lamb's high feast we sing
praise to our victorious King,
who hath washed us in the tide
flowing from his piercèd side;
praise we him, whose love divine‿
gives his sacred blood for wine,
gives his body for the feast,
Christ the victim, Christ the priest.

*2

Where the paschal blood is poured,
death's dark angel sheathes his sword;
Israel's hosts triumphant go
through the wave that drowns the foe.
Praise we Christ, whose blood was shed,
paschal victim, paschal bread;
with sincerity and love
eat we manna from above.

3

Mighty victim from the sky,
hell's fierce powers beneath thee lie;
thou hast conquered in the fight,
thou hast brought us life and light.
Now no more can death appal,
now no more the grave enthral:
thou hast opened Paradise,
and in thee thy saints shall rise.

4

Easter triumph, Easter joy,
sin alone can this destroy;
from sin's power do thou set free
souls new-born, O Lord, in thee.
Hymns of glory and of praise,
risen Lord, to thee we raise;
holy Father, praise to thee,
with the Spirit, ever be.

Latin, tr. R. Campbell (1814–68)

82 (AMR **140**)

St. Albinus 7 8.7 8. with Alleluia H. J. Gauntlett (1805–76)

Jesus lives! thy terrors now‿
can no more, O death, appal us;
Jesus lives! by this we know
thou, O grave, canst not enthral us.
Alleluia.

2

Jesus lives! henceforth is death‿
but the gate of life immortal:
this shall calm our trembling breath,
when we pass its gloomy portal.
Alleluia.

3

Jesus lives! for us he died;
then, alone to Jesus living,
pure in heart may we abide,
glory to our Saviour giving.
Alleluia.

4

Jesus lives! our hearts know well‿
naught from us his love shall sever;
life nor death nor powers of hell
tear us from his keeping ever.
Alleluia.

5

Jesus lives! to him the throne‿
over all the world is given:
may we go where he is gone,
rest and reign with him in heaven.
Alleluia.

C. F. Gellert (1715–69)
tr. Frances E. Cox* (1812–97)

83 (AMR **141**)
Savannah 77.77. John Wesley's *Foundery Collection*, 1742

Love's redeeming work is done;
fought the fight, the battle won:
lo, our Sun's eclipse is o'er,
lo, he sets in blood no more.

2

Vain the stone, the watch, the seal;
Christ has burst the gates of hell;
death in vain forbids his rise;
Christ has opened Paradise.

3

Lives again our glorious King;
where, O death, is now thy sting?
Dying once, he all doth save;
where thy victory, O grave?

4

Soar we now where Christ has led,
following our exalted Head;
made like him, like him we rise;
ours the cross, the grave, the skies.

5

Hail the Lord of earth and heaven!
praise to thee by both be given:
thee we greet triumphant now;
hail, the Resurrection thou!

CHARLES WESLEY (1707–88)

84 (AMR **142**)
St. Michael S.M.

Adapted from
Anglo-Genevan Psalms, 1561

The Lord is risen indeed:
now is his work performed;
now is the mighty captive freed,
and death's strong castle stormed.

2

The Lord is risen indeed:
then hell has lost his prey;
with him is risen the ransomed seed
to reign in endless day.

3

The Lord is risen indeed:
he lives, to die no more;
he lives, the sinner's cause to plead,
whose curse and shame he bore.

4

The Lord is risen indeed:
attending angels, hear!
up to the courts of heaven with speed
the joyful tidings bear.

5

Then take your golden lyres,
and strike each cheerful chord;
join, all ye bright celestial choirs,
to sing our risen Lord.

T. Kelly (1769–1855)

85 (AMR **603**)
Gelobt sei Gott — M. Vulpius
8 8 8. with Alleluias — (*Gesangbuch*, 1609)

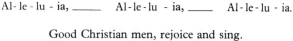

Al-le-lu-ia, Al-le-lu-ia, Al-le-lu-ia.

Good Christian men, rejoice and sing.
Now is the triumph of our King.
To all the world glad news we bring:
Alleluia.

2

The Lord of Life is risen for ay:
bring flowers of song to strew his way;
let all mankind rejoice and say
Alleluia.

3

Praise we in songs of victory
that Love, that Life, which cannot die,
and sing with hearts uplifted high
Alleluia.

4

Thy name we bless, O risen Lord,
and sing to-day with one accord
the life laid down, the life restored:
Alleluia.

C. A. Alington (1872–1955)

86 (AMR **146**)
Metzler's Redhead C.M. R. Redhead (1820–1901)

1 Jesu, our hope, our heart's desire,
thy work of grace we sing;
Redeemer of the world art thou,
its Maker and its King.

2 How vast the mercy and the love
which laid our sins on thee,
and led thee to a cruel death,
to set thy people free!

3 But now the bonds of death are burst,
the ransom has been paid;
and thou art on thy Father's throne,
in glorious robes arrayed.

4 O may thy mighty love prevail
our sinful souls to spare;
O may we stand around thy throne,
and see thy glory there.

5 Jesu, our only joy be thou,
as thou our prize wilt be;
in thee be all our glory now
and through eternity.

6 All praise to thee who art gone up
triumphantly to heaven;
all praise to God the Father's name,
and Holy Ghost be given.

Latin, tr. J. CHANDLER (1806–76)

87 (AMR **147**) FIRST TUNE

Llanfair 7 7.7 7. with Alleluias Welsh Hymn Melody

Al — le - lu - ia.
Al — le - lu - ia.
Al — le - lu - ia.
SECOND TUNE
Chislehurst 7 7.7 7. with Alleluias
S. H. Nicholson (1875–1947)
Hail the day that sees him rise, *Al - le - lu - ia.*
to his throne a - bove the skies; *Al - le - lu - ia.*
Christ, the Lamb for sin-ners given,
en-ters now the high-est heaven. *Al - le - lu - ia, Al - le - lu - ia, Al - le - lu - ia.*

Alternative Tune: *Orientis partibus* (302)

Hail the day that sees him rise,
Alleluia.
to his throne above the skies;
Alleluia.
Christ, the Lamb for sinners given,
Alleluia.
enters now the highest heaven.
Alleluia.

2

There for him high triumph waits;
lift your heads, eternal gates!
he hath conquered death and sin;
take the King of Glory in!

3

Lo, the heaven its Lord receives,
yet he loves the earth he leaves;
though returning to his throne,
still he calls mankind his own.

4

See, he lifts his hands above;
see, he shews the prints of love;
hark, his gracious lips bestow
blessings on his Church below.

5

Still for us he intercedes,
his prevailing death he pleads;
near himself prepares our place,
he the first-fruits of our race.

6

Lord, though parted from our sight,
far above the starry height,
grant our hearts may thither rise,
seeking thee above the skies.

CHARLES WESLEY (1707–88)
T. COTTERILL (1779–1823) and others

88 (AMR **148**)
Rex Gloriae 8 7.8 7. D. Henry Smart (1813–79)

See the Conqueror mounts in triumph,
see the King in royal state
riding on the clouds his chariot
to his heavenly palace gate;
hark, the choirs of angel voices
joyful alleluias sing,
and the portals high are lifted
to receive their heavenly King.

2

Who is this that comes in glory,
with the trump of jubilee?
Lord of battles, God of armies,
he has gained the victory;
he who on the Cross did suffer,
he who from the grave arose,
he has vanquished sin and Satan,
he by death has spoiled his foes.

3

He has raised our human nature
  on the clouds to God's right hand;
there we sit in heavenly places,
  there with him in glory stand:
Jesus reigns, adored by angels;
  man with God is on the throne;
mighty Lord, in thine ascension
  we by faith behold our own.

*4

See him who is gone before us
  heavenly mansions to prepare,
see him who is ever pleading‿
  for us with prevailing prayer,
see him who with sound of trumpet
  and with his angelic train,
summoning the world to judgement,
  on the clouds will come again.

*5

Glory be to God the Father;
  glory be to God the Son,
dying, ris'n, ascending for us,
  who the heavenly realm has won;
glory to the Holy Spirit:
  to One God in Persons Three
glory both in earth and heaven,
  glory, endless glory be.

CHRISTOPHER WORDSWORTH (1807–85)

89 (AMR 153)
Warrington L.M. R. Harrison (1748–1810)

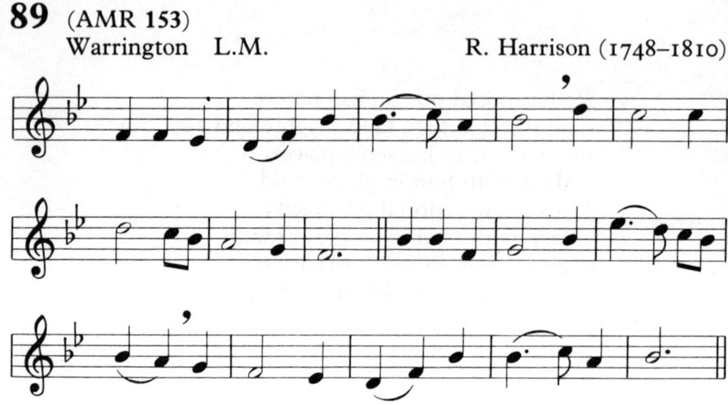

Spirit of mercy, truth, and love,
O shed thine influence from above,
and still from age to age convey‿
the wonders of this sacred day.

2

In every clime, by every tongue,
be God's surpassing glory sung;
let all the listening earth be taught
the acts our great Redeemer wrought.

3

Unfailing comfort, heavenly guide,
still o'er thy holy Church preside;
still let mankind thy blessings prove,
Spirit of mercy, truth, and love.

Foundling Hospital Collection, 1774

90 (AMR **154**)
Winchester Old C.M. T. Este (*Psalms*, 1592)

ALTERNATIVE VERSION

T. Ravenscroft (1621)

This version may be used for verses 5 and 6

When God of old came down from heaven,
  in power and wrath he came;
before his feet the clouds were riven,
  half darkness and half flame.

*2

But when he came the second time,
  he came in power and love;
softer than gale at morning prime
  hovered his holy Dove.

*3

The fires, that rushed on Sinai down
in sudden torrents dread,
now gently light, a glorious crown,
on every sainted head.

*4

And as on Israel's awestruck ear
the voice exceeding loud,
the trump that angels quake to hear,
thrilled from the deep, dark cloud;

5

So, when the Spirit of our God
came down his flock to find,
a voice from heaven was heard abroad,
a rushing, mighty wind.

6

It fills the Church of God; it fills‿
the sinful world around:
only in stubborn hearts and wills
no place for it is found.

7

Come, Lord, come Wisdom, Love, and Power,
open our ears to hear;
let us not miss the accepted hour:
save, Lord, by love or fear.

JOHN KEBLE (1792–1866)

91 (AMR 155)
Naphill 7 7.7 7. D. Harold Darke (1888–1976)

Our Lord, his Passion ended,
hath gloriously ascended,
yet though from him divided,
he leaves us not unguided;
  all his benefits to crown
  he hath sent his Spirit down,
  burning like a flame of fire
  his disciples to inspire.

2

God's Spirit is directing;
no more they sit expecting;
but forth to all the nation
they go with exultation;
  that which God in them hath wrought
  fills their life and soul and thought;
  so their witness now can do
  work as great in others too.

*3

The centuries go gliding,
but still we have abiding‿
with us that Spirit holy
to make us brave and lowly –
  lowly, for we feel our need:
  God alone is strong indeed;
  brave, for with the Spirit's aid
  we can venture unafraid.

4

O Lord of every nation,
fill us with inspiration;
we know our own unfitness,
yet for thee would bear witness.
  By thy Spirit now we raise
  to the heavenly Father praise:
  Holy Spirit, Father, Son,
  make us know thee, ever One.

F. C. Burkitt (1864–1935)

92 (AMR 156)
Veni, sancte Spiritus 777. D. S. Webbe the elder (1740–1816)

Come, thou Holy Spirit, come,
and from thy celestial home
  shed a ray of light divine;
come, thou Father of the poor,
come, thou source of all our store,
  come, within our bosoms shine:

2

Thou of comforters the best,
thou the soul's most welcome guest,
  sweet refreshment here below;
in our labour rest most sweet,
grateful coolness in the heat,
  solace in the midst of woe.

3

O most blessèd Light divine,
shine within these hearts of thine,
  and our inmost being fill;
where thou art not, man hath naught,
nothing good in deed or thought,
  nothing free from taint of ill.

4

Heal our wounds; our strength renew;
on our dryness pour thy dew;
  wash the stains of guilt away;
bend the stubborn heart and will;
melt the frozen, warm the chill;
  guide the steps that go astray.

5

On the faithful, who adore‿
and confess thee, evermore‿
  in thy sevenfold gifts descend:
give them virtue's sure reward,
give them thy salvation, Lord,
  give them joys that never end.

STEPHEN LANGTON (d. 1228)
tr. E. CASWALL* (1814–78)

93 (AMR 157)

Veni, Creator Spiritus L.M. Mode viii

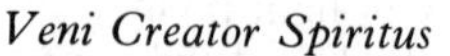
Veni Creator Spiritus

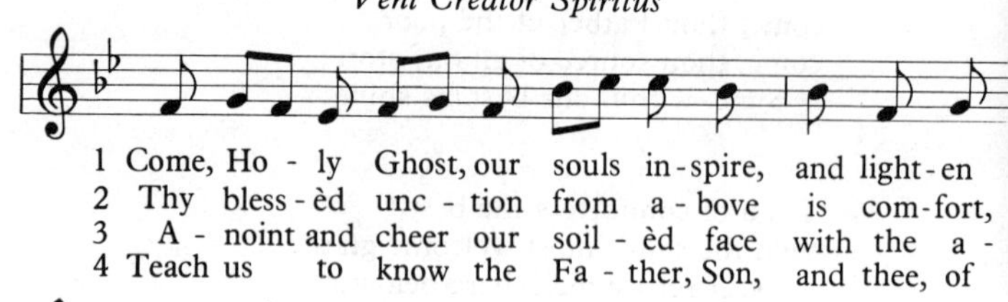
1 Come, Ho - ly Ghost, our souls in-spire, and light-en
2 Thy bless-èd unc - tion from a - bove is com-fort,
3 A - noint and cheer our soil - èd face with the a -
4 Teach us to know the Fa - ther, Son, and thee, of

with ce - les - tial fire; thou the a - noint-ing
life, and fire of love; en - a - ble with per -
-bun-dance of thy grace: keep far our foes, give
both, to be but one; that through the a - ges

Spi - rit art, who dost thy seven-fold gifts im-part.
-pet - ual light the dull-ness of our blind-ed sight.
peace at home; where thou art guide no ill can come.
all a - long this____ may be our end - less song,

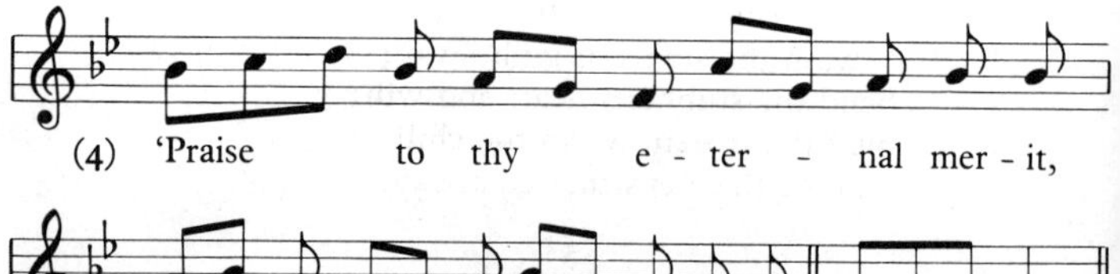
(4) 'Praise to thy e - ter - nal mer - it,

Fa - ther, Son, and Ho - ly Spi-rit.' A - - men.

Latin, par. JOHN COSIN (1594–1672)

94 (AMR **158**)
Chartres (Angers) 11 11 11.5. Chartres Antiphoner, 1784

Father most holy, merciful and loving,
Jesu, Redeemer, ever to be worshipped,
life-giving Spirit, Comforter most gracious,
God everlasting;

2

Three in a wondrous Unity unbroken,
One perfect Godhead, love that never faileth,
light of the angels, succour of the needy,
hope of all living;

3

all thy creation serveth its Creator,
thee every creature praiseth without ceasing;
we too would sing thee psalms of true devotion:
hear, we beseech thee.

4

Lord God Almighty, unto thee be glory,
One in three Persons, over all exalted.
Thine, as is meet, be honour, praise and blessing
now and for ever.

Latin, before 10th cent.
tr. A. E. Alston (1862–1927)

95 (AMR **160**)

Nicaea 11 12.12 10. J. B. Dykes (1823–76)

Holy, holy, holy! Lord God Almighty!
  early in the morning our song shall rise to thee;
Holy, holy, holy! merciful and mighty!
  God in three Persons, blessèd Trinity!

2

Holy, holy, holy! all the saints adore thee,
  casting down their golden crowns around the glassy sea;
cherubim and seraphim falling down before thee,
  which wert and art and evermore shalt be.

3

Holy, holy, holy! though the darkness hide thee,
  though the eye of sinful man thy glory may not see,
only thou art holy, there is none beside thee
  perfect in power, in love, and purity.

4

Holy, holy, holy! Lord God Almighty!
  all thy works shall praise thy name in earth and sky and sea;
Holy, holy, holy! merciful and mighty!
  God in three Persons, blessèd Trinity!

REGINALD HEBER (1783–1826)

96 (AMR **161**)

Laus Deo 8 7.8 7. R. Redhead (1820–1901)

The descant may be sung for verses 3 and 6

1

Bright the vision that delighted‿
once the sight of Judah's seer;
Sweet the countless tongues united
to entrance the prophet's ear.

2

Round the Lord in glory seated
cherubim and seraphim‿
Filled his temple, and repeated‿
each to each the alternate hymn:

3

'Lord, thy glory fills the heaven;
earth is with its fulness stored;
unto thee be glory given,
Holy, holy, holy, Lord.'

4

Heaven is still with glory ringing,
earth takes up the angels' cry,
'Holy, holy, holy,' singing,
'Lord of hosts, the Lord most high.'

5

With his seraph train before him,
with his holy Church below,
thus unite we to adore him,
bid we thus our anthem flow:

6

'Lord, thy glory fills the heaven;
earth is with its fulness stored;
unto thee be glory given,
Holy, holy, holy, Lord.'

This hymn is based on the account of Isaiah's vision in Isaiah 6.

RICHARD MANT (1776–1848)

97 (AMR **164**)

FIRST TUNE

Rivaulx L.M. — J. B. Dykes (1823–76)

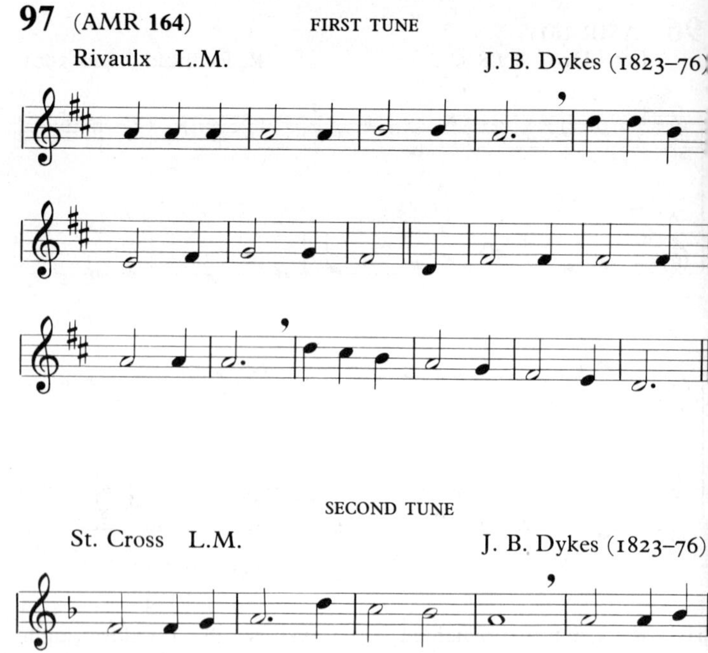

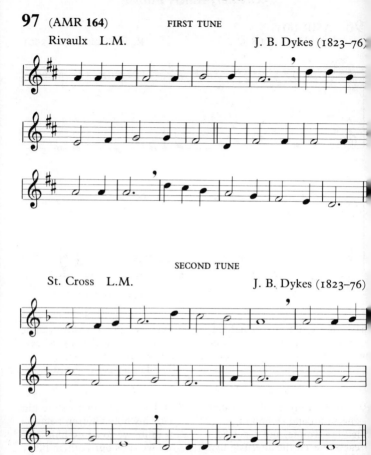

SECOND TUNE

St. Cross L.M. — J. B. Dykes (1823–76)

Father of heaven, whose love profound
a ransom for our souls hath found,
before thy throne we sinners bend,
to us thy pardoning love extend.

2

Almighty Son, incarnate Word,
our Prophet, Priest, Redeemer, Lord,
before thy throne we sinners bend,
to us thy saving grace extend.

3

Eternal Spirit, by whose breath
the soul is raised from sin and death,
before thy throne we sinners bend,
to us thy quickening power extend.

4

Thrice Holy! Father, Spirit, Son;
mysterious Godhead, Three in One,
before thy throne we sinners bend,
grace, pardon, life to us extend.

E. COOPER (1770–1833)

98 (AMR **630**) FIRST TUNE

Lasst uns erfreuen
(Easter Song)
8 8.4 4.8 8. and Alleluias

Melody from
Geistliche Kirchengesang (Cologne, 1623)

Version in AMR

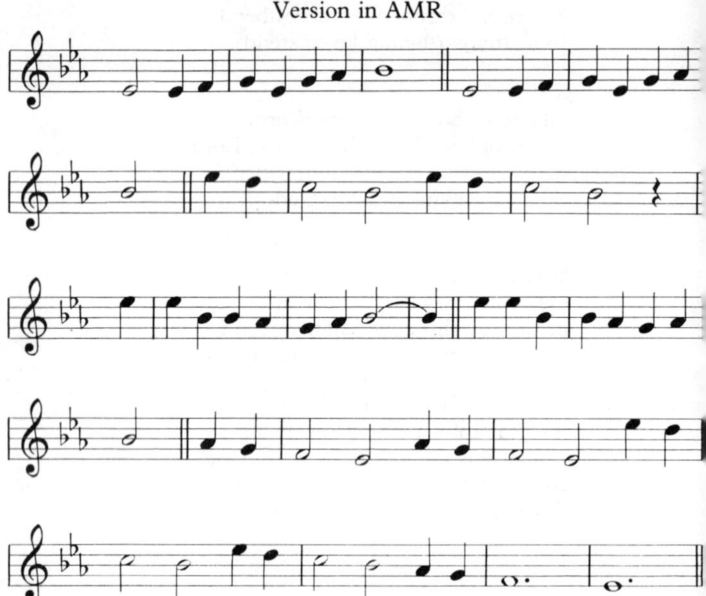

Another version of this tune is at 105

SECOND TUNE

Illsley (Bishop) L.M. J. Bishop (1665–1737)

In the AMR version the last line is

From all that dwell below the skies
let the Creator's praise arise:
Alleluia.
let the Redeemer's name be sung
through every land by every tongue.
Alleluia.

2

Eternal are thy mercies, Lord;
eternal truth attends thy word:
Alleluia.
Thy praise shall sound from shore to shore,
till suns shall rise and set no more.
Alleluia.

ISAAC WATTS (1674–1748)
Psalm 117

In the second tune Alleluia *is omitted*

99 (AMR **165**)
St. Anne C.M. *Supplement to the New Version*, 1708
(modern form)

The descant may be sung for verse 6

Man frail and God eternal

O God, our help in ages past,
  our hope for years to come,
our shelter from the stormy blast,
  and our eternal home;

2

beneath the shadow of thy throne
  thy saints have dwelt secure;
sufficient is thine arm alone,
  and our defence is sure.

3

Before the hills in order stood,
  or earth received her frame,
from everlasting thou art God,
  to endless years the same.

4

A thousand ages in thy sight
  are like an evening gone;
short as the watch that ends the night
  before the rising sun.

*5

Time, like an ever-rolling stream,
  bears all its sons away;
they fly forgotten, as a dream‿
  dies at the opening day.

6

O God, our help in ages past,
  our hope for years to come,
be thou our guard while troubles last,
  and our eternal home.

ISAAC WATTS* (1674–1748)
Psalm 90

100 (AMR **166**)
Old 100th L.M. Melody in Genevan Psalter, 1551

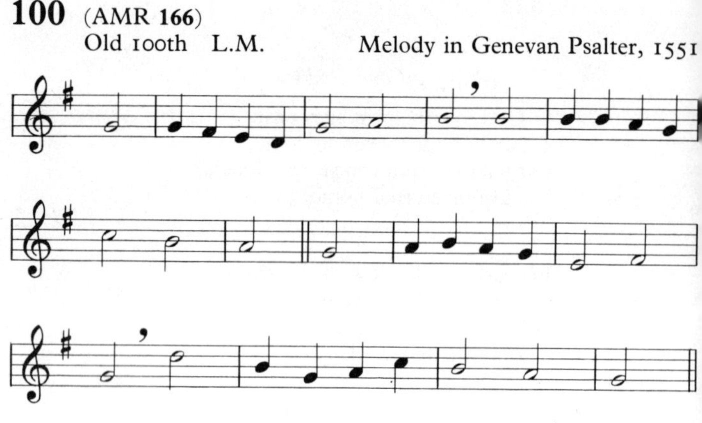

ALTERNATIVE VERSION
(melody in the tenor part)

John Dowland (1563–1626)

This version may be used for verses 2 and 4

All people that on earth do dwell,
sing to the Lord with cheerful voice;
him serve with fear, his praise forth tell,
come ye before him, and rejoice.

2

The Lord, ye know, is God indeed;
without our aid he did us make;
we are his folk, he doth us feed,
and for his sheep he doth us take.

3

O enter then his gates with praise,
approach with joy his courts unto;
praise, laud, and bless his name always,
for it is seemly so to do.

4

For why? the Lord our God is good;
his mercy is for ever sure;
his truth at all times firmly stood,
and shall from age to age endure.

5

To Father, Son, and Holy Ghost,
the God whom heaven and earth adore,
from men and from the angel-host
be praise and glory evermore.

W. Kethe (d. 1594)
in *Anglo-Genevan Psalter* (1560)
Psalm 100

Another version of this psalm is at 197

101 (AMR **167**)

Hanover
10 10.11 11.

Supplement to the New Version, 1708
descant by Alan Gray (1855–1935)

The descant may be sung for verse 6

Alternative Tune: *Old 104th* (298)

O worship the King all glorious above;
O gratefully sing his power and his love;
our shield and defender, the Ancient of Days,
pavilioned in splendour and girded with praise.

2

O tell of his might, O sing of his grace,
whose robe is the light, whose canopy space;
his chariots of wrath the deep thunder clouds form,
and dark is his path on the wings of the storm.

*3

The earth with its store of wonders untold,
almighty, thy power hath founded of old;
hath stablished it fast by a changeless decree,
and round it hath cast, like a mantle, the sea.

4

Thy bountiful care what tongue can recite?
it breathes in the air, it shines in the light;
it streams from the hills, it descends to the plain,
and sweetly distils in the dew and the rain.

5

Frail children of dust and feeble as frail,
in thee do we trust, nor find thee to fail;
thy mercies how tender, how firm to the end!
our maker, defender, redeemer, and friend.

6

O measureless might, ineffable love,
while angels delight to hymn thee above,
thy humbler creation, though feeble their lays,
with true adoration shall sing to thy praise.

ROBERT GRANT (1779–1838)
Psalm 104

In verse 6 line 3, for Grant's 'humbler', *AMR has* 'ransomed'.

102 (AMR 169)

Westminster C.M. James Turle (1802–82)

Our heavenly Father

My God, how wonderful thou art,
  thy majesty how bright,
how beautiful thy mercy-seat,
  in depths of burning light!

2

How dread are thine eternal years,
  O everlasting Lord,
by prostrate spirits day and night
  incessantly adored!

3

How wonderful, how beautiful,
  the sight of thee must be,
thine endless wisdom, boundless power,
  and aweful purity!

4

O how I fear thee, living God,
with deepest, tenderest fears,
and worship thee with trembling hope,
and penitential tears!

5

Yet I may love thee too, O Lord,
almighty as thou art,
for thou hast stooped to ask of me‿
the love of my poor heart.

6

No earthly father loves like thee,
no mother, e'er so mild,
bears and forbears as thou hast done‿
with me thy sinful child.

7

Father of Jesus, love's reward,
what rapture will it be,
prostrate before thy throne to lie,
and gaze and gaze on thee!

F. W. Faber (1814–63)

103 (AMR 170)

Addison's (London) D.L.M. J. Sheeles (1688–1761)

The spacious firmament on high,
with all the blue ethereal sky,
and spangled heavens, a shining frame,
their great Original proclaim.
The unwearied sun from day to day
does his Creator's power display,
and publishes to every land
the work of an almighty hand.

2

Soon as the evening shades prevail
the moon takes up the wondrous tale,
and nightly to the listening earth
repeats the story of her birth;
whilst all the stars that round her burn,
and all the planets in their turn,
confirm the tidings, as they roll,
and spread the truth from pole to pole.

3

What though in solemn silence all‿
move round the dark terrestrial ball;
what though nor reàl voice nor sound
amid their radiant orbs be found;
in reason's ear they all rejoice,
and utter forth a glorious voice,
for ever singing as they shine,
'The hand that made us is divine.'

JOSEPH ADDISON (1672–1719)
Psalm 19. 1–6

The last line of each verse is repeated

104 (AMR **171**)
Dix 7 7·7 7·7 7·   Adapted from C. Kocher (1786–1872)
by W. H. Monk (1823–89)

The descant may be sung for verses 3 and 5

Creator, Ruler, Father

The sacrifice of praise

For the beauty of the earth,
  for the beauty of the skies,
for the love which from our birth
  over and around us lies,
Lord of all, to thee we raise‿
this our sacrifice of praise.

2

For the beauty of each hour‿
  of the day and of the night,
hill and vale and tree and flower,
  sun and moon and stars of light:

3

For the joy of human love,
  brother, sister, parent, child,
friends on earth, and friends above,
  pleasures pure and undefiled:

4

For each perfect gift of thine,
  to our race so freely given,
graces human and divine,
  flowers of earth and buds of heaven:

5

For thy Church which evermore‿
  lifteth holy hands above,
offering up on every shore
  her pure sacrifice of love,
Lord of all, to thee we raise‿
this our sacrifice of praise.

F. S. PIERPOINT* (1835–1917)

In the refrain, for the author's 'sacrifice' *AMR has* 'grateful hymn'

105 (AMR **172**)
Lasst uns erfreuen
(Easter Song)
8 8.4 4.8 8. and Alleluias

Geistliche Kirchengesang
(Cologne, 1623)
arr. R. Vaughan Williams
(1872–1958)

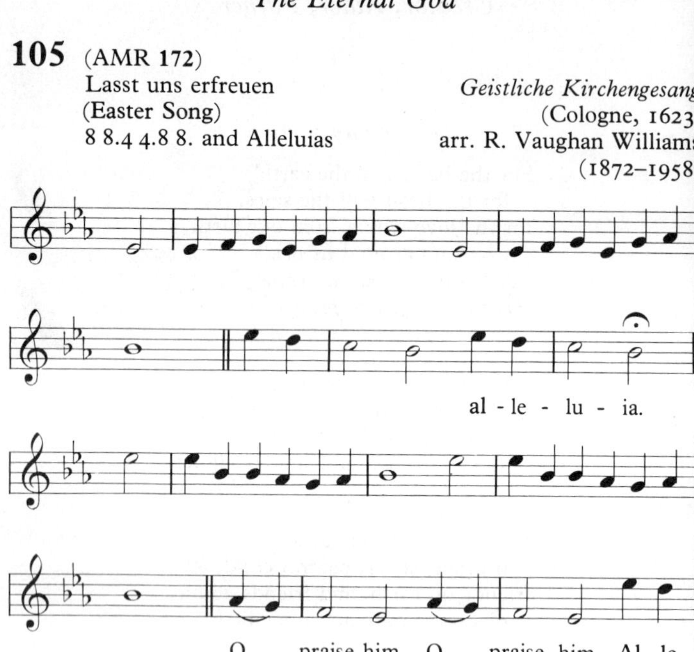
al - le - lu - ia.
O___ praise him, O___ praise him, Al - le -
lu - ia, al - le - lu - ia, al - le - lu - ia.

The AMR version of this tune is at 98

1 All creatures of our God and King,
lift up your voice and with us sing
Alleluia, alleluia.
Thou burning sun with golden beam,
thou silver moon with softer gleam,
O praise him, O praise him,
Alleluia, alleluia, alleluia.

2 Thou rushing wind that art so strong,
ye clouds that sail in heaven along,
  O praise him, alleluia.
Thou rising morn, in praise rejoice,
ye lights of evening, find a voice;

3 Thou flowing water, pure and clear,
make music for thy Lord to hear,
  Alleluia, alleluia.
Thou fire so masterful and bright,
that givest man both warmth and light:

*4 Dear mother earth, who day by day
unfoldest blessings on our way,
  O praise him, alleluia.
The flowers and fruits that in thee grow,
let them his glory also show:

5 And all ye men of tender heart,
forgiving others, take your part,
  O sing ye alleluia.
Ye who long pain and sorrow bear,
praise God and on him cast your care:

*6 And thou, most kind and gentle death,
waiting to hush our latest breath,
  O praise him, alleluia.
Thou leadest home the child of God,
and Christ our Lord the way hath trod:

7 Let all things their Creator bless,
and worship him in humbleness;
  O praise him, alleluia.
Praise, praise the Father, praise the Son,
and praise the Spirit, Three in One;
  O praise him, O praise him,
  Alleluia, alleluia, alleluia.

W. H. Draper (1855–1933)
Based on St. Francis of Assisi's
Canticle of the Sun

106 (AMR 174)
St. Audrey 8 7.8 7.8 7. Basil Harwood (1859–1949)

Alternative Tune: *Regent Square* (185)

Creator, Ruler, Father

Lord of beauty, thine the splendour
shewn in earth and sky and sea,
burning sun and moonlight tender,
hill and river, flower and tree:
lest we fail our praise to render
touch our eyes that they may see.

2

Lord of wisdom, whom obeying
mighty waters ebb and flow,
while unhasting, undelaying,
planets on their courses go:
in thy laws thyself displaying,
teach our minds thyself to know.

3

Lord of life, alone sustaining
all below and all above,
Lord of love, by whose ordaining
sun and stars sublimely move:
in our earthly spirits reigning,
lift our hearts that we may love.

4

Lord of beauty, bid us own thee,
Lord of truth, our footsteps guide,
till as Love our hearts enthrone thee,
and, with vision purified,
Lord of all, when all have known thee,
thou in all art glorified.

C. A. ALINGTON (1872–1955)

107 (AMR 175)

Ivyhatch L.M. B. Luard Selby (1853–1918)

Alternative Tunes:
Church Triumphant (20), *Niagara* (NS 491, MHT 158)

1 The Lord is King! lift up thy voice,
O earth, and all ye heavens, rejoice;
from world to world the joy shall ring,
'The Lord omnipotent is King'.

2 The Lord is King! who then shall dare‿
resist his will, distrust his care,
or murmur at his wise decrees,
or doubt his royal promises?

3 He reigns! ye saints, exalt your strains;
your God is King, your Father reigns;
and he is at the Father's side,
the Man of Love, the Crucified.

*4 Alike pervaded by his eye
all parts of his dominion lie:
this world of ours and worlds unseen,
and thin the boundary between.

5 One Lord one empire all secures;
he reigns, and life and death are yours;
through earth and heaven one song shall ring,
'The Lord omnipotent is King'.

J. Conder (1789–1855)

108 (AMR 176)

Offertorium 7 6.7 6. D.

Adapted from Michael Haydn (1737–1806)

Joy and peace in believing

1

Sometimes a light surprises
the Christian while he sings:
it is the Lord who rises
with healing in his wings;
when comforts are declining,
he grants the soul again
a season of clear shining
to cheer it after rain.

2

In holy contemplation
we sweetly then pursue
the theme of God's salvation,
and find it ever new:
set free from present sorrow,
we cheerfully can say,
'E'en let the unknown morrow
bring with it what it may,

3

it can bring with it nothing
but he will bear us through;
who gives the lilies clothing
will clothe his people too:
beneath the spreading heavens
no creature but is fed;
and he who feeds the ravens
will give his children bread.'

4

Though vine nor fig-tree neither
their wonted fruit should bear,
though all the fields should wither,
nor flocks nor herds be there;
yet, God the same abiding,
his praise shall tune my voice;
for, while in him confiding,
I cannot but rejoice.

William Cowper (1731–1800)

109 (AMR 177)

Contemplation C.M. F. A. G. Ouseley (1825–89)

When all thy mercies, O my God,
  my rising soul surveys,
transported with the view, I'm lost‿
  in wonder, love, and praise.

2

Unnumbered comforts to my soul
  thy tender care bestowed,
before my infant heart conceived
  from whom those comforts flowed.

3

When in the slippery paths of youth
  with heedless steps I ran,
thine arm unseen conveyed me safe,
  and led me up to man.

*4

Ten thousand thousand precious gifts
  my daily thanks employ,
and not the least a cheerful heart
  which tastes those gifts with joy.

5

Through every period of my life
  thy goodness I'll pursue,
and after death in distant worlds
  the glorious theme renew.

6

Through all eternity to thee‿
  a joyful song I'll raise;
for O, eternity's too short
  to utter all thy praise.

JOSEPH ADDISON (1672–1719)

110 (AMR **178**)
University C.M. C. Collignon (1725–85)

The God of love my shepherd is,
and he that doth me feed;
while he is mine and I am his,
what can I want or need?

2

He leads me to the tender grass,
where I both feed and rest;
then to the streams that gently pass:
in both I have the best.

3

Or if I stray, he doth convert,
and bring my mind in frame,
and all this not for my desert,
but for his holy name.

4

Yea, in death's shady black abode
well may I walk, not fear;
for thou art with me, and thy rod
to guide, thy staff to bear.

5

Surely thy sweet and wondrous love
shall measure all my days;
and, as it never shall remove,
so neither shall my praise.

George Herbert (1593–1632)
Psalm 23

111 (AMR **179**)

Surrey 8 8.8 8.8 8. Henry Carey (*c*. 1690–1743)

1 The Lord my pasture shall prepare,
and feed me with a shepherd's care;
his presence shall my wants supply,
and guard me with a watchful eye;
my noonday walks he shall attend,
and all my midnight hours defend.

2 When in the sultry glebe I faint,
or on the thirsty mountain pant,
to fertile vales and dewy meads
my weary wandering steps he leads,
where peaceful rivers, soft and slow,
amid the verdant landscape flow.

3 Though in a bare and rugged way
through devious lonely wilds I stray,
thy bounty shall my pains beguile;
the barren wilderness shall smile
with sudden greens and herbage crowned,
and streams shall murmur all around.

4 Though in the paths of death I tread,
with gloomy horrors overspread,
my steadfast heart shall fear no ill,
for thou, O Lord, art with me still:
thy friendly crook shall give me aid,
and guide me through the dreadful shade.

JOSEPH ADDISON (1672–1719)
Psalm 23

112 (AMR 181)

London New C.M. *Psalms* (Edinburgh, 1635)

Light shining out of darkness

1

God moves in a mysterious way
his wonders to perform;
he plants his footsteps in the sea,
and rides upon the storm.

2

Deep in unfathomable mines
of never-failing skill
he treasures up his bright designs,
and works his sovereign will.

3

Ye fearful saints, fresh courage take;
the clouds ye so much dread
are big with mercy, and shall break
in blessings on your head.

4

Judge not the Lord by feeble sense,
but trust him for his grace;
behind a frowning providence
he hides a smiling face.

5

His purposes will ripen fast,
unfolding every hour;
the bud may have a bitter taste,
but sweet will be the flower.

6

Blind unbelief is sure to err,
and scan his work in vain;
God is his own interpreter,
and he will make it plain.

William Cowper (1731–1800)

113 (AMR 182)

Marching 8 7.8 7. Martin Shaw (1875–1958)

Father, hear the prayer we offer:
  not for ease that prayer shall be,
but for strength that we may ever‿
  live our lives courageously.

2

Not for ever in green pastures
  do we ask our way to be;
but the steep and rugged pathway
  may we tread rejoicingly.

3

Not for ever by still waters
  would we idly rest and stay;
but would smite the living fountains‿
  from the rocks along our way.

4

Be our strength in hours of weakness,
  in our wanderings be our guide;
through endeavour, failure, danger,
  Father, be thou at our side.

L. M. Willis (1824–1908)

114 (AMR **183**)
Ein' feste Burg 8 7.8 7.6 6.6 6 7. Martin Luther
(A stronghold sure) (1483–1546)

A safe stronghold our God is still,
a trusty shield and weapon;
he'll keep us clear from all the ill
that hath us now o'ertaken.
The ancient prince of hell
hath risen with purpose fell;
strong mail of craft and power
he weareth in this hour;
on earth is not his fellow.

2

With force of arms we nothing can,
  full soon were we down-ridden;
but for us fights the proper Man,
  whom God himself hath bidden.
    Ask ye, Who is this same?
    Christ Jesus is his name,
    the Lord Sabaoth's Son;
    he, and no other one,
  shall conquer in the battle.

*3

And were this world all devils o'er,
  and watching to devour us,
we lay it not to heart so sore;
  not they can overpower us.
    And let the prince of ill
    look grim as e'er he will,
    he harms us not a whit;
    for why? his doom is writ;
  a word shall quickly slay him.

*4

God's word, for all their craft and force,
  one moment will not linger,
but, spite of hell, shall have its course;
  'tis written by his finger.
    And though they take our life,
    goods, honour, children, wife,
    yet is their profit small;
    these things shall vanish all:
  the City of God remaineth.

MARTIN LUTHER (1483–1546)
tr. THOMAS CARLYLE (1795–1881)

115 (AMR **184**)
Repton 8 6. 8 8 6. C. Hubert H. Parry (1848–1918)

The last line of each verse is repeated

Dear Lord and Father of mankind,
  forgive our foolish ways;
re-clothe us in our rightful mind,
in purer lives thy service find,
  in deeper reverence praise.

2

In simple trust like theirs who heard,
  beside the Syrian sea,
the gracious calling of the Lord,
let us, like them, without a word
  rise up and follow thee.

*3

O Sabbath rest by Galilee!
  O calm of hills above,
where Jesus knelt to share with thee
the silence of eternity,
  interpreted by love!

4

Drop thy still dews of quietness,
  till all our strivings cease;
take from our souls the strain and stress,
and let our ordered lives confess
  the beauty of thy peace.

5

Breathe through the heats of our desire
  thy coolness and thy balm;
let sense be dumb, let flesh retire;
speak through the earthquake, wind, and fire,
  O still small voice of calm.

J. G. Whittier (1807–92)

116 (AMR 442)

FIRST TUNE

Royal Oak

7 6.7 6. with refrain

English Traditional Melody
adapted by Martin Shaw (1875–1958)

Refrain
1 All things bright and beau-ti-ful, all crea-tures great and
small, all things wise and won-der-ful, the
Lord God made them all.
Verses
2 Each lit-tle flower that
o-pens, each lit-tle bird that sings, he
back to Refrain
made their glow-ing col-ours, he made their ti-ny wings.

Maker of heaven and earth

I

All things bright and beautiful,
all creatures great and small,
all things wise and wonderful,
the Lord God made them all.

2

Each little flower that opens,
each little bird that sings,
he made their glowing colours,
he made their tiny wings:

3

The purple-headed mountain,
  the river running by,
the sunset, and the morning
  that brightens up the sky:

4

The cold wind in the winter,
  the pleasant summer sun,
the ripe fruits in the garden,
  he made them every one:

*5

The tall trees in the greenwood,
  the meadows where we play,
the rushes by the water
  we gather every day:

6

He gave us eyes to see them,
  and lips that we might tell
how great is God almighty,
  who has made all things well:

7

All things bright and beautiful,
  all creatures great and small,
all things wise and wonderful,
  the Lord God made them all.

CECIL FRANCES ALEXANDER (1818–95)

116 (AMR 442) SECOND TUNE

All things bright and beautiful W. H. Monk (1823–8

7 6.7 6. with refrain

Refrain
1 All things bright and beau - ti-ful, all crea-tures great and
small, all things wise and won - der-ful, the
Lord God made them all.
Verses
back to Refrai

Maker of heaven and earth

1

All things bright and beautiful,
all creatures great and small,
all things wise and wonderful,
the Lord God made them all.

2

Each little flower that opens,
each little bird that sings,
he made their glowing colours,
he made their tiny wings:

3

The purple-headed mountain,
  the river running by,
the sunset, and the morning
  that brightens up the sky:

4

The cold wind in the winter,
  the pleasant summer sun,
the ripe fruits in the garden,
  he made them every one:

*5

The tall trees in the greenwood,
  the meadows where we play,
the rushes by the water
  we gather every day:

6

He gave us eyes to see them,
  and lips that we might tell
how great is God almighty,
  who has made all things well:

7

All things bright and beautiful,
  all creatures great and small,
all things wise and wonderful,
  the Lord God made them all.

CECIL FRANCES ALEXANDER (1818–95)

117 (AMR **185**) FIRST TUNE

Gerontius C.M. J. B. Dykes (1823–76)

SECOND TUNE

Somervell C.M. Arthur Somervell (1863–1937)

Alternative Tunes:
Richmond (125), *Billing* (NS 490, MHT 157)

Praise to the Holiest in the height,
  and in the depth be praise:
in all his words most wonderful,
  most sure in all his ways.

2

O loving wisdom of our God!
  when all was sin and shame,
a second Adam to the fight
  and to the rescue came.

3

O wisest love! that flesh and blood,
  which did in Adam fail,
should strive afresh against the foe,
  should strive and should prevail;

4

and that a higher gift than grace
  should flesh and blood refine,
God's presence and his very self,
  and essence all-divine.

5

O generous love! that he, who smote‿
  in Man for man the foe,
the double agony in Man
  for man should undergo;

6

and in the garden secretly,
  and on the cross on high,
should teach his brethren, and inspire‿
  to suffer and to die.

7

Praise to the Holiest in the height,
  and in the depth be praise:
in all his words most wonderful,
  most sure in all his ways.

J. H. Newman (1801–90)

118 (AMR **186**)
Halton Holgate 8 7.8 7.

Later form of melody by
William Boyce (*c.* 1710–79)

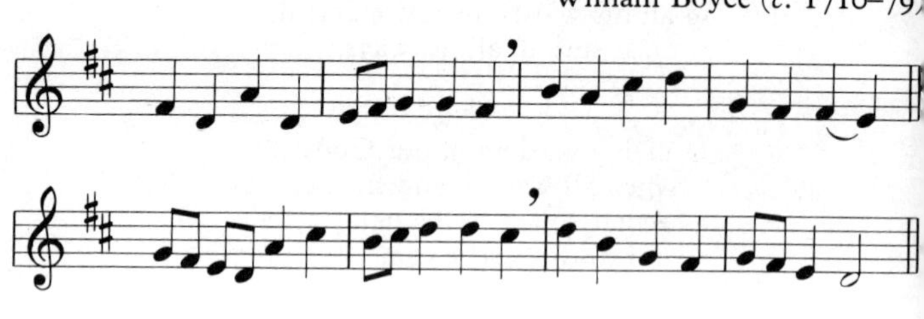

Firmly I believe and truly
  God is Three and God is One;
and I next acknowledge duly
  Manhood taken by the Son.

2

And I trust and hope most fully
  in that Manhood crucified;
and each thought and deed unruly‿
  do to death, as he has died.

3

Simply to his grace and wholly
  light and life and strength belong,
and I love supremely, solely,
  him the holy, him the strong.

4

And I hold in veneration,
  for the love of him alone,
holy Church as his creation,
  and her teachings as his own.

5

Adoration ay be given,
  with and through the angelic host,
to the God of earth and heaven,
  Father, Son, and Holy Ghost.

J. H. Newman (1801–90)

119 (AMR 187)
Eisenach L.M. J. H. Schein (1586–1628)

Version in AMR

O love, how deep, how broad, how high!
It fills the heart with ecstasy,
that God, the Son of God, should take
our mortal form for mortals' sake.

2

He sent no angel to our race
of higher or of lower place,
but wore the robe of human frame‿
himself, and to this lost world came.

3

For us he was baptized, and bore‿
his holy fast, and hungered sore;
for us temptations sharp he knew;
for us the tempter overthrew.

4

For us to wicked men betrayed,
scourged, mocked, in purple robe arrayed,
he bore the shameful cross and death;
for us at length gave up his breath.

5

For us he rose from death again,
for us he went on high to reign,
for us he sent his Spirit here
to guide, to strengthen, and to cheer.

6

To him whose boundless love has won
salvation for us through his Son,
to God the Father, glory be
both now and through eternity.

Ascribed to THOMAS À KEMPIS (c. 1379–1471)
tr. BENJAMIN WEBB* (1819–85)

120 (AMR **189**)
Metzler's Redhead C.M. R. Redhead (1820–1901)

PART ONE

Jesu, the very thought of thee
with sweetness fills the breast;
but sweeter far thy face to see,
and in thy presence rest.

2

No voice can sing, no heart can frame,
nor can the memory find,
a sweeter sound than Jesu's name,
the Saviour of mankind.

3

O hope of every contrite heart,
O joy of all the meek,
to those who ask how kind thou art,
how good to those who seek!

4

But what to those who find? Ah, this
nor tongue nor pen can show;
the love of Jesus, what it is
none but his loved ones know.

5

Jesu, our only joy be thou,
as thou our prize wilt be;
in thee be all our glory now,
and through eternity.

PART TWO

6

O Jesu, King most wonderful,
  thou Conqueror renowned,
thou sweetness most ineffable,
  in whom all joys are found!

7

When once thou visitest the heart,
  then truth begins to shine,
then earthly vanities depart,
  then kindles love divine.

8

Thee, Jesu, may our voices bless,
  thee may we love alone,
and ever in our lives express
  the image of thine own.

9

Abide with us, and let thy light‿
  shine, Lord, on every heart;
dispel the darkness of our night,
  and joy to all impart.

10

Jesu, our love and joy, to thee,
  the Virgin's holy Son,
all might and praise and glory be
  while endless ages run.

Latin, c. 12th cent.
tr. E. CASWALL (1814–78)

121 (AMR **190**)
Oriel 8 7.8 7.8 7. C. Ett, *Cantica Sacra*, 1840
descant by Alan Gray (1855–1935)

The descant may be sung for verses 2 and 6

To the name of our salvation
laud and honour let us pay,
which for many a generation
hid in God's foreknowledge lay,
but with holy exultation
we may sing aloud to-day.

2

Jesus is the name we treasure,
name beyond what words can tell;
name of gladness, name of pleasure,
ear and heart delighting well;
name of sweetness passing measure,
saving us from sin and hell.

*3

'Tis the name for adoration,
name for songs of victory,
name for holy meditation
in this vale of misery,
name for joyful veneration
by the citizens on high.

4

'Tis the name that whoso preacheth
speaks like music to the ear;
who in prayer this name beseecheth
sweetest comfort findeth near;
who its perfect wisdom reacheth
heavenly joy possesseth here.

5

Jesus is the name exalted
over every other name;
in this name, whene'er assaulted,
we can put our foes to shame:
strength to them who else had halted,
eyes to blind, and feet to lame.

6

Therefore we in love adoring
this most blessèd name revere,
holy Jesu, thee imploring
so to write it in us here,
that hereafter heavenward soaring
we may sing with angels there.

Latin, c. 15th cent.
tr. J. M. NEALE* (1818–66)

122 (AMR **192**)

St. Peter C.M. A. R. Reinagle (1799–1877

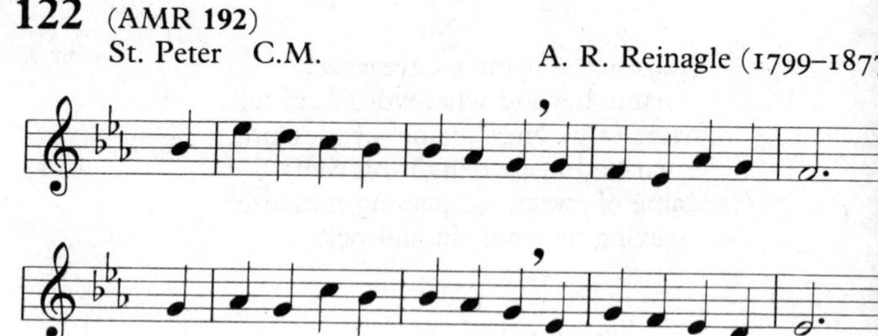

His Holy Name

The name of Jesus

How sweet the name of Jesus sounds
  in a believer's ear!
It soothes his sorrows, heals his wounds,
  and drives away his fear.

2

It makes the wounded spirit whole,
  and calms the troubled breast;
'tis manna to the hungry soul,
  and to the weary rest.

3

Dear name! the rock on which I build,
  my shield and hiding-place,
my never-failing treasury filled‿
  with boundless stores of grace.

4

Jesus! my Shepherd, Brother, Friend,
  my Prophet, Priest, and King,
my Lord, my Life, my Way, my End,
  accept the praise I bring.

5

Weak is the effort of my heart,
  and cold my warmest thought;
but when I see thee as thou art,
  I'll praise thee as I ought.

6

Till then I would thy love proclaim
  with every fleeting breath;
and may the music of thy name
  refresh my soul in death.

JOHN NEWTON* (1725–1807)

123 (AMR **193**) FIRST TUNE

Hollingside 7 7.7 7. D. J. B. Dykes (1823–76)

SECOND TUNE

Aberystwyth 7 7.7 7. D. Joseph Parry (1841–1903)

In temptation

Jesu, lover of my soul,
  let me to thy bosom fly,
while the gathering waters roll,
  while the tempest still is high:
hide me, O my Saviour, hide,
  till the storm of life is past;
safe into the haven guide,
  O receive my soul at last.

2

Other refuge have I none;
  hangs my helpless soul on thee;
leave, ah, leave me not alone,
  still support and comfort me.
All my trust on thee is stayed,
  all my help from thee I bring;
cover my defenceless head
  with the shadow of thy wing.

3

Plenteous grace with thee is found,
  grace to cleanse from every sin;
let the healing streams abound;
  make and keep me pure within:
thou of life the fountain art;
  freely let me take of thee;
spring thou up within my heart,
  rise to all eternity.

CHARLES WESLEY* (1707–88)

124 (AMR **195**)
Cornwall 8 8 6. D. S. S. Wesley (1810–76)

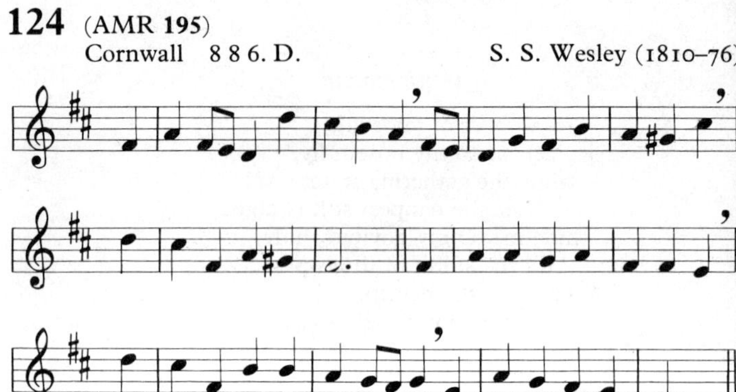

Desiring to love

O love divine, how sweet thou art!
When shall I find my longing heart
  all taken up by thee?
I thirst, I faint and die to prove‿
the greatness of redeeming love,
  the love of Christ to me.

2

Stronger his love than death or hell;
its riches are unsearchable:
  the first-born sons of light‿
desire in vain its depth to see;
they cannot reach the mystery,
  the length and breadth and height.

*3

God only knows the love of God;
O that it now were shed abroad
  in this poor stony heart!
For love I sigh, for love I pine;
this only portion, Lord, be mine,
  be mine this better part.

4

For ever would I take my seat‿
with Mary at the Master's feet:
  be this my happy choice;
my only care, delight, and bliss,
my joy, my heaven on earth, be this,
  to hear the Bridegroom's voice.

CHARLES WESLEY* (1707–88)

125 (AMR **196**) FIRST TUNE

Richmond C.M.

Adapted from T. Haweis (1734–1820)

SECOND TUNE

Selby C.M.

A. J. Eyre (1853–1919)

O for a thousand tongues to sing
  my dear Redeemer's praise,
the glories of my God and King,
  the triumphs of his grace!

2

Jesus! the name that charms our fears,
  that bids our sorrows cease;
'tis music in the sinner's ears,
  'tis life and health and peace.

3

He speaks; and, listening to his voice,
  new life the dead receive,
the mournful broken hearts rejoice,
  the humble poor believe.

4

Hear him, ye deaf; his praise, ye dumb,
  your loosened tongues employ;
ye blind, behold your Saviour come;
  and leap, ye lame, for joy!

5

My gracious Master and my God,
  assist me to proclaim
and spread through all the earth abroad
  the honours of thy name.

CHARLES WESLEY (1707–88)

126 (AMR 197)

Dominus regit me   8 7.8 7.   J. B. Dykes (1823–76

The descant may be sung for verse 6

The King of love my shepherd is,
whose goodness faileth never;
I nothing lack if I am his
and he is mine for ever.

2

Where streams of living water flow
my ransomed soul he leadeth,
and where the verdant pastures grow
with food celestial feedeth.

3

Perverse and foolish oft I strayed,
but yet in love he sought me,
and on his shoulder gently laid,
and home rejoicing brought me.

4

In death's dark vale I fear no ill
with thee, dear Lord, beside me;
thy rod and staff my comfort still,
thy cross before to guide me.

5

Thou spread'st a table in my sight;
thy unction grace bestoweth;
and O what transport of delight
from thy pure chalice floweth!

6

And so through all the length of days
thy goodness faileth never:
good Shepherd, may I sing thy praise
within thy house for ever.

H. W. Baker (1821–77)
Psalm 23

127 (AMR **198**)
St. George S.M. H. J. Gauntlett (1805–76)

To Christ, the Prince of Peace,
and Son of God most high,
the Father of the world to come,
we lift our joyful cry.

2

Deep in his heart for us
the wound of love he bore,
that love which he enkindles still
in hearts that him adore.

3

O Jesu, victim blest,
what else but love divine
could thee constrain to open thus‿
that sacred heart of thine?

4

O wondrous fount of love,
O well of waters free,
O heavenly flame, refining fire,
O burning charity!

5

Hide us in thy dear heart,
Jesu, our Saviour blest,
so shall we find thy plenteous grace,
and heaven's eternal rest.

Latin, 18th cent.
tr. E. CASWALL* (1814–78)

28 (AMR **199**)

St. James C.M. R. Courteville (?1675–1772)

Thou art the Way: by thee alone‿
from sin and death we flee;
and he who would the Father seek
must seek him, Lord, by thee.

2

Thou art the Truth: thy word alone‿
true wisdom can impart;
thou only canst inform the mind
and purify the heart.

3

Thou art the Life: the rending tomb‿
proclaims thy conquering arm;
and those who put their trust in thee
nor death nor hell shall harm.

4

Thou art the Way, the Truth, the Life:
grant us that Way to know,
that Truth to keep, that Life to win,
whose joys eternal flow.

G. W. Doane (1799–1859)

129 (AMR 200) FIRST TUNE

St. Paul's S.M. John Stainer (1840–1901)

SECOND TUNE

Southwell (Damon) S.M. W. Damon (*Psalms*, 1579)

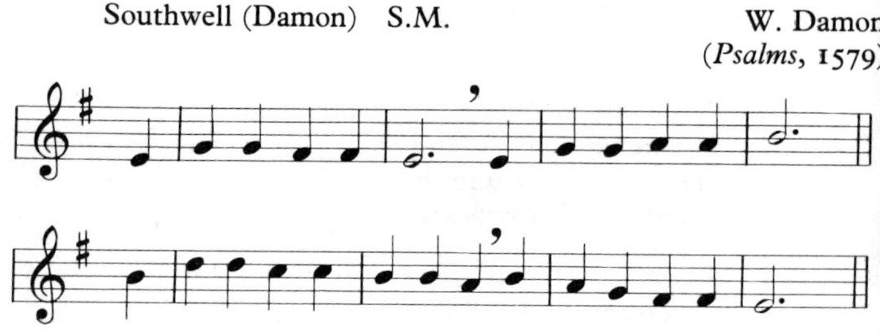

Lord Jesus, think on me,
and purge away my sin;
from earthborn passions set me free,
and make me pure within.

2

Lord Jesus, think on me
with many a care opprest;
let me thy loving servant be,
and taste thy promised rest.

3

Lord Jesus, think on me,
nor let me go astray;
through darkness and perplexity
point thou the heavenly way.

4

Lord Jesus, think on me,
that, when the flood is past,
I may the eternal brightness see,
and share thy joy at last.

SYNESIUS OF CYRENE (c. 365–c. 414)
tr. A. W. CHATFIELD (1808–96)

130 (AMR **204**)
Wareham L.M. W. Knapp (1698–1768

In AMR this hymn is set to *Almsgiving*

Where high the heavenly temple stands,
the house of God not made with hands,
a great High Priest our nature wears,
the guardian of mankind appears.

2

He who for men their surety stood,
and poured on earth his precious blood,
pursues in heaven his mighty plan,
the Saviour and the Friend of man.

3

Though now ascended up on high,
he bends on earth a brother's eye;
partaker of the human name,
he knows the frailty of our frame.

4

In every pang that rends the heart
the Man of Sorrows had a part;
he sympathizes with our grief,
and to the sufferer sends relief.

5

With boldness therefore at the throne
let us make all our sorrows known;
and ask the aid of heavenly power
to help us in the evil hour.

M. Bruce (1746–67)
Hebrews 4. 14–16

131 (AMR **205**)
Love Divine 8 7.8 7. John Stainer (1840–1901)

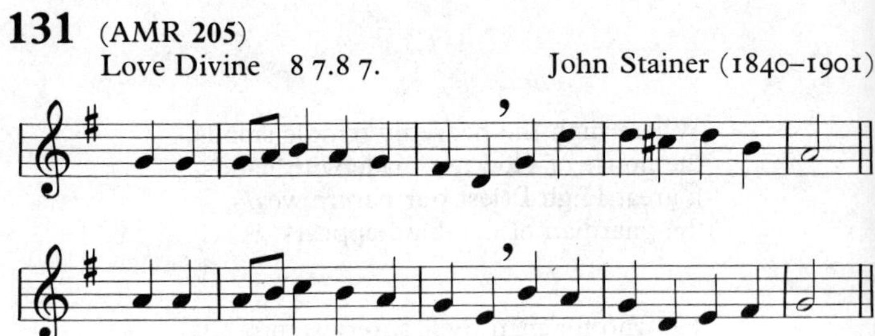

Alternative Tune: *Blaenwern* (NS 464, MHT 131)

Lord of Light, Life and Love

Love divine, all loves excelling,
joy of heaven, to earth come down,
fix in us thy humble dwelling,
all thy faithful mercies crown.

2

Jesu, thou art all compassion,
pure unbounded love thou art;
visit us with thy salvation,
enter every trembling heart.

3

Come, almighty to deliver,
let us all thy grace receive;
suddenly return, and never,
never more thy temples leave.

4

Thee we would be always blessing,
serve thee as thy hosts above;
pray, and praise thee, without ceasing,
glory in thy perfect love.

5

Finish then thy new creation:
pure and spotless let us be;
let us see thy great salvation,
perfectly restored in thee;

6

changed from glory into glory,
till in heaven we take our place,
till we cast our crowns before thee,
lost in wonder, love, and praise.

CHARLES WESLEY* (1707–88)

132 (AMR 207)
Everton 8 7.8 7. D. Henry Smart (1813–79

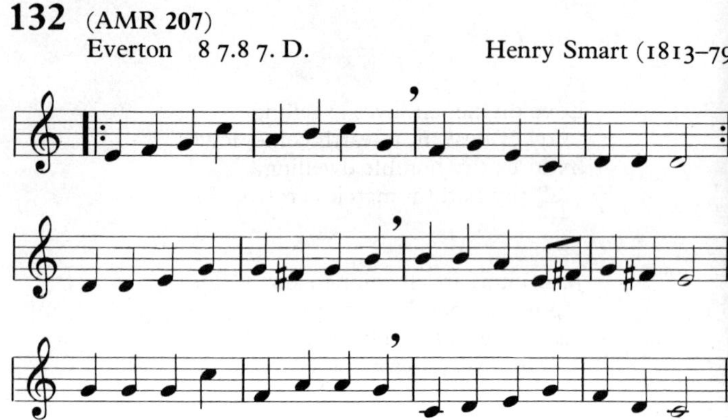

Lord of Light, Life and Love

Son of God, eternal Saviour,
  source of life and truth and grace,
Son of Man, whose birth incarnate
  hallows all our human race,
thou, our Head, who, throned in glory,
  for thine own dost ever plead,
fill us with thy love and pity;
  heal our wrongs, and help our need.

*2

As thou, Lord, hast lived for others,
  so may we for others live;
freely have thy gifts been granted,
  freely may thy servants give:
thine the gold and thine the silver,
  thine the wealth of land and sea,
we but stewards of thy bounty,
  held in solemn trust for thee.

3

Come, O Christ, and reign among us,
  King of love, and Prince of peace;
hush the storm of strife and passion,
  bid its cruel discords cease;
by thy patient years of toiling,
  by thy silent hours of pain,
quench our fevered thirst of pleasure,
  shame our selfish greed of gain.

4

Son of God, eternal Saviour,
  source of life and truth and grace,
Son of Man, whose birth incarnate
  hallows all our human race,
thou who prayedst, thou who willest,
  that thy people should be one,
grant, O grant our hope's fruition:
  here on earth thy will be done.

S. C. Lowry (1855–1932)

133 (AMR **208**)
Bishopthorpe C.M. *Select Portions of the Psalr*
(H. Gardner, c. 178

Immortal Love for ever full,
for ever flowing free,
for ever shared, for ever whole,
a never-ebbing sea.

2

Our outward lips confess the name
all other names above;
love only knoweth whence it came
and comprehendeth love.

3

We may not climb the heavenly steeps
  to bring the Lord Christ down;
in vain we search the lowest deeps,
  for him no depths can drown:

4

but warm, sweet, tender, even yet‿
  a present help is he;
and faith has still its Olivet,
  and love its Galilee.

*5

The healing of his seamless dress
  is by our beds of pain;
we touch him in life's throng and press,
  and we are whole again.

*6

Through him the first fond prayers are said
  our lips of childhood frame;
the last low whispers of our dead
  are burdened with his name.

7

Alone, O Love ineffable,
  thy saving name is given;
to turn aside from thee is hell,
  to walk with thee is heaven.

J. G. WHITTIER (1807–92)

134 (AMR 444)

Buckland 7 7·7 7· L. G. Hayne (1836–83

Loving Shepherd of thy sheep,
keep thy lamb, in safety keep;
nothing can thy power withstand,
none can pluck me from thy hand.

2

Loving Saviour, thou didst give‿
thine own life that we might live,
and the hands outstretched to bless
bear the cruel nails' impress.

3

I would praise thee every day,
gladly all thy will obey,
like thy blessèd ones above
happy in thy precious love.

4

Loving Shepherd, ever near,
teach thy lamb thy voice to hear;
suffer not my steps to stray
from the straight and narrow way.

5

Where thou leadest I would go,
walking in thy steps below,
till before my Father's throne
I shall know as I am known.

JANE E. LEESON (1809–81)

35 (AMR **210**)
Petra 77·77·77· R. Redhead (1820–1901)

A living and dying prayer

Rock of ages, cleft for me,
let me hide myself in thee;
let the water and the blood,
from thy riven side which flowed,
be of sin the double cure:
cleanse me from its guilt and power.

2

Not the labours of my hands
can fulfil thy law's demands;
could my zeal no respite know,
could my tears for ever flow,
all for sin could not atone:
thou must save, and thou alone.

3

Nothing in my hand I bring,
simply to thy cross I cling;
naked, come to thee for dress;
helpless, look to thee for grace;
foul, I to the fountain fly;
wash me, Saviour, or I die.

4

While I draw this fleeting breath,
when my eyelids close in death,
when I soar through tracts unknown,
see thee on thy judgement throne;
Rock of ages, cleft for me,
let me hide myself in thee.

A. M. Toplady* (1740–78)

136 (AMR 211)

Song 13 7 7.7 7. Orlando Gibbons (1583–1625

Jesu, grant me this, I pray,
ever in thy heart to stay;
let me evermore abide
hidden in thy wounded side.

2

If the world or Satan lay‿
tempting snares about my way,
I am safe when I abide
in thy heart and wounded side.

3

If the flesh, more dangerous still,
tempt my soul to deeds of ill,
naught I fear when I abide
in thy heart and wounded side.

4

Death will come one day to me;
Jesu, cast me not from thee:
dying let me still abide
in thy heart and wounded side.

Latin, 17th cent.
tr. H. W. BAKER (1821–77)

137 (AMR 214)
Horsley C.M. W. Horsley (1774–1858)

There is a green hill far away,
without a city wall,
where the dear Lord was crucified,
who died to save us all.

2

We may not know, we cannot tell,
what pains he had to bear,
but we believe it was for us
he hung and suffered there.

3

He died that we might be forgiven,
he died to make us good,
that we might go at last to heaven,
saved by his precious blood.

4

There was no other good enough
to pay the price of sin;
he only could unlock the gate‿
of heaven, and let us in.

5

O dearly, dearly has he loved,
and we must love him too,
and trust in his redeeming blood,
and try his works to do.

Cecil Frances Alexander (1818–95)

138 (AMR 215)

Bow Brickhill L.M. S. H. Nicholson (1875–1947)

Alternative Tune: *Breslau* (237)

1 We sing the praise of him who died,
of him who died upon the cross;
the sinner's hope let men deride,
for this we count the world but loss.

2 Inscribed upon the cross we see
in shining letters, 'God is love;'
he bears our sins upon the Tree;
he brings us mercy from above.

3 The Cross! it takes our guilt away:
it holds the fainting spirit up;
it cheers with hope the gloomy day,
and sweetens every bitter cup.

4 It makes the coward spirit brave,
and nerves the feeble arm for fight;
it takes its terror from the grave,
and gilds the bed of death with light:

5 the balm of life, the cure of woe,
the measure and the pledge of love,
the sinner's refuge here below,
the angels' theme in heaven above.

T. Kelly (1769–1855)

39 (AMR **216**)
Gopsal 6 6 6 6.8 8. G. F. Handel (1685—1759)

Rejoice! the Lord is King.
Your Lord and King adore;
mortals, give thanks and sing,
and triumph evermore:
lift up your heart, lift up your voice;
rejoice, again I say, rejoice.

2

Jesus, the Saviour, reigns,
the God of truth and love;
when he had purged our stains,
he took his seat above:

3

His kingdom cannot fail;
he rules o'er earth and heaven;
the keys of death and hell
are to our Jesus given:

4

He sits at God's right hand
till all his foes submit,
and bow to his command,
and fall beneath his feet:
lift up your heart, lift up your voice;
rejoice, again I say, rejoice.

CHARLES WESLEY (1707–88)

140 (AMR 217) FIRST TUNE

Miles Lane C.M. W. Shrubsole (1760–1806)

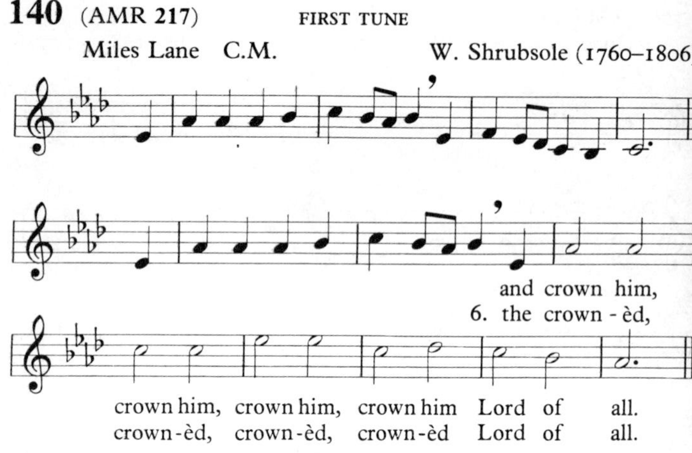
and crown him,
6. the crown - èd,
crown him, crown him, crown him Lord of all.
crown-èd, crown-èd, crown-èd Lord of all.

SECOND TUNE

Ladywell D.C.M. W. H. Ferguson (1872–1950)

All hail the power of Jesus' name!
let angels prostrate fall;
bring forth the royal diadem
and crown him Lord of all.

*2

Crown him, ye morning stars of light,
who fixed this floating ball;
now hail the Strength of Israel's might,
and crown him Lord of all.

*3

Crown him, ye martyrs of your God,
who from his altar call;
extol the Stem-of-Jesse's Rod,
and crown him Lord of all.

4

Ye seed of Israel's chosen race,
ye ransomed of the fall,
hail him who saves you by his grace,
and crown him Lord of all.

5

Sinners, whose love can ne'er forget
the wormwood and the gall,
go spread your trophies at his feet,
and crown him Lord of all.

6

Let every tribe and every tongue
before him prostrate fall,
and shout in universal song
the crownèd Lord of all.

E. PERRONET (c. 1726–92)

141 (AMR **218**)
St. Magnus C.M. Jeremiah Clarke (*c.* 1673–1707

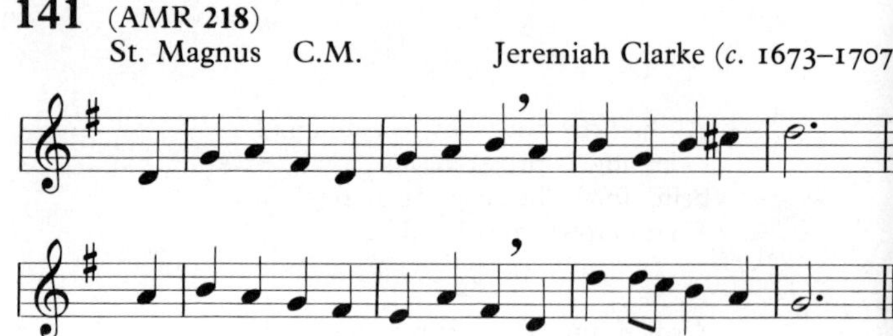

His Power and Glory

Perfect through sufferings

The head that once was crowned with thorns
  is crowned with glory now:
a royal diadem adorns‿
  the mighty Victor's brow.

2

The highest place that heaven affords
  is his, is his by right,
the King of kings, and Lord of lords,
  and heaven's eternal Light;

3

the joy of all who dwell above,
  the joy of all below,
to whom he manifests his love,
  and grants his name to know.

4

To them the Cross, with all its shame,
  with all its grace, is given:
their name an everlasting name,
  their joy the joy of heaven.

5

They suffer with their Lord below,
  they reign with him above;
their profit and their joy to know‿
  the mystery of his love.

6

The Cross he bore is life and health,
  though shame and death to him;
his people's hope, his people's wealth,
  their everlasting theme.

T. Kelly (1769–1855)
Hebrews 2. 10

142 (AMR **219**)
Crüger
7 6.7 6. D.

Adapted from J. Crüger (1598–1662
by W. H. Monk (1823–89

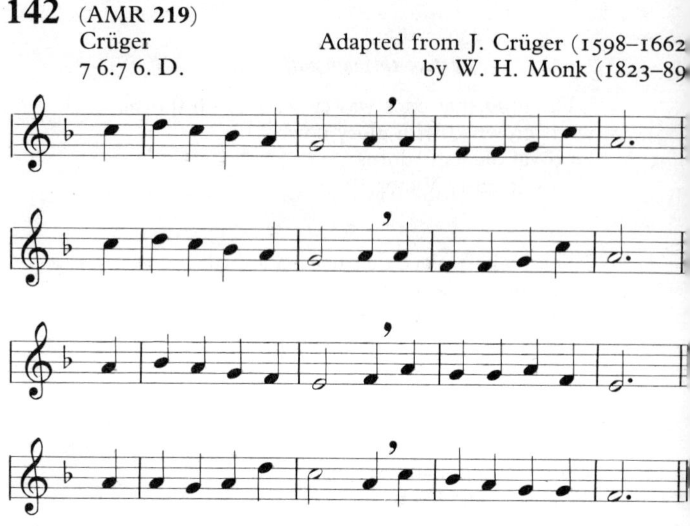

Hail to the Lord's Anointed,
  great David's greater Son!
Hail, in the time appointed,
  his reign on earth begun!
He comes to break oppression,
  to set the captive free,
to take away transgression,
  and rule in equity.

*2

He comes with succour speedy
  to those who suffer wrong;
to help the poor and needy,
  and bid the weak be strong;
to give them songs for sighing,
  their darkness turn to light,
whose souls, condemned and dying,
  were precious in his sight.

His Power and Glory

3

He shall come down like showers
  upon the fruitful earth,
and love, joy, hope, like flowers,
  spring in his path to birth:
before him on the mountains
  shall peace, the herald, go;
and righteousness in fountains
  from hill to valley flow.

*4

Arabia's desert-ranger
  to him shall bow the knee;
the Ethiopian stranger
  his glory come to see;
with offerings of devotion
  ships from the isles shall meet,
to pour the wealth of ocean‿
  in tribute at his feet.

5

Kings shall bow down before him,
  and gold and incense bring;
all nations shall adore him,
  his praise all people sing:
to him shall prayer unceasing
  and daily vows ascend;
his kingdom still increasing,
  a kingdom without end.

6

O'er every foe victorious,
  he on his throne shall rest;
from age to age more glorious,
  all-blessing and all-blest:
the tide of time shall never‿
  his covenant remove;
his name shall stand for ever,
  his changeless name of love.

J. MONTGOMERY* (1771–1854)
Psalm 72

143 (AMR **220**) FIRST TUNE

Truro L.M. Melody from T. Williams's *Psalmodia Evangelica*, 1789

SECOND TUNE

Galilee L.M. P. Armes (1836–1908)

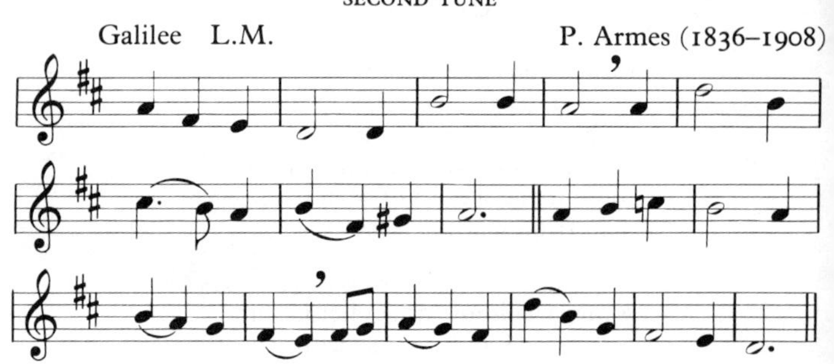

The Kingdom of Christ

Jesus shall reign where'er the sun‿
does his successive journeys run;
his kingdom stretch from shore to shore,
till moons shall wax and wane no more.

2

People and realms of every tongue
dwell on his love with sweetest song,
and infant voices shall proclaim‿
their early blessings on his name.

3

Blessings abound where'er he reigns:
the prisoner leaps to lose his chains;
the weary find eternal rest,
and all the sons of want are blest.

4

To him shall endless prayer be made,
and praises throng to crown his head;
his name like incense shall arise
with every morning sacrifice.

5

Let every creature rise and bring‿
peculiar honours to our King;
angels descend with songs again,
and earth repeat the loud Amen.

ISAAC WATTS* (1674–1748)
Psalm 72

144 (AMR 221)

Nativity C.M. H. Lahee (1826–1912)

Come, let us join our cheerful songs
with angels round the throne;
ten thousand thousand are their tongues,
but all their joys are one.

2

'Worthy the Lamb that died,' they cry,
'to be exalted thus;'
'worthy the Lamb,' our lips reply,
'for he was slain for us.'

3

Jesus is worthy to receive‿
honour and power divine;
and blessings, more than we can give,
be, Lord, for ever thine.

4

Let all creation join in one
to bless the sacred name‿
of him that sits upon the throne,
and to adore the Lamb.

ISAAC WATTS* (1674–1748)
Revelation 5. 11–13

145 (AMR 222)
Neander (Unser Herrscher) J. Neander (1640–80)
8 7.8 7.8 7.

The descant may be sung for verse 6

Come, ye faithful, raise the anthem,
  cleave the skies with shouts of praise;
sing to him who found the ransom,
  Ancient of eternal days,
God of God, the Word incarnate,
  whom the heaven of heaven obeys.

2

Ere he raised the lofty mountains,
formed the seas, or built the sky,
love eternal, free, and boundless,
moved the Lord of Life to die,
fore-ordained the Prince of princes
for the throne of Calvary.

3

There, for us and our redemption,
see him all his life-blood pour!
there he wins our full salvation,
dies that we may die no more;
then, arising, lives for ever,
reigning where he was before.

4

High on yon celestial mountains
stands his sapphire throne, all bright,
midst unending alleluias
bursting from the sons of light;
Sion's people tell his praises,
victor after hard-won fight.

*5

Bring your harps, and bring your incense,
sweep the string and pour the lay;
let the earth proclaim his wonders,
King of that celestial day;
he the Lamb once slain is worthy,
who was dead, and lives for ay.

*6

Laud and honour to the Father,
laud and honour to the Son,
laud and honour to the Spirit,
ever Three and ever One,
consubstantial, co-eternal,
while unending ages run.

J. Hupton (1762–1849)
and J. M. Neale (1818–66)

146 (AMR 223) FIRST TUNE

Laudes Domini 6 6 6. D. Joseph Barnby (1838–96)

SECOND TUNE

Ludgate 6 6 6. D. J. Dykes Bower (1905–1981)

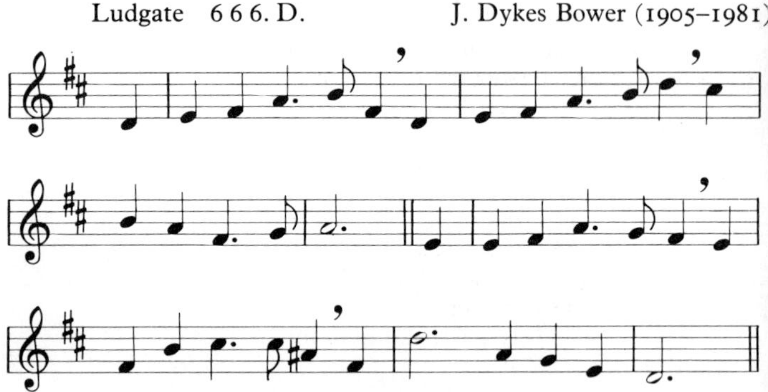

When morning gilds the skies,
my heart awaking cries,
may Jesus Christ be praised:
alike at work and prayer
to Jesus I repair;
may Jesus Christ be praised.

2

Whene'er the sweet church bell
peals over hill and dell,
  may Jesus Christ be praised:
O hark to what it sings,
as joyously it rings,
  may Jesus Christ be praised.

3

My tongue shall never tire
of chanting with the choir,
  may Jesus Christ be praised:
this song of sacred joy,
it never seems to cloy,
  may Jesus Christ be praised.

4

Does sadness fill my mind?
a solace here I find,
  may Jesus Christ be praised:
or fades my earthly bliss?
my comfort still is this,
  may Jesus Christ be praised.

*5

The night becomes as day,
when from the heart we say,
  may Jesus Christ be praised:
the powers of darkness fear,
when this sweet chant they hear,
  may Jesus Christ be praised.

6

Be this, while life is mine,
my canticle divine,
  may Jesus Christ be praised:
be this the eternal song
through ages all along,
  may Jesus Christ be praised.

German, 19th cent.
tr. E. CASWALL* (1814–78)

147 (AMR 224)
Diademata D.S.M. G. J. Elvey (1816–9

Crown him with many crowns,
the Lamb upon his throne;
hark, how the heavenly anthem drowns‿
all music but its own:
awake, my soul, and sing
of him who died for thee,
and hail him as thy matchless King
through all eternity.

2

Crown him the Virgin's Son,
the God incarnate born,
whose arm those crimson trophies won
which now his brow adorn:
Fruit of the mystic Rose,
as of that Rose the Stem;
the Root whence mercy ever flows,
the Babe of Bethlehem.

3

Crown him the Lord of love;
behold his hands and side,
those wounds yet visible above
in beauty glorified:
no angel in the sky
can fully bear that sight,
but downward bends his burning eye
at mysteries so bright.

4

Crown him the Lord of peace,
whose power a sceptre sways
from pole to pole, that wars may cease,
and all be prayer and praise:
his reign shall know no end,
and round his piercèd feet
fair flowers of paradise extend‿
their fragrance ever sweet.

5

Crown him the Lord of years,
the Potentate of time,
Creator of the rolling spheres,
ineffably sublime:
all hail, Redeemer, hail!
for thou hast died for me;
thy praise shall never, never fail
throughout eternity.

The expression 'mystic Rose' in verse 2, *line* 5, *is a medieval title for the Blessed Virgin, and is combined here with a reference to Isaiah* 11.1

MATTHEW BRIDGES* (1800–94)
Revelation 19. 12

148 (AMR 225)

Evelyns 6 5.6 5. D. W. H. Monk (1823–89)

At the name of Jesus
every knee shall bow,
every tongue confess him
King of glory now:
'tis the Father's pleasure‿
we should call him Lord,
who from the beginning
was the mighty Word.

*2

At his voice creation‿
sprang at once to sight,
all the angel faces,
all the hosts of light,
thrones and dominations,
stars upon their way,
all the heavenly orders,
in their great array.

3

Humbled for a season,
to receive a name
from the lips of sinners
unto whom he came,
faithfully he bore it
spotless to the last,
brought it back victorious,
when from death he passed:

4

Bore it up triumphant
with its human light,
through all ranks of creatures,
to the central height,
to the throne of Godhead,
to the Father's breast;
filled it with the glory‿
of that perfect rest.

5

Name him, brothers, name him,
with love strong as death,
but with awe and wonder
and with bated breath:
he is God the Saviour,
he is Christ the Lord,
ever to be worshipped,
trusted, and adored.

*6

In your hearts enthrone him;
there let him subdue‿
all that is not holy,
all that is not true:
crown him as your Captain
in temptation's hour;
let his will enfold you
in its light and power.

*7

Brothers, this Lord Jesus
shall return again,
with his Father's glory,
with his angel train;
for all wreaths of empire
meet upon his brow,
and our hearts confess him
King of glory now.

CAROLINE M. NOEL (1817–77)

Verse 5, line 2: AMR has 'with love as strong as death'.

149 (AMR 226)

Paderborn 10 10.11 11. *Paderborn Gesangbuch*, 1765

Ye servants of God, your Master proclaim,
and publish abroad his wonderful name;
the name all-victorious of Jesus extol:
his kingdom is glorious, and rules over all.

2

God ruleth on high, almighty to save;
and still he is nigh: his presence we have;
the great congregation his triumph shall sing,
ascribing salvation to Jesus our King.

3

Salvation to God who sits on the throne!
let all cry aloud, and honour the Son.
The praises of Jesus the angels proclaim,
fall down on their faces, and worship the Lamb.

4

Then let us adore, and give him his right:
all glory and power, all wisdom and might,
and honour and blessing, with angels above,
and thanks never-ceasing, and infinite love.

CHARLES WESLEY (1707–88)

50 (AMR **229**)
Narenza S.M.

Adapted from J. Leisentritt,
Catholicum Hymnologium, 1584

The active Christian

1 Ye servants of the Lord,
each in his office wait,
observant of his heavenly word,
and watchful at his gate.

2 Let all your lamps be bright,
and trim the golden flame;
gird up your loins as in his sight,
for aweful is his name.

3 Watch! 'tis your Lord's command,
and while we speak, he's near;
mark the first signal of his hand,
and ready all appear.

4 O happy servant he
in such a posture found!
he shall his Lord with rapture see,
and be with honour crowned.

5 Christ shall the banquet spread
with his own royal hand,
and raise that faithful servant's head
amid the angelic band.

PHILIP DODDRIDGE* (1720–51)
Luke 12. 35–8

151 (AMR 230)

St. Cuthbert 8 6.8 4. J. B. Dykes (1823–76

Our blest Redeemer, ere he breathed
his tender last farewell,
a Guide, a Comforter, bequeathed
with us to dwell.

2

He came sweet influence to impart,
a gracious willing guest,
while he can find one humble heart
wherein to rest.

3

And his that gentle voice we hear,
soft as the breath of even,
that checks each fault, that calms each fear,
and speaks of heaven.

4

And every virtue we possess,
and every conquest won,
and every thought of holiness,
are his alone.

5

Spirit of purity and grace,
our weakness, pitying, see:
O make our hearts thy dwelling-place,
and worthier thee.

HARRIET AUBER (1773–1862)

The Holy Spirit

52 (AMR **231**)
Tallis's Ordinal C.M. Thomas Tallis (*c.* 1505–85)

O Holy Spirit, Lord of grace,
eternal fount of love,
inflame, we pray, our inmost hearts
with fire from heaven above.

2

As thou in bond of love dost join
the Father and the Son,
so fill us all with mutual love,
and knit our hearts in one.

3

All glory to the Father be,
all glory to the Son,
all glory, Holy Ghost, to thee,
while endless ages run.

C. Coffin (1676–1749)
tr. J. Chandler (1808–76)

153 (AMR **232**)
Hawkhurst L.M. H. J. Gauntlett (1805–7

Alternative Tune: *Eisenach* (119)

Come, gracious Spirit, heavenly Dove,
with light and comfort from above;
be thou our guardian, thou our guide,
o'er every thought and step preside.

2

The light of truth to us display,
and make us know and choose thy way;
plant holy fear in every heart,
that we from God may ne'er depart.

3

Lead us to Christ, the living Way,
nor let us from his pastures stray;
lead us to holiness, the road‿
that we must take to dwell with God.

4

Lead us to heaven, that we may share‿
fulness of joy for ever there;
lead us to God, our final rest,
to be with him for ever blest.

S. BROWNE (1680–1732
and other

154 (AMR 233)

FIRST TUNE

Charity 777.5. John Stainer (1840–1901)

SECOND TUNE

Capetown 777.5. F. Filitz (1804–76)

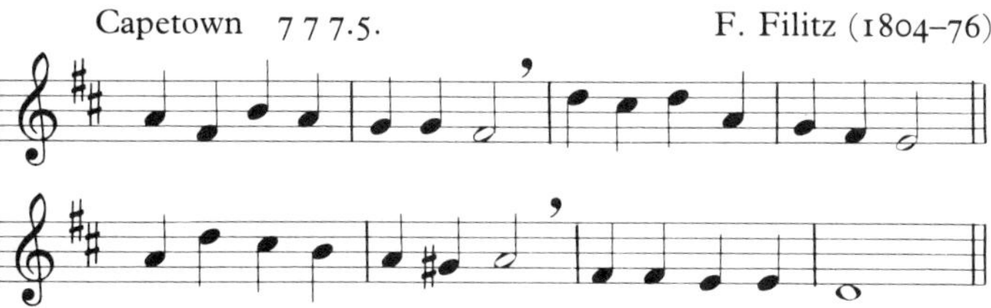

1

Gracious Spirit, Holy Ghost,
taught by thee, we covet most
of thy gifts at Pentecost,
holy, heavenly love.

2

Love is kind, and suffers long,
love is meek, and thinks no wrong,
love than death itself more strong;
therefore give us love.

3

Prophecy will fade away,
melting in the light of day;
love will ever with us stay;
therefore give us love.

4

Faith will vanish into sight;
hope be emptied in delight;
love in heaven will shine more bright;
therefore give us love.

5

Faith and hope and love we see
joining hand in hand agree;
but the greatest of the three,
and the best, is love.

*6

From the overshadowing‿
of thy gold and silver wing
shed on us, who to thee sing,
holy, heavenly love.

CHRISTOPHER WORDSWORTH (1807–85)
1 Corinthians 13; Psalm 68. 13

155 (AMR 234)
St. Timothy C.M. H. W. Baker (1821–77)

O Holy Ghost, thy people bless
who long to feel thy might,
and fain would grow in holiness
as children of the light.

2

To thee we bring, who art the Lord,
our selves to be thy throne;
let every thought and deed and word
thy pure dominion own.

3

Life-giving Spirit, o'er us move,
as on the formless deep;
give life and order, light and love,
where now is death or sleep.

4

Great gift of our ascended King,
his saving truth reveal;
our tongues inspire his praise to sing,
our hearts his love to feel.

*5

True wind of heaven, from south or north,
for joy or chastening, blow;
the garden-spices shall spring forth
if thou wilt bid them flow.

6

O Holy Ghost, of sevenfold might,
all graces come from thee;
grant us to know and serve aright
One God in Persons Three.

H. W. BAKER (1821–77)

156 (AMR 235)

FIRST TUNE

Down Ampney 66.11. D. R. Vaughan Willian
(1872–195

SECOND TUNE

North Petherton 66.11. D. William H. Harri
(1883–1973

Come down, O Love divine,
seek thou this soul of mine,
and visit it with thine own ardour glowing;
O Comforter, draw near,
within my heart appear,
and kindle it, thy holy flame bestowing.

2

O let it freely burn,
till earthly passions turn‿
to dust and ashes in its heat consuming;
and let thy glorious light
shine ever on my sight,
and clothe me round, the while my path illuming.

3

Let holy charity
mine outward vesture be,
and lowliness become mine inner clothing:
true lowliness of heart,
which takes the humbler part,
and o'er its own shortcomings weeps with loathing.

4

And so the yearning strong,
with which the soul will long,
shall far outpass the power of human telling;
for none can guess its grace,
till he become the place
wherein the Holy Spirit makes his dwelling.

BIANCO DA SIENA (d. 1434)
tr. R. F. LITTLEDALE (1833–90)

157 (AMR **236**) FIRST TUNE

Carlisle S.M. C. Lockhart (1745–181

SECOND TUNE

Wirksworth S.M. Adapted from J. Chetha
(Aylesbury) (*Psalms*, 171

Breathe on me, Breath of God,
fill me with life anew,
that I may love what thou dost love,
and do what thou wouldst do.

2

Breathe on me, Breath of God,
until my heart is pure;
until with thee I will one will,
to do and to endure.

3

Breathe on me, Breath of God,
till I am wholly thine;
until this earthly part of me
glows with thy fire divine.

4

Breathe on me, Breath of God:
so shall I never die,
but live with thee the perfect life
of thine eternity.

EDWIN HATCH (1835–89)

58 (AMR 237) FIRST TUNE

Amen Court 6 6.8 4. J. Dykes Bower (1905–81)

SECOND TUNE

Temple 6 6.8 4. Walford Davies (1869–1941)

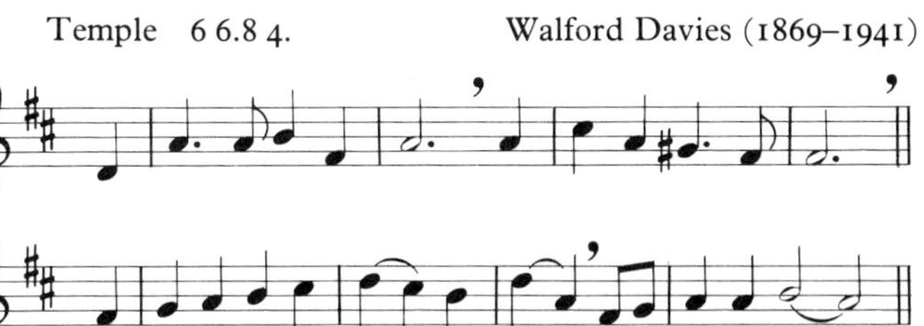

O King enthroned on high,
thou Comforter divine,
blest Spirit of all truth, be nigh‿
and make us thine.

2

Thou art the source of life,
thou art our treasure-store;
give us thy peace, and end our strife‿
for evermore.

3

Descend, O heavenly Dove,
abide with us alway;
and in the fulness of thy love
cleanse us, we pray.

Greek, c. 8th cent.
tr. J. Brownlie (1857–1925)

159 (AMR 238)

Song 22 10 10.10 10. Orlando Gibbons (1583–1625)

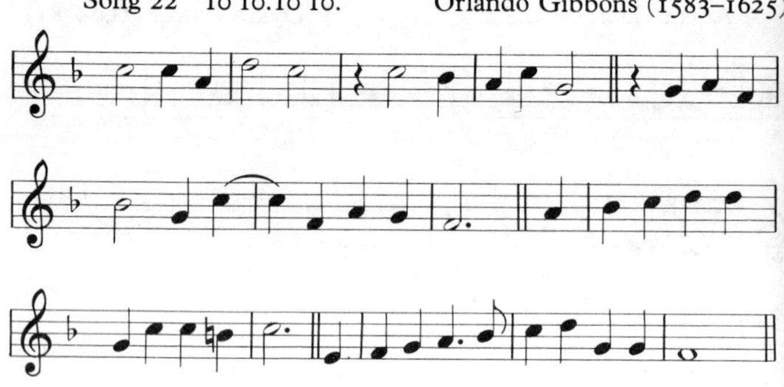

1 Love of the Father, Love of God the Son,
from whom all came, in whom was all begun;
who formest heavenly beauty out of strife,
creation's whole desire and breath of life:

2 Thou the all-holy, thou supreme in might,
thou dost give peace, thy presence maketh right;
thou with thy favour all things dost enfold,
with thine all-kindness free from harm wilt hold.

*3 Hope of all comfort, splendour of all aid,
that dost not fail nor leave the heart afraid:
to all that cry thou dost all help accord,
the angels' armour, and the saints' reward.

4 Purest and highest, wisest and most just,
there is no truth save only in thy trust;
thou dost the mind from earthly dreams recall,
and bring, through Christ, to him for whom are all.

5 Eternal glory, all men thee adore,
who art and shalt be worshipped evermore:
us whom thou madest, comfort with thy might,
and lead us to enjoy thy heavenly light.

ROBERT BRIDGES (1844–1930)
based on *Amor Patris et Filii*, 12th cent.

60 (AMR 242)

Quam Dilecta 6 6.6 6. H. L. Jenner (1820–98)

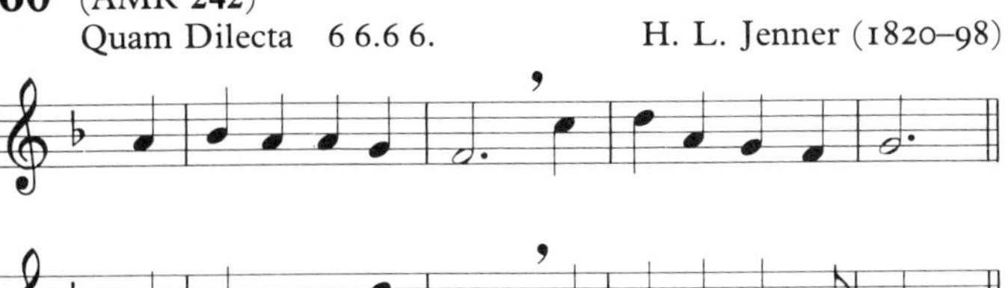

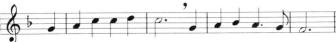

We love the place, O God,
wherein thine honour dwells;
the joy of thine abode
all earthly joy excels.

2

't is the house of prayer,
wherein thy servants meet;
ınd thou, O Lord, art there
thy chosen flock to greet.

3

We love the sacred font;
for there the holy Dove
:o pour is ever wont‿
his blessing from above.

4

We love thine altar, Lord;
O what on earth so dear?
for there, in faith adored,
we find thy presence near.

5

We love the word of life,
the word that tells of peace,
of comfort in the strife,
and joys that never cease.

6

We love to sing below
for mercies freely given;
but O, we long to know‿
the triumph-song of heaven.

7

Lord Jesus, give us grace
on earth to love thee more,
in heaven to see thy face,
and with thy saints adore.

W. Bullock (1798–1874)
H. W. Baker (1821–77)

161 (AMR **243**)
Harewood 6 6.6 6.4 4.4 4. S. S. Wesley (1810–76)

Christ is our corner-stone,
on him alone we build;
with his true saints alone
the courts of heaven are filled:
on his great love
our hopes we place
of present grace
and joys above.

2

O then with hymns of praise
these hallowed courts shall ring;
our voices we will raise
the Three in One to sing;
and thus proclaim
in joyful song,
both loud and long,
that glorious name.

3

Here, gracious God, do thou‿
for evermore draw nigh;
accept each faithful vow,
and mark each suppliant sigh;
in copious shower
on all who pray
each holy day
thy blessings pour.

4

Here may we gain from heaven
the grace which we implore;
and may that grace, once given,
be with us evermore,
until that day
when all the blest
to endless rest
are called away.

Latin, before 9th cent.
tr. J. CHANDLER (1806–76)

162 (AMR **245**)
Wareham L.M. W. Knapp (1698–176

The House of God

Jesus, where'er thy people meet,
there they behold thy mercy-seat;
where'er they seek thee thou art found,
and every place is hallowed ground.

2

For thou, within no walls confined,
inhabitest the humble mind;
such ever bring thee when they come,
and, going, take thee to their home.

3

Dear Shepherd of thy chosen few,
thy former mercies here renew;
here to our waiting hearts proclaim
the sweetness of thy saving name.

4

Here may we prove the power of prayer
to strengthen faith and sweeten care,
to teach our faint desires to rise,
and bring all heaven before our eyes.

5

Lord, we are few, but thou art near;
nor short thine arm, nor deaf thine ear:
O rend the heavens, come quickly down,
and make a thousand hearts thine own.

William Cowper (1731–1800)

163 (AMR **246**)

Angel Voices 85. 85. 843. E. G. Monk (1819–190

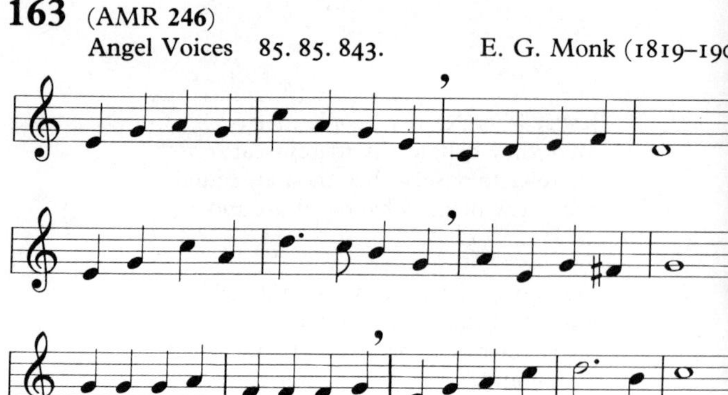

Angel-voices ever singing
round thy throne of light,
angel-harps for ever ringing,
rest not day nor night;
thousands only live to bless thee
and confess thee
Lord of might.

2

Thou who art beyond the farthest‿
mortal eye can scan,
can it be that thou regardest‿
songs of sinful man?
can we know that thou art near us,
and wilt hear us?
yea, we can.

3

Yea, we know that thou rejoicest‿
  o'er each work of thine;
thou didst ears and hands and voices
  for thy praise design;
craftsman's art and music's measure
    for thy pleasure
      all combine.

4

In thy house, great God, we offer‿
  of thine own to thee;
and for thine acceptance proffer
  all unworthily
hearts and minds and hands and voices
    in our choicest
      psalmody.

5

Honour, glory, might, and merit
  thine shall ever be,
Father, Son, and Holy Spirit,
  blessèd Trinity.
Of the best that thou hast given
    earth and heaven
      render thee.

F. Pott (1832–1909)

164 (AMR 247)
Oswald's Tree C.M. Walford Davies (1869–1941

Alternative Tune: *St. Flavian* (272)

Great Shepherd of thy people, hear,
thy presence now display;
as thou hast given a place for prayer,
so give us hearts to pray.

2

Within these walls let holy peace
and love and concord dwell;
here give the troubled conscience ease,
the wounded spirit heal.

3

May we in faith receive thy word,
in faith present our prayers,
and in the presence of our Lord
unbosom all our cares.

4

The hearing ear, the seeing eye,
the contrite heart, bestow;
and shine upon us from on high,
that we in grace may grow.

JOHN NEWTON* (1725–1807)

165 (AMR **248**)

Croft's 136th 6 6.6 6.4 4.4 4. William Croft (1678–1727)

Longing for the House of God

Lord of the worlds above
how pleasant and how fair
the dwellings of thy love,
thy earthly temples, are!
To thine abode
my heart aspires,
with warm desires
to see my God.

2

O happy souls that pray
where God appoints to hear!
O happy men that pay‿
their constant service there!
They praise thee still;
and happy they
that love the way
to Zion's hill.

3

They go from strength to strength
through this dark vale of tears,
till each arrives at length,
till each in heaven appears:
O glorious seat!
when God our King
shall thither bring
our willing feet.

ISAAC WATTS (1674–1748)
Psalm 84

166 (AMR 250)

Ravenshaw 6 6.6 6.

Adapted from a German Medieval Melody by W. H. Monk (1823–89)

Lord, thy word abideth,
and our footsteps guideth;
who its truth believeth
light and joy receiveth.

2

When our foes are near us,
then thy word doth cheer us,
word of consolation,
message of salvation.

3

When the storms are o'er us,
and dark clouds before us,
then its light directeth,
and our way protecteth.

4

Who can tell the pleasure,
who recount the treasure,
by thy word imparted
to the simple-hearted?

5

Word of mercy, giving‿
succour to the living;
word of life, supplying‿
comfort to the dying.

6

O that we discerning‿
its most holy learning,
Lord, may love and fear thee,
evermore be near thee.

H. W. BAKER (1821–77)

167 (AMR 251)

Collingwood C.M. H. A. Bate (b. 1899)

Alternative Tune: *Southwell* (187)
In AMR this hymn is set to *Angmering*

Father of mercies, in thy word‿
what endless glory shines!
For ever be thy name adored
for these celestial lines.

2

Here may the blind and hungry come,
and light and food receive;
here shall the lowliest guest have room,
and taste and see and live.

3

Here springs of consolation rise
to cheer the fainting mind,
and thirsting souls receive supplies,
and sweet refreshment find.

4

Here the Redeemer's welcome voice
spreads heavenly peace around,
and life and everlasting joys
attend the blissful sound.

5

O may these heavenly pages be‿
my ever dear delight,
and still new beauties may I see,
and still increasing light.

6

Divine instructor, gracious Lord,
be thou for ever near;
teach me to love thy sacred word,
and view my Saviour here.

Anne Steele (1717–78)

168 (AMR 252)

Alfreton L.M. *Supplement to the New Version*, 17

Alternative Tune: *Brockham* (23)

The glory and success of the Gospel

1 The heavens declare thy glory, Lord;
in every star thy wisdom shines;
but when our eyes behold thy word,
we read thy name in fairer lines.

2 Sun, moon, and stars convey thy praise
round the whole earth, and never stand;
so, when thy truth began its race,
it touched and glanced on every land.

3 Nor shall thy spreading Gospel rest
till through the world thy truth has run;
till Christ has all the nations blest
that see the light or feel the sun.

4 Great Sun of Righteousness, arise;
bless the dark world with heavenly light;
thy Gospel makes the simple wise,
thy laws are pure, thy judgements right.

5 Thy noblest wonders here we view,
in souls renewed and sins forgiven:
Lord, cleanse my sins, my soul renew,
and make thy word my guide to heaven.

Isaac Watts (1674–1748
Psalm 1

169 (AMR 254)

University C.M. C. Collignon (1725–85)

1 The Church of God a kingdom is,
where Christ in power doth reign;
where spirits yearn till, seen in bliss,
their Lord shall come again.

2 Glad companies of saints possess‿
this Church below, above;
and God's perpetual calm doth bless‿
their paradise of love.

3 An altar stands within the shrine
whereon, once sacrificed,
is set, immaculate, divine,
the Lamb of God, the Christ.

4 There rich and poor, from countless lands,
praise Christ on mystic rood;
there nations reach forth holy hands
to take God's holy food.

5 There pure life-giving streams o'erflow‿
the sower's garden-ground;
and faith and hope fair blossoms show,
and fruits of love abound.

6 O King, O Christ, this endless grace
to us and all men bring,
to see the vision of thy face
in joy, O Christ, our King.

L. B. C. L. Muirhead (1845–1925)

170 (AMR 255) FIRST TUNE

Aurelia 7 6.7 6. D. S. S. Wesley (1810–76

The Church's one foundation
  is Jesus Christ her Lord;
she is his new creation
  by water and the word:
from heaven he came and sought her
  to be his holy Bride;
with his own blood he bought her,
  and for her life he died.

2

Elect from every nation,
  yet one o'er all the earth,
her charter of salvation
  one Lord, one faith, one birth;
one holy name she blesses,
  partakes one holy food,
and to one hope she presses
  with every grace endued.

*3

Though with a scornful wonder
  men see her sore opprest,
by schisms rent asunder,
  by heresies distrest,
yet saints their watch are keeping,
  their cry goes up, 'How long?'
and soon the night of weeping
  shall be the morn of song.

4

Mid toil and tribulation,
  and tumult of her war,
she waits the consummation‿
  of peace for evermore;
till with the vision glorious
  her longing eyes are blest,
and the great Church victorious
  shall be the Church at rest.

5

Yet she on earth hath union
  with God the Three in One,
and mystic sweet communion
  with those whose rest is won:
O happy ones and holy!
  Lord, give us grace that we,
like them the meek and lowly,
  on high may dwell with thee.

S. J. Stone (1839–1900)

170 (AMR 255) SECOND TUNE

King's Lynn 7 6.7 6. D. English Traditional Melod
arr. R. Vaughan Williams (1872–195

The Church's one foundation
  is Jesus Christ her Lord;
she is his new creation
  by water and the word:
from heaven he came and sought her
  to be his holy Bride;
with his own blood he bought her,
  and for her life he died.

2

Elect from every nation,
  yet one o'er all the earth,
her charter of salvation
  one Lord, one faith, one birth;
one holy name she blesses,
  partakes one holy food,
and to one hope she presses
  with every grace endued.

*3

Though with a scornful wonder
  men see her sore opprest,
by schisms rent asunder,
  by heresies distrest,
yet saints their watch are keeping,
  their cry goes up, 'How long?'
and soon the night of weeping
  shall be the morn of song.

4

Mid toil and tribulation,
  and tumult of her war,
she waits the consummation‿
  of peace for evermore;
till with the vision glorious
  her longing eyes are blest,
and the great Church victorious
  shall be the Church at rest.

5

Yet she on earth hath union
  with God the Three in One,
and mystic sweet communion
  with those whose rest is won:
O happy ones and holy!
  Lord, give us grace that we,
like them the meek and lowly,
  on high may dwell with thee.

S. J. Stone (1839–1900)

171 (AMR 256)

Thornbury 7 6.7 6. D. Basil Harwood (1859–1949)

Thy hand, O God, has guided‿
thy flock, from age to age;
the wondrous tale is written,
full clear, on every page;
our fathers owned thy goodness,
and we their deeds record;
and both of this bear witness:
one Church, one faith, one Lord.

2

Thy heralds brought glad tidings
to greatest, as to least;
they bade men rise, and hasten
to share the great King's feast;
and this was all their teaching,
in every deed and word,
to all alike proclaiming
one Church, one faith, one Lord.

*3

When shadows thick were falling,
  and all seemed sunk in night,
thou, Lord, didst send thy servants,
  thy chosen sons of light.
On them and on thy people
  thy plenteous grace was poured,
and this was still their message:
  one Church, one faith, one Lord.

4

Through many a day of darkness,
  through many a scene of strife,
the faithful few fought bravely,
  to guard the nation's life.
Their Gospel of redemption,
  sin pardoned, man restored,
was all in this enfolded:
  one Church, one faith, one Lord.

*5

And we, shall we be faithless?
  shall hearts fail, hands hang down?
shall we evade the conflict,
  and cast away our crown?
Not so: in God's deep counsels
  some better thing is stored;
we will maintain, unflinching,
  one Church, one faith, one Lord.

6

Thy mercy will not fail us,
  nor leave thy work undone;
with thy right hand to help us,
  the victory shall be won;
and then, by men and angels,
  thy name shall be adored,
and this shall be their anthem:
  one Church, one faith, one Lord.

E. H. Plumptre (1821–91)

172 (AMR 257) FIRST TUNE

Abbot's Leigh 8 7.8 7. D. C. V. Taylor (b. 1907)

Optional version for verse 4 over page

The City of God

Glorious things of thee are spoken,
  Zion, city of our God;
he whose word cannot be broken
  formed thee for his own abode.
On the Rock of ages founded,
  what can shake thy sure repose?
With salvation's walls surrounded,
  thou may'st smile at all thy foes.

2

See, the streams of living waters,
springing from eternal love,
well supply thy sons and daughters,
and all fear of want remove.
Who can faint while such a river‿
ever flows their thirst to assuage:
grace which, like the Lord the giver,
never fails from age to age?

*3

Round each habitation hovering,
see the cloud and fire appear
for a glory and a covering,
showing that the Lord is near.
Thus they march, the pillar leading,
light by night and shade by day;
daily on the manna feeding
which he gives them when they pray.

4

Saviour, if of Zion's city
I through grace a member am,
let the world deride or pity,
I will glory in thy name.
Fading is the worldling's pleasure,
all his boasted pomp and show;
solid joys and lasting treasure
none but Zion's children know.

JOHN NEWTON* (1725–1807)
Isaiah 33. 20–21

In verse 4, line 1, for Newton's 'if', *AMR has* 'since'

172 (AMR 257)

Optional version for verse 4

John Wilson (198

DESCANT

4 Sa - viour, if of Zi - on's ci - ty
I thro' grace a mem-ber am, let the
world de - ride or pi - ty, I will glo - ry
in thy name. Fa - ding is the world-ling's
plea - sure, all his boast - ed pomp and
show; so - lid joys and last - ing
trea - sure none but Zi - on's chil - dren know.

SECOND TUNE

Austria 8 7.8 7. D. J. Haydn (1732–1809)

The City of God

1

lorious things of thee are spoken
Zion, city of our God;
e whose word cannot be broken
formed thee for his own abode.
n the Rock of ages founded,
what can shake thy sure repose?
/ith salvation's walls surrounded,
thou may'st smile at all thy foes.

2

ee, the streams of living waters,
springing from eternal love,
'ell supply thy sons and daughters,
and all fear of want remove.
/ho can faint while such a river‿
ever flows their thirst to assuage:
race which, like the Lord the giver,
never fails from age to age?

*3

Round each habitation hovering,
see the cloud and fire appear
for a glory and a covering,
showing that the Lord is near.
Thus they march, the pillar leading,
light by night and shade by day;
daily on the manna feeding
which he gives them when they pray.

4

Saviour, if of Zion's city
I through grace a member am,
let the world deride or pity,
I will glory in thy name.
Fading is the worldling's pleasure,
all his boasted pomp and show;
solid joys and lasting treasure
none but Zion's children know.

JOHN NEWTON* (1725–1807)
Isaiah 33. 20–21

In verse 4, line 1, for Newton's 'if', *AMR has* 'since'

173 (AMR 258)

Richmond C.M.

Adapted fron
T. Haweis (1734–182c

City of God, how broad and far‿
outspread thy walls sublime!
the true thy chartered freemen are
of every age and clime:

2

one holy Church, one army strong,
one steadfast, high intent;
one working band, one harvest-song,
one King omnipotent.

3

How purely hath thy speech come down
from man's primeval youth!
how grandly hath thine empire grown
of freedom, love, and truth!

4

How gleam thy watch-fires through the night
with never-fainting ray!
how rise thy towers, serene and bright,
to meet the dawning day!

5

In vain the surge's angry shock,
in vain the drifting sands:
unharmed upon the eternal Rock
the eternal city stands.

S. Johnson (1822–82)

74 (AMR 259)

Old 120th 6 6.6 6.6 6. *Psalms*, 1570

The kingdom of God within

O thou not made with hands,
not throned above the skies,
nor walled with shining walls,
nor framed with stones of price,
more bright than gold or gem,
God's own Jerusalem!

2

Where'er the gentle heart
finds courage from above;
where'er the heart forsook
warms with the breath of love;
where faith bids fear depart,
City of God, thou art.

3

Thou art where'er the proud‿
in humbleness melts down;
where self itself yields up;
where martyrs win their crown;
where faithful souls possess‿
themselves in perfect peace;

4

where in life's common ways
with cheerful feet we go;
where in his steps we tread,
who trod the way of woe;
where he is in the heart,
City of God, thou art.

5

Not throned above the skies,
nor golden-walled afar,
but where Christ's two or three‿
in his name gathered are,
be in the midst of them,
God's own Jerusalem.

F. T. PALGRAVE (1824–97)

175 (AMR **260**)

Hyfrydol 8 7.8 7. D. R. H. Prichard (1811–87)

Ye that know the Lord is gracious,
  ye for whom a Corner-stone‿
stands, of God elect and precious,
  laid that ye may build thereon,
see that on that sure foundation
  ye a living temple raise,
towers that may tell forth salvation,
  walls that may re-echo praise.

2

Living stones, by God appointed
  each to his allotted place,
kings and priests, by God anointed,
  shall ye not declare his grace?
Ye, a royal generation,
  tell the tidings of your birth,
tidings of a new creation
  to an old and weary earth.

3

Tell the praise of him who called you
  out of darkness into light,
broke the fetters that enthralled you,
  gave you freedom, peace and sight:
tell the tale of sins forgiven,
  strength renewed and hope restored,
till the earth, in tune with heaven,
  praise and magnify the Lord.

C. A. Alington (1872–1955)

176 (AMR 261)

Binchester C.M. William Croft (1678–172

1 Happy are they, they that love God,
whose hearts have Christ confest,
who by his Cross have found their life,
and 'neath his yoke their rest.

2 Glad is the praise, sweet are the songs,
when they together sing;
and strong the prayers that bow the ear‿
of heaven's eternal King.

3 Christ to their homes giveth his peace,
and makes their loves his own:
but ah, what tares the evil one
hath in his garden sown!

4 Sad were our lot, evil this earth,
did not its sorrows prove‿
the path whereby the sheep may find
the fold of Jesus' love.

5 Then shall they know, they that love him,
how all their pain is good;
and death itself cannot unbind
their happy brotherhood.

ROBERT BRIDGES (1844-1930
based on *O quam juvat*,
C. COFFIN (1676–1749

177 (AMR 262)

St. Cecilia 6 6.6 6. L. G. Hayne (1836–83)

1

Thy kingdom come, O God,
thy rule, O Christ, begin;
break with thine iron rod
the tyrannies of sin.

2

Where is thy reign of peace
and purity and love?
When shall all hatred cease,
as in the realms above?

3

When comes the promised time
that war shall be no more,
and lust, oppression, crime
shall flee thy face before?

4

We pray thee, Lord, arise,
and come in thy great might;
revive our longing eyes,
which languish for thy sight.

5

Men scorn thy sacred name,
and wolves devour thy fold;
by many deeds of shame
we learn that love grows cold.

6

O'er lands both near and far
thick darkness broodeth yet:
arise, O morning star,
arise, and never set.

L. Hensley (1824–1905)

In verse 6, line 1, AMR has 'O'er heathen lands afar'

178 (AMR **263**)
Irish C.M. *Hymns and Sacred Poems* (Dublin, 174

1 Thy kingdom come! on bended knee
the passing ages pray;
and faithful souls have yearned to see
on earth that kingdom's day.

2 But the slow watches of the night
not less to God belong;
and for the everlasting right
the silent stars are strong.

3 And lo, already on the hills
the flags of dawn appear;
gird up your loins, ye prophet souls,
proclaim the day is near:

4 the day in whose clear-shining light
all wrong shall stand revealed,
when justice shall be throned in might,
and every hurt be healed;

5 when knowledge, hand in hand with peace,
shall walk the earth abroad:
the day of perfect righteousness,
the promised day of God.

F. L. Hosmer (1840–1929)

79 (AMR **264**)
Heathlands 7 7·7 7·7 7· Henry Smart (1813–79)

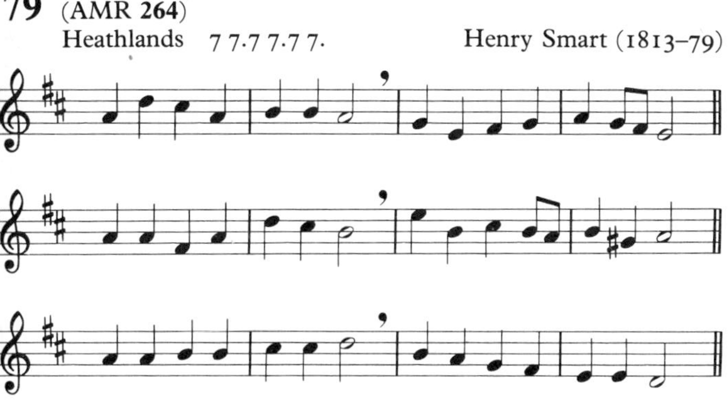

God of mercy, God of grace,
show the brightness of thy face;
shine upon us, Saviour, shine,
fill thy Church with light divine;
and thy saving health extend‿
unto earth's remotest end.

2

Let the people praise thee, Lord;
be by all that live adored;
let the nations shout and sing
glory to their Saviour King;
at thy feet their tribute pay,
and thy holy will obey.

3

Let the people praise thee, Lord;
earth shall then her fruits afford;
God to man his blessing give,
man to God devoted live;
all below, and all above,
one in joy and light and love.

H. F. Lyte (1793–1847)
Psalm 67

180 (AMR **266**)
Moscow 6 6 4.6 6 6 4. F. Giardini (1716–96

1

Thou, whose almighty word
chaos and darkness heard,
  and took their flight;
hear us, we humbly pray,
and where the Gospel-day‿
sheds not its glorious ray,
  let there be light.

2

Thou, who didst come to bring
on thy redeeming wing
  healing and sight,
health to the sick in mind,
sight to the inly blind,
O now to all mankind
  let there be light.

3

Spirit of truth and love,
life-giving, holy Dove,
  speed forth thy flight;
move on the water's face,
bearing the lamp of grace,
and in earth's darkest place
  let there be light.

4

Holy and blessèd Three,
glorious Trinity,
  Wisdom, Love, Might;
boundless as ocean's tide
rolling in fullest pride,
through the earth far and wide
  let there be light.

J. Marriott (1780–1825)

81 (AMR **636**)
Waltham 8 7.8 7. H. Albert (1604–51)

May the grace of Christ our Saviour,
  and the Father's boundless love,
with the Holy Spirit's favour,
  rest upon us from above.

2

Thus may we abide in union
  with each other and the Lord,
and possess, in sweet communion,
  joys which earth cannot afford.

JOHN NEWTON (1725–1807)
2 Corinthians 13.14

182 (AMR 272)
Dundee C.M. *Psalms* (Edinburgh, 1615

ALTERNATIVE VERSION

T. Ravenscroft (1621

The Communion of Saints

Let saints on earth in concert sing
with those whose work is done;
for all the servants of our King
in heaven and earth are one.

2

One family, we dwell in him,
one Church, above, beneath;
though now divided by the stream,
the narrow stream of death.

3

One army of the living God,
to his command we bow:
part of the host have crossed the flood,
and part are crossing now.

4

E'en now to their eternal home
there pass some spirits blest;
while others to the margin come,
waiting their call to rest.

5

Jesu, be thou our constant guide;
then, when the word is given,
bid Jordan's narrow stream divide,
and bring us safe to heaven.

CHARLES WESLEY (1707–88)
and others

183 (AMR 274) FIRST TUNE

Invitation (Devonshire) L.M. J. F. Lampe (1703–51

SECOND TUNE

Uffingham L.M. Jeremiah Clarke (*c.* 1673–1707)

The Communion of Saints

He wants not friends that hath thy love,
  and may converse and walk with thee,
and with thy saints here and above,
  with whom for ever I must be.

2

In the blest fellowship of saints
  is wisdom, safety, and delight;
and when my heart declines and faints,
  it's raisèd by their heat and light.

3

As for my friends, they are not lost;
  the several vessels of thy fleet,
though parted now, by tempests tost,
  shall safely in the haven meet.

4

Still we are centred all in thee,
  members, though distant, of one Head;
in the same family we be,
  by the same faith and spirit led.

5

Before thy throne we daily meet
  as joint-petitioners to thee;
in spirit we each other greet,
  and shall again each other see.

6

The heavenly hosts, world without end,
  shall be my company above;
and thou, my best and surest Friend,
  who shall divide me from thy love?

RICHARD BAXTER (1615–91)

184 (AMR **278**)
Ewing 7 6.7 6. D. A. Ewing (1830–9

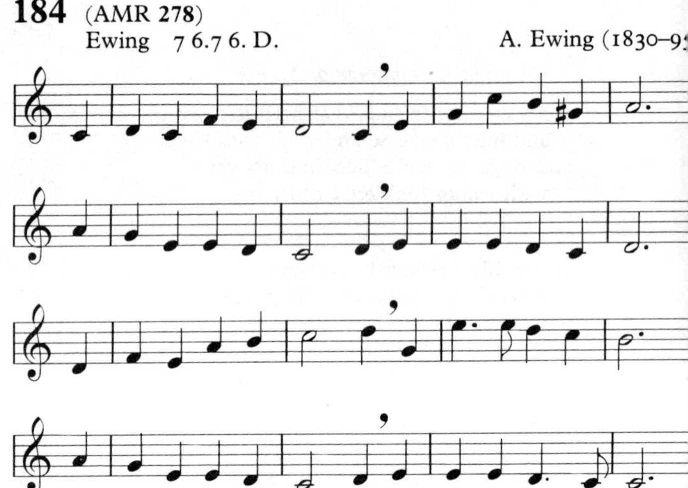

Jerusalem the golden,
with milk and honey blest,
beneath thy contemplation
sink heart and voice opprest.
I know not, O I know not
what joys await us there,
what radiancy of glory,
what bliss beyond compare.

2

They stand, those halls of Sion,
all jubilant with song,
and bright with many an angel,
and all the martyr throng;
the Prince is ever with them,
the daylight is serene,
the pastures of the blessèd
are decked in glorious sheen.

3

There is the throne of David;
and there, from care released,
the shout of them that triumph,
the song of them that feast;
and they, who with their Leader
have conquered in the fight,
for ever and for ever
are clad in robes of white.

4

O sweet and blessèd country,
the home of God's elect!
O sweet and blessèd country
that eager hearts expect!
Jesu, in mercy bring us‿
to that dear land of rest;
who art, with God the Father
and Spirit, ever blest.

BERNARD OF CLUNY (12th Century)
tr. J. M. NEALE* (1818–66)

185 (AMR 279)

Regent Square 8 7.8 7.8 7. Henry Smart (1813–79

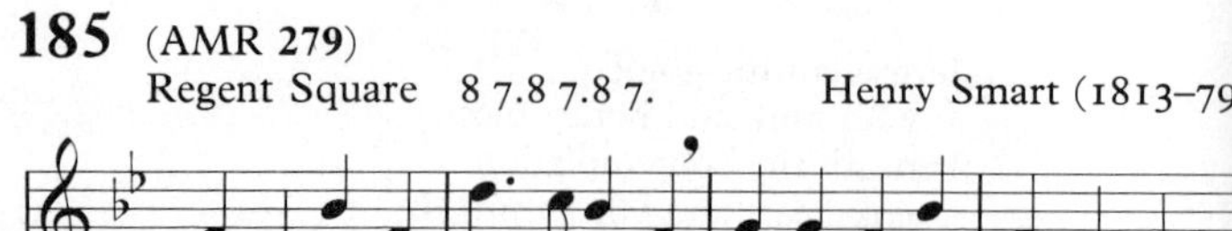

Light's abode, celestial Salem,
  vision whence true peace doth spring,
brighter than the heart can fancy,
  mansion of the highest King;
O how glorious are the praises
  which of thee the prophets sing!

2

There for ever and for ever
  alleluia is outpoured;
for unending, for unbroken
  is the feast-day of the Lord;
all is pure and all is holy
  that within thy walls is stored.

3

There no cloud or passing vapour
 dims the brightness of the air;
endless noon-day, glorious noon-day,
 from the Sun of suns is there;
there no night brings rest from labour,
 for unknown are toil and care.

*4

O how glorious and resplendent,
 fragile body, shalt thou be,
when endued with so much beauty,
 full of health and strong and free,
full of vigour, full of pleasure
 that shall last eternally.

*5

Now with gladness, now with courage,
 bear the burden on thee laid,
that hereafter these thy labours
 may with endless gifts be paid;
and in everlasting glory
 thou with brightness be arrayed.

6

Laud and honour to the Father,
 laud and honour to the Son,
laud and honour to the Spirit,
 ever Three and ever One,
consubstantial, co-eternal,
 while unending ages run.

Ascribed to THOMAS À KEMPIS (c. 1380–1471)
tr. J. M. NEALE* (1818–66)

186 (AMR **281**)

O quanta qualia 10 10.10 10. La Feillée, *Méthode*, 1808

O what their joy and their glory must be,
those endless sabbaths the blessèd ones see;
crown for the valiant, to weary ones rest;
God shall be all, and in all ever blest.

*2

What are the Monarch, his court, and his throne?
what are the peace and the joy that they own?
O that the blest ones, who in it have share,
all that they feel could as fully declare.

3

Truly Jerusalem name we that shore,
'Vision of peace,' that brings joy evermore.
Wish and fulfilment can severed be ne'er,
nor the thing prayed for come short of the prayer.

4

There, where no troubles distraction can bring,
we the sweet anthems of Sion shall sing,
while for thy grace, Lord, their voices of praise
thy blessèd people eternally raise.

*5

There dawns no sabbath, no sabbath is o'er,
those sabbath-keepers have one evermore;
one and unending is that triumph-song
which to the angels and us shall belong.

6

Now in the meanwhile, with hearts raised on high,
we for that country must yearn and must sigh;
seeking Jerusalem, dear native land,
through our long exile on Babylon's strand.

7

Low before him with our praises we fall,
of whom, and in whom, and through whom are all:
of whom, the Father; and in whom, the Son;
through whom, the Spirit, with them ever One.

PETER ABELARD (1079–1142)
tr. J. M. NEALE* (1818–66)

187 (AMR **282**)

Southwell (Irons) C.M. H. S. Irons (1834–1905)

Jerusalem, my happy home,
  name ever dear to me,
when shall my labours have an end?
  thy joys when shall I see?

2

When shall these eyes thy heaven-built walls
  and pearly gates behold?
thy bulwarks with salvation strong,
  and streets of shining gold?

3

Apostles, martyrs, prophets, there‿
  around my Saviour stand;
and all I love in Christ below
  will join the glorious band.

4

Jerusalem, my happy home,
  when shall I come to thee?
when shall my labours have an end?
  thy joys when shall I see?

5

O Christ, do thou my soul prepare
  for that bright home of love;
that I may see thee and adore,
  with all thy saints above.

Based on 'F.B.P.' (c. 1600)

188 (AMR **283**)
St. Sebastian 10 10.7. P. C. Buck (1871–1947

Sing alleluia forth in duteous praise,
ye citizens of heaven; O sweetly raise‿
an endless alleluia.

2

Ye powers who stand before the eternal Light,
in hymning choirs re-echo to the height
an endless alleluia.

3

The holy city shall take up your strain,
and with glad songs resounding wake again
an endless alleluia.

4

In blissful antiphons ye thus rejoice
to render to the Lord with thankful voice
an endless alleluia.

5

Ye who have gained at length your palms in bliss,
victorious ones, your chant shall still be this:
an endless alleluia.

*6

There, in one grand acclaim, for ever ring
the strains which tell the honour of your King:
an endless alleluia.

*7

This is sweet rest for weary ones brought back,
this is glad food and drink which ne'er shall lack:
an endless alleluia.

*8

While thee, by whom were all things made, we praise‿
for ever, and tell out in sweetest lays
an endless alleluia.

9

Almighty Christ, to thee our voices sing‿
glory for evermore; to thee we bring‿
an endless alleluia. Amen.

Mozarabic (5th–8th cent.)
tr. J. ELLERTON (1828–93)

189 (AMR **284**)
Alford 7 6.8 6. D. J. B. Dykes (1823–76)

The Church Triumphant

Ten thousand times ten thousand,
  in sparkling raiment bright,
the armies of the ransomed saints
  throng up the steeps of light:
'tis finished! all is finished,
  their fight with death and sin;
fling open wide the golden gates,
  and let the victors in.

*2

What rush of alleluias
  fills all the earth and sky,
what ringing of a thousand harps
  bespeaks the triumph nigh!
O day, for which creation
  and all its tribes were made!
O joy, for all its former woes
  a thousand-fold repaid!

3

O then what raptured greetings
  on Canaan's happy shore,
what knitting severed friendships up,
  where partings are no more!
Then eyes with joy shall sparkle
  that brimmed with tears of late:
orphans no longer fatherless,
  nor widows desolate.

4

Bring near thy great salvation,
  thou Lamb for sinners slain,
fill up the roll of thine elect,
  then take thy power and reign:
appear, Desire of Nations;
  thine exiles long for home;
show in the heavens thy promised sign;
  thou Prince and Saviour, come.

H. ALFORD (1810–71)

190 (AMR 285)

Beulah C.M. G. M. Garrett (1834–97)

A prospect of heaven makes death easy

1 There is a land of pure delight,
where saints immortal reign;
infinite day excludes the night,
and pleasures banish pain.

2 There everlasting spring abides,
and never-withering flowers;
death, like a narrow sea, divides‿
that heavenly land from ours.

3 Sweet fields beyond the swelling flood
stand dressed in living green;
so to the Jews old Canaan stood,
while Jordan rolled between.

4 But timorous mortals start and shrink
to cross the narrow sea,
and linger shivering on the brink,
and fear to launch away.

5 O could we make our doubts remove,
those gloomy doubts that rise,
and see the Canaan that we love
with unbeclouded eyes;

6 could we but climb where Moses stood,
and view the landscape o'er,
not Jordan's stream, nor death's cold flood,
should fright us from the shore.

Isaac Watts (1674–1748)

191 (AMR **286**)

Christus der ist mein Leben   M. Vulpius (*c.* 1560–1615)
7 6.7 6.

My soul, there is a country
  far beyond the stars,
where stands a wingèd sentry
  all skilful in the wars.

2

There above noise, and danger,
  sweet peace sits crowned with smiles,
and One born in a manger
  commands the beauteous files.

3

He is thy gracious Friend,
  and – O my soul, awake! –
did in pure love descend,
  to die here for thy sake.

4

If thou canst get but thither,
  there grows the flower of peace,
the Rose that cannot wither,
  thy fortress and thy ease.

5

Leave then thy foolish ranges,
  for none can thee secure
but one who never changes,
  thy God, thy life, thy cure.

HENRY VAUGHAN (1622–95)

192 (AMR **365**)

Praise, My Soul 8 7.8 7.8 7. John Goss (1800–80)

Praise, my soul, the King of heaven,
to his feet thy tribute bring;
ransomed, healed, restored, forgiven,
who like me his praise should sing?
Alleluia, Alleluia,
praise the everlasting King.

2

Praise him for his grace and favour
to our fathers in distress;
praise him still the same as ever,
slow to chide, and swift to bless:
Alleluia, Alleluia,
glorious in his faithfulness.

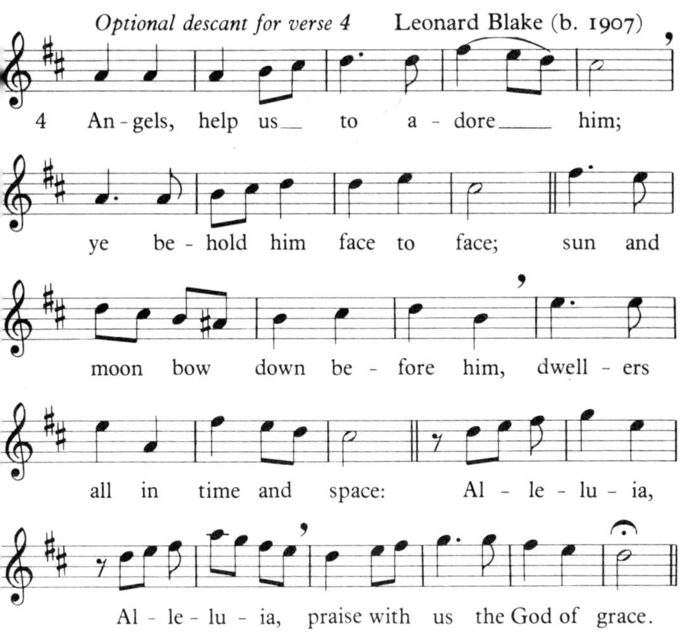
Optional descant for verse 4
Leonard Blake (b. 1907)
4 An - gels, help us to a - dore him;
ye be - hold him face to face; sun and
moon bow down be - fore him, dwell - ers
all in time and space: Al - le - lu - ia,
Al - le - lu - ia, praise with us the God of grace.

3

Father-like, he tends and spares us,
well our feeble frame he knows;
in his hands he gently bears us,
rescues us from all our foes:
Alleluia, Alleluia,
widely as his mercy flows.

4

Angels, help us to adore him;
ye behold him face to face;
sun and moon, bow down before him,
dwellers all in time and space:
Alleluia, Alleluia,
praise with us the God of grace.

H. F. LYTE (1793–1847)
Psalm 103

193 (AMR 366) FIRST TUNE

Luther's Hymn — 8 7.8 7.887.

Later form of melody *Geistliche Lieder* (1533 or earli

SECOND TUNE

Palace Green 8 7.8 7.8 8 7. Michael Fleming (b. 192

Alternative Tune: *Mit Freuden zart* (273)

Sing praise to God who reigns above,
the God of all creation,
the God of power, the God of love,
the God of our salvation;
with healing balm my soul he fills,
and every faithless murmur stills:
to God all praise and glory.

2

The Lord is never far away,
but, through all grief distressing,
an ever-present help and stay,
our peace and joy and blessing;
as with a mother's tender hand,
he leads his own, his chosen band:
to God all praise and glory.

3

Thus all my gladsome way along
I sing aloud thy praises,
that men may hear the grateful song
my voice unwearied raises;
be joyful in the Lord, my heart;
both soul and body bear your part:
to God all praise and glory.

J. J. SCHÜTZ (1640–90)
tr. FRANCES E. COX (1812–97)

194 (AMR 367)

Gwalchmai 7 4.7 4. D. J. D. Jones (1827–70

King of glory, King of peace,
I will love thee;
and, that love may never cease,
I will move thee.
Thou hast granted my request,
thou hast heard me;
thou didst note my working breast,
thou hast spared me.

2

Wherefore with my utmost art
I will sing thee,
and the cream of all my heart
I will bring thee.
Though my sins against me cried,
thou didst clear me,
and alone, when they replied,
thou didst hear me.

3

Seven whole days, not one in seve
I will praise thee;
in my heart, though not in heaven
I can raise thee.
Small it is, in this poor sort
to enrol thee:
e'en eternity's too short
to extol thee.

George Herbert (1593–1632)

95 (AMR **368**)
Austria 8 7.8 7. D. J. Haydn (1732–1809)

Praise the Lord! ye heavens, adore him;
praise him, angels, in the height;
sun and moon, rejoice before him,
praise him, all ye stars and light.
Praise the Lord! for he hath spoken;
worlds his mighty voice obeyed:
laws, which never shall be broken,
for their guidance he hath made.

2

Praise the Lord! for he is glorious;
never shall his promise fail:
God hath made his saints victorious;
sin and death shall not prevail.
Praise the God of our salvation;
hosts on high, his power proclaim;
heaven and earth and all creation,
laud and magnify his name!

Foundling Hospital Collection, c. 1796
Psalm 148

196 (AMR **369**)
Northampton 77.77. C. J. King (1859–1934

1 Songs of praise the angels sang,
heaven with alleluias rang,
when creation was begun,
when God spake and it was done.

2 Songs of praise awoke the morn
when the Prince of Peace was born;
songs of praise arose when he‿
captive led captivity.

3 Heaven and earth must pass away;
songs of praise shall crown that day:
God will make new heavens and earth;
songs of praise shall hail their birth.

4 And will man alone be dumb
till that glorious kingdom come?
No, the Church delights to raise‿
psalms and hymns and songs of praise.

5 Saints below, with heart and voice,
still in songs of praise rejoice;
learning here, by faith and love,
songs of praise to sing above.

6 Hymns of glory, songs of praise,
Father, unto thee we raise,
Jesu, glory unto thee,
with the Spirit, ever be.

James Montgomery* (1771–1854)

97 (AMR **370**)
Old 100th L.M. Melody in Genevan Psalter, 1551

An alternative version of this tune is at 100

Before Jehovah's aweful throne,
ye nations, bow with sacred joy;
know that the Lord is God alone:
he can create, and he destroy.

2

His sovereign power, without our aid,
made us of clay, and formed us men;
and, when like wandering sheep we strayed,
he brought us to his fold again.

3

We'll crowd thy gates with thankful songs,
high as the heavens our voices raise;
and earth, with her ten thousand tongues,
shall fill thy courts with sounding praise.

4

Wide as the world is thy command,
vast as eternity thy love;
firm as a rock thy truth shall stand,
when rolling years shall cease to move.

Isaac Watts (1674–1748)
Psalm 100

Another version of this psalm is at 100

198 (AMR 371)

Darwall's 148th 6 6.6 6.4 4.4 4. J. Darwall (1731–8

DESCANT
4 My soul, bear thou thy part, tri - umph in God a
- bove, and with a well - tuned heart sing
thou the songs of love; let all thy days
till life shall end, what - e'er he send, be filled with praise.

Ye holy angels bright,
  who wait at God's right hand,
or through the realms of light
  fly at your Lord's command,
    assist our song,
      for else the theme‿
      too high doth seem
    for mortal tongue.

2

Ye blessèd souls at rest,
  who ran this earthly race,
and now, from sin released,
  behold the Saviour's face,
    his praises sound,
      as in his light
      with sweet delight
    ye do abound.

3

Ye saints, who toil below,
  adore your heavenly King,
and onward as ye go
  some joyful anthem sing;
    take what he gives
      and praise him still,
      through good and ill,
    who ever lives.

4

My soul, bear thou thy part,
  triumph in God above,
and with a well-tuned heart
  sing thou the songs of love;
    let all thy days
      till life shall end,
      what'er he send,
    be filled with praise.

RICHARD BAXTER (1615–91)
and J. H. GURNEY (1802–62)

199 (AMR 372)

St. Denio 11 11.11 11. Welsh Hymn Melody (183

Immortal, invisible, God only wise,
in light inaccessible hid from our eyes,
most blessèd, most glorious, the Ancient of Days,
almighty, victorious, thy great name we praise.

2

Unresting, unhasting, and silent as light,
nor wanting, nor wasting, thou rulest in might;
thy justice like mountains high soaring above
thy clouds which are fountains of goodness and love.

3

To all life thou givest, to both great and small;
in all life thou livest, the true life of all;
we blossom and flourish as leaves on the tree,
and wither and perish; but naught changeth thee.

4

Great Father of glory, pure Father of light,
thine angels adore thee, all veiling their sight;
all laud we would render: O help us to see‿
'tis only the splendour of light hideth thee.

W. CHALMERS SMITH (1824–1908)
1 Timothy 1. 17

200 (AMR **373**)
Richmond C.M.

Adapted fro
T. Haweis (1734–182

Fill thou my life, O Lord my God,
in every part with praise,
that my whole being may proclaim
thy being and thy ways.

2

Not for the lip of praise alone,
nor e'en the praising heart,
I ask, but for a life made up‿
of praise in every part:

3

praise in the common things of life,
its goings out and in;
praise in each duty and each deed,
however small and mean.

4

Fill every part of me with praise:
let all my being speak‿
of thee and of thy love, O Lord,
poor though I be and weak.

*5

So shalt thou, Lord, receive from me
the praise and glory due;
and so shall I begin on earth
the song for ever new.

*6

So shall each fear, each fret, each care,
be turnèd into song;
and every winding of the way
the echo shall prolong.

7

So shall no part of day or night
unblest or common be;
but all my life, in every step,
be fellowship with thee.

H. Bonar* (1808–89)

201 (AMR **374**)
Carlisle S.M. C. Lockhart (1745–1815

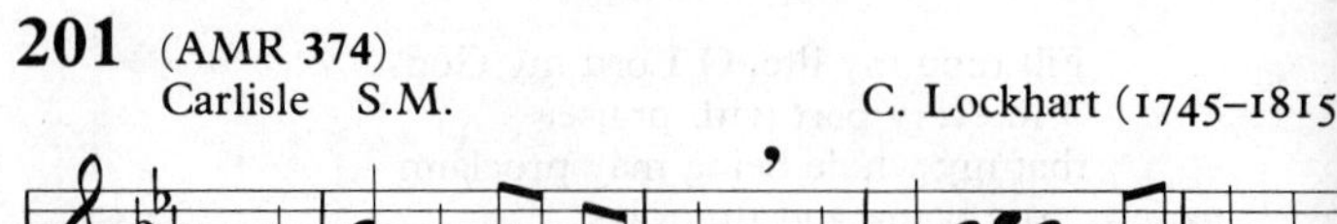

Stand up, and bless the Lord,
ye people of his choice;
stand up, and bless the Lord your God
with heart and soul and voice.

2

Though high above all praise,
above all blessing high,
who would not fear his holy name,
and laud and magnify?

3

O for the living flame
from his own altar brought,
to touch our lips, our mind inspire,
and wing to heaven our thought.

4

God is our strength and song,
and his salvation ours;
then be his love in Christ proclaimed
with all our ransomed powers.

5

Stand up, and bless the Lord,
the Lord your God adore;
stand up, and bless his glorious name
henceforth for evermore.

JAMES MONTGOMERY (1771–1854)

02 (AMR 375)
Luckington — Basil Harwood (1859–1949
10 4.6 6.6 6.10 4.

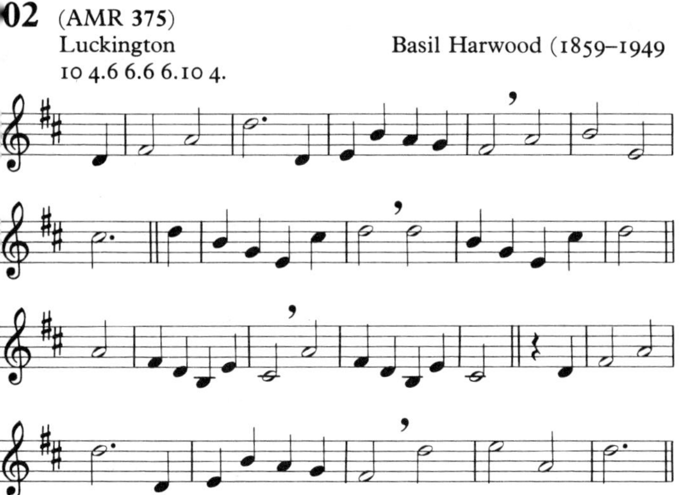

Antiphon

Let all the world in every corner sing,
my God and King.
The heavens are not too high,
his praise may thither fly:
the earth is not too low,
his praises there may grow.
Let all the world in every corner sing,
my God and King.

2

Let all the world in every corner sing,
my God and King.
The Church with psalms must shout,
no door can keep them out;
but above all the heart
must bear the longest part.
Let all the world in every corner sing,
my God and King.

George Herbert (1593–1632)

203 (**AMR 376**) **FIRST TUNE**

Laudate Dominum (Parry) C. Hubert H. Pa

10 10.11 11. (1848–19

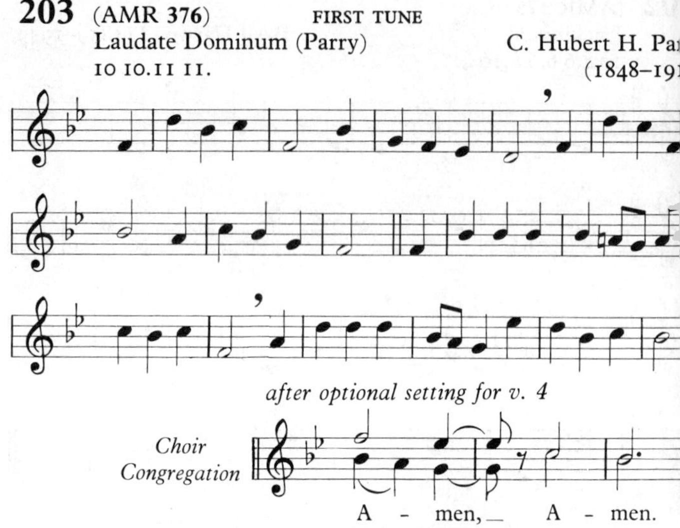

1 O praise ye the Lord! praise him in the height;
rejoice in his word, ye angels of light;
ye heavens adore him by whom ye were made,
and worship before him, in brightness arrayed.

2 O praise ye the Lord! praise him upon earth,
in tuneful accord, ye sons of new birth;
praise him who hath brought you his grace from above,
praise him who hath taught you to sing of his love.

3 O praise ye the Lord, all things that give sound;
each jubilant chord re-echo around;
loud organs, his glory forth tell in deep tone,
and, sweet harp, the story of what he hath done.

4 O praise ye the Lord! thanksgiving and song
to him be outpoured all ages along:
for love in creation, for heaven restored,
for grace of salvation, O praise ye the Lord! (Amen)

H. W. Baker (1821–7
based on Psalm 15

SECOND TUNE

Laudate Dominum (Gauntlett) H. J. Gauntlett (1805–76)
10 10.11 11.

1 O praise ye the Lord! praise him in the height;
rejoice in his word, ye angels of light;
ye heavens adore him by whom ye were made,
and worship before him, in brightness arrayed.

2 O praise ye the Lord! praise him upon earth,
in tuneful accord, ye sons of new birth;
praise him who hath brought you his grace from above,
praise him who hath taught you to sing of his love.

3 O praise ye the Lord, all things that give sound;
each jubilant chord re-echo around;
loud organs, his glory forth tell in deep tone,
and, sweet harp, the story of what he hath done.

4 O praise ye the Lord! thanksgiving and song
to him be outpoured all ages along:
for love in creation, for heaven restored,
for grace of salvation, O praise ye the Lord!

H. W. Baker (1821–77)
based on Psalm 150

204 (AMR 377) John Antes (1740–1811
Monkland 77.77 arr. J. Wilkes (1861

1 Let us, with a gladsome mind,
praise the Lord, for he is kind:
for his mercies ay endure,
ever faithful, ever sure.

2 Let us blaze his name abroad,
for of gods he is the God:

3 He with all-commanding might
filled the new-made world with light:

4 He the golden-tressèd sun
caused all day his course to run:

5 And the hornèd moon at night
'mid her spangled sisters bright:

6 All things living he doth feed,
his full hand supplies their need:

7 Let us, with a gladsome mind,
praise the Lord, for he is kind:
for his mercies ay endure,
ever faithful, ever sure.

John Milton* (1608–74)
Psalm 136

5 (AMR **379**)
Nun danket — Later form of a melody from J. Crüger's
6 7.6 7.6 6.6 6. — *Praxis Pietatis Melica* (*c.* 1647)

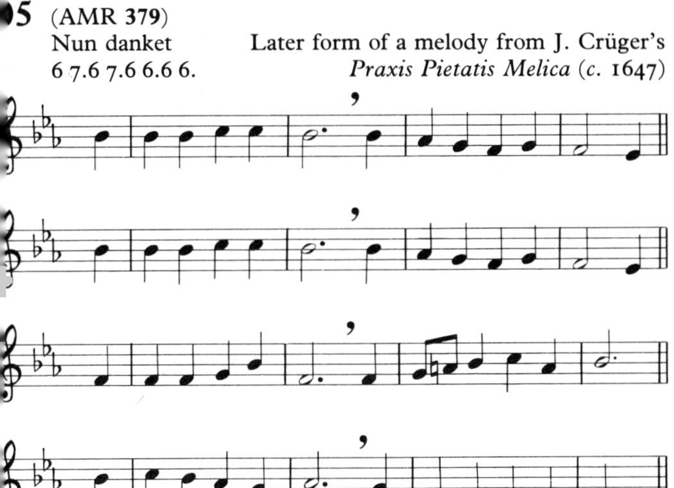

Now thank we all our God,
with heart and hands and voices,
who wondrous things hath done,
in whom his world rejoices;
who from our mother's arms
hath blessed us on our way
with countless gifts of love,
and still is ours to-day.

2

O may this bounteous God
rough all our life be near us,
with ever joyful hearts
d blessèd peace to cheer us;
and keep us in his grace,
and guide us when perplexed,
and free us from all ills
in this world and the next.

3

All praise and thanks to God
the Father now be given,
the Son, and him who reigns
with them in highest heaven,
the one eternal God,
whom earth and heaven adore,
for thus it was, is now,
and shall be evermore.

M. Rinkart (1586–1649)
tr. Catherine Winkworth (1827–78)

206 (AMR 380)

Old 124th 10 10.10 10.10. *Genevan Psalter* (155

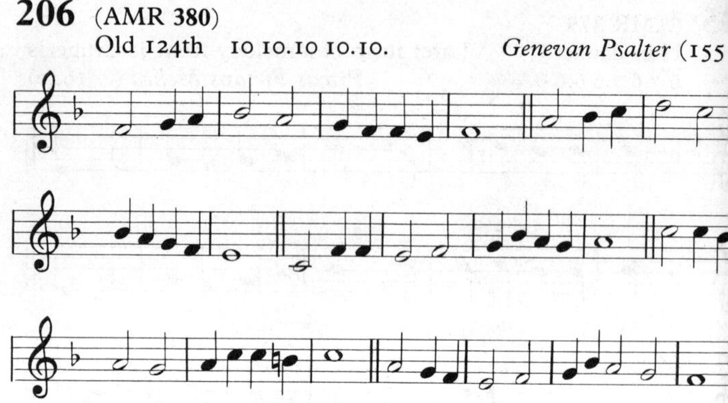

We would extol thee, ever-blessèd Lord;
thy holy name for ever be adored;
each day we live to thee our psalm we raise:
thou, God and King, art worthy of our praise,
great and unsearchable in all thy ways.

2

Age shall to age pass on the endless song,
telling the wonders which to thee belong,
thy mighty acts with joy and fear relate;
laud we thy glory while on thee we wait,
glad in the knowledge of thy love so great.

3

Thou, Lord, art gracious, merciful to all,
nigh to thy children when on thee they call;
slow unto anger, pitiful and kind,
thou to compassion ever art inclined:
we love thee with our heart and strength and mind.

NICHOL GRIEVE (1868–1954)
Psalm 145

207 (AMR **382**)
Lobe den Herren 14 14.4 7.8. *Praxis Pietatis Melica*
(Praxis pietatis) (1668)

Praise to the Lord, the Almighty, the King of creation;
O my soul, praise him, for he is thy health and salvation:
all ye who hear,
now to his temple draw near,
joining in glad adoration.

2

Praise to the Lord, who o'er all things so wondrously reigneth,
shieldeth thee gently from harm, or when fainting sustaineth:
hast thou not seen‿
how thy heart's wishes have been‿
granted in what he ordaineth?

3

Praise to the Lord, who doth prosper thy work and defend thee;
surely his goodness and mercy shall daily attend thee:
ponder anew
what the Almighty can do,
if to the end he befriend thee.

4

Praise to the Lord! O let all that is in me adore him!
All that hath life and breath, come now with praises before him!
let the Amen
sound from his people again:
gladly for ay we adore him.

J. Neander (1650–80)
tr. Catherine Winkworth (1827–78)

208 (AMR **289**)
Kocher 7 6.7 6. J. H. Knecht (1752–181

O happy band of pilgrims,
  if onward ye will tread
with Jesus as your fellow
  to Jesus as your Head.

2

O happy if ye labour
  as Jesus did for men;
O happy if ye hunger
  as Jesus hungered then.

3

The cross that Jesus carried
  he carried as your due:
the crown that Jesus weareth
  he weareth it for you.

4

The faith by which ye see him,
  the hope in which ye yearn,
the love that through all troubles
  to him alone will turn,

5

the trials that beset you,
  the sorrows ye endure,
the manifold temptations
  that death alone can cure,

6

what are they but his jewels
  of right celestial worth?
what are they but the ladder
  set up to heaven on earth?

7

O happy band of pilgrims,
  look upward to the skies,
where such a light affliction
  shall win so great a prize.

J. M. Neale (1818–66

209 (AMR **290**)
Wiltshire C.M. G. T. Smart (1776–1867)

Through all the changing scenes of life,
in trouble and in joy,
the praises of my God shall still
my heart and tongue employ.

2

O magnify the Lord with me,
with me exalt his name;
when in distress to him I called,
he to my rescue came.

3

The hosts of God encamp around‿
the dwellings of the just;
deliverance he affords to all
who on his succour trust.

4

O make but trial of his love:
experience will decide‿
how blest are they, and only they,
who in his truth confide.

5

Fear him, ye saints, and you will then‿
have nothing else to fear;
make you his service your delight,
your wants shall be his care.

6

To Father, Son, and Holy Ghost,
the God whom we adore,
be glory, as it was, is now,
and shall be evermore.

Psalm 34 in *New Version* (Tate and Brady, 1696)

210 (**AMR 291**)
University College 7 7.7 7. H. J. Gauntlett (1805–7

Oft in danger, oft in woe,
onward, Christians, onward go;
bear the toil, maintain the strife,
strengthened with the bread of life.

2

Onward, Christians, onward go,
join the war, and face the foe;
will ye flee in danger's hour?
know ye not your Captain's power?

3

Let not sorrow dim your eye;
soon shall every tear be dry:
let not fears your course impede;
great your strength, if great your need.

4

Let your drooping hearts be glad;
march in heavenly armour clad;
fight, nor think the battle long:
soon shall victory wake your song.

5

Onward then in battle move;
more than conquerors ye shall prove:
though opposed by many a foe,
Christian soldiers, onward go.

H. Kirke White (1785–1806)
and others

211 (AMR **292**). FIRST TUNE

Rustington 8 7.8 7. D. C. Hubert H. Parry (1848–1918

SECOND TUNE

St. Oswald 8 7.8 7. J. B. Dykes (1823–76)

In the second tune the descant may be sung for the second half of verses 2 and 4

Alternative Tune: *Marching* (113)

Pilgrimage

Through the night of doubt and sorrow
  onward goes the pilgrim band,
singing songs of expectation,
  marching to the promised land.
Clear before us through the darkness
  gleams and burns the guiding light;
brother clasps the hand of brother,
  stepping fearless through the night.

2

One the light of God's own presence
  o'er his ransomed people shed,
chasing far the gloom and terror,
  brightening all the path we tread:
one the object of our journey,
  one the faith which never tires,
one the earnest looking forward,
  one the hope our God inspires:

*3

one the strain that lips of thousands
  lift as from the heart of one:
one the conflict, one the peril,
  one the march in God begun:
one the gladness of rejoicing
  on the far eternal shore,
where the one almighty Father
  reigns in love for evermore.

4

Onward, therefore, pilgrim brothers,
  onward with the Cross our aid;
bear its shame, and fight its battle,
  till we rest beneath its shade.
Soon shall come the great awaking,
  soon the rending of the tomb;
then the scattering of all shadows,
  and the end of toil and gloom.

B. S. Ingemann (1789–1862)
tr. S. Baring-Gould (1834–1924)

212 (AMR 293) FIRST TUNE

Monks Gate
6 5.6 5.6 6.6 5.

Adapted from an
English Traditional Melody
by R. Vaughan Williams (1872–1958)

SECOND TUNE

Bunyan 6 5.6 5.6 6.6 5. *Christen-schatz* (Basle, 1745)

Pilgrimage

Who would true valour see,
  let him come hither;
one here will constant be,
  come wind, come weather;
there's no discouragement
shall make him once relent
his first avowed intent
    to be a pilgrim.

2

Whoso beset him round
  with dismal stories,
do but themselves confound;
  his strength the more is.
No lion can him fright;
he'll with a giant fight,
but he will have the right
    to be a pilgrim.

3

No goblin nor foul fiend
  can daunt his spirit;
he knows he at the end
  shall life inherit.
Then, fancies, fly away;
he'll not fear what men say;
he'll labour night and day
    to be a pilgrim.

JOHN BUNYAN* (1628–88)

213 (AMR 295)

FIRST TUNE

Harts 7 7·7 7· Benjamin Milgrove (1731–181

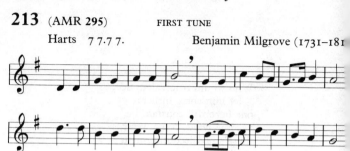

SECOND TUNE

Bewdley 7 7·7 7· F. A. G. Ouseley (1825–8

Pilgrimage

Encouragement to praise

Children of the heavenly King,
as ye journey, sweetly sing;
sing your Saviour's worthy praise,
glorious in his works and ways.

2

We are travelling home to God
in the way the fathers trod;
they are happy now, and we‿
soon their happiness shall see.

3

Lift your eyes, ye sons of light!
Sion's city is in sight;
there our endless home shall be,
there our Lord we soon shall see.

4

Fear not, brethren! joyful stand
on the borders of your land;
Jesus Christ, your Father's Son,
bids you undismayed go on.

5

Lord, obedient we would go,
gladly leaving all below;
only thou our leader be,
and we still will follow thee.

JOHN CENNICK* (1718–55)

214 (AMR 296) FIRST TUNE

Pilgrimage 8 7.8 7.4 7. G. J. Elvey (1816–9

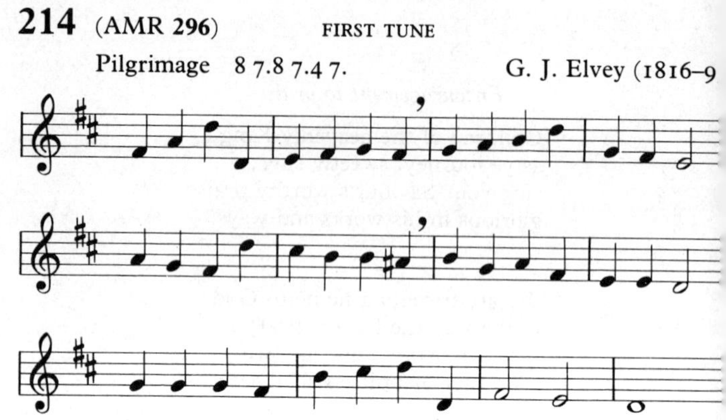

SECOND TUNE

Cwm Rhondda 8 7.8 7.4 7. John Hughes (1873–1932

Pilgrimage

Guide me, O thou great Redeemer,
  pilgrim through this barren land;
I am weak, but thou art mighty;
  hold me with thy powerful hand:
    bread of heaven,
feed me now and evermore.

2

Open now the crystal fountain
  whence the healing stream doth flow;
let the fiery cloudy pillar
  lead me all my journey through:
    strong deliverer,
be thou still my strength and shield.

3

When I tread the verge of Jordan,
  bid my anxious fears subside;
death of death, and hell's destruction,
  land me safe on Canaan's side:
    songs and praises
I will ever give to thee.

W. WILLIAMS (1717–91)
tr. P. and W. WILLIAMS*

215 (AMR 298)

FIRST TUNE

Alberta 10 4.10 4.10 10. William H. Harris (1883–197

SECOND TUNE

Lux benigna 10 4.10 4.10 10. J. B. Dykes (1823–7

Pilgrimage

Lead, kindly Light, amid the encircling gloom,
        lead thou me on;
the night is dark, and I am far from home;
        lead thou me on.
Keep thou my feet; I do not ask to see‿
the distant scene; one step enough for me.

2

I was not ever thus, nor prayed that thou‿
        shouldst lead me on;
I loved to choose and see my path; but now‿
        lead thou me on.
I loved the garish day, and, spite of fears,
pride ruled my will: remember not past years.

3

So long thy power hath blest me, sure it still‿
        will lead me on,
o'er moor and fen, o'er crag and torrent, till‿
        the night is gone,
and with the morn those angel faces smile,
which I have loved long since, and lost awhile.

J. H. NEWMAN (1801–90)

216 (AMR **299**)

Martyrdom C.M. H. Wilson (1766–1824)

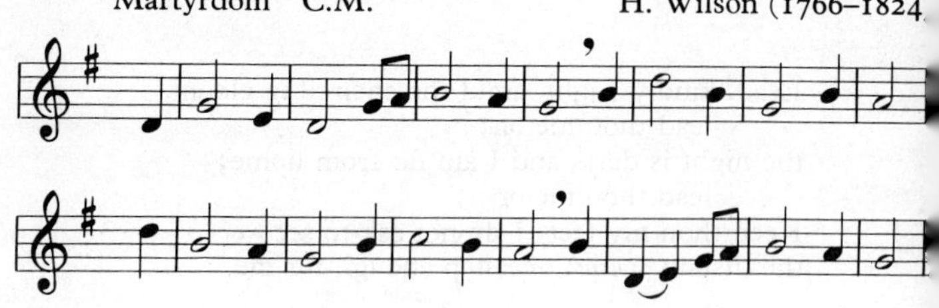

Jacob's vow

O God of Bethel, by whose hand‿
thy people still are fed,
who through this weary pilgrimage
hast all our fathers led;

2

our vows, our prayers, we now present
before thy throne of grace;
God of our fathers, be the God‿
of their succeeding race.

3

Through each perplexing path of life
our wandering footsteps guide;
give us each day our daily bread,
and raiment fit provide.

4

O spread thy covering wings around,
till all our wanderings cease,
and at our Father's loved abode
our souls arrive in peace.

PHILIP DODDRIDGE (1702–51)
Genesis 28. 20–22

217 (AMR 300)

Abridge C.M. I. Smith (1734–1805)

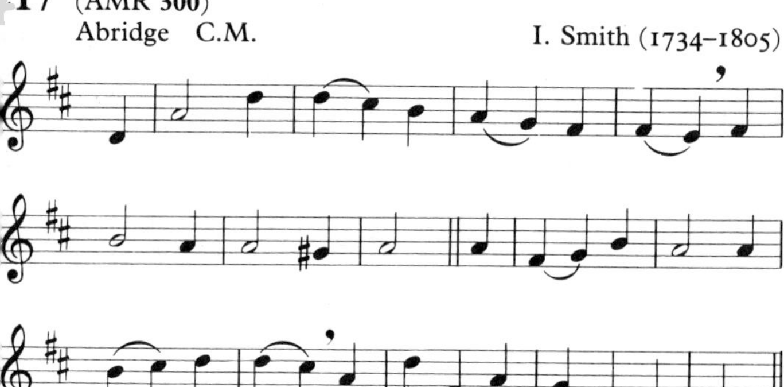

Lead us not into temptation

Be thou my guardian and my guide,
  and hear me when I call;
let not my slippery footsteps slide,
  and hold me lest I fall.

2

The world, the flesh, and Satan dwell‿
  around the path I tread;
O save me from the snares of hell,
  thou quickener of the dead.

3

And if I tempted am to sin,
  and outward things are strong,
do thou, O Lord, keep watch within,
  and save my soul from wrong.

4

Still let me ever watch and pray,
  and feel that I am frail;
that if the tempter cross my way,
  yet he may not prevail.

Isaac Williams (1802–65)

218 (AMR **301**)
York C.M. *Scottish Psalter* (161

The Shepherd-Boy's Song
in the Valley of Humiliation

He that is down needs fear no fall,
he that is low no pride;
he that is humble ever shall‿
have God to be his guide.

2

I am content with what I have,
little be it or much;
and, Lord, contentment still I crave,
because thou savest such.

3

Fullness to such a burden is
that go on pilgrimage;
here little, and hereafter bliss,
is best from age to age.

JOHN BUNYAN (1628–88

219 (AMR **303**)

St. Ethelwald S.M. W. H. Monk (1823–89)

The whole armour of God

1 Soldiers of Christ, arise,
and put your armour on,
strong in the strength which God supplies,
through his eternal Son;

2 strong in the Lord of Hosts,
and in his mighty power:
who in the strength of Jesus trusts
is more than conqueror.

3 Stand then in his great might,
with all his strength endued;
and take, to arm you for the fight,
the panoply of God.

4 From strength to strength go on,
wrestle and fight and pray;
tread all the powers of darkness down,
and win the well-fought day;

5 that, having all things done,
and all your conflicts past,
ye may o'ercome, through Christ alone,
and stand entire at last.

Charles Wesley (1707–88)
Ephesians 6.10–18

220 (AMR 304)

Duke Street L.M.

Late 18th c. melod
attributed to J. Hatton (d. 1793

Fight the good fight with all thy might;
Christ is thy strength, and Christ thy right;
lay hold on life, and it shall be‿
thy joy and crown eternally.

2

Run the straight race through God's good grace,
lift up thine eyes, and seek his face;
life with its way before us lies;
Christ is the path, and Christ the prize.

3

Cast care aside, lean on thy guide;
his boundless mercy will provide;
trust, and thy trusting soul shall prove
Christ is its life, and Christ its love.

4

Faint not nor fear, his arms are near;
he changeth not, and thou art dear;
only believe, and thou shalt see
that Christ is all in all to thee.

J. S. B. MONSELL* (1811–75)

221 (AMR **307**)
Morning Light 7 6.7 6. D. G. J. Webb (1803–

Stand up, stand up for Jesus,
ye soldiers of the Cross!
lift high his royal banner,
it must not suffer loss.
From victory unto victory
his army he shall lead,
till every foe is vanquished,
and Christ is Lord indeed.

*2

:and up, stand up for Jesus,
the solemn watchword hear;
while ye sleep he suffers,
away with shame and fear.
'here'er ye meet with evil,
within you or without,
ıarge for the God of battles,
and put the foe to rout.

3

:and up, stand up for Jesus,
the trumpet call obey;
ırth to the mighty conflict
in this his glorious day.
e that are men now serve him
against unnumbered foes;
t courage rise with danger
and strength to strength oppose.

4

Stand up, stand up for Jesus,
stand in his strength alone;
the arm of flesh will fail you,
ye dare not trust your own.
Put on the Gospel armour,
each piece put on with prayer;
when duty calls or danger
be never wanting there.

5

Stand up, stand up for Jesus,
the strife will not be long;
this day the noise of battle,
the next the victor's song.
To him that overcometh
a crown of life shall be;
he with the King of Glory
shall reign eternally.

G. DUFFIELD (1818–88)

222 (AMR **309**) FIRST TUNE

St. Mary C.M. E. Prys's *Llyfr y Psalmau* (162

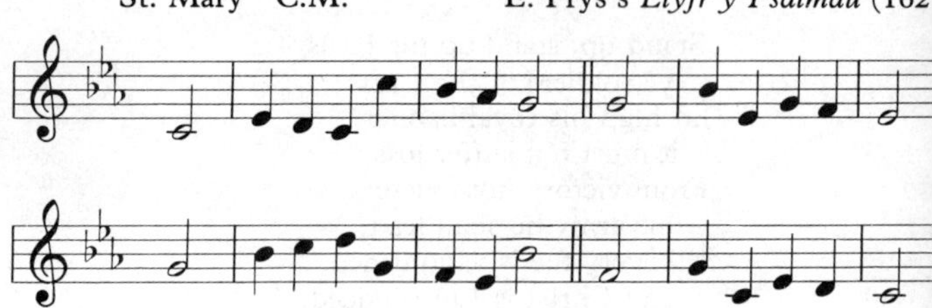

SECOND TUNE

(Old) Martyrs C.M. *Psalms* (Edinburgh, 161

Warfare

O God of truth, whose living word
upholds whate'er hath breath,
look down on thy creation, Lord,
enslaved by sin and death.

2

Set up thy standard, Lord, that we‿
who claim a heavenly birth
may march with thee to smite the lies
that vex thy groaning earth.

3

Ah, would we join that blest array,
and follow in the might‿
of him, the Faithful and the True,
in raiment clean and white?

4

We fight for truth? we fight for God?
poor slaves of lies and sin!
he who would fight for thee on earth
must first be true within.

5

Then, God of truth, for whom we long,
thou who wilt hear our prayer,
do thine own battle in our hearts,
and slay the falsehood there.

6

Yea, come! then, tried as in the fire,
from every lie set free,
thy perfect truth shall dwell in us,
and we shall live in thee.

THOMAS HUGHES (1822–96)

In verse 2, line 4, for the original 'groaning' *AMR has* 'ransomed'

223 (AMR 310)
Doncaster S.M. S. Wesley (1766–18

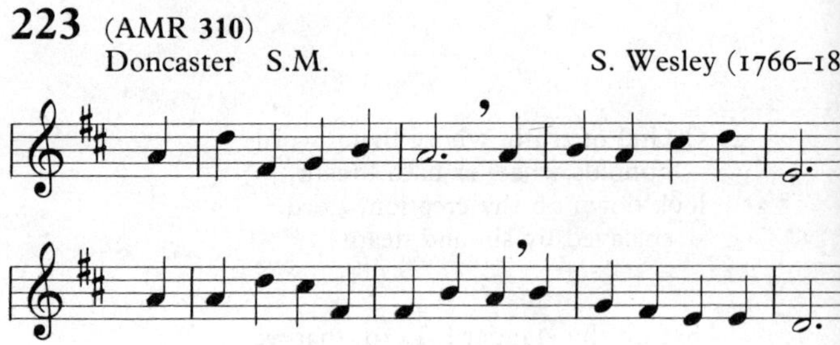

Faith, Hope and Love

Put thou thy trust in God,
in duty's path go on;
walk in his strength with faith and hope,
so shall thy work be done.

2

Commit thy ways to him,
thy works into his hands,
and rest on his unchanging word,
who heaven and earth commands.

3

Though years on years roll on,
his covenant shall endure;
though clouds and darkness hide his path,
the promised grace is sure.

4

Give to the winds thy fears;
hope, and be undismayed:
God hears thy sighs and counts thy tears;
God shall lift up thy head.

5

Through waves and clouds and storms
his power will clear thy way:
wait thou his time; the darkest night‿
shall end in brightest day.

6

Leave to his sovereign sway
to choose and to command;
so shalt thou, wondering, own his way,
how wise, how strong his hand.

P. GERHARDT (1607–76)
tr. JOHN WESLEY (1703–91) and others.

224 (AMR **311**)

Mannheim 8 7.8 7.8 7. F. Filitz's *Choralbuch* (1847

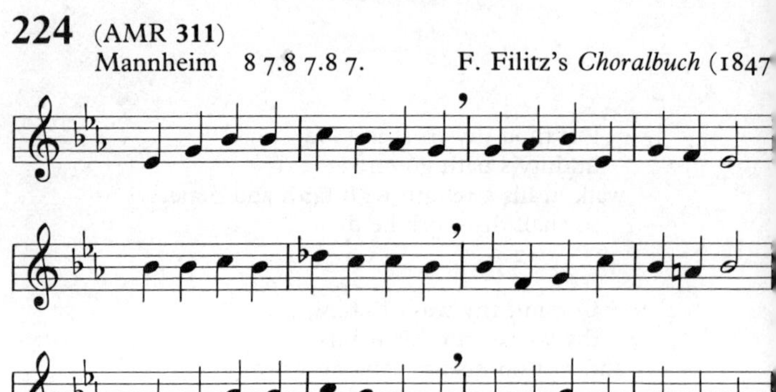

Lead us, heavenly Father, lead us
  o'er the world's tempestuous sea;
guard us, guide us, keep us, feed us,
  for we have no help but thee;
yet possessing every blessing,
  if our God our Father be.

2

Saviour, breathe forgiveness o'er us:
  all our weakness thou dost know;
thou didst tread this earth before us,
  thou didst feel its keenest woe;
lone and dreary, faint and weary,
  through the desert thou didst go.

3

Spirit of our God, descending,
  fill our hearts with heavenly joy,
love with every passion blending,
  pleasure that can never cloy:
thus provided, pardoned, guided,
  nothing can our peace destroy.

J. Edmeston (1791–1867)

25 (AMR **313**)
St. Aëlred 8 8 8.3. J. B. Dykes (1823–76)

Fierce raged the tempest o'er the deep,
watch did thine anxious servants keep,
but thou wast wrapped in guileless sleep,
calm and still.

2

'Save, Lord, we perish,' was their cry,
'O save us in our agony!'
Thy word above the storm rose high,
'Peace, be still.'

3

The wild winds hushed; the angry deep‿
sank, like a little child, to sleep;
the sullen billows ceased to leap,
at thy will.

4

So, when our life is clouded o'er,
and storm-winds drift us from the shore,
say, lest we sink to rise no more,
'Peace, be still.'

Godfrey Thring (1823–1903)

226 (AMR 314)

Martyrdom C.M. H. Wilson (1766–182.

As pants the hart for cooling streams
  when heated in the chase,
so longs my soul, O God, for thee,
  and thy refreshing grace.

2

For thee, my God, the living God,
  my thirsty soul doth pine:
O when shall I behold thy face,
  thou majesty divine?

3

Why restless, why cast down, my soul?
  hope still, and thou shalt sing‿
the praise of him who is thy God,
  thy health's eternal spring.

4

To Father, Son, and Holy Ghost,
  the God whom we adore,
be glory, as it was, is now,
  and shall be evermore.

Psalm 42 in *New Version*
(TATE and BRADY, 1696)

27 (AMR **317**)

St. Hugh C.M. E. J. Hopkins (1818–1901)

The preparations of the heart in man

Lord, teach us how to pray aright
with reverence and with fear;
though dust and ashes in thy sight,
we may, we must, draw near.

2

We perish if we cease from prayer:
O grant us power to pray;
and, when to meet thee we prepare,
Lord, meet us by the way.

3

iod of all grace, we bring to thee‿
a broken, contrite heart;
ive what thine eye delights to see,
truth in the inward part;

4

faith in the only sacrifice‿
that can for sin atone,
to cast our hopes, to fix our eyes,
on Christ, on Christ alone;

5

patience to watch and wait and weep,
though mercy long delay;
courage our fainting souls to keep,
and trust thee though thou slay.

6

Give these, and then thy will be done;
thus, strengthened with all might,
we, through thy Spirit and thy Son,
shall pray, and pray aright.

James Montgomery (1771–1854)

228 (AMR 318)

St. Etheldreda C.M. Thomas Turton (1780–1864)

Desiring to pray

1

Shepherd divine, our wants relieve
in this our evil day;
to all thy tempted followers give
the power to watch and pray.

2

Long as our fiery trials last,
long as the cross we bear,
O let our souls on thee be cast
in never-ceasing prayer.

3

The Spirit's interceding grace
give us in faith to claim;
to wrestle till we see thy face,
and know thy hidden name.

4

Till thou thy perfect love impart
till thou thyself bestow,
be this the cry of every heart,
'I will not let thee go.'

5

I will not let thee go, unless‿
thou tell thy name to me;
with all thy great salvation bless,
and make me all like thee.

6

Then let me on the mountain-top
behold thy open face;
where faith in sight is swallowed up,
and prayer in endless praise.

Charles Wesley* (1707–88)

The latter part of this hymn makes reference to Jacob's encounter with the angel (Genesis 32. 24–30)

29 (AMR 324)

Old 120th 6 6.6 6.6 6. Melody from *Psalms*, 1570

In AMR this hymn is set to *Remission* and *Waltham*

Not for our sins alone
 thy mercy, Lord, we sue;
let fall thy pitying glance
 on our devotions too,
what we have done for thee,
 and what we think to do.

2

The holiest hours we spend
 in prayer upon our knees,
the times when most we deem
 our songs of praise will please,
thou searcher of all hearts,
 forgiveness pour on these.

3

And all the gifts we bring,
 and all the vows we make,
and all the acts of love
 we plan for thy dear sake,
into thy pardoning thought,
 O God of mercy, take.

4

And most, when we, thy flock,
 before thine altar bend,
and strange, bewildering thoughts
 with those sweet moments blend,
by him whose death we plead,
 good Lord, thy help extend.

5

Bow down thine ear and hear,
 open thine eyes and see;
our very love is shame,
 and we must come to thee
to make it of thy grace
 what thou wouldst have it be.

HENRY TWELLS (1823–1900)

230 (AMR 325)

Stockton C.M. T. Wright (1763–182

Version in AMR

Make me a clean heart

O for a heart to praise my God,
a heart from sin set free;
a heart that's sprinkled with the blood
so freely shed for me:

2

a heart resigned, submissive, meek,
my great Redeemer's throne;
where only Christ is heard to speak,
where Jesus reigns alone:

3

a humble, lowly, contrite heart,
believing, true, and clean,
which neither life nor death can part
from him that dwells within:

4

a heart in every thought renewe
and full of love divine;
perfect and right and pure and go
a copy, Lord, of thine.

5

Thy nature, gracious Lord, impa
come quickly from above;
write thy new name upon my he
thy new best name of love.

CHARLES WESLEY* (1707–88
Psalm 51. 1

231 (AMR 326)

Caithness C.M. *Scottish Psalter* (1635)

Walking with God

1 O for a closer walk with God,
a calm and heavenly frame;
a light to shine upon the road
that leads me to the Lamb.

2 What peaceful hours I once enjoyed,
how sweet their memory still!
but they have left an aching void
the world can never fill.

3 Return, O holy Dove, return,
sweet messenger of rest:
I hate the sins that made thee mourn,
and drove thee from my breast.

4 The dearest idol I have known,
whate'er that idol be,
help me to tear it from thy throne,
and worship only thee.

5 So shall my walk be close with God,
calm and serene my frame;
so purer light shall mark the road
that leads me to the Lamb.

William Cowper (1731–1800)
Genesis 5. 24

232 (AMR 327)
Eden 6 6.6 6. O. M. Feilden (1837–1924

Alternative Tune: *Quam dilecta* (160)

Lord, be thy word my rule,
in it may I rejoice;
thy glory be my aim,
thy holy will my choice;

2

thy promises my hope,
thy providence my guard,
thine arm my strong support,
thyself my great reward.

CHRISTOPHER WORDSWORTH (1807–85)

33 (AMR **329**)
Hereford L.M. S. S. Wesley (1810–76)

O thou who camest from above
  the fire celestial to impart,
kindle a flame of sacred love
  on the mean altar of my heart.

2

There let it for thy glory burn
  with inextinguishable blaze,
and trembling to its source return
  in humble prayer and fervent praise.

3

Jesus, confirm my heart's desire
  to work and speak and think for thee;
still let me guard the holy fire
  and still stir up the gift in me.

4

Still let me prove thy perfect will,
  my acts of faith and love repeat;
till death thy endless mercies seal,
  and make the sacrifice complete.

CHARLES WESLEY* (1707–88)
Leviticus 6. 13

234 (AMR **330**)
Newington 7 7.7 7. W. D. Maclagan (1826–191

Thine for ever! God of love,
hear us from thy throne above;
thine for ever may we be
here and in eternity.

2

Thine for ever! Lord of life,
shield us through our earthly strife;
thou the Life, the Truth, the Way,
guide us to the realms of day.

3

Thine for ever! O how blest
they who find in thee their rest!
Saviour, guardian, heavenly friend,
O defend us to the end.

*4

Thine for ever! Shepherd, keep‿
us thy frail and trembling sheep;
safe alone beneath thy care,
let us all thy goodness share.

5

Thine for ever! thou our guide,
all our wants by thee supplied,
all our sins by thee forgiven,
lead us, Lord, from earth to heaven.

M. F. Maude (1819–1913)

235 (AMR 331)

Wolvercote 7 6.7 6. D. W. H. Ferguson (1874–1950

O Jesus, I have promised
to serve thee to the end;
be thou for ever near me,
my Master and my Friend:
I shall not fear the battle
if thou art by my side,
nor wander from the pathway
if thou wilt be my guide.

Dedication

*2

O let me feel thee near me:
  the world is ever near;
I see the sights that dazzle,
  the tempting sounds I hear;
my foes are ever near me,
  around me and within;
but, Jesus, draw thou nearer,
  and shield my soul from sin.

3

O let me hear thee speaking
  in accents clear and still,
above the storms of passion,
  the murmurs of self-will;
O speak to reassure me,
  to hasten or control;
O speak, and make me listen,
  thou guardian of my soul.

4

O Jesus, thou hast promised
  to all who follow thee,
that where thou art in glory
  there shall thy servant be;
and, Jesus, I have promised
  to serve thee to the end:
O give me grace to follow,
  my Master and my Friend.

5

O let me see thy foot-marks,
  and in them plant mine own;
my hope to follow duly
  is in thy strength alone:
O guide me, call me, draw me,
  uphold me to the end;
and then in heaven receive me,
  my Saviour and my Friend.

J. E. Bode (1816–74)

236 (AMR **332**)

God be in my head
Walford Davies (1869–194
Org.
God be in my head,
and in my un - der stand - ing; God be in mine
eyes, and in my look - ing; God be in my
mouth, and in my speak - ing; God be in my
heart, and in my think - ing;
God be at mine end, and at my de - part - ing.

God be in my head
and in my understanding;

2 God be in mine eyes,
and in my looking;

3 God be in my mouth,
and in my speaking;

4 God be in my heart,
and in my thinking;

5 God be at mine end,
and at my departing.

PYNSON'S *Horae*, 151.

237 (AMR 333)

Breslau L.M. German Traditional Melody

1 Take up thy cross, the Saviour said,
  if thou wouldst my disciple be;
deny thyself, the world forsake,
  and humbly follow after me.

2 Take up thy cross—let not its weight‿
  fill thy weak spirit with alarm:
his strength shall bear thy spirit up,
  and brace thy heart, and nerve thine arm.

3 Take up thy cross, nor heed the shame,
  nor let thy foolish pride rebel:
thy Lord for thee the Cross endured,
  to save thy soul from death and hell.

4 Take up thy cross then in his strength,
  and calmly every danger brave;
'twill guide thee to a better home,
  and lead to victory o'er the grave.

5 Take up thy cross, and follow Christ,
  nor think till death to lay it down;
for only he who bears the cross
  may hope to wear the glorious crown.

6 To thee, great Lord, the One in Three,
  all praise for evermore ascend:
O grant us in our home to see
  the heavenly life that knows no end.

C. W. Everest (1814–77)

238 (AMR 335)

Franconia S.M. *Harmonischer Liederschatz* (1738)
adapted by W. H. Havergal (1793–1870)

Blest are the pure in heart,
for they shall see our God;
the secret of the Lord is theirs,
their soul is Christ's abode.

2

The Lord, who left the heavens
our life and peace to bring,
to dwell in lowliness with men,
their pattern and their King;

3

still to the lowly soul
he doth himself impart,
and for his dwelling and his throne
chooseth the pure in heart.

4

Lord, we thy presence seek;
may ours this blessing be;
give us a pure and lowly heart,
a temple meet for thee.

JOHN KEBLE (1792–1866) and others

39 (AMR 336)
Song 34 L.M. Orlando Gibbons (1583–1625)

Before work

Forth in thy name, O Lord, I go,
  my daily labour to pursue;
thee, only thee, resolved to know,
  in all I think or speak or do.

2

The task thy wisdom hath assigned
  O let me cheerfully fulfil;
in all my works thy presence find,
  and prove thy good and perfect will.

3

Thee may I set at my right hand,
  whose eyes my inmost substance see,
and labour on at thy command,
  and offer all my works to thee.

4

Give me to bear thy easy yoke,
  and every moment watch and pray,
and still to things eternal look,
  and hasten to thy glorious day;

5

for thee delightfully employ
  whate'er thy bounteous grace hath given,
and run my course with even joy,
  and closely walk with thee to heaven.

CHARLES WESLEY* (1707–88)

240 (AMR 337)

Sandys S.M. W. Sandys' *Christmas Carols* (1833)

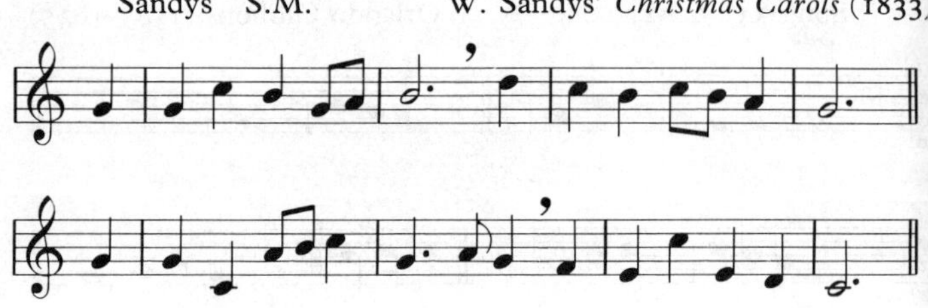

The Elixir

1 Teach me, my God and King,
in all things thee to see;
and what I do in anything
to do it as for thee.

2 A man that looks on glass,
on it may stay his eye;
or, if he pleaseth, through it pass,
and then the heaven espy.

3 All may of thee partake;
nothing can be so mean
which, with this tincture, *For thy sake*,
will not grow bright and clean.

4 A servant with this clause
makes drudgery divine;
who sweeps a room, as for thy laws,
makes that and the action fine.

5 This is the famous stone
that turneth all to gold;
for that which God doth touch and own
cannot for less be told.

George Herbert (1593–1632)

241 (AMR **341**)

Woodlands 10 10.10 10. W. Greatorex (1877–1949)

1 'Lift up your hearts!' We lift them, Lord, to thee;
here at thy feet none other may we see:
'Lift up your hearts!' E'en so, with one accord,
we lift them up, we lift them to the Lord.

Above the level of the former years,
the mire of sin, the slough of guilty fears,
the mist of doubt, the blight of love's decay,
O Lord of light, lift all our hearts to-day.

*3 Above the swamps of subterfuge and shame,
the deeds, the thoughts, that honour may not name,
the halting tongue that dares not tell the whole,
O Lord of truth, lift every Christian soul.

4 Lift every gift that thou thyself hast given:
low lies the best till lifted up to heaven;
low lie the bounding heart, the teeming brain,
till, sent from God, they mount to God again.

5 Then, as the trumpet-call in after years,
'Lift up your hearts!' rings pealing in our ears,
still shall those hearts respond with full accord,
'We lift them up, we lift them to the Lord.'

H. Montagu Butler (1833–1918)

242 (AMR **342**)

St. Hugh C.M. E. J. Hopkins (1818–1901)

God and the Soul

The Covenant and Confidence of Faith

Lord, it belongs not to my care
  whether I die or live:
to love and serve thee is my share,
  and this thy grace must give.

2

Christ leads me through no darker rooms
  than he went through before;
he that unto God's kingdom comes
  must enter by this door.

3

Come, Lord, when grace hath made me meet
  thy blessèd face to see;
for if thy work on earth be sweet,
  what will thy glory be!

4

Then I shall end my sad complaints
  and weary, sinful days,
and join with the triumphant saints
  that sing my Saviour's praise.

5

My knowledge of that life is small,
  the eye of faith is dim;
but 'tis enough that Christ knows all,
  and I shall be with him.

RICHARD BAXTER* (1615–91)

243 (AMR 343)

Colchester 8 8.8 8.8 8. S. S. Wesley (1810–

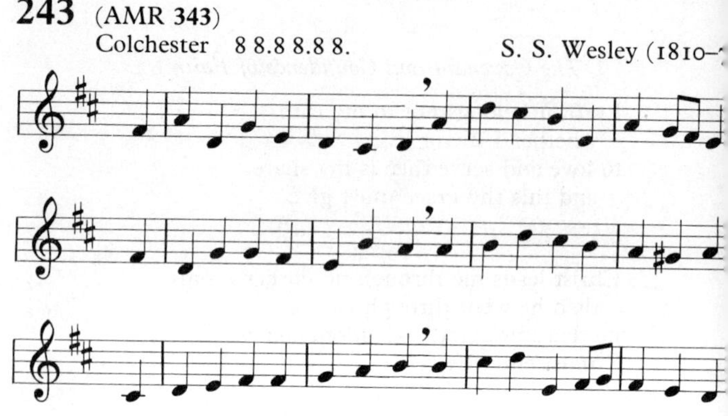

In AMR this hymn is set to *Wrestling Jacob*

Wrestling Jacob

Come, O thou Traveller unknown,
  whom still I hold, but cannot see;
my company before is gone,
  and I am left alone with thee;
with thee all night I mean to stay,
and wrestle till the break of day.

2

I need not tell thee who I am,
  my misery or sin declare;
thyself hast called me by my name;
  look on thy hands, and read it there.
But who, I ask thee, who art thou?
tell me thy name, and tell me now.

3

In vain thou strugglest to get free;
  I never will unloose my hold.
Art thou the man that died for me?
  the secret of thy love unfold:
wrestling, I will not let thee go,
till I thy name, thy nature know.

4

Yield to me now, for I am weak,
  but confident in self-despair;
speak to my heart, in blessings speak,
  be conquered by my instant prayer.
Speak, or thou never hence shalt move,
and tell me if thy name is Love?

5

'Tis love! 'tis love! thou diedst for me!
  I hear thy whisper in my heart!
the morning breaks, the shadows flee;
  pure universal Love thou art:
to me, to all, thy mercies move;
thy nature and thy name is Love.

CHARLES WESLEY (1707–88)

This hymn is based on the story of Jacob's encounter with the angel in Genesis 32. 24–30

244 (AMR 344)
St. Bees 7 7·7 7· J. B. Dykes (1823–7

Lovest thou me?

Hark, my soul, it is the Lord;
'tis thy Saviour, hear his word;
Jesus speaks, and speaks to thee,
'Say, poor sinner, lov'st thou me?

2

'I delivered thee when bound,
and, when wounded, healed thy wound;
sought thee wandering, set thee right,
turned thy darkness into light.

3

'Can a woman's tender care
cease towards the child she bare?
yes, she may forgetful be,
yet will I remember thee.

4

'Mine is an unchanging love,
higher than the heights above,
deeper than the depths beneath,
free and faithful, strong as death.

5

'Thou shalt see my glory soon,
when the work of grace is done:
partner of my throne shalt be:
say, poor sinner, lov'st thou me

6

Lord, it is my chief complaint
that my love is weak and faint;
yet I love thee, and adore;
O for grace to love thee more!

William Cowper (1731–1800
John 21. 16

45 (**AMR 347**)
Nun danket all C.M. *Praxis Pietatis*, 1647

Jesus, these eyes have never seen
  that radiant form of thine;
the veil of sense hangs dark between‿
  thy blessèd face and mine.

2

I see thee not, I hear thee not,
  yet art thou oft with me;
and earth hath ne'er so dear a spot
  as where I meet with thee.

3

Yet, though I have not seen, and still‿
  must rest in faith alone,
I love thee, dearest Lord, and will,
  unseen, but not unknown.

4

When death these mortal eyes shall seal,
  and still this throbbing heart,
the rending veil shall thee reveal
  all glorious as thou art.

Ray Palmer (1808–87)
John 20. 29; 1 Peter 1. 8

246 (AMR 349)

FIRST TUNE

Saffron Walden 8 8 8.6. A. H. Brown (1830–19

SECOND TUNE

Misericordia 8 8 8.6. Henry Smart (1813–7

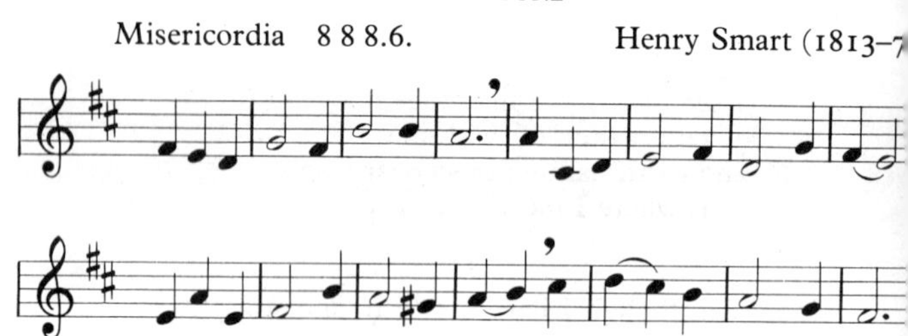

Just as I am, without one plea
but that thy blood was shed for me,
and that thou bidst me come to thee,
    O Lamb of God, I come.

2

Just as I am, though tossed about
with many a conflict, many a doubt,
fightings and fears within, without,
    O Lamb of God, I come.

3

Just as I am, poor, wretched, blind;
sight, riches, healing of the mind,
yea, all I need, in thee to find,
    O Lamb of God, I come.

4

Just as I am, thou wilt receive,
wilt welcome, pardon, cleanse, relieve:
because thy promise I believe,
    O Lamb of God, I come.

5

Just as I am (thy love unknown
has broken every barrier down),
now to be thine, yea, thine alone,
    O Lamb of God, I come.

6

Just as I am, of that free love‿
the breadth, length, depth, and height to prove,
here for a season, then above,
    O Lamb of God, I come.

CHARLOTTE ELLIOTT (1789–1871)

247 (AMR 351)

FIRST TUNE

Vox dilecti D.C.M. — J. B. Dykes (1823–76

SECOND TUNE

Kingsfold D.C.M. — English Traditional Melody

I heard the voice of Jesus say,
'Come unto me and rest;
lay down, thou weary one, lay down
thy head upon my breast:'
I came to Jesus as I was,
so weary, worn and sad;
I found in him a resting-place,
and he has made me glad.

2

I heard the voice of Jesus say,
'Behold, I freely give
the living water, thirsty one;
stoop down and drink and live:'
I came to Jesus, and I drank
of that life-giving stream;
my thirst was quenched, my soul revived,
and now I live in him.

3

I heard the voice of Jesus say,
'I am this dark world's light;
look unto me, thy morn shall rise,
and all thy day be bright:'
I looked to Jesus, and I found
in him my star, my sun;
and in that light of life I'll walk
till travelling days are done.

H. Bonar (1808–89)

In verse 1, line 6, AMR has 'weary and worn'

248 (AMR **360**)
North Coates 6 5.6 5. T. R. Matthews (1826–1910

O my Saviour, lifted
from the earth for me,
draw me, in thy mercy,
nearer unto thee.

2

Lift my earth-bound longings,
fix them, Lord, above;
draw me with the magnet
of thy mighty love.

3

Lord, thine arms are stretching
ever far and wide,
to enfold thy children
to thy loving side.

4

And I come, O Jesus:
dare I turn away?
No, thy love hath conquered,
and I come to-day,

5

bringing all my burdens,
sorrow, sin, and care;
at thy feet I lay them,
and I leave them there.

W. Walsham How (1823–97

249 (AMR 361) FIRST TUNE

Innocents 7 7.7 7. *The Parish Choir*, 1850

SECOND TUNE

Consecration 7 7.7 7. W. H. Havergal (1793–1870)

1

ke my life, and let it be
nsecrated, Lord, to thee;
e my moments and my days,
them flow in ceaseless praise.

2

ke my hands, and let them move
the impulse of thy love;
e my feet, and let them be
ift and beautiful for thee.

3

ke my voice, and let me sing
vays, only, for my King;
e my lips, and let them be
ed with messages from thee.

*4

Take my silver and my gold;
not a mite would I withhold;
take my intellect, and use
every power as thou shalt choose.

5

Take my will, and make it thine:
it shall be no longer mine;
take my heart: it is thine own;
it shall be thy royal throne.

6

Take my love; my Lord, I pour
at thy feet its treasure-store;
take myself, and I will be
ever, only, all for thee.

FRANCES R. HAVERGAL (1836–79)

250 (AMR **363**)

Margaret   Irregular   T. R. Matthews (1826–1910

Thou didst leave thy throne and thy kingly crown,
  when thou camest to earth for me;
but in Bethlehem's home was there found no room
  for thy holy nativity:
    O come to my heart, Lord Jesus;
    there is room in my heart for thee.

2

Heaven's arches rang when the angels sang,
  proclaiming thy royal degree;
but in lowly birth didst thou come to earth,
  and in great humility:

3

The foxes found rest, and the bird had its nest
  in the shade of the cedar tree;
but thy couch was the sod, O thou Son of God,
  in the desert of Galilee:

4

Thou camest, O Lord, with the living word
  that should set thy people free;
but with mocking scorn and with crown of thorn
  they bore thee to Calvary:

5

When the heavens shall ring, and the angels sing,
  at thy coming to victory,
let thy voice call me home, saying, 'Yet there is room,
  there is room at my side for thee:'
    O come to my heart, Lord Jesus;
    there is room in my heart for thee.

EMILY E. S. ELLIOTT (1836–97)
Luke 2. 7

251 (AMR **364**)

Gott will's machen 8 7.8 7. J. L. Steiner (1688–176

*1

Souls of men, why will ye scatter
like a crowd of frightened sheep?
Foolish hearts, why will ye wander
from a love so true and deep?

*2

Was there ever kindest shepherd
half so gentle, half so sweet,
as the Saviour who would have us
come and gather round his feet?

3

There's a wideness in God's mercy
like the wideness of the sea;
there's a kindness in his justice
which is more than liberty.

4

There is no place where earth's sorrows
  are more felt than up in heaven;
there is no place where earth's failings
  have such kindly judgement given.

5

There is plentiful redemption
  in the blood that has been shed;
there is joy for all the members
  in the sorrows of the Head.

6

For the love of God is broader
  than the measures of man's mind;
and the heart of the Eternal
  is most wonderfully kind.

7

Pining souls, come nearer Jesus,
  and oh, come not doubting thus,
but with faith that trusts more bravely
  his huge tenderness for us.

8

If our love were but more simple,
  we should take him at his word;
and our lives would be all sunshine
  in the sweetness of our Lord.

F. W. Faber (1814–63)

252 (AMR 383) FIRST TUNE

Pange lingua 8 7.8 7.8 7. Mode ii

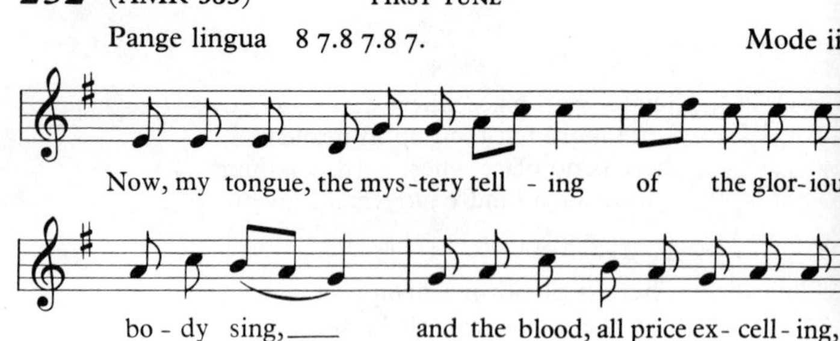
Now, my tongue, the mys-tery tell - ing of the glor-iou
bo - dy sing, and the blood, all price ex- cell - ing,

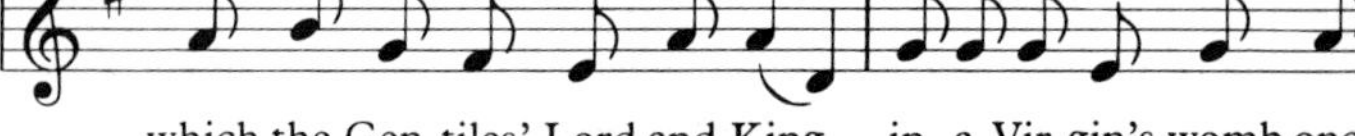
which the Gen-tiles' Lord and King, in a Vir-gin's womb once

dwell-ing, shed for this world's ran- som-ing. A - men.

This tune is set as in AMR 97

PART ONE

Now, my tongue, the mystery telling
  of the glorious body sing,
and the blood, all price excelling,
  which the Gentiles' Lord and King,
in a Virgin's womb once dwelling,
  shed for this world's ransoming.

2

Given for us, and condescending‿
  to be born for us below,
he, with men in converse blending,
  dwelt the seed of truth to sow,
till he closed with wondrous ending
  his most patient life of woe.

3

That last night, at supper lying,
  'mid the Twelve, his chosen band,
Jesus, with the law complying,
  keeps the feast its rites demand;
then, more precious food supplying,
  gives himself with his own hand.

4

Word-made-flesh, true bread he maketh
  by his word his flesh to be,
wine his blood; which whoso taketh
  must from carnal thoughts be free:
faith alone, though sight forsaketh,
  shows true hearts the mystery.

PART TWO

5

Therefore we, before him bending,
  this great sacrament revere:
types and shadows have their ending,
  for the newer rite is here;
faith, our outward sense befriending,
  makes our inward vision clear.

6

Glory let us give and blessing
  to the Father and the Son,
honour, might, and praise addressing,
  while eternal ages run;
ever too his love confessing,
  who, from both, with both is one. Amen.

St. Thomas Aquinas (1227–74)
tr. J. M. Neale, E. Caswall, and others

252 (AMR **383**) SECOND TUNE

Tantum ergo (Grafton) 8 7.8 7.8 7. French Melody, 18

PART ONE

Now, my tongue, the mystery telling
 of the glorious body sing,
and the blood, all price excelling,
 which the Gentiles' Lord and King,
in a Virgin's womb once dwelling,
 shed for this world's ransoming.

2

Given for us, and condescending‿
 to be born for us below,
he, with men in converse blending,
 dwelt the seed of truth to sow,
till he closed with wondrous ending
 his most patient life of woe.

3

That last night, at supper lying,
  'mid the Twelve, his chosen band,
Jesus, with the law complying,
  keeps the feast its rites demand;
then, more precious food supplying,
  gives himself with his own hand.

4

Word-made-flesh, true bread he maketh
  by his word his flesh to be,
wine his blood; which whoso taketh
  must from carnal thoughts be free:
faith alone, though sight forsaketh,
  shows true hearts the mystery.

PART TWO

5

Therefore we, before him bending,
  this great sacrament revere:
types and shadows have their ending,
  for the newer rite is here;
faith, our outward sense befriending,
  makes our inward vision clear.

6

Glory let us give and blessing
  to the Father and the Son,
honour, might, and praise addressing,
  while eternal ages run;
ever too his love confessing,
  who, from both, with both is one.

St. Thomas Aquinas (1227–74)
tr. J. M. Neale, E. Caswall, and others

253 (AMR 384) FIRST TUNE

Verbum supernum prodiens L.M. Mode vi

1 The heaven-ly Word, pro-ceed-ing forth yet leav-ing not
2 By false dis-ci-ple to be given to foe-men for
3 He gave him-self_ in ei-ther kind, his pre-cious flesh,
4 By birth their fel-low-man was he, their meat, when sit-

Part 2

5 O sav-ing Vic-tim, ope-ning wide the gate of heaven
6 All praise and thanks to thee as-cend for ev-er-more,

1 the Fa-ther's side, ac-com-plish-ing his work on earth
2 his life a-thirst, him-self, the ve-ry bread of heaven
3 his pre-cious blood; in love's own ful-ness thus de-signed
4 -ting at the board; he died, their ran-som-er to be;
5 to man be-low, our foes press on from ev-ery side:
6 blest One in Three; O grant us life that shall not end

1 had reached at length life's e-ven-tide.
2 he gave to his dis-ci-ples first.
3 of the whole man to be the food.
4 he ev-er reigns, their great re-ward.
5 thine aid sup-ply, thy strength be-stow.
6 in our true na-tive land with thee. A-men.

PART ONE

The heavenly Word, proceeding forth
yet leaving not the Father's side,
accomplishing his work on earth
had reached at length life's eventide.

2

By false disciple to be given
to foemen for his life athirst,
himself, the very bread of heaven,
he gave to his disciples first.

3

He gave himself in either kind,
his precious flesh, his precious blood;
in love's own fulness thus designed
of the whole man to be the food.

4

By birth their fellow-man was he,
their meat, when sitting at the board;
he died, their ransomer to be;
he ever reigns, their great reward.

PART TWO

5

O saving Victim, opening wide
the gate of heaven to man below,
our foes press on from every side:
thine aid supply, thy strength bestow.

6

All praise and thanks to thee ascend
for evermore, blest One in Three;
O grant us life that shall not end
in our true native land with thee. Amen.

St. Thomas Aquinas (1227–74)
tr. J. M. Neale, E. Caswall, and others

253 (AMR 384) SECOND TUNE

Solemnis Haec Festivitas L.M. *Paris Gradual* (168

PART ONE

The heavenly Word, proceeding forth
yet leaving not the Father's side,
accomplishing his work on earth
had reached at length life's eventide.

2

By false disciple to be given
to foemen for his life athirst,
himself, the very bread of heaven,
he gave to his disciples first.

3

He gave himself in either kind,
his precious flesh, his precious blood;
in love's own fulness thus designed
of the whole man to be the food.

4

By birth their fellow-man was he,
their meat, when sitting at the board;
he died, their ransomer to be;
he ever reigns, their great reward.

PART TWO

5

O saving Victim, opening wide‿
the gate of heaven to man below,
our foes press on from every side:
thine aid supply, thy strength bestow.

6

All praise and thanks to thee ascend
for evermore, blest One in Three;
O grant us life that shall not end
in our true native land with thee.

St. Thomas Aquinas (1227–74)
tr. J. M. Neale, E. Caswall, and others

254 (AMR **385**) FIRST TUNE

Adoro te devote 10 10.10 10 Mode v

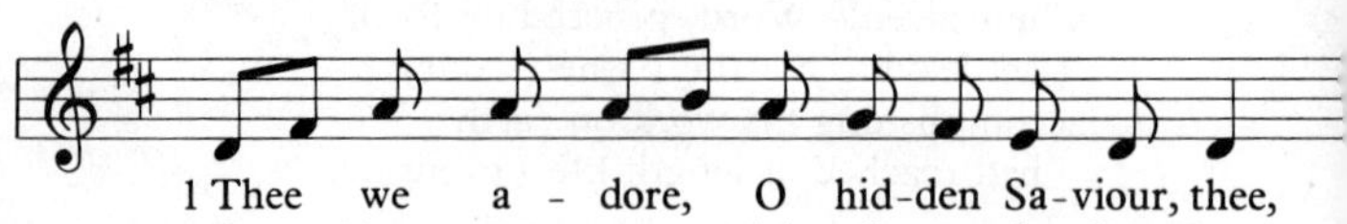

1 Thee we a - dore, O hid-den Sa-viour, thee,
2 O blest mem - or - ial of our dy - ing Lord,
3 Foun - tain of good - ness, Je - su, Lord and God,
4 O Christ, whom now be-neath a veil we see,

1 who in thy sa - cra-ment dost deign to be;
2 who liv-ing bread to men doth here af - ford;
3 cleanse us, un-clean, with thy most clean-sing blood;
4 may what we thirst for soon our por-tion be:

1 both flesh and spi - rit at thy pre-sence fail,
2 O may our souls for ev - er feed on thee,
3 in-crease our faith and love, that we may know
4 to gaze on thee un-veiled, and see thy face,

1 yet here thy pre-sence we de-vout-ly hail.
2 and thou, O Christ, for ev - er pre-cious be.
3 the hope and peace which from thy pre-sence flow.
4 the vi - sion of thy glo - ry and thy grace. A - men.

SECOND TUNE

Sheldonian 10 10.10 10. Cyril V. Taylor (b. 1907)

Thee we adore, O hidden Saviour, thee,
who in thy sacrament dost deign to be;
both flesh and spirit at thy presence fail,
yet here thy presence we devoutly hail.

2

O blest memorial of our dying Lord,
who living bread to men doth here afford;
O may our souls for ever feed on thee,
and thou, O Christ, for ever precious be.

3

Fountain of goodness, Jesu, Lord and God,
cleanse us, unclean, with thy most cleansing blood;
increase our faith and love, that we may know‿
the hope and peace which from thy presence flow.

4

O Christ, whom now beneath a veil we see,
may what we thirst for soon our portion be:
to gaze on thee unveiled, and see thy face,
the vision of thy glory and thy grace.

St. Thomas Aquinas (1227–74)
tr. J. R. Woodford (1820–85)

255 (AMR **387**)
St Sepulchre L.M. G. Cooper (1820–76

Alternative Tune: *Invitation* (*Devonshire*) (45)

Jesu, thou joy of loving hearts,
  thou fount of life, thou light of men;
from the best bliss that earth imparts
  we turn unfilled to thee again.

2

Thy truth unchanged hath ever stood;
  thou savest those that on thee call;
to them that seek thee thou art good,
  to them that find thee all in all.

3

We taste thee, O thou living bread,
  and long to feast upon thee still;
we drink of thee, the fountain-head,
  and thirst our souls from thee to fill.

4

Our restless spirits yearn for thee,
  where'er our changeful lot is cast,
glad when thy gracious smile we see,
  blest when our faith can hold thee fast.

5

O Jesu, ever with us stay;
  make all our moments calm and bright;
chase the dark night of sin away;
  shed o'er the world thy holy light.

Jesu, dulcis memoria
tr. Ray Palmer (1808–87)

256 (AMR **390**)
Picardy 8 7.8 7.8 7. French Carol Melod
(French Carol)

Let all mortal flesh keep silence
  and with fear and trembling stand;
ponder nothing earthly-minded,
  for with blessing in his hand
Christ our God to earth descendeth,
  our full homage to demand.

2

King of kings, yet born of Mary,
  as of old on earth he stood,
Lord of lords, in human vesture –
  in the body and the blood –
he will give to all the faithful
  his own self for heavenly food.

3

Rank on rank the host of heaven
  spreads its vanguard on the way,
as the Light of light descendeth
  from the realms of endless day,
that the powers of hell may vanish
  as the darkness clears away.

4

At his feet the six-winged seraph;
  cherubim with sleepless eye
veil their faces to the Presence,
  as with ceaseless voice they cry,
Alleluia, Alleluia,
  Alleluia, Lord most high.

Liturgy of St. James
tr. G. Moultrie (1829–85)

257 (AMR **393**)

Schmücke dich 8 8.8 8. D. J. Crüger (1598–166

Holy Communion

PART ONE

1 Deck thyself, my soul, with gladness,
leave the gloomy haunts of sadness;
come into the daylight's splendour,
there with joy thy praises render
unto him whose grace unbounded
hath this wondrous banquet founded:
high o'er all the heavens he reigneth,
yet to dwell with thee he deigneth.

2 Now I sink before thee lowly,
filled with joy most deep and holy,
as with trembling awe and wonder
on thy mighty works I ponder:
how, by mystery surrounded,
depth no man hath ever sounded,
none may dare to pierce unbidden
secrets that with thee are hidden.

PART TWO

3 Sun, who all my life dost brighten,
Light, who dost my soul enlighten,
Joy, the sweetest man e'er knoweth,
Fount, whence all my being floweth,
at thy feet I cry, my Maker,
let me be a fit partaker
of this blessèd food from heaven,
for our good, thy glory, given.

4 Jesus, Bread of Life, I pray thee,
let me gladly here obey thee;
never to my hurt invited,
be thy love with love requited:
from this banquet let me measure,
Lord, how vast and deep its treasure;
through the gifts thou here dost give me,
as thy guest in heaven receive me.

J. Franck (1618–77)
tr. Catherine Winkworth (1827–78)

258 (AMR **394**) FIRST TUNE

Gweedore 6 6.6 6.8 8. S. S. Wesley (1810–7

Author of life divine
  who hast a table spread,
furnished with mystic wine
  and everlasting bread,
preserve the life thyself hast given,
and feed and train us up for heaven.

2

Our needy souls sustain
  with fresh supplies of love,
till all thy life we gain,
  and all thy fulness prove,
and, strengthened by thy perfect grace,
behold without a veil thy face.

Charles Wesley (1707–88)

SECOND TUNE

Lawes' Psalm 47 6 6.6 6.8 8. Henry Lawes (1596–1662)

Author of life divine
  who hast a table spread,
furnished with mystic wine
  and everlasting bread,
preserve the life thyself hast given,
and feed and train us up for heaven.

2

Our needy souls sustain
  with fresh supplies of love,
till all thy life we gain,
  and all thy fulness prove,
and, strengthened by thy perfect grace,
behold without a veil thy face.

CHARLES WESLEY (1707–88)

259 (AMR **396**)

Rockingham L.M. Adapted by E. Miller (1730–180

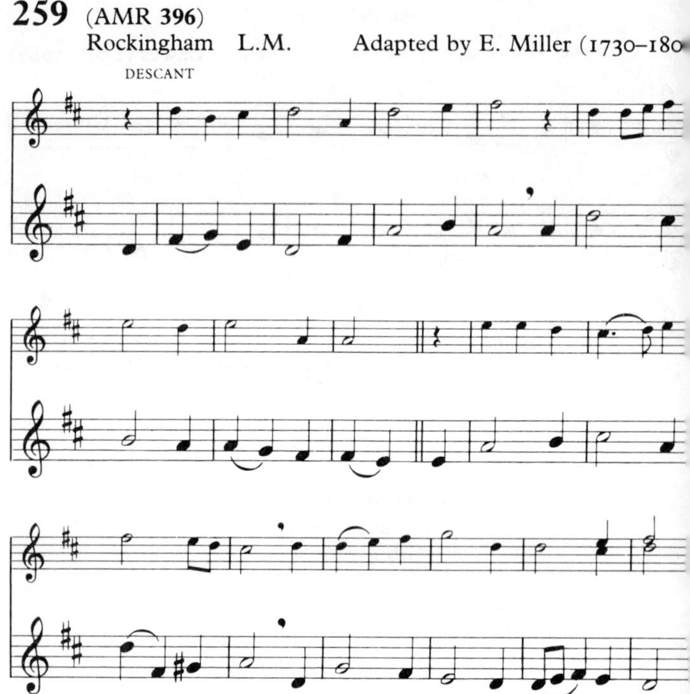

The descant may be used for verse 4

My God, and is thy table spread,
  and doth thy cup with love o'erflow?
thither be all thy children led,
  and let them all thy sweetness know.

2

Hail, sacred feast which Jesus makes,
  rich banquet of his flesh and blood!
thrice happy he who here partakes
  that sacred stream, that heavenly food.

*3

Why are its bounties all in vain
  before unwilling hearts displayed?
was not for them the Victim slain?
  are they forbid the children's bread?

4

O let thy table honoured be,
  and furnished well with joyful guests;
and may each soul salvation see,
  that here its sacred pledges tastes.

PHILIP DODDRIDGE (1702–51)

260 (AMR **397**) FIRST TUNE

Song 1 10 10.10 10.10 10. Orlando Gibbons (1583–162

SECOND TUNE

Unde et memores W. H. Monk (1823–89

10 10.10 10.10 10.

And now, O Father, mindful of the love
  that bought us, once for all, on Calvary's tree,
and having with us him that pleads above,
  we here present, we here spread forth to thee
that only offering perfect in thine eyes,
the one true, pure, immortal sacrifice.

2

Look, Father, look on his anointed face,
  and only look on us as found in him;
look not on our misusings of thy grace,
  our prayer so languid, and our faith so dim:
for lo, between our sins and their reward
we set the Passion of thy Son our Lord.

*3

And then for those, our dearest and our best,
  by this prevailing presence we appeal:
O fold them closer to thy mercy's breast,
  O do thine utmost for their souls' true weal;
from tainting mischief keep them white and clear,
and crown thy gifts with strength to persevere.

*4

And so we come: O draw us to thy feet,
  most patient Saviour, who canst love us still;
and by this food, so aweful and so sweet,
  deliver us from every touch of ill:
in thine own service make us glad and free,
and grant us never more to part with thee.

William Bright (1824–1901)

261 (AMR **398**)

Albano C.M. Vincent Novello (1781–186

Once, only once, and once for all,
his precious life he gave;
before the Cross our spirits fall,
and own it strong to save.

2

'One offering, single and complete,'
with lips and heart we say;
but what he never can repeat
he shows forth day by day.

3

For, as the priest of Aaron's line
within the holiest stood,
and sprinkled all the mercy-shrine
with sacrificial blood;

4

so he who once atonement wrought,
  our Priest of endless power,
presents himself for those he bought‿
  in that dark noontide hour.

5

His manhood pleads where now it lives
  on heaven's eternal throne,
and where in mystic rite he gives‿
  its presence to his own.

6

And so we show thy death, O Lord,
  till thou again appear;
and feel, when we approach thy board,
  we have an altar here.

*7

All glory to the Father be,
  all glory to the Son,
all glory, Holy Ghost, to thee,
  while endless ages run.

William Bright (1824–1901)

262 (AMR **399**)
Hyfrydol 8 7.8 7. D. R. H. Prichard (1811–8

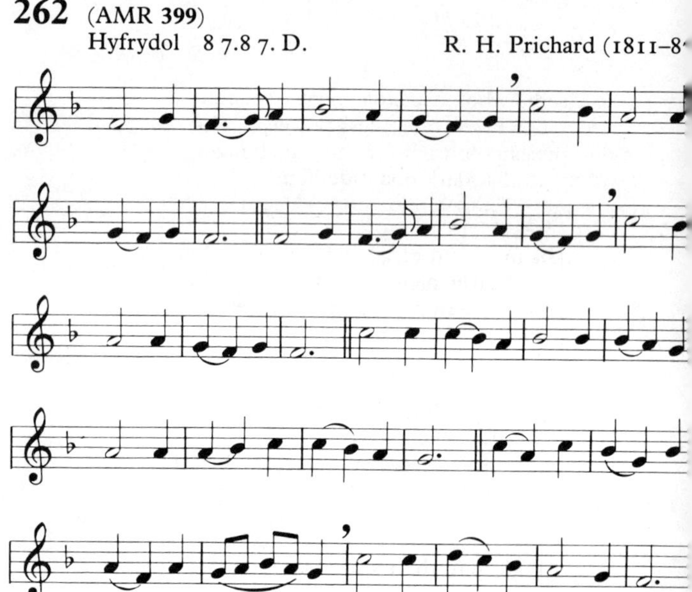

Alleluia, sing to Jesus!
his the sceptre, his the throne;
Alleluia, his the triumph,
his the victory alone:
hark, the songs of peaceful Sion
thunder like a mighty flood;
Jesus out of every nation
hath redeemed us by his blood.

2

Alleluia, not as orphans‿
are we left in sorrow now;
Alleluia, he is near us,
faith believes, nor questions how:
though the cloud from sight received him,
when the forty days were o'er,
shall our hearts forget his promise,
'I am with you evermore'?

3

Alleluia, bread of angels,
thou on earth our food, our stay;
Alleluia, here the sinful‿
flee to thee from day to day:
Intercessor, Friend of sinners,
earth's Redeemer, plead for me,
where the songs of all the sinless
sweep across the crystal sea.

4

Alleluia, King eternal,
thee the Lord of lords we own;
Alleluia, born of Mary,
earth thy footstool, heaven thy throne:
thou within the veil hast entered,
robed in flesh, our great High Priest;
thou on earth both Priest and Victim
in the eucharistic feast.

W. Chatterton Dix (1837–98)

263 (AMR **400**) FIRST TUNE

St. Helen 8 7.8 7.8 7. G. C. Martin (1844–191

SECOND TUNE

Rhuddlan 8 7.8 7.8 7. Welsh Traditional Melod

Lord, enthroned in heavenly splendour,
  first-begotten from the dead,
thou alone, our strong defender,
  liftest up thy people's head.
      Alleluia,
    Jesu, true and living bread.

2

Here our humblest homage pay we,
  here in loving reverence bow;
here for faith's discernment pray we,
  lest we fail to know thee now.
      Alleluia,
    thou art here, we ask not how.

3

Though the lowliest form doth veil thee
  as of old in Bethlehem,
here as there thine angels hail thee,
  Branch and Flower of Jesse's Stem.
      Alleluia,
    we in worship join with them.

4

Paschal Lamb, thine offering, finished‿
  once for all when thou wast slain,
in its fulness undiminished
  shall for evermore remain,
      Alleluia,
    cleansing souls from every stain.

5

Life-imparting heavenly Manna,
  stricken Rock with streaming side,
heaven and earth with loud hosanna
  worship thee, the Lamb who died,
      Alleluia,
    risen, ascended, glorified.

G. H. Bourne (1840–1925)

264 (AMR 401)

Dies Dominica 7 6.7 6. D. J. B. Dykes (1823–7

Alternative Tune: *Offertorium* (266)

We pray thee, heavenly Father,
  to hear us in thy love,
and pour upon thy children
  the unction from above;
that so in love abiding,
  from all defilement free,
we may in pureness offer‿
  our Eucharist to thee.

2

Be thou our guide and helper,
  O Jesus Christ, we pray;
so may we well approach thee,
  if thou wilt be the Way:
thou, very Truth, hast promised
  to help us in our strife,
food of the weary pilgrim,
  eternal source of life.

3

And thou, creator Spirit,
  look on us, we are thine;
renew in us thy graces,
  upon our darkness shine;
that, with thy benediction
  upon our souls outpoured,
we may receive in gladness
  the body of the Lord.

4

O Trinity of Persons,
  O Unity most high,
on thee alone relying
  thy servants would draw nigh:
unworthy in our weakness,
  on thee our hope is stayed,
and blessed by thy forgiveness
  we will not be afraid.

V. S. S. Coles (1845–1929)

265 (AMR **402**)

Song 1   10 10.10 10.10 10.   Orlando Gibbons (1583–162

O thou, who at thy Eucharist didst pray
  that all thy Church might be for ever one,
grant us at every Eucharist to say
  with longing heart and soul, 'Thy will be done:'
O may we all one bread, one body be,
through this blest sacrament of unity.

2

For all thy Church, O Lord, we intercede;
  make thou our sad divisions soon to cease;
draw us the nearer each to each, we plead,
  by drawing all to thee, O Prince of peace:
thus may we all one bread, one body be,
through this blest sacrament of unity.

*3

Wè pray thee too for wanderers from thy fold;
  O bring them back, good Shepherd of the sheep,
back to the faith which saints believed of old,
  back to the Church which still that faith doth keep:
soon may we all one bread, one body be,
through this blest sacrament of unity.

4

So, Lord, at length when sacraments shall cease,
  may we be one with all thy Church above,
one with thy saints in one unbroken peace,
  one with thy saints in one unbounded love:
more blessèd still, in peace and love to be
one with the Trinity in Unity.

W. H. Turton (1856–1938)

266 (AMR 403) Adapted fron
Offertorium 7 6.7 6. D. Michael Haydn (1737–1806

Alternative Tune: *Crüger* (142)

We hail thy presence glorious,
  O Christ our great High Priest,
o'er sin and death victorious,
  at thy thanksgiving feast:
as thou art interceding
  for us in heaven above,
thy Church on earth is pleading
  thy perfect work of love.

2

Through thee in every nation
  thine own their hearts upraise,
off'ring one pure oblation,
  one sacrifice of praise:
with thee in blest communion
  the living and the dead
are joined in closest union,
  one Body with one Head.

*3

O living bread from heaven,
  Jesu, our Saviour good,
who thine own self hast given
  to be our souls' true food;
for us thy body broken
  hung on the Cross of shame:
this bread its hallowed token
  we break in thy dear name.

*4

O stream of love unending,
  poured from the one true vine,
with our weak nature blending
  the strength of life divine;
our thankful faith confessing
  in thy life-blood outpoured,
we drink this cup of blessing
  and praise thy name, O Lord.

5

May we thy word believing
  thee through thy gifts receive,
that, thou within us living,
  we all to God may live;
draw us from earth to heaven
  till sin and sorrow cease,
forgiving and forgiven,
  in love and joy and peace.

R. G. Parsons (1882–1948)

267 (AMR **405**)
St. Mark L.M.

W. Crowfoot (1724–8
from Crisp's *Divine Harmony*, 17

Alternative Tune: *Ludborough* (282)

Almighty Father, Lord most high,
who madest all, who fillest all,
thy name we praise and magnify,
for all our needs on thee we call.

2

We offer to thee of thine own
ourselves and all that we can bring,
in bread and cup before thee shown,
our universal offering.

3

All that we have we bring to thee,
yet all is naught when all is done,
save that in it thy love can see‿
the sacrifice of thy dear Son.

4

By his command in bread and cup
his body and his blood we plead:
what on the Cross he offered up
is here our sacrifice indeed.

5

For all thy gifts of life and grace,
here we thy servants humbly pray
that thou would'st look upon the face‿
of thine anointed Son to-day.

V. S. S. Coles (1845–1929)

268 (AMR 407)

Standish Irregular J. Dykes Bower (1905–81

After the second verse

O sweet-est Je - su, O gra-cious Je - su, O Je - su,

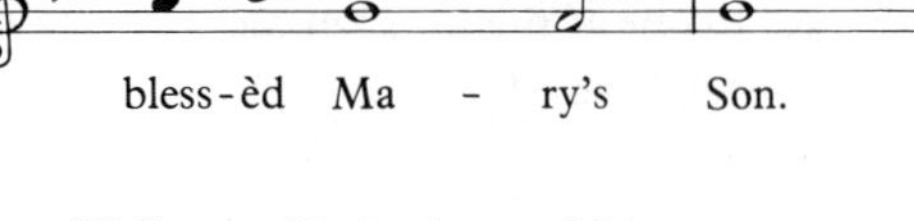

Hail, true Body, born of Mary,
by a wondrous virgin-birth.
Thou who on the Cross wast offered
to redeem the sons of earth;

2

thou whose side became a fountain
pouring forth thy precious blood,
give us now, and at our dying,
thine own self to be our food.

O sweetest Jesu,
O gracious Jesu,
O Jesu, blessèd Mary's Son.

14th cent.
tr. H. N. OXENHAM (1829–88)

69 (AMR **408**)
Liebster Jesu 7 8.7 8.8 8. J. R. Ahle (1625–73)

Dearest Jesu, we are here,
at thy call, thy presence owning;
pleading now in holy fear
that great sacrifice atoning:
Word incarnate, much in wonder
on this mystery deep we ponder.

2

Jesu, strong to save – the same‿
yesterday, to-day, for ever –
make us fear and love thy name,
serving thee with best endeavour:
in this life, O ne'er forsake us,
but to bliss hereafter take us.

G. R. Woodward (1848–1934)
after T. Clausnitzer (1619–84)

270 (AMR **409**) FIRST TUNE

Rendez à Dieu 9 8.9 8. D. *La Forme des Prière*
Strasbourg, 154

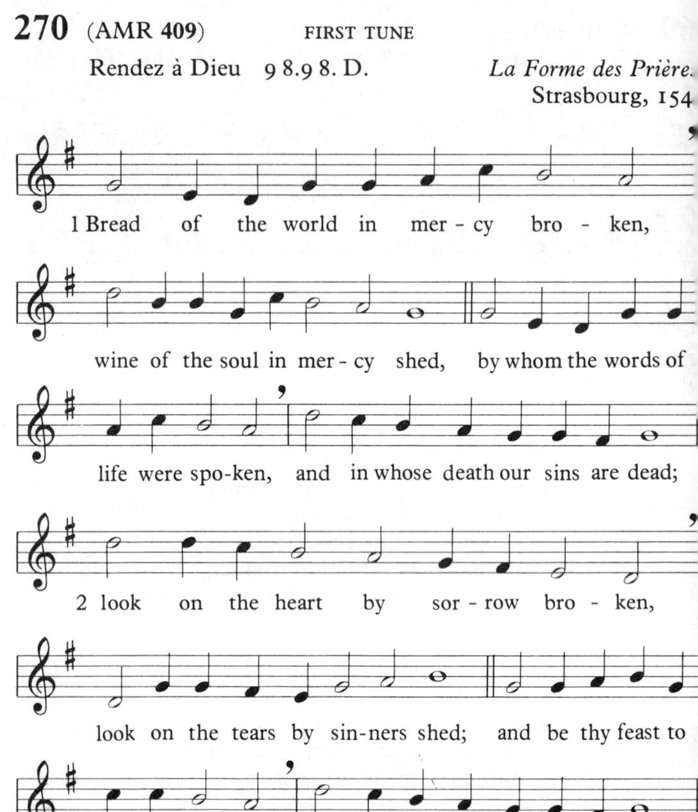
1 Bread of the world in mer - cy bro - ken,
wine of the soul in mer - cy shed, by whom the words of
life were spo-ken, and in whose death our sins are dead;
2 look on the heart by sor - row bro - ken,
look on the tears by sin-ners shed; and be thy feast to
us the to - ken that by thy grace our souls are fed.

SECOND TUNE

Les Commandemens 9 8.9 8. (Commandments)

La Forme des Prières, Strasbourg, 1545

Bread of the world in mercy broken,
  wine of the soul in mercy shed,
by whom the words of life were spoken,
  and in whose death our sins are dead;

2

look on the heart by sorrow broken,
  look on the tears by sinners shed;
and be thy feast to us the token
  that by thy grace our souls are fed.

REGINALD HEBER (1783–1826)

271 (AMR 411)

Bread of Heaven 7 7·7 7·7 7· W. D. Maclagan (1826–1910)

Bread of heaven, on thee we feed,
for thy flesh is meat indeed;
ever may our souls be fed
with this true and living bread;
day by day with strength supplied
through the life of him who died.

2

Vine of heaven, thy blood supplies‿
this blest cup of sacrifice;
Lord, thy wounds our healing give,
to thy Cross we look and live:
Jesus, may we ever be‿
grafted, rooted, built in thee.

J. CONDER (1789–1855)

72 (AMR **412**)

St. Flavian C.M. Adapted from *Psalms*, 1562

O God, unseen yet ever near,
  thy presence may we feel;
and, thus inspired with holy fear,
  before thine altar kneel.

2

Here may thy faithful people know‿
  the blessings of thy love,
the streams that through the desert flow,
  the manna from above.

3

We come, obedient to thy word,
  to feast on heavenly food;
our meat the body of the Lord,
  our drink his precious blood.

4

Thus may we all thy word obey,
  for we, O God, are thine;
and go rejoicing on our way,
  renewed with strength divine.

E. Osler (1798–1863)

273 (AMR **423**)

Mit Freuden zart 8 7.8 7.8 8 7. Hymn Melody of the Bohemian Brethren, 1566

Version in AMR

Let us employ all notes of joy
  and praise that never endeth
to God above, whose mighty love‿
  our hearts and minds defendeth;
who by his grace, in every place,
to all who need and duly plead
  his power and presence lendeth.

2

For, ere he died, the Crucified‿
  wrought things eternal for us
by bread and wine, which love divine‿
  hath given to assure us:
O taste and see; find him to be‿
our great reward, our living Lord
  most willing to restore us.

3

The word he spoke, the bread he broke
  shall fill our lives with glory,
if we are true and loving too
  and for our sins are sorry:
O do his will, and praise him still,
and still proclaim his glorious name
  and deathless Gospel story.

ADAM FOX (1883–1977)

274 (AMR 414)

Farley Castle 10 10.10 10. Henry Lawes (1596–1662

Here, O my Lord, I see thee face to face;
here faith would touch and handle things unseen;
here grasp with firmer hand the eternal grace,
and all my weariness upon thee lean.

2

Here would I feed upon the bread of God;
here drink with thee the royal wine of heaven;
here would I lay aside each earthly load;
here taste afresh the calm of sin forgiven.

3

I have no help but thine; nor do I need‿
another arm save thine to lean upon:
it is enough, my Lord, enough indeed,
my strength is in thy might, thy might alone.

H. Bonar (1808–89)

75 (AMR **416**)
Christe Fons Jugis 11 11 11.5. Attributed to P. G. Dubois (1624–94)

Wherefore, O Father, we thy humble servants
here bring before thee Christ thy well-belovèd,
all perfect offering, sacrifice immortal,
spotless oblation.

2

See now thy children, making intercession
through him our Saviour, Son of God incarnate,
for all thy people, living and departed,
pleading before thee.

W. H. H. Jervois (1852–1905)

276 (AMR 417)

Sheen 14 14.14 15. Gustav Holst (1874–193

From glory to glory advancing, we praise thee, O Lord;
thy name with the Father and Spirit be ever adored.
From strength unto strength we go forward on Sion's highway,
to appear before God in the city of infinite day.

2

Thanksgiving and glory and worship and blessing and love,
one heart and one song have the saints upon earth and above.
Evermore, O Lord, to thy servants thy presence be nigh;
ever fit us by service on earth for thy service on high.

Liturgy of St. Jame
tr. C. W. Humphreys (1840–1921

77 (AMR **421**)
Hosanna in Excelsis 7 7.4 4.7. D. S. H. Nicholson
(1875–1947)

1 Glory in highest heaven
to our exalted Saviour,
who left behind
for all mankind
these tokens of his favour:
his bleeding love and mercy,
his all-redeeming passion;
who here displays,
and gives the grace
which brings us our salvation.

Louder than gathered waters,
or bursting peals of thunder,
we lift our voice
and speak our joys,
and shout our loving wonder.
Shout, all our elder brethren,
while we record the story
of him that came
and suffered shame,
to carry us to glory.

3 Angels in fixed amazement
around our altars hover,
with eager gaze
adore the grace
of our eternal Lover,
himself and all his fulness
who gives to the believer;
and by this bread
whoe'er are fed
shall live with God for ever.

In the first line AMR has Hosanna in the highest

CHARLES WESLEY* (1707–88)

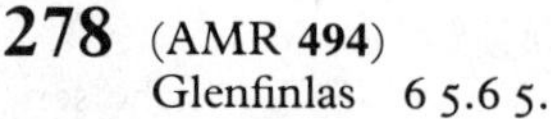

278 (AMR **494**)
Glenfinlas 6 5.6 5. K. G. Finlay (1882–1974

Alternative Tune: *North Coates* (248)

Hands that have been handling‿
holy things and high
still, Lord, in thy service
bless and fortify.

2

Ears which heard the message
of the words of life
keep thou closed and guarded
from the noise of strife.

3

Eyes whose contemplation‿
looked upon thy love,
let them gaze expectant
on the world above.

4

'Holy, Holy, Holy,'
thee our lips confessed:
on those lips for ever
let no falsehood rest.

5

Feet which trod the pavement
round about God's board,
let them walk in glory
where God's light is poured.

6

Bodies that have tasted
of the living Bread,
be they re-created
in their living Head.

*7

Be we all one Body,
all our members one,
measured by the stature
of God's full-grown Son.

ADAM FOX (1883–1977)
based on Liturgy of Malabar

Another translation of these words is at NS 421

79 (AMR **459**)

St. Peter C.M. A. R. Reinagle (1799–1877)

My God, accept my heart this day,
  and make it always thine,
that I from thee no more may stray,
  no more from thee decline.

2

Before the Cross of him who died,
  behold, I prostrate fall;
let every sin be crucified,
  and Christ be all in all.

3

Anoint me with thy heavenly grace,
  and seal me for thine own;
that I may see thy glorious face,
  and worship near thy throne.

4

Let every thought and work and word
  to thee be ever given:
then life shall be thy service, Lord,
  and death the gate of heaven.

*5

All glory to the Father be,
  all glory to the Son,
all glory, Holy Ghost, to thee,
  while endless ages run.

MATTHEW BRIDGES (1800–94)

280 (AMR 463)

Felix 11 10.11 10. F. Mendelssohn-Bartholdy (1809–4

Alternative Tune: *Strength and Stay* (7)

O perfect Love, all human thought transcending,
lowly we kneel in prayer before thy throne,
that theirs may be the love which knows no ending,
whom thou for evermore dost join in one.

2

O perfect Life, be thou their full assurance
of tender charity and steadfast faith,
of patient hope, and quiet brave endurance,
with childlike trust that fears nor pain nor death.

3

Grant them the joy which brightens earthly sorrow,
grant them the peace which calms all earthly strife;
and to life's day the glorious unknown morrow
that dawns upon eternal love and life.

DOROTHY F. GURNEY (1858–1932

81 (AMR **469**) FIRST TUNE

Eudoxia 6 5.6 5. S. Baring-Gould (1834–1924)

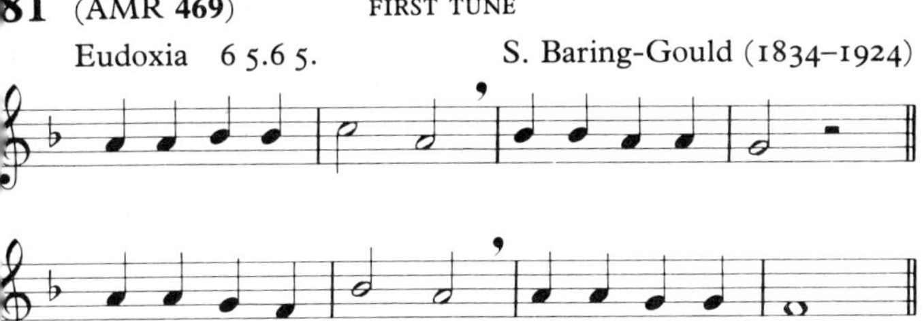

SECOND TUNE

Caswall 6 5.6 5. F. Filitz (1804–76)

Jesu, Son of Mary,
 fount of life alone,
here we hail thee present
 on thine altar-throne:

humbly we adore thee,
 Lord of endless might,
in the mystic symbols
 veiled from earthly sight.

Think, O Lord, in mercy
 on the souls of those‿
who, in faith gone from us,
 now in death repose.

Here 'mid stress and conflict
 toils can never cease;
there, the warfare ended,
 bid them rest in peace.

5 Often were they wounded
 in the deadly strife;
heal them, good Physician,
 with the balm of life.

6 Every taint of evil,
 frailty, and decay,
good and gracious Saviour,
 cleanse and purge away.

7 Rest eternal grant them,
 after weary fight;
shed on them the radiance
 of thy heavenly light.

8 Lead them onward, upward,
 to the holy place,
where thy saints made perfect
 gaze upon thy face.

From the Swahili
tr. E. S. Palmer (1856–1931)

282 (AMR 473)
Ludborough L.M. T. R. Matthews (1826–191

Alternative Tune: *Melcombe* (2)

Ordination

Lord, pour thy Spirit from on high,
  and thine assembled servants bless;
graces and gifts to each supply,
  and clothe thy priests with righteousness.

2

Within thy temple when they stand,
  to teach the truth as taught by thee,
Saviour, like stars in thy right hand
  let all thy Church's pastors be.

3

Wisdom and zeal and faith impart,
  firmness with meekness, from above,
to bear thy people in their heart,
  and love the souls whom thou dost love;

4

to watch and pray and never faint,
  by day and night their guard to keep,
to warn the sinner, cheer the saint,
  to feed thy lambs and tend thy sheep.

5

So, when their work is finished here,
  may they in hope their charge resign;
when the Chief Shepherd shall appear,
  O God, may they and we be thine.

JAMES MONTGOMERY (1771–1854)

In line 2 for 'assembled' *AMR has* 'ordainèd'.

283 (AMR **474**)
Oriel 8 7.8 7.8 7. C. Ett, *Cantica Sacra*, 18
descant by Alan Gray (1855–193

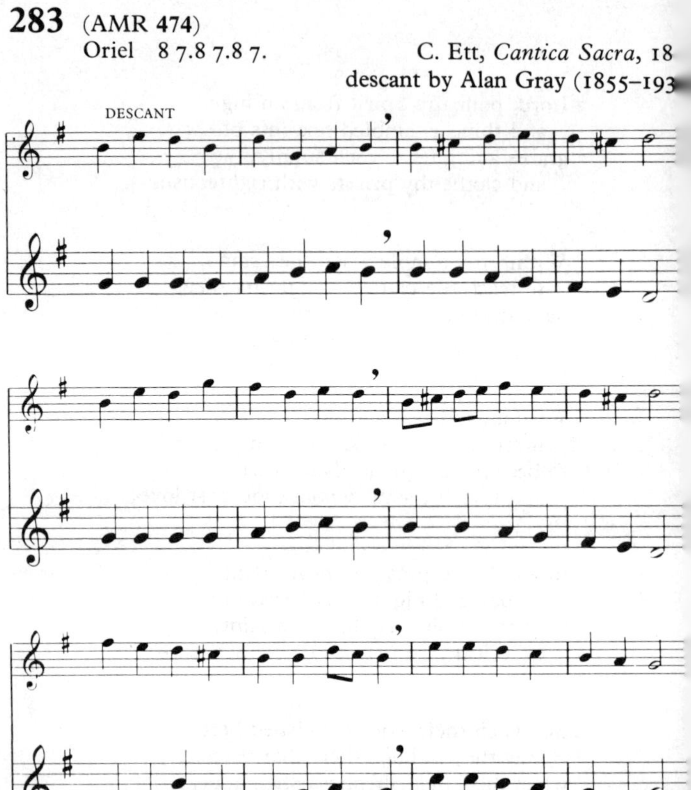

Alternative Tune: *Westminster Abbey* (332)

1

Blessèd city, heavenly Salem,
vision dear of peace and love,
who of living stones art builded
in the height of heaven above,
and by angel hosts encircled
as a bride dost earthward move.

2

Christ is made the sure foundation,
Christ the head and corner-stone,
chosen of the Lord, and precious,
binding all the Church in one,
holy Sion's help for ever,
and her confidence alone.

3

To this temple, where we call thee,
come, O Lord of hosts, to-day;
with thy wonted loving-kindness
hear thy servants as they pray;
and thy fullest benediction
shed within its walls alway.

4

Here vouchsafe to all thy servants
what they ask of thee to gain,
what they gain from thee for ever
with the blessèd to retain,
and hereafter in thy glory
evermore with thee to reign.

Latin, before 9th cent.
tr. J. M. NEALE (1818–66)

A longer version is at 332

284 (AMR **476**)

Was Lebet Irregular *Rheinhardt MS* (Üttingen, 175·

In our day of thanksgiving one psalm let us offer
  for the saints who before us have found their reward;
when the shadow of death fell upon them, we sorrowed,
  but now we rejoice that they rest in the Lord.

2

In the morning of life, and at noon, and at even,
  he called them away from our worship below;
but not till his love, at the font and the altar,
  had girt them with grace for the way they should go.

3

These stones that have echoed their praises are holy,
  and dear is the ground where their feet have once trod;
yet here they confessed they were strangers and pilgrims,
  and still they were seeking the city of God.

4

Sing praise, then, for all who here sought and here found him,
  whose journey is ended, whose perils are past:
they believed in the light; and its glory is round them,
  where the clouds of earth's sorrow are lifted at last.

W. H. Draper (1855–1933)

285 (AMR **478**)
St. Matthew D.C.M. William Croft (1678–172

The Sick

Thine arm, O Lord, in days of old
  was strong to heal and save;
it triumphed o'er disease and death,
  o'er darkness and the grave:
to thee they went, the blind, the dumb,
  the palsied and the lame,
the leper with his tainted life,
  the sick with fevered frame.

2

And lo, thy touch brought life and health,
  gave speech and strength and sight;
and youth renewed and frenzy calmed
  owned thee, the Lord of light:
and now, O Lord, be near to bless,
  almighty as of yore,
in crowded street, by restless couch,
  as by Gennesareth's shore.

3

Be thou our great deliverer still,
  thou Lord of life and death;
restore and quicken, soothe and bless,
  with thine almighty breath:
to hands that work, and eyes that see,
  give wisdom's heavenly lore,
that whole and sick, and weak and strong,
  may praise thee evermore.

E. H. Plumptre (1821–91)

286 (AMR 479)

Belgrave C.M.

W. Horsley (1774–18

From thee all skill and science flow,
  all pity, care, and love,
all calm and courage, faith and hope:
  O pour them from above.

2

And part them, Lord, to each and all,
  as each and all shall need,
to rise, like incense, each to thee,
  in noble thought and deed.

3

And hasten, Lord, that perfect day
  when pain and death shall cease,
and thy just rule shall fill the earth
  with health and light and peace.

*4

When ever blue the sky shall gleam,
  and ever green the sod,
and man's rude work deface no more
  the paradise of God.

CHARLES KINGSLEY (1819–75)

287 (AMR **480**)
Almsgiving 8 8 8.4. J. B. Dykes (1823–7

Alternative Tune: *Es ist kein Tag* (NS 399, HHT 66)

O Lord of heaven and earth and sea,
to thee all praise and glory be.
How shall we show our love to thee,
who givest all?

*2

The golden sunshine, vernal air,
sweet flowers and fruit, thy love declare;
when harvests ripen, thou art there,
who givest all.

3

For peaceful homes, and healthful days,
for all the blessings earth displays,
we owe thee thankfulness and praise,
who givest all.

4

Thou didst not spare thine only Son,
but gav'st him for a world undone,
and freely with that blessèd One
thou givest all.

5

Thou giv'st the Holy Spirit's dower,
Spirit of life and love and power,
and dost his sevenfold graces shower
upon us all.

6

For souls redeemed, for sins forgiven,
for means of grace and hopes of heaven,
Father, what can to thee be given,
who givest all?

*7

We lose what on ourselves we spend,
we have as treasure without end
whatever, Lord, to thee we lend,
who givest all:

8

To thee, from whom we all derive‿
our life, our gifts, our power to give:
O may we ever with thee live,
who givest all.

CHRISTOPHER WORDSWORTH (1807–85)

288 (AMR **481**)
Monkland 7 7.7 7. John Antes (1740–181
arr. J. Wilkes (186

Harvest

Praise, O praise our God and King;
hymns of adoration sing:
  for his mercies still endure
  ever faithful, ever sure.

2

Praise him that he made the sun
day by day his course to run:

3

And the silver moon by night,
shining with her gentle light:

4

Praise him that he gave the rain
to mature the swelling grain:

5

And hath bid the fruitful field
crops of precious increase yield:

6

Praise him for our harvest-store;
he hath filled the garner-floor:

7

And for richer food than this,
pledge of everlasting bliss:

8

Glory to our bounteous King;
glory let creation sing:
  glory to the Father, Son,
  and blest Spirit, Three in One.

H. W. Baker (1821–77)

289 (AMR **482**)

St. George 7 7.7 7. D. G. J. Elvey (1816–

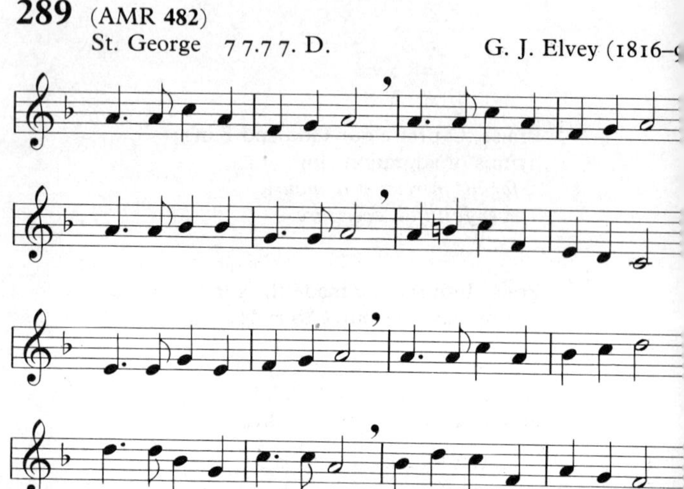

Harvest

Come, ye thankful people, come,
raise the song of harvest-home:
all is safely gathered in,
ere the winter storms begin;
God, our maker, doth provide‿
for our wants to be supplied:
come to God's own temple, come;
raise the song of harvest-home.

2

All this world is God's own field,
fruit unto his praise to yield;
wheat and tares therein are sown,
unto joy or sorrow grown;
ripening with a wondrous power
till the final harvest-hour:
grant, O Lord of life, that we‿
holy grain and pure may be.

3

For we know that thou wilt come,
and wilt take thy people home;
from thy field wilt purge away
all that doth offend, that day;
and thine angels charge at last
in the fire the tares to cast,
but the fruitful ears to store‿
in thy garner evermore.

4

Come then, Lord of mercy, come,
bid us sing thy harvest-home:
let thy saints be gathered in,
free from sorrow, free from sin:
all upon the golden floor
praising thee for evermore:
come, with all thine angels come,
bid us sing thy harvest-home.

H. ALFORD* (1810–71)

290 (AMR **483**)

Wir pflügen 7 6.7 6. D. 6 6.8 4. J. A. P. Schul
(1747–180

We plough the fields, and scatter
the good seed on the land,
but it is fed and watered
by God's almighty hand:
he sends the snow in winter,
the warmth to swell the grain,
the breezes, and the sunshine,
and soft, refreshing rain.
All good gifts around us
are sent from heaven above;
then thank the Lord, O thank the Lord,
for all his love.

2

He only is the maker‿
  of all things near and far;
he paints the wayside flower,
  he lights the evening star;
the winds and waves obey him,
  by him the birds are fed;
much more to us, his children,
  he gives our daily bread.
    All good gifts around us
      are sent from heaven above;
    then thank the Lord, O thank the Lord,
      for all his love.

3

We thank thee then, O Father,
  for all things bright and good,
the seed-time and the harvest,
  our life, our health, our food.
Accept the gifts we offer
  for all thy love imparts,
and, what thou most desirest,
  our humble, thankful hearts.
    All good gifts around us
      are sent from heaven above;
    then thank the Lord, O thank the Lord,
      for all his love.

M. CLAUDIUS (1740–1815)
tr. JANE MONTGOMERY CAMPBELL (1817–78)

291 (AMR **484**)
Golden Sheaves 8 7.8 7. D.

Arthur Sullivan
(1842–1900)

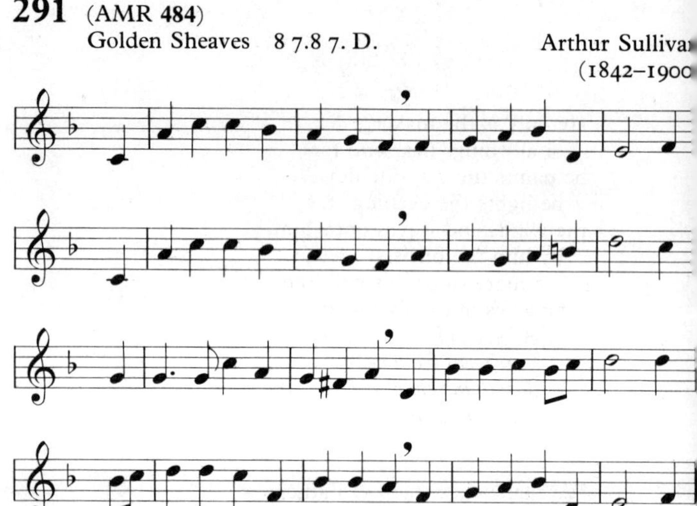

Harvest

To thee, O Lord, our hearts we raise
  in hymns of adoration,
to thee bring sacrifice of praise
  with shouts of exultation:
bright robes of gold the fields adorn,
  the hills with joy are ringing,
the valleys stand so thick with corn
  that even they are singing.

2

And now, on this our festal day,
  thy bounteous hand confessing,
upon thine altar, Lord, we lay‿
  the first-fruits of thy blessing:
by thee the souls of men are fed
  with gifts of grace supernal;
thou who dost give us earthly bread;
  give us the bread eternal.

3

We bear the burden of the day,
  and often toil seems dreary;
but labour ends with sunset ray,
  and rest comes for the weary:
may we, the angel-reaping o'er,
  stand at the last accepted,
Christ's golden sheaves for evermore
  to garners bright elected.

4

O blessèd is that land of God,
  where saints abide for ever;
where golden fields spread far and broad,
  where flows the crystal river:
the strains of all its holy throng
  with ours to-day are blending;
thrice blessèd is that harvest-song
  which never hath an ending.

W. Chatterton Dix (1837–98)

292 (AMR 487)
Melita 8 8.8 8.8 8. J. B. Dykes (1823–76

Those at Sea

1

Eternal Father, strong to save,
whose arm hath bound the restless wave,
who bidd'st the mighty ocean deep
its own appointed limits keep:
  O hear us when we cry to thee
  for those in peril on the sea.

2

O Christ, whose voice the waters heard
and hushed their raging at thy word,
who walkedst on the foaming deep,
and calm amid the storm didst sleep:
  O hear us when we cry to thee
  for those in peril on the sea.

3

O Holy Spirit, who didst brood‿
upon the waters dark and rude,
and bid their angry tumult cease,
and give, for wild confusion, peace:
  O hear us when we cry to thee
  for those in peril on the sea.

4

O Trinity of love and power,
our brethren shield in danger's hour;
from rock and tempest, fire and foe,
protect them wheresoe'er they go:
  thus evermore shall rise to thee
  glad hymns of praise from land and sea.

W. WHITING (1825–78)

293 (AMR 577)
National Anthem 6 6 4.6 6 6 4. *Thesaurus Musicus,* c. 1743

National Anthem

God save our gracious Queen,
long live our noble Queen,
God save the Queen.
Send her victorious,
happy and glorious,
long to reign over us:
God save the Queen.

*2

O Lord our God, arise,
scatter our enemies,
and make them fall;
confound their politics,
frustrate their knavish tricks;
on thee our hopes we fix:
God save us all.

3

Thy choicest gifts in store
on her be pleased to pour,
long may she reign.
May she defend our laws,
and ever give us cause
to sing with heart and voice,
God save the Queen.

ANON

SECOND VERSION

God save our gracious Queen,
long live our noble Queen,
    God save the Queen.
Send her victorious,
happy and glorious,
long to reign over us:
    God save the Queen.

2

Nor on this land alone,
but be God's mercies known
    from shore to shore.
Lord, make the nations see
that all should brothers be
and form one family
    the wide world o'er.

1 ANON.
2 W. E. HICKSON* (1803–70)

294 (AMR 578)

Jerusalem D.L.M. C. Hubert H. Parry (1848–1918)

Slow but with animation
3
mf
And did those feet in an - cient
p
time walk up-on Eng-land's moun-tains green? And was the
ho - ly Lamb of God on Eng-land's plea-sant pas - tures
mf
poco cresc.
seen? And did the coun - te-nance di - vine shine forth up -
f
- on our cloud-ed hills? And was Je - ru - sa-lem build - ed
poco rit.
2
here a-mong those dark sa-tan - ic mills?
mf
Bring me my bow of burn-ing gold! Bring me my
ar-rows of de - sire! Bring me my spear! O clouds, un -

p
-fold! Bring me my cha - ri - ot of fire! I will not
cease from men - tal fight, nor shall my sword sleep in my
allargando
ff
rit.
hand, till we have built Je - ru - sa - lem in Eng-land's
green and plea - sant land.

Jerusalem

And did those feet in ancient time
  walk upon England's mountains green?
And was the holy Lamb of God
  on England's pleasant pastures seen?
And did the countenance divine
  shine forth upon our clouded hills?
And was Jerusalem builded here
  among those dark satanic mills?

2

Bring me my bow of burning gold!
  Bring me my arrows of desire!
Bring me my spear! O clouds, unfold!
  Bring me my chariot of fire!
I will not cease from mental fight,
  nor shall my sword sleep in my hand,
till we have built Jerusalem
  in England's green and pleasant land.

William Blake (1757–1827)

295 (AMR 579)
Thaxted 13 13.13 13.13 13. Gustav Holst (1874–1934
(adapted from his Suite *The Planet*

National

The Two Fatherlands

I vow to thee, my country, all earthly things above,
entire and whole and perfect, the service of my love:
the love that asks no question, the love that stands the test,
that lays upon the altar the dearest and the best;
the love that never falters, the love that pays the price,
the love that makes undaunted the final sacrifice.

2

And there's another country, I've heard of long ago,
most dear to them that love her, most great to them that know;
we may not count her armies, we may not see her King;
her fortress is a faithful heart, her pride is suffering;
and soul by soul and silently her shining bounds increase,
and her ways are ways of gentleness and all her paths are peace.

CECIL SPRING-RICE (1859–1918)

296 (AMR 582)

Wareham L.M. W. Knapp (1698–176

Rejoice, O land, in God thy might;
his will obey, him serve aright;
for thee the saints uplift their voice:
fear not, O land, in God rejoice.

2

Glad shalt thou be, with blessing crowned,
with joy and peace thou shalt abound;
yea, love with thee shall make his home
until thou see God's kingdom come.

3

He shall forgive thy sins untold:
remember thou his love of old;
walk in his way, his word adore,
and keep his truth for evermore.

ROBERT BRIDGES (1844–1930)

297 (AMR 503) FIRST TUNE

Aeterna Christi Munera L.M. Mode

1 The e - ter - nal gifts of Christ the King
2 For they the Church 's prin - ces are,
3 Theirs is the stead - fast faith of saint
4 In them the Fa - ther's glo - ry shon
5 To thee, Re - deem - er, now we cry,
the a - pos - tles' glo - ry, let us sing;
tri - umph - ant lead - ers in the war,
and hope that nev - er yields nor faints,
in them the will of God the Son,
that thou wouldst join to them on high
and all, with hearts of glad - ness, raise
in heaven-ly courts a war - rior band,
and love of Christ in per - fect glow
in them ex - ults the Ho - ly Ghost,
thy ser - vants, who this grace im - plore,
due hymns of thank - ful love and praise.
true lights to light - en ev - ery land.
that lays the prince of this world low.
through them re - joice the heaven - ly host.
for ev - er and for ev - er - more. A - men.

SECOND TUNE

Illsley (Bishop) L.M. J. Bishop (1665–1737)

The eternal gifts of Christ the King,
the apostles' glory, let us sing;
and all, with hearts of gladness, raise‿
due hymns of thankful love and praise.

2

For they the Church's princes are,
triumphant leaders in the war,
in heavenly courts a warrior band,
true lights to lighten every land.

3

Theirs is the steadfast faith of saints,
and hope that never yields nor faints,
and love of Christ in perfect glow
that lays the prince of this world low.

4

In them the Father's glory shone,
in them the will of God the Son,
in them exults the Holy Ghost,
through them rejoice the heavenly host.

5

To thee, Redeemer, now we cry,
that thou wouldst join to them on high
thy servants, who this grace implore,
for ever and for evermore.

St. Ambrose (c. 340–97)
tr. J. M. Neale* (1818–66)

298 (AMR 506)

Old 104th   10 10.11 11.   T. Ravenscroft, *Psalmes*, 16

descant by Alan Gray (1855–193

The descant may be sung for verse 6

Alternative Tune: *Hanover* (101)

Apostles

Disposer supreme, and Judge of the earth,
who choosest for thine the meek and the poor;
to frail earthen vessels, and things of no worth,
entrusting thy riches which ay shall endure;

2

those vessels soon fail, though full of thy light,
and at thy decree are broken and gone;
thence brightly appeareth thy truth in its might,
as through the clouds riven the lightnings have shone.

3

Like clouds are they borne to do thy great will,
and swift as the winds about the world go:
the Word with his wisdom their spirits doth fill;
they thunder, they lighten, the waters o'erflow.

4

Their sound goeth forth, 'Christ Jesus the Lord!'
then Satan doth fear, his citadels fall;
as when the dread trumpets went forth at thy word,
and one long blast shattered the Canaanite's wall.

5

O loud be their trump, and stirring their sound,
to rouse us, O Lord, from slumber of sin:
the lights thou hast kindled in darkness around,
O may they awaken our spirits within.

6

All honour and praise, dominion and might,
to God, Three in One, eternally be,
who round us hath shed his own marvellous light,
and called us from darkness his glory to see.

J. B. de Santeuil (1630–97)
tr. Isaac Williams (1802–65)

299 (AMR 507)
University College 77.77. H. J. Gauntlett (1805–7

1

Captains of the saintly band,
lights who lighten every land,
princes who with Jesus dwell,
judges of his Israel;

2

on the nations sunk in night
ye have shed the Gospel light;
sin and error flee away,
truth reveals the promised day.

3

Not by warrior's spear and sword,
not by art of human word,
preaching but the cross of shame,
rebel hearts for Christ ye tame.

4

Earth, that long in sin and pai
groaned in Satan's deadly chai
now to serve its God is free
in the law of liberty.

5

Distant lands with one acclaim
tell the honour of your name,
who, wherever man has trod,
teach the mysteries of God.

6

Glory to the Three in One
while eternal ages run,
who from deepest shades of nig
called us to his glorious light.

J. B. DE SANTEUIL (1630–9
tr. H. W. BAKER (1821–7

0 (AMR **508**)

Evangelists 8 8 7. D.
(Alles ist an
Gottes Segen)

Adapted from
J. S. Bach's version of a chorale
by J. Löhner (1691) and others

1 Come, pure hearts, in sweetest measures
sing of those who spread the treasures
in the holy gospels shrined:
blessèd tidings of salvation,
peace on earth, their proclamation,
love from God to lost mankind.

2 Thou, by whom the words were given
for our light and guide to heaven,
Spirit, on our darkness shine;
graft them in our hearts, increasing‿
faith, hope, love, and joy unceasing,
till our hearts are wholly thine.

3 O that we, thy truth confessing
and thy holy word possessing,
Jesu, may thy love adore;
unto thee our voices raising,
thee with all thy ransomed praising
ever and for evermore.

R. Campbell (1814–68) and others
based on Adam of St. Victor (12th century)

301 (AMR 510) FIRST TUNE

Venice S.M. W. Amps (1824–191

SECOND TUNE

St. Thomas S.M. Aaron Williams (1731–7

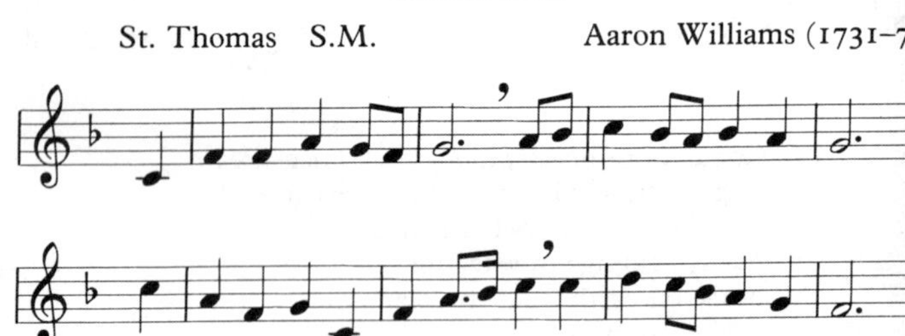

How beauteous are their feet,
who stand on Sion's hill,
who bring salvation on their tongues
and words of peace instil.

2

How happy are our ears
that hear this happy sound,
which kings and prophets waited for,
and sought, but never found.

3

How blessèd are our eyes
that see this heavenly light.
prophets and kings desired it long,
but died without the sight.

4

The Lord makes bare his arm
through all the earth abroad:
let every nation now behold
their Saviour and their God.

ISAAC WATTS (1674–1748)
Matthew 13. 16–17

302 (AMR 524)

Orientis Partibus 7 7.7 7. Office of P. de Corb
(d. 12

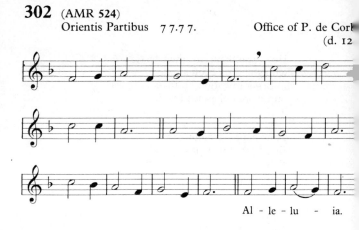

Al - le - lu - ia.

Version in AMR

Any Saint

Soldiers, who are Christ's below,
strong in faith resist the foe:
boundless is the pledged reward
unto them who serve the Lord.

2

'Tis no palm of fading leaves
that the conqueror's hand receives;
joys are his, serene and pure,
light that ever shall endure.

3

For the souls that overcome
waits the beauteous heavenly home,
where the blessèd evermore
tread on high the starry floor.

4

Passing soon and little worth
are the things that tempt on earth;
heavenward lift thy soul's regard:
God himself is thy reward.

5

Father, who the crown dost give,
Saviour, by whose death we live,
Spirit, who our hearts dost raise,
Three in One, thy name we praise.

Latin, 18th cent.
tr. J. H. Clark (1839–88)

303 (AMR 525) FIRST TUNE

Deus Tuorum Militum L.M. *Grenoble Antiphoner*, 175
(Grenoble)

SECOND TUNE

Whitehall (Sandys' Psalm 8) Henry Lawes
L.M. (1596–1662)

Any Saint

Lo, round the throne, a glorious band,
the saints in countless myriads stand,
of every tongue redeemed to God,
arrayed in garments washed in blood.

2

Through tribulation great they came;
they bore the cross, despised the shame;
from all their labours now they rest,
in God's eternal glory blest.

3

They see their Saviour face to face,
and sing the triumphs of his grace;
him day and night they ceaseless praise,
to him the loud thanksgiving raise:

4

'Worthy the Lamb, for sinners slain,
through endless years to live and reign;
thou hast redeemed us by thy blood,
and made us kings and priests to God.'

5

O may we tread the sacred road
that saints and holy martyrs trod;
wage to the end the glorious strife,
and win, like them, a crown of life.

ROWLAND HILL (1744–1833)
and others

304 (AMR 526)

Deerhurst 8 7.8 7. D. J. Langran (1835–190

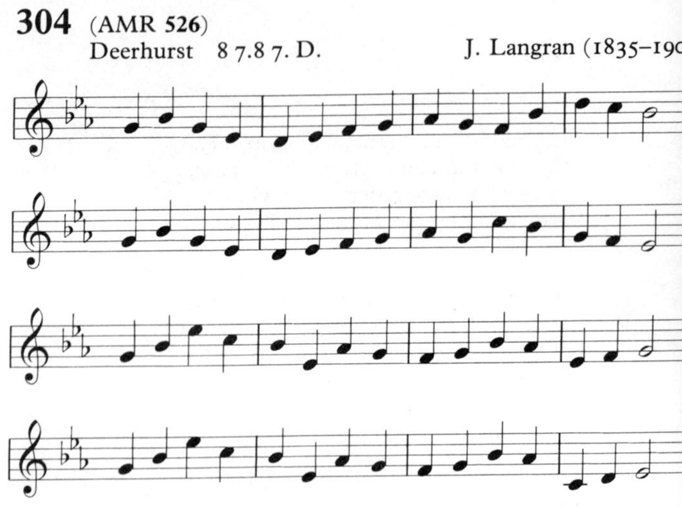

Hark! the sound of holy voices,
chanting at the crystal sea
Alleluia, Alleluia,
Alleluia, Lord, to thee:
multitude, which none can number,
like the stars in glory stands,
clothed in white apparel, holding‿
palms of victory in their hands.

*2

Patriarch, and holy prophet,
who prepared the way of Christ,
king, apostle, saint, confessor,
martyr, and evangelist,
saintly maiden, godly matron,
widows who have watched to prayer,
joined in holy concert, singing‿
to the Lord of all, are there.

*3

They have come from tribulation,
and have washed their robes in blood,
washed them in the blood of Jesus;
tried they were, and firm they stood:
mocked, imprisoned, stoned, tormented,
sawn asunder, slain with sword,
they have conquered death and Satan
by the might of Christ the Lord.

4

Marching with thy cross their banner,
they have triumphed following‿
thee, the Captain of Salvation,
thee their Saviour and their King:
gladly, Lord, with thee they suffered;
gladly, Lord, with thee they died,
and by death to life immortal
they were born, and glorified.

5

Now they reign in heavenly glory,
now they walk in golden light,
now they drink, as from a river,
holy bliss and infinite;
love and peace they taste for ever,
and all truth and knowledge see
in the beatific vision
of the blessèd Trinity.

6

God of God, the One-begotten,
Light of Light, Emmanuel,
in whose Body joined together
all the saints for ever dwell,
pour upon us of thy fulness,
that we may for evermore
God the Father, God the Son, and‿
God the Holy Ghost adore.

Christopher Wordsworth (1807–85)

305 (AMR 527)

Sine Nomine 10 10.10 4. R. Vaughan William[s] (1872–195[8])

For all the saints who from their labours rest,
who thee by faith before the world confessed,
thy name, O Jesu, be for ever blest.
Alleluia.

2

Thou wast their rock, their fortress, and their might;
thou, Lord, their Captain in the well-fought fight;
thou, in the darkness, still their one true Light.
Alleluia.

3

O may thy soldiers, faithful, true, and bold,
fight as the saints who nobly fought of old,
and win, with them, the victor's crown of gold.
Alleluia.

4

O blest communion, fellowship divine!
we feebly struggle, they in glory shine;
yet all are one in thee, for all are thine.
Alleluia.

5

And when the strife is fierce, the warfare long,
steals on the ear the distant triumph-song,
and hearts are brave again and arms are strong.
Alleluia.

6

The golden evening brightens in the west;
soon, soon to faithful warriors comes their rest:
sweet is the calm of Paradise the blest.
Alleluia.

7

But lo, there breaks a yet more glorious day;
the saints triumphant rise in bright array:
the King of Glory passes on his way.
Alleluia.

8

From earth's wide bounds, from ocean's farthest coast,
through gates of pearl streams in the countless host,
singing to Father, Son, and Holy Ghost
Alleluia.

W. Walsham How (1823–97)

306 (AMR 528) FIRST TUNE

Sennen Cove C.M. William H. Harris (1883–197

SECOND TUNE

Stracathro C.M. C. Hutcheson (1792–186

The business and blessedness of glorified saints

How bright these glorious spirits shine!
whence all their white array?
How came they to the blissful seats
of everlasting day?

2

Lo, these are they from sufferings great
who came to realms of light;
and in the blood of Christ have washed‿
those robes that shine so bright.

3

Now with triumphal palms they stand
  before the throne on high,
and serve the God they love amidst‿
  the glories of the sky.

4

Hunger and thirst are felt no more,
  nor suns with scorching ray;
God is their sun, whose cheering beams
  diffuse eternal day.

5

The Lamb, which dwells amidst the throne,
  shall o'er them still preside,
feed them with nourishment divine,
  and all their footsteps guide.

6

Midst pastures green he'll lead his flock,
  where living streams appear;
and God the Lord from every eye
  shall wipe off every tear.

*7

To Father, Son, and Holy Ghost,
  the God whom we adore,
be glory, as it was, is now,
  and shall be evermore.

Isaac Watts (1674–1748) and others
Revelation 7. 13–17

307 (AMR 530)

Palms of Glory 77.77. W. D. Maclagan (1826–1910)

Palms of glory, raiment bright,
crowns that never fade away,
gird and deck the saints in light:
priests and kings and conquerors they.

2

Yet the conquerors bring their palms
to the Lamb amidst the throne,
and proclaim in joyful psalms
victory through his Cross alone.

3

Kings for harps their crowns resign,
crying, as they strike the chords,
'Take the kingdom, it is thine,
King of kings and Lord of lords.'

4

Round the altar priests confess,
if their robes are white as snow,
'twas the Saviour's righteousness,
and his blood, that made them so.

5

They were mortal too like us:
O, when we like them must die,
may our souls translated thus
triumph, reign, and shine on high.

JAMES MONTGOMERY (1771–1854)

308 (AMR 531)
Mount Ephraim S.M. B. Milgrove (1731–1810)

1 For all thy saints, O Lord,
who strove in thee to live,
who followed thee, obeyed, adored,
our grateful hymn receive.

2 For all thy saints, O Lord,
who strove in thee to die,
and found in thee a full reward,
accept our thankful cry.

3 Thine earthly members fit
to join thy saints above,
in one communion ever knit,
one fellowship of love.

4 Jesu, thy name we bless,
and humbly pray that we‿
may follow them in holiness,
who lived and died for thee.

5 All might, all praise, be thine,
Father, co-equal Son,
and Spirit, bond of love divine,
while endless ages run.

RICHARD MANT (1776–1848)

309 (AMR 512)
Puer Nobis Nascitur L.M. M. Praetorius (1571–162

Alternative Tunes: *Wareham* (296), *Warrington* (89)

The God whom earth and sea and sky‿
adore and laud and magnify,
whose might they own, whose praise they tell,
in Mary's body deigned to dwell.

2

O Mother blest, the chosen shrine‿
wherein the Architect divine,
whose hand contains the earth and sky,
vouchsafed in hidden guise to lie:

3

blest in the message Gabriel brought;
blest in the work the Spirit wrought;
most blest, to bring to human birth
the long Desired of all the earth.

4

O Lord, the Virgin-born, to thee
eternal praise and glory be,
whom with the Father we adore
and Holy Ghost for evermore.

VENANTIUS FORTUNATUS (c. 530–c. 600)
tr. J. M. NEALE* (1818–66)

310 (AMR **513**)
Farley Castle 10 10.10 10. Henry Lawes (1596–1662

The Blessed Virgin Mary

Her Virgin eyes saw God incarnate born,
when she to Bethlem came that happy morn:
how high her raptures then began to swell,
none but her own omniscient Son can tell.

2

As Eve, when she her fontal sin reviewed,
wept for herself and all she should include,
blest Mary, with man's Saviour in embrace,
joyed for herself and for all human race.

3

All saints are by her Son's dear influence blest;
she kept the very fountain at her breast:
the Son adored and nursed by the sweet Maid
a thousandfold of love for love repaid.

4

Heaven with transcendent joys her entrance graced,
near to his throne her Son his Mother placed;
and here below, now she's of heaven possest,
all generations are to call her blest.

THOMAS KEN (1637–1711)

311 (AMR 514)

Quem pastores 8 8 8.7. German Medieval Melody

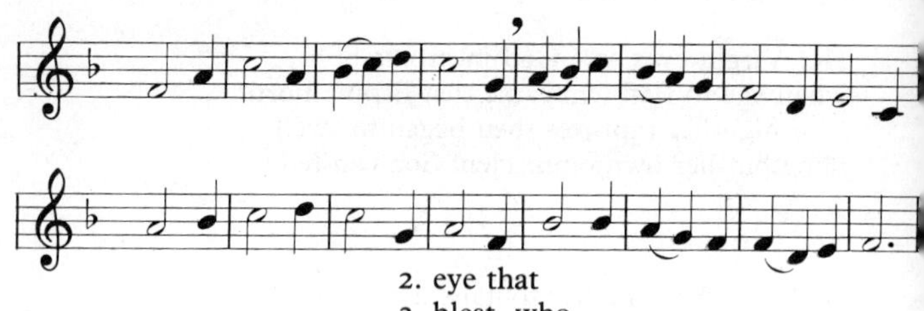

Virgin-born, we bow before thee:
blessèd was the womb that bore thee;
Mary, maid and mother mild,
blessèd was she in her child.

2

Blessèd was the breast that fed thee;
blessèd was the hand that led thee;
blessèd was the parent's eye
that watched thy slumbering infancy.

3

Blessèd she by all creation,
who brought forth the world's Salvation;
blessèd they, for ever blest,
who love thee most and serve thee best.

4

Virgin-born, we bow before thee:
blessèd was the womb that bore thee;
Mary, maid and mother mild,
blessèd was she in her child.

Reginald Heber (1783–1826)

12 (AMR 533)
St. Andrew 8 7.8 7. E. H. Thorne (1834–1916)

Alternative Tune: *Merton* (24)

Jesus calls us: o'er the tumult‿
of our life's wild restless sea
day by day his sweet voice soundeth,
saying, 'Christian, follow me;'

2

as of old Saint Andrew heard it
by the Galilean lake,
turned from home and toil and kindred,
leaving all for his dear sake.

3

Jesus calls us from the worship‿
of the vain world's golden store,
from each idol that would keep us,
saying, 'Christian, love me more.'

4

In our joys and in our sorrows,
days of toil and hours of ease,
still he calls, in cares and pleasures,
that we love him more than these.

5

Jesus calls us: by thy mercies,
Saviour, make us hear thy call,
give our hearts to thine obedience,
serve and love thee best of all.

CECIL FRANCES ALEXANDER (1818–95)

313 (AMR 541)

Ellacombe 7 6.7 6. D. *Württemberg Gesangbuch*, 1784

Conversion of St. Paul

We sing the glorious conquest
  before Damascus' gate,
when Saul, the Church's spoiler,
  came breathing threats and hate;
the ravening wolf rushed forward
  full early to the prey;
but lo, the Shepherd met him,
  and bound him fast to-day.

*2

O glory most excelling
  that smote across his path!
O light that pierced and blinded
  the zealot in his wrath!
O voice that spake within him
  the calm reproving word!
O love that sought and held him
  the bondman of his Lord!

3

O Wisdom, ordering all things
  in order strong and sweet,
what nobler spoil was ever
  cast at the Victor's feet?
what wiser master-builder
  e'er wrought at thine employ
than he, till now so furious
  thy building to destroy?

4

Lord, teach thy Church the lesson,
  still in her darkest hour
of weakness and of danger
  to trust thy hidden power:
thy grace by ways mysterious
  the wrath of man can bind,
and in thy boldest foeman
  thy chosen saint can find.

JOHN ELLERTON (1826–93)

314 (AMR **544**)
Old 120th 6 6.6 6.6 6. *Psalms*, 157

Hail to the Lord who comes,
comes to his temple gate,
not with his angel host,
not in his kingly state:
no shouts proclaim him nigh,
no crowds his coming wait.

2

But borne upon the throne‿
of Mary's gentle breast,
watched by her duteous love,
in her fond arms at rest;
thus to his Father's house
he comes, the heavenly guest.

3

There Joseph at her side
in reverent wonder stands;
and, filled with holy joy,
old Simeon in his hands
takes up the promised Child,
the glory of all lands.

*4

Hail to the great First-born,
whose ransom-price they pay,
the Son before all worlds,
the Child of man to-day,
that he might ransom us
who still in bondage lay.

5

O Light of all the earth,
thy children wait for thee:
come to thy temples here,
that we, from sin set free,
before thy Father's face
may all presented be.

JOHN ELLERTON (1826–93)

15 (AMR 551)
Lobet den Herren 11 11 11.5. J. Crüger (1598–1662)

Sing we the praises of the great forerunner,
tell forth the mighty wonders of his story:
so may his Master cleanse our lips and make them
fit to extol him.

2

Lo, God's high herald, swift from heaven descending,
gives to thy father tidings of thy coming,
telling thy name and all the tale of marvels
that shall befall thee.

3

Oft had the prophets in the time before thee
spoken in vision of the Daystar's coming;
but when he came, 'twas thou that didst proclaim him
Saviour of all men.

PAUL THE DEACON (730–99)
tr. C. S. PHILLIPS (1883–1949)

The descant may be sung for verse 5

St. John the Baptist

Lo, from the desert homes,
  where he hath hid so long,
the new Elijah comes,
  in sternest wisdom strong:
    the voice that cries
      of Christ from high,
      and judgement nigh
    from opening skies.

2

our God e'en now doth stand
at heaven's opening door;
s fan is in his hand,
  and he will purge his floor;
    the wheat he claims
      and with him stows,
      the chaff he throws
    to quenchless flames.

3

Ye haughty mountains, bow‿
  your sky-aspiring heads;
ye valleys, hiding low,
  lift up your gentle meads;
    make his way plain
      your King before,
      for evermore
    he comes to reign.

*4

May thy dread voice around,
  thou harbinger of Light,
on our dull ears still sound,
  lest here we sleep in night,
    till judgement come,
      and on our path
      the Lamb's dread wrath
    shall burst in doom.

5

O God, with love's sweet might,
  who dost anoint and arm‿
Christ's soldier for the fight
  with grace that shields from harm:
    thrice blessèd Three,
      heaven's endless days
      shall sing thy praise
    eternally.

C. Coffin (1676–1749)
tr. Isaac Williams (1802–65)

317 (AMR 555)

Love Unknown 6 6.6 6.8 8. John Ireland (1879–196

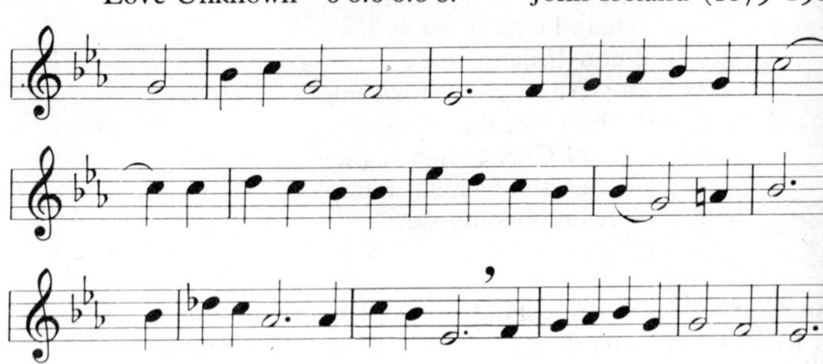

1 'Thou art the Christ, O Lord,
the Son of God most high:'
for ever be adored
that name in earth and sky,
in which, though mortal strength may fail,
the saints of God at last prevail.

2 O surely he was blest
with blessedness unpriced,
who, taught of God, confessed
the Godhead in the Christ;
for of thy Church, Lord, thou didst own
thy saint a true foundation-stone.

3 Thrice fallen, thrice restored,
the bitter lesson learnt,
that heart for thee, O Lord,
with triple ardour burnt.
The cross he took he laid not down
until he grasped the martyr's crown.

4 O bright triumphant faith,
O courage void of fears,
O love most strong in death,
O penitential tears!
By these, Lord, keep us lest we fall,
and make us go where thou shalt call.

W. Walsham How (1823–97

18 (AMR **560**)
Carlisle S.M. C. Lockhart (1745–1815)

'Tis good, Lord, to be here,
thy glory fills the night;
thy face and garments, like the sun,
shine with unborrowed light.

2

'Tis good, Lord, to be here,
thy beauty to behold,
where Moses and Elijah stand,
thy messengers of old.

3

Fulfiller of the past,
promise of things to be,
we hail thy body glorified,
and our redemption see.

4

Before we taste of death,
we see thy kingdom come;
we fain would hold the vision bright,
and make this hill our home.

5

'Tis good, Lord, to be here,
yet we may not remain;
but since thou bidst us leave the mount,
come with us to the plain.

J. Armitage Robinson (1858–1933)

319 (AMR 288)

Trisagion 10 10.10 10. Henry Smart (1813–

1 Stars of the morning, so gloriously bright,
filled with celestial virtue and light,
these that, where night never followeth day,
praise the Thrice-Holy for ever and ay:

2 these are thy ministers, these dost thou own,
Lord God of Sabaoth, nearest thy throne;
these are thy messengers, these dost thou send,
help of the helpless ones, man to defend.

*3 These keep the guard amidst Salem's dear bowers,
Thrones, Principalities, Virtues, and Powers,
where, with the Living Ones, mystical four,
cherubim, seraphim, bow and adore.

4 Then, when the earth was first poised in mid space,
then, when the planets first sped on their race,
then, when was ended the six days' employ,
then all the sons of God shouted for joy.

5 Still let them succour us; still let them fight,
Lord of angelic hosts, battling for right;
till, where their anthems they ceaselessly pour,
we with the angels may bow and adore.

St. Joseph the Hymnographer (d. 883)
par. J. M. Neale* (1818–66)

20 (AMR **448**)
Solothurn L.M. Swiss Traditional Melody

Around the throne of God a band
of glorious angels ever stand;
bright things they see, sweet harps they hold,
and on their heads are crowns of gold.

2

Some wait around him, ready still
to sing his praise and do his will;
and some, when he commands them, go
to guard his servants here below.

3

Lord, give thy angels every day
command to guide us on our way,
and bid them every evening keep
their watch around us while we sleep.

4

So shall no wicked thing draw near,
to do us harm or cause us fear;
and we shall dwell, when life is past,
with angels round thy throne at last.

J. M. Neale (1818–66)

321 (AMR **564**)
Coelites Plaudant 11 11 11.5. *Rouen Antiphoner*, 17
(Rouen)

1 Christ, the fair glory of the holy angels,
ruler of all men, author of creation,
grant us in mercy grace to win by patience
joys everlasting.

2 Send thine archangel Michael from thy presence:
peacemaker blessèd, may he hover o'er us,
hallow our dwellings, that for us thy children
all things may prosper.

3 Send thine archangel, Gabriel the mighty:
on strong wings flying, may he come from heaven,
drive from thy temple Satan the old foeman,
succour our weakness.

4 Send thine archangel, Raphael the healer:
through him with wholesome med'cines of salvation
heal our backsliding, and in paths of goodness
guide our steps daily.

5 Father almighty, Son, and Holy Spirit,
Godhead eternal, grant us our petition;
thine be the glory through the whole creation
now and for ever.

Ascribed to RABANUS MAURUS (776–856
tr. C. S. PHILLIPS (1883–1949

322 (AMR **569**)
St. Alphege 7 6.7 6. H. J. Gauntlett (1805–76)

1

O heavenly Jerusalem
of everlasting halls,
thrice blessèd are the people
thou storest in thy walls.

2

Thou art the golden mansion
where saints for ever sing,
the seat of God's own chosen,
the palace of the King.

3

There God for ever sitteth,
himself of all the crown:
the Lamb, the light that shineth
and never goeth down.

4

Naught to this seat approacheth
their sweet peace to molest;
they sing their God for ever,
nor day nor night they rest.

5

Sure hope doth thither lead us;
our longings thither tend:
may short-lived toil ne'er daunt us
for joys that cannot end.

6

To Christ the sun that lightens
his Church above, below,
to Father, and to Spirit,
all things created bow.

Latin, 18th cent.
tr. Isaac Williams (1802–65)

323 (AMR 570)
All Saints
8 7.8 7.7 7.

from *Geistreiches Gesangbuch*
(Darmstadt, 1698
adapted by W. H. Monk (1823–89

Who are these like stars appearing,
these, before God's throne who stand?
each a golden crown is wearing:
who are all this glorious band?
Alleluia, hark, they sing,
praising loud their heavenly King.

*2

Who are these in dazzling brightness,
clothed in God's own righteousness,
these, whose robes of purest whiteness
shall their lustre still possess,
still untouched by time's rude hand?
whence came all this glorious band?

3

These are they who have contended
  for their Saviour's honour long,
wrestling on till life was ended,
  following not the sinful throng;
    these, who well the fight sustained,
    triumph by the Lamb have gained.

*4

These are they whose hearts were riven,
  sore with woe and anguish tried,
who in prayer full oft have striven
  with the God they glorified;
    now, their painful conflict o'er,
    God has bid them weep no more.

5

These, the Almighty contemplating,
  did as priests before him stand,
soul and body always waiting
  day and night at his command:
    now in God's most holy place
    blest they stand before his face.

H. T. SCHENCK (1656–1727)
tr. FRANCES E. COX (1812–97)

324 (AMR 571) FIRST TUNE

Song 67 C.M. E. Prys, *Psalms*, 16

SECOND TUNE

San Rocco C.M. Derek Williams (b. 194

In key C at 493

The Examples of Christ and the Saints

Give us the wings of faith to rise‿
within the veil, and see‿
the saints above, how great their joys,
how bright their glories be.

2

Once they were mourning here below,
their couch was wet with tears;
they wrestled hard, as we do now,
with sins and doubts and fears.

3

We ask them whence their victory came:
they, with united breath,
ascribe the conquest to the Lamb,
their triumph to his death.

4

They marked the footsteps that he trod,
his zeal inspired their breast,
and, following their incarnate God,
they reached the promised rest.

5

Our glorious Leader claims our praise
for his own pattern given;
while the great cloud of witnesses
show the same path to heaven.

ISAAC WATTS* (1674–1748)

325 (AMR **591**)

Corde natus 8 7.8 7.8 7. 7.
(Divinum Mysterium)

Later form c
Plainsong Melody as i
Piae Cantiones (Nyland, 158

The AMR setting is in E at 33

1

Of the Father's love begotten
 ere the worlds began to be,
he is Alpha and Omega,
 he the source, the ending he,
of the things that are, that have been,
 and that future years shall see,
 evermore and evermore.

*2

At his word they were created;
 he commanded; it was done:
heaven and earth and depths of ocean
 in their threefold order one;
all that grows beneath the shining
 of the light of moon and sun,
 evermore and evermore.

3

O that birth for ever blessèd
 when the Virgin, full of grac
by the Holy Ghost conceiving,
 bare the Saviour of our race,
and the Babe, the world's Rede
 first revealed his sacred face,
 evermore and evermore.

4

O ye heights of heaven, adore
 angel-hosts, his praises sing;
powers, dominions, bow before
 and extol our God and King
let no tongue on earth be silen
 every voice in concert ring,
 evermore and evermore.

5

This is he whom seers and sages
sang of old with one accord;
whom the writings of the prophets
promised in their faithful word;
now he shines, the long-expected:
let creation praise its Lord,
evermore and evermore.

*6

Hail, thou Judge of souls departed!
hail, thou King of them that live!
on the Father's throne exalted
none in might with thee may strive;
who at last in judgement coming
sinners from thy face shalt drive,
evermore and evermore.

*7

Now let old and young men's voices
join with boys' thy name to sing,
matrons, virgins, little maidens
in glad chorus answering;
let their guileless songs re-echo,
and the heart its praises bring,
evermore and evermore.

8

Christ, to thee, with God the Father,
and, O Holy Ghost, to thee,
hymn and chant and high thanksgiving
and unwearied praises be,
honour, glory, and dominion,
and eternal victory,
evermore and evermore.

PRUDENTIUS (348–c. 413) tr. J. M. NEALE (1818–66)
H. W. BAKER (1821–77) and others

326 (AMR 593)
Adeste Fideles Irregular
Probably
J. F. Wade (c. 1711–8
1 O come, all ye faith-ful, joy - ful and tri - um-phant, O
2 God of God, Light of Light,
3 See how the shep-herds sum-moned to his cra - dle,
4 Lo, star-led chief-tains, ma - gi, Christ a - dor - ing,
come ye, O come ye to Beth - le - hem;
lo, he ab - hors not the Vir - gin's womb;
leav - ing their flocks, draw nigh to gaze;
of - fer him in - cense, gold, and myrrh;
come and be - hold him born, the King of an-gels:
ve - ry God, be - got - ten, not cre - a - ted: O
we too will thi - ther bend our joy - ful foot-steps:
we to the Christ-child bring our hearts' ob - la - tions:
come, let us a - dore him, O come, let us a - dore him, O
come, let us a - dore him, Christ the Lord.
DESCANT
7 Yea, Lord; we greet thee, born this hap-py morn-ing;
5 Child, for us sin - ners poor and in the man-ger,
6 Sing, choirs of an - gels, sing in ex - ul - ta - tion,
7 Yea, Lord, we greet thee, born this hap-py morn-ing;

Je - su, to thee be glo - ry given;
fain we em - brace thee with love and awe;
sing, all ye ci - ti - zens of heaven a - bove:
Je - su, to thee be glo - ry given:
Word of the Fa - ther, now in flesh ap - pear - ing: O
who would not love thee, lov - ing us so dear - ly?
'Glo - ry to God in the high - est:' O
Word of the Fa - ther, now in flesh ap - pear - ing:
come, O come, O
come, let us a - dore him, O come, let us a - dore him, O
come, let us a - dore him, Christ the Lord!
come, let us a - dore him, Christ the Lord.

Latin, 18th cent. tr. F. Oakeley (1802–80)
W. T. Brooke (1848–1917) and others

327 (AMR 595)

Evelyns 6 5.6 5. D. W. H. Monk (1823–89)

This tune is in a higher key at 148

1 From the eastern mountains
   pressing on they come,
wise men in their wisdom,
   to his humble home;
stirred by deep devotion,
   hasting from afar,
ever journeying onward,
   guided by a star.

2 There their Lord and Saviour
   meek and lowly lay,
wondrous light that led them
   onward on their way,
ever now to lighten
   nations from afar,
as they journey homeward
   by that guiding star.

3 Thou who in a manger
  once hast lowly lain,
who dost now in glory
  o'er all kingdoms reign,
gather in the peoples,
  who in lands afar
ne'er have seen the brightness
  of thy guiding star.

*4 Gather in the outcasts,
  all who've gone astray;
throw thy radiance o'er them,
  guide them on their way:
those who never knew thee,
  those who've wandered far,
guide them by the brightness
  of thy guiding star.

5 Onward through the darkness
  of the lonely night,
shining still before them
  with thy kindly light,
guide them, Jew and Gentile,
  homeward from afar,
young and old together,
  by thy guiding star.

*6 Until every nation,
  whether bond or free,
'neath thy star-lit banner,
  Jesu, follow thee
o'er the distant mountains
  to that heavenly home,
where nor sin nor sorrow
  evermore shall come.

GODFREY THRING (1823–1903)

In verse 3, line 5, AMR has 'heathen'

328 (AMR 597)
St. Theodulph 7 6.7 6. D. M. Teschner (16

Fi

D.C

ANOTHER VERSION

arr. J. S. Bach (1685–1750

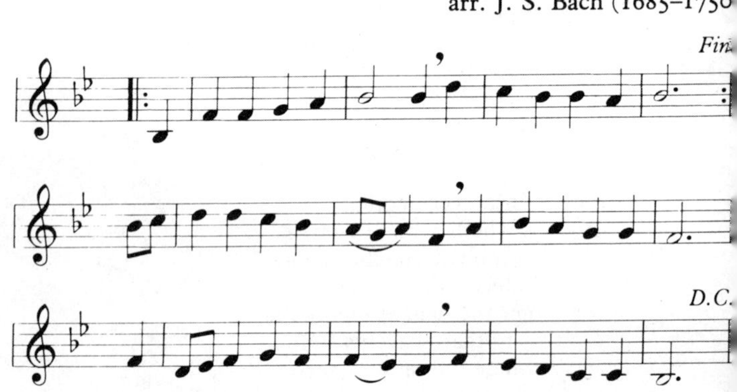

Palm Sunday

1

glory, laud, and honour
thee, Redeemer, King,
whom the lips of children
made sweet hosannas ring.

2

ou art the King of Israel,
hou David's royal Son,
o in the Lord's name comest,
he King and blessèd one:

3

e company of angels
re praising thee on high,
l mortal men and all things‿
created make reply:

4

e people of the Hebrews
with palms before thee went:
r praise and prayer and anthems
before thee we present:

5

To thee before thy passion
 they sang their hymns of praise:
to thee now high exalted
 our melody we raise:

6

Thou didst accept their praises,
 accept the prayers we bring,
who in all good delightest,
 thou good and gracious King:

7

Thy sorrow and thy triumph
 grant us, O Christ, to share,
that to the holy city
 together we may fare:

8

For homage may we bring thee
 our victory o'er the foe,
that in the Conqueror's triumph
 this strain may ever flow:

9

All glory, laud, and honour
to thee, Redeemer, King,
to whom the lips of children
made sweet hosannas ring.

THEODULPH OF ORLEANS (d. 821)
tr. J. M. NEALE (1818–66)

329 (AMR **602**)

Lasst uns erfreuen
(Easter Song)
8 8.4 4.8 8. and Alleluias

Melody adapted fro
Geistliche Kirchengesang (Cologne, 162
arr. R. Vaughan Williar
(1872–195

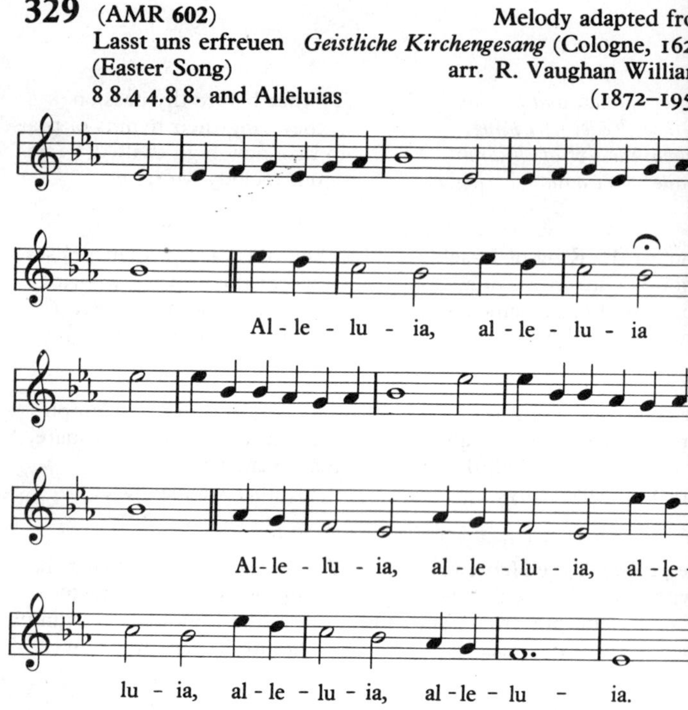
Al - le - lu - ia, al - le - lu - ia
Al- le - lu - ia, al - le - lu - ia, al - le -
lu - ia, al - le - lu - ia, al - le - lu - ia.

The AMR version of this tune is at 98

Light's glittering morn bedecks the sky;
heaven thunders forth its victor-cry:
Alleluia.
The glad earth shouts her triumph high,
and groaning hell makes wild reply:
Alleluia.

2

While he, the King, the mighty King,
despoiling death of all its sting,
and trampling down the powers of night,
brings forth his ransomed saints to light:

3

His tomb of late the threefold guard‿
of watch and stone and seal had barred;
but now, in pomp and triumph high,
he comes from death to victory:

4

The pains of hell are loosed at last,
the days of mourning now are past;
an angel robed in light hath said,
'The Lord is risen from the dead:'

PART TWO

5

O bitter the apostles' pain
for their dear Lord so lately slain,
by rebel servants doomed to die
a death of cruel agony:

6

With gentle voice the angel gave‿
the women tidings at the grave:
'Fear not, your Master shall ye see;
he goes before to Galilee:'

7

Then, hastening on their eager way
the joyful tidings to convey,
their Lord they met, their living Lord,
and falling at his feet adored:

8

His faithful followers with speed
to Galilee forthwith proceed,
that there once more they may behold
the Lord's dear face, as he foretold:

Continued over page

329 (AMR **602**) *contd.*

Al - le - lu - ia, al - le - lu - ia
Al - le - lu - ia, al - le - lu - ia, al - le -
lu - ia, al - le - lu - ia, al - le - lu - ia.

PART THREE

9

That Eastertide with joy was bright,
the sun shone out with fairer light,
when, to their longing eyes restored,
the glad apostles saw their Lord:

10

He bade them see his hands, his side,
where yet the glorious wounds abide;
the tokens true which made it plain
their Lord indeed was risen again:

11

Jesu, the King of gentleness,
do thou thyself our hearts possess,
that we may give thee all our days
the tribute of our grateful praise:

This Doxology may be sung at the end of any part, or of the whole hymn

12

O Lord of all, with us abide
in this our joyful Eastertide;
from every weapon death can wield
thine own redeemed for ever shield:

13

All praise be thine, O risen Lord,
from death to endless life restored;
all praise to God the Father be
and Holy Ghost eternally:

Latin, tr. J. M. NEALE* (1818–66)

330 (AMR **606**)
Croft's 136th 6 6.6 6.4 4.4 4. William Croft (1678–1727)

To thee our God we fly
  for mercy and for grace;
O hear our lowly cry,
  and hide not thou thy face.
O Lord, stretch forth thy mighty hand,
and guard and bless our fatherland.

2

Arise, O Lord of Hosts,
  be jealous for thy name,
and drive from out our coasts
  the sins that put to shame:

3

Thy best gifts from on high
  in rich abundance pour,
that we may magnify
  and praise thee more and more:

4

The powers ordained by thee
with heavenly wisdom bless;
may they thy servants be,
and rule in righteousness:

5

The Church of thy dear Son
inflame with love's pure fire,
bind her once more in one,
and life and truth inspire:

*6

The pastors of thy fold
with grace and power endue,
that faithful, pure, and bold,
they may be pastors true:

7

O let us love thy house,
and sanctify thy day,
bring unto thee our vows,
and loyal homage pay:

8

Give peace, Lord, in our time;
O let no foe draw nigh,
nor lawless deed of crime
insult thy majesty:

*9

Though vile and worthless, still‿
thy people, Lord, are we;
and for our God we will‿
none other have but thee.
O Lord, stretch forth thy mighty hand,
and guard and bless our fatherland.

W. Walsham How (1823–97)

331 (AMR **631**)
Leoni 6 6.8 4. D. Traditional Hebrew Melody

The God of Abraham praise
who reigns enthroned above,
Ancient of everlasting Days,
and God of love:
Jehovah, great I AM,
by earth and heaven confest;
we bow and bless the sacred name
for ever blest.

*2

The God of Abraham praise,
at whose supreme command
from earth we rise, and seek the joys
at his right hand:
we all on earth forsake,
its wisdom, fame, and power;
and him our only portion make,
our shield and tower.

3

Though nature's strength decay,
and earth and hell withstand,
to Canaan's bounds we urge our way
at his command
the watery deep we pass,
with Jesus in our view;
and through the howling wilderness
our way pursue.

4

The goodly land we see,
with peace and plenty blest:
a land of sacred liberty
and endless rest;
there milk and honey flow,
and oil and wine abound,
and trees of life for ever grow,
with mercy crowned.

5

There dwells the Lord our King,
the Lord our Righteousness,
triumphant o'er the world of sin,
the Prince of peace:
on Sion's sacred height
his kingdom he maintains,
and glorious with his saints in light
for ever reigns.

Continued over page

331 (AMR **631**) *contd.*

*6

He keeps his own secure,
he guards them by his side,
arrays in garment white and pure
his spotless Bride:
with streams of sacred bliss,
beneath serener skies,
with all the fruits of Paradise,
he still supplies.

*7

Before the great Three-One
they all exulting stand,
and tell the wonders he hath done
through all their land:
the listening spheres attend,
and swell the growing fame,
and sing in songs which never end
the wondrous name.

*8

The God who reigns on high
the great archangels sing,
and 'Holy, Holy, Holy,' cry,
'almighty King,
who was, and is the same,
and evermore shall be:
Jehovah, Father, great I AM,
we worship thee.'

9

Before the Saviour's face
the ransomed nations bow,
o'erwhelmed at his almighty grace
for ever new;
he shows his prints of love –
they kindle to a flame,
and sound through all the worlds above
the slaughtered Lamb.

10

The whole triumphant host
give thanks to God on high;
hail, Father, Son, and Holy Ghost,
they ever cry:
hail, Abraham's God, and mine,
(I join the heavenly lays)
all might and majesty are thine,
and endless praise.

THOMAS OLIVERS (1725–99)
based on the Hebrew *Yigdal*

332 (AMR **620**)
Westminster Abbey
8 7.8 7.8 7.

Adapted from an anthem
Henry Purcell (*c.* 1659–169

Alternative Tune: *Oriel* (121)

PART ONE

Blessèd city, heavenly Salem,
vision dear of peace and love,
who of living stones art builded
in the height of heaven above,
and, with angel hosts encircled,
as a bride dost earthward move.

2

From celestial realms descending,
bridal glory round thee shed,
meet for him whose love espoused thee,
to thy Lord shalt thou be led;
all thy streets and all thy bulwarks
of pure gold are fashionèd.

3

Bright thy gates of pearl are shining,
they are open evermore;
and by virtue of his merits
thither faithful souls do soar,
who for Christ's dear name in this world
pain and tribulation bore.

4

Many a blow and biting sculpture
  polished well those stones elect,
in their places now compacted
  by the heavenly Architect,
who therewith hath willed for ever
  that his palace should be decked.

PART TWO

5

rist is made the sure foundation,
Christ the head and corner-stone,
osen of the Lord, and precious,
binding all the Church in one,
ly Sion's help for ever,
and her confidence alone.

6

All that dedicated city,
  dearly loved of God on high,
in exultant jubilation
  pours perpetual melody,
God the One in Three adoring
  in glad hymns eternally.

PART THREE

7

this temple, where we call thee,
come, O Lord of Hosts, to-day;
th thy wonted loving-kindness
hear thy servants as they pray,
d thy fullest benediction
shed within its walls alway.

8

Here vouchsafe to all thy servants
  what they ask of thee to gain,
what they gain from thee for ever
  with the blessèd to retain,
and hereafter in thy glory
  evermore with thee to reign.

This Doxology may be sung at the end of any part, or of the whole hymn

9

Laud and honour to the Father,
  laud and honour to the Son,
laud and honour to the Spirit,
  ever Three, and ever One,
consubstantial, co-eternal,
  while unending ages run.

Latin, 7th–8th Cent.
tr. J. M. NEALE* (1818–66)

333 (AMR **629**)

St. Gertrude 6 5.6 5. Ter. Arthur Sullivan (1842–190

On-ward, Christ-ian sol - diers, march-ing as to_ war,
with the Cross of Je - sus go - ing on be - fore.

Onward, Christian soldiers,
marching as to war,
with the Cross of Jesus
going on before.
Christ the royal Master
leads against the foe;
forward into battle,
see, his banners go:
Onward, Christian soldiers,
marching as to war,
with the Cross of Jesus
going on before.

*2

At the sign of triumph
Satan's host doth flee;
on then, Christian soldiers,
on to victory.
Hell's foundations quiver
at the shout of praise;
brothers, lift your voices,
loud your anthems raise:

*3

ike a mighty army
moves the Church of God;
:others, we are treading
where the saints have trod:
'e are not divided,
all one body we,
ıe in hope and doctrine,
one in charity:

4

Crowns and thrones may perish,
kingdoms rise and wane,
but the Church of Jesus
constant will remain:
gates of hell can never
'gainst that Church prevail;
we have Christ's own promise,
and that cannot fail:

5

Onward, then, ye people,
join our happy throng,
blend with ours your voices
in the triumph song:
glory, laud, and honour
unto Christ the King,
this through countless ages
men and angels sing:
Onward, Christian soldiers,
marching as to war,
with the Cross of Jesus
going on before.

S. Baring-Gould (1834–1924)

New Standard Edition
Part Two

100 Hymns for Today	334–433
More Hymns for Today	434–533

Hymns in the following Supplements are arranged alphabetically.

In making choice, reference may be made to the Subject Index.

334 (HHT 1)

Tyrol D.C.M. Tyrolean Meloc

Lively

The Man for Others

A Man there lived in Galilee
  unlike all men before,
for he alone from first to last
  our flesh unsullied wore;
a perfect life of perfect deeds
  once to the world was shown,
that all mankind might mark his steps
  and in them plant their own.

2

A Man there died on Calvary
  above all others brave;
his fellow-men he saved and blessed,
  himself he scorned to save.
No thought can gauge the weight of woe
  on him, the sinless, laid;
we only know that with his blood
  our ransom price was paid.

3

A Man there reigns in glory now,
  divine, yet human still;
that human which is all divine
  death sought in vain to kill.
All power is his; supreme he rules‿
  the realms of time and space;
yet still our human cares and needs
  find in his heart a place.

S. C. Lowry* (1855–1932)

335 (HHT 2)

Surrey 8 8.8 8.8 8. Henry Carey (c. 1690–174

The Stranger

A stranger once did bless the earth
who never caused a heart to mourn,
whose very voice gave sorrow mirth;
and how did earth his worth return?
it spurned him from its lowliest lot:
the meanest station owned him not.

2

An outcast thrown in sorrow's way,
a fugitive that knew no sin,
yet in lone places forced to stray;
men would not take the stranger in.
Yet peace, though much himself he mourned,
was all to others he returned.

3

His presence was a peace to all,
  he bade the sorrowful rejoice.
Pain turned to pleasure at his call,
  health lived and issued from his voice;
he healed the sick, and sent abroad
the dumb rejoicing in the Lord.

4

The blind met daylight in his eye,
  the joys of everlasting day;
the sick found health in his reply,
  the cripple threw his crutch away.
Yet he with troubles did remain,
and suffered poverty and pain.

5

It was for sin he suffered all
  to set the world-imprisoned free,
to cheer the weary when they call;
  and who could such a stranger be?
The God, who hears each human cry,
and came, a Saviour, from on high.

JOHN CLARE* (1793–1864)

336 (HHT 3)
Michael 8 7.8 7.3 3 7. Herbert Howells (1892–1983

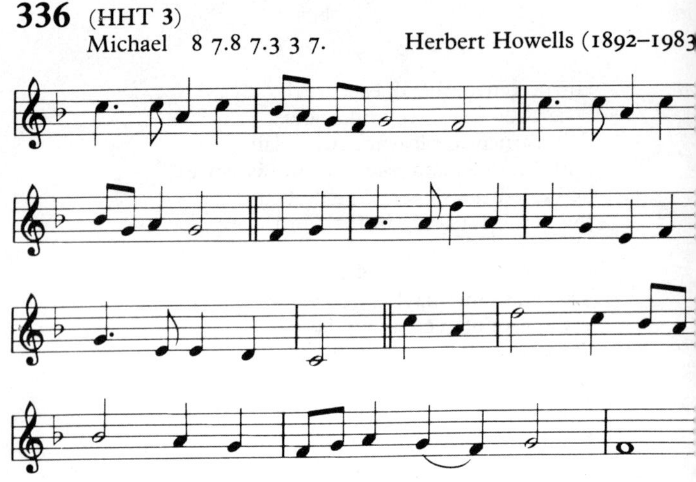

God our hope

All my hope on God is founded;
he doth still my trust renew.
Me through change and chance he guideth,
only good and only true.
God unknown,
he alone
calls my heart to be his own.

*2

Pride of man and earthly glory,
sword and crown betray his trust;
what with care and toil he buildeth,
tower and temple, fall to dust.
But God's power,
hour by hour,
is my temple and my tower.

3

God's great goodness aye endureth,
  deep his wisdom, passing thought:
splendour, light, and life attend him,
  beauty springeth out of naught.
      Evermore
      from his store
  new-born worlds rise and adore.

4

Daily doth th' Almighty giver
  bounteous gifts on us bestow;
his desire our soul delighteth,
  pleasure leads us where we go.
      Love doth stand‿
      at his hand;
  joy doth wait on his command.

5

Still from man to God eternal
  sacrifice of praise be done,
high above all praises praising
  for the gift of Christ his Son.
      Christ doth call‿
      one and all:
  ye who follow shall not fall.

ROBERT BRIDGES (1844–1930)
based on the German of J. NEANDER (1650–80)

337 (HHT 4)

Engelberg 10 10 10.4. C. V. Stanford (1852–1924)

verses 1–4
last verse
Al - - le - lu - ia.
Al - - le - lu - ia.

Alternative Tune: *Sine Nomine* (305)

Humility and glory

All praise to thee, for thou, O King divine,
didst yield the glory that of right was thine,
that in our darkened hearts thy grace might shine:
Alleluia.

2

Thou cam'st to us in lowliness of thought;
by thee the outcast and the poor were sought,
and by thy death was God's salvation wrought:
Alleluia.

3

Let this mind be in us which was in thee,
who wast a servant that we might be free,
humbling thyself to death on Calvary:
Alleluia.

4

Wherefore, by God's eternal purpose, thou
art high exalted o'er all creatures now,
and giv'n the name to which all knees shall bow:
Alleluia.

5

Let ev'ry tongue confess with one accord
in heav'n and earth that Jesus Christ is Lord;
and God the Father be by all adored:
Alleluia.

F. Bland Tucker (1895–1984)
based on Philippians 2. 5–11

338 (HHT 5)

Annue Christe 12 12.12 12. La Feillée, *Méthode*, 18c

The claims of love

Almighty Father, who for us thy Son didst give,
that men and nations through his precious death might live,
in mercy guard us, lest by sloth and selfish pride
we cause to stumble those for whom the Saviour died.

2

We are thy stewards; thine our talents, wisdom, skill;
our only glory that we may thy trust fulfil;
that we thy pleasure in our neighbours' good pursue,
if thou but workest in us both to will and do.

3

On just and unjust thou thy care dost freely shower;
make us, thy children, free from greed and lust for power,
lest human justice, yoked with man's unequal laws,
oppress the needy and neglect the humble cause.

4

Let not our worship blind us to the claims of love,
but let thy manna lead us to the feast above,
to seek the country which by faith we now possess,
where Christ, our treasure, reigns in peace and righteousness.

GEORGE B. CAIRD (1917–84)

339 (HHT **6**)

Kingsfold D.C.M. English Traditional Melod

The healing Christ

And didst thou travel light, dear Lord,
was thine so smooth a road
that thou upon thy shoulders broad
could hoist our heavy load?
too frail each other's woes to bear
without thy help are we;
can we each other's burdens share
if we not burden thee?

2

O wonder of the world withstood!
that night of prayer and doom
was not the sunset red with blood,
the dawn pale as a tomb?
in agony and bloody sweat,
in tears of love undried,
O undespairing Lord, and yet‿
with man identified.

3

As in dark drops the pitting rain‿
falls on a dusty street,
so tears shall fall and fall again
to wash thy wounded feet.
But thy quick hands to heal are strong,
O love, thy patients we,
who sing with joy the pilgrims' song
and walk, dear Lord, with thee.

GEOFFREY DEARMER (b. 1893)

340 (HHT 7)

Bridegroom 8 7.8 7.6. Peter Cutts (b. 1937

A & B may be sung by contrasted groups of voices

Belonging

As the bridegroom to his chosen,
  as the king unto his realm,
as the keep unto the castle,
  as the pilot to the helm,
so, Lord, art thou to me.

2

As the fountain in the garden,
  as the candle in the dark,
as the treasure in the coffer,
  as the manna in the ark,
so, Lord, art thou to me.

3

As the music at the banquet,
  as the stamp unto the seal,
as the medicine to the fainting,
  as the wine-cup at the meal,
so, Lord, art thou to me.

4

As the ruby in the setting,
  as the honey in the comb,
as the light within the lantern,
  as the father in the home,
so, Lord, art thou to me.

5

As the sunshine in the heavens,
  as the image in the glass,
as the fruit unto the fig-tree,
  as the dew unto the grass,
so, Lord, art thou to me.

Par. from (?) John Tauler (1300–61)
by Emma Frances Bevan (1827–1909)

341 (HHT **8**)

Diva servatrix 11 11 11.5. *Bayeux Antiphoner, 173*

The tune is sung twice for each verse, with first and second endings

The love-feast

As the disciples, when thy Son had left them,
  met in a love-feast, joyfully conversing,
all the stored memory of the Lord's last supper
    fondly rehearsing;
so may we here, who gather now in friendship,
  seek for the spirit of those earlier Churches,
welcoming him who stands and for an entrance‿
    patiently searches.

2

As, when their converse closed and supper ended,
  taking the bread and wine they made thanksgiving,
breaking and blessing, thus to have communion‿
    with Christ the living;
so may we here, a company of brothers,
  make this our love-feast and commemoration,
that in his Spirit we may have more worthy‿
    participation.

3

And as they prayed and sang to thee rejoicing,
  ere in the night-fall they embraced and parted,
in their hearts singing as they journeyed homeward,
    brave and true-hearted;
so may we here, like corn that once was scattered‿
  over the hill-side, now one bread united,
led by the Spirit, do thy work rejoicing,
    lamps filled and lighted.

PERCY DEARMER (1867–1936)

342 (HHT **9**)
Deus tuorum militum (Grenoble)
L.M. *Grenoble Antiphoner, 175*

The new life

Awake, awake: fling off the night!
for God has sent his glorious light;
  and we who live in Christ's new day
  must works of darkness put away.

2

Awake and rise, like men renewed,
men with the Spirit's power endued.
  The light of life in us must glow,
  and fruits of truth and goodness show.

3

Let in the light; all sin expose‿
to Christ, whose life no darkness knows.
  Before his cross for guidance kneel;
  his light will judge and, judging, heal.

4

Awake, and rise up from the dead,
and Christ his light on you will shed.
  Its power will wrong desires destroy,
  and your whole nature fill with joy.

5

Then sing for joy, and use each day;
give thanks for everything alway.
  Lift up your hearts; with one accord
  praise God through Jesus Christ our Lord.

J. R. Peacey (1896–1971)
based on Ephesians 5. 6–20
(possibly a hymn for baptism)

343 (HHT **10**)

Slane 10 11.11 11. Irish Traditional Melo

First and Last

Be thou my vision, O Lord of my heart,
be all else but naught to me, save that thou art;
be thou my best thought in the day and the night,
both waking and sleeping, thy presence my light.

2

Be thou my wisdom, be thou my true word,
be thou ever with me, and I with thee, Lord;
be thou my great Father, and I thy true son;
be thou in me dwelling, and I with thee one.

3

Be thou my breastplate, my sword for the fight;
be thou my whole armour, be thou my true might;
be thou my soul's shelter, be thou my strong tower:
O raise thou me heavenward, great Power of my power.

4

Riches I heed not, nor man's empty praise:
be thou mine inheritance now and always;
be thou and thou only the first in my heart;
O Sovereign of heaven, my treasure thou art.

5

High King of heaven, thou heaven's bright Sun,
O grant me its joys after vict'ry is won;
great Heart of my own heart, whatever befall,
still be thou my vision, O Ruler of all.

Irish, c. 8th century tr. MARY BYRNE (1880–1931)
versified, ELEANOR HULL (1860–1935)

344 (HHT 11)

Milton Abbas 6 6 4.6 6 6 4. Eric Thiman (1900–75)

Christ for the world

Christ for the world we sing!
The world to Christ we bring
with fervent prayer;
the wayward and the lost,
by restless passions tossed,
redeemed at countless cost‿
from dark despair.

2

Christ for the world we sing!
The world to Christ we bring
with one accord;
with us the work to share,
with us reproach to dare,
with us the cross to bear,
for Christ our Lord.

3

Christ for the world we sing!
The world to Christ we bring
with joyful song;
the new-born souls, whose days,
reclaimed from error's ways,
inspired with hope and praise,
to Christ belong.

SAMUEL WOLCOTT (1813–86)

345 (HHT 12)

Gelobt sei Gott — M. Vulpius

8 8 8. with Alleluias — *Gesangbuch*, 160

Al - le - lu - ia. Al - le - lu - ia. Al - le - lu - ia.

Christ the King

Christ is the King! O friends rejoice;
brothers and sisters with one voice
make all men know he is your choice.
Alleluia.

2

O magnify the Lord, and raise‿
anthems of joy and holy praise
for Christ's brave saints of ancient days.
Alleluia.

3

They with a faith for ever new
followed the King, and round him drew‿
thousands of faithful men and true.
Alleluia.

4

O Christian women, Christian men,
all the world over, seek again‿
the Way disciples followed then.
Alleluia.

5

Christ through all ages is the same:
place the same hope in his great name,
with the same faith his word proclaim.
Alleluia.

6

Let Love's unconquerable might
your scattered companies unite
in service to the Lord of light.
Alleluia.

7

So shall God's will on earth be done,
new lamps be lit, new tasks begun,
and the whole Church at last be one.
Alleluia.

G. K. A. BELL* (1883–1958)

346 (HHT 13)

Darmstadt 6 7.6 7.6 6.6 6. A. Fritsch (1679

Alternative Tune: *Nun danket* (205)

The hope of the world

Christ is the world's true light,
  its captain of salvation,
the daystar clear and bright
  of every man and nation;
new life, new hope awakes,
  where'er men own his sway:
freedom her bondage breaks,
  and night is turned to day.

2

In Christ all races meet,
  their ancient feuds forgetting,
the whole round world complete,
  from sunrise to its setting:
when Christ is throned as Lord,
  men shall forsake their fear,
to ploughshare beat the sword,
  to pruning-hook the spear.

3

One Lord, in one great name
  unite us all who own thee;
cast out our pride and shame
  that hinder to enthrone thee;
the world has waited long,
  has travailed long in pain;
to heal its ancient wrong,
  come, Prince of Peace, and reign!

G. W. Briggs (1875–1959)

347 (HHT **14**)

Cambridge 6 6.6 5.6 5. Charles Wood (1866–1926

The hope of glory

Christ, who knows all his sheep,
will all in safety keep:
he will not lose one soul,
  nor ever fail us:
nor we the promised goal,
  whate'er assail us.

2

We know our God is just;
to him we wholly trust‿
all that we have and claim,
  and all we hope for:
all's sure and seen to him,
  which here we grope for.

3

Fear not the world of light,
though out of mortal sight;
there shall we know God more,
  where all is holy:
there is no grief or care,
  no sin or folly.

4

O blessèd company,
where all in harmony
God's joyous praises sing,
  in love unceasing;
and all obey their King,
  with perfect pleasing.

Adapted from RICHARD BAXTER (1615–91)

48 (HHT 15) FIRST TUNE

Quedgeley 7 6.7 6. John Dykes Bower (1905–81)

SECOND TUNE

Melling 7 6.7 6. John Fawcett (1789–1867)

The Gospel

Come, Lord, to our souls come down,
  through the Gospel speaking;
let your words, your cross and crown,
  lighten all our seeking.

2

Drive out darkness from the heart,
  banish pride and blindness;
plant in every inward part
  truthfulness and kindness.

3

Eyes be open, spirits stirred,
  minds new truth receiving;
make us, Lord, by your own Word,
  more and more believing.

H. C. A. Gaunt (1902–83)

349 (HHT **16**)

Blackbird Leys 10 10.10 10. Peter Cutts (b. 193

Alternative Tunes: *Adoro te* and *Sheldonian* (254)

The breaking of bread

Come, risen Lord, and deign to be our guest;
nay, let us be thy guests; the feast is thine;
thyself at thine own board make manifest,
in thine own sacrament of bread and wine.

2

We meet, as in that upper room they met;
thou at the table, blessing, yet dost stand:
'This is my body': so thou givest yet:
faith still receives the cup as from thy hand.

3

One body we, one body who partake,
one church united in communion blest;
one name we bear, one bread of life we break,
with all thy saints on earth and saints at rest.

4

One with each other, Lord, for one in thee,
who art one Saviour and one living Head;
then open thou our eyes, that we may see;
be known to us in breaking of the bread.

G. W. Briggs (1875–1959

50 (HHT 17)
Watchman S.M. James Leach (1762–98)

Alternative Tune: *Narenza* (150)

Daily work

1 Come, workers for the Lord
and lift up heart and hand;
praise God, all skill at bench and board,
praise, all that brain has planned.

2 When Christ to manhood came
a craftsman was he made
and served his glad apprentice time
bound to the joiner's trade.

3 When Christ on Calvary
drank down his cruel draught,
the men who nailed him to the tree
were men of his own craft.

4 So, God, our labour take,
from spite and greed set free;
may nothing that we do or make
bring ill to man or thee.

5 All workers for the Lord,
come sing with voice and heart;
in strength of hands be God adored
and praised in power of art.

NORMAN NICHOLSON (b. 1914)

351 (HHT **18**)

Agincourt L.M. English Melody, 15th ce

Alternative Tune: *Breslau* (397)

The unknown God

Creator of the earth and skies,
  to whom all truth and power belong,
grant us your truth to make us wise;
  grant us your power to make us strong.

2

We have not known you: to the skies‿
  our monuments of folly soar,
and all our self-wrought miseries
  have made us trust ourselves the more.

3

We have not loved you: far and wide‿
  the wreckage of our hatred spreads,
and evils wrought by human pride
  recoil on unrepentant heads.

4

We long to end this worldwide strife:
  how shall we follow in your way?
speak to mankind your words of life,
  until our darkness turns to day.

DONALD WYNN HUGHES* (1911–67)

352 (HHT **19**)
Song 24 — Orlando Gibbons (1583–162
10 10.10 10.10 10.

Alternative Tune: *Song 1* (353)

Bread and Wine

He took

Dear Lord, to you again our gifts we bring,
  this bread our toil, this wine our ecstasy,
  poor and imperfect though they both must be;
yet you will take a heart-free offering.
Yours is the bounty, ours the unfettered will
to make or mar, to fashion good or ill.

He blessed 2

Yes, you will take and bless, and grace impart
  to make again what once your goodness gave,
  what we half crave, and half refuse to have,
a sturdier will, a more repentant heart.
You have on earth no hands, no hearts but ours;
bless them as yours, ourselves, our will, our powers.

He broke 3

Break bread, O Lord, break down our wayward wills,
  break down our prized possessions, break them down;
  let them be freely given as your own
to all who need our gifts, to heal their ills.
Break this, the bread we bring, that all may share
in your one living body, everywhere.

He gave 4

Our lips receive your wine, our hands your bread;
  you give us back the selves we offered you,
  won by the Cross, by Calvary made new,
a heart enriched, a life raised from the dead.
Grant us to take and guard your treasure well,
that we in you, and you in us may dwell.

H. C. A. Gaunt (1902–83)

353 (HHT **20**)

Song 1 — Orlando Gibbons (1583–1625)

10 10.10 10.10 10.

Unity in the Spirit

Eternal Ruler of the ceaseless round
 of circling planets singing on their way;
guide of the nations from the night profound
 into the glory of the perfect day;
rule in our hearts, that we may ever be
guided and strengthened and upheld by thee.

2

We are of thee, the children of thy love,
 the brothers of thy well-belovèd Son;
descend, O Holy Spirit, like a dove,
 into our hearts, that we may be as one:
as one with thee, to whom we ever tend;
as one with him, our Brother and our Friend.

3

We would be one in hatred of all wrong,
 one in our love of all things sweet and fair,
one with the joy that breaketh into song,
 one with the grief that trembles into prayer,
one in the power that makes thy children free
to follow truth, and thus to follow thee.

4

O clothe us with thy heavenly armour, Lord,
 thy trusty shield, thy sword of love divine;
our inspiration be thy constant word;
 we ask no victories that are not thine:
give or withhold, let pain or pleasure be;
enough to know that we are serving thee.

J. W. Chadwick (1840–1904)

354 (HHT 21)

Every Star | Sydney Carter (b. 1915

Solo (or a few voices)
All
God a - bove, Man be - low, Ho - ly is the_ name I__ know

A carol of the universe

Solo (or a few voices)
Every star shall sing a carol;
  every creature, high or low,
come and praise the King of Heaven,
  by whatever name you know:

All
God above, Man below,
  Holy is the name I know.

2

When the King of all creation‿
  had a cradle on the earth,
holy was the human body,
  holy was the human birth:

3

Who can tell what other cradle
  high above the milky way
still may rock the King of Heaven
  on another Christmas Day?

4

Who can count how many crosses
  still to come or long ago
crucify the King of Heaven?
  holy is the name I know:

5

Who can tell what other body
  he will hallow for his own?
I will praise the Son of Mary,
  brother of my blood and bone:

6

Every star and every planet,
  every creature high and low,
come and praise the King of Heaven,
  by whatever name you know:

SYDNEY CARTER (b. 1915)

355(i) (HHT **22**(i)) *Rheinhardt M.*
Was lebet 12 10.12 10. (Üttingen, 175.

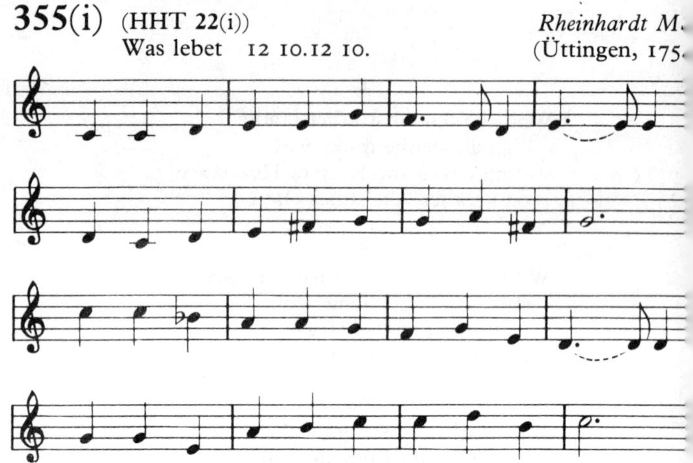

The two parts of this hymn may be used separately. If both parts are combined, verses 2, 4 and 6 may be sung by soloist or choir.

Alive for God

PART I

1 Father all-pow-erful, thine is the kingdom,
thine is the pow-er, the glory of love;
gently thou carest for each of thy children,
lovingly sending thy Son from above.

3 Crucified Jesus, thou bearest our wickedness,
now thou art risen that all men may live;
mighty Redeemer, despite our unworthiness,
thou in thy mercy our sins dost forgive.

5 Comforter, Spirit, thou camest at Pentecost,
pouring thy grace on thy Church here below;
still thou dost feed us by prayer and by sacrament,
till all creation thy glory shall know.

7 Holiest Trinity, perfect in Unity,
bind in thy love every nation and race:
may we adore thee for time and eternity,
Father, Redeemer, and Spirit of grace.

5(ii) (HHT 22(ii))
Was lebet 12 10.12 10.

Rheinhardt MS.
(Üttingen, 1754)

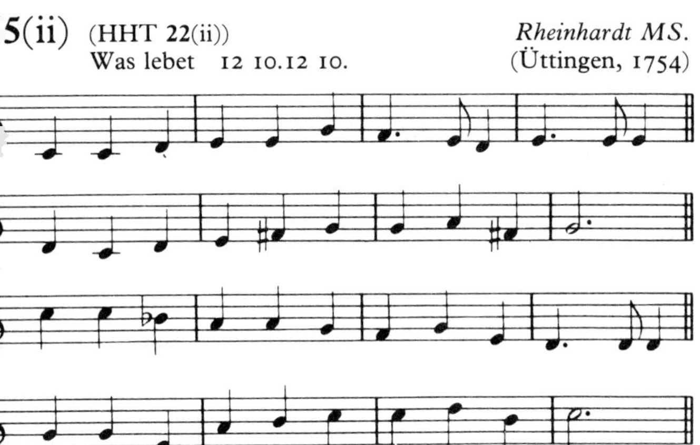

The two parts of this hymn may be used separately.
If both parts are combined, verses 2, 4 and 6 may be sung by soloist or choir.

Alive for God

PART 2

2 Father all-loving, thou rulest in majesty,
judgment is thine, and condemneth our pride;
stir up our rulers and peoples to penitence,
sorrow for sins that for vengeance have cried.

4 Blessèd Lord Jesus, thou camest in poverty,
sharing a stable with beasts at thy birth;
stir us to work for thy justice and charity,
truly to care for the poor upon earth.

6 Come, Holy Spirit, create in us holiness,
lift up our lives to thy standard of right;
stir every will to new ventures of faithfulness,
flood the whole Church with thy glorious light.

7 Holiest Trinity, perfect in Unity,
bind in thy love every nation and race:
may we adore thee for time and eternity,
Father, Redeemer, and Spirit of grace.

Patrick Appleford (b. 1924)

356 (HHT 23)

Abbot's Leigh 8 7.8 7.D. Cyril Taylor (b. 190

A descant to this tune is at 172

Renewal

Father, Lord of all Creation,
  Ground of Being, Life and Love;
height and depth beyond description
  only life in you can prove:
you are mortal life's dependence:
  thought, speech, sight are ours by grace;
yours is every hour's existence,
  sovereign Lord of time and space.

2

Jesus Christ, the Man for Others,
  we, your people, make our prayer:
give us grace to love as brothers‿
  all whose burdens we can share.
Where your name binds us together
  you, Lord Christ, will surely be;
where no selfishness can sever
  there your love may all men see.

3

Holy Spirit, rushing, burning‿
  wind and flame of Pentecost,
fire our hearts afresh with yearning‿
  to regain what we have lost.
May your love unite our action,
  nevermore to speak alone:
God, in us abolish faction,
  God, through us your love make known.

STEWART CROSS (b. 1928)

357 (HHT **24**)
Les Commandemens 9 8.9 8. Strasbourg, 1545
(Commandments)

The Living Bread

Father, we thank thee who hast planted‿
thy holy name within our hearts.
Knowledge and faith and life immortal
Jesus thy Son to us imparts.

2

Thou, Lord, didst make all for thy pleasure,
didst give man food for all his days,
giving in Christ the bread eternal;
thine is the power, be thine the praise.

3

Watch o'er thy Church, O Lord, in mercy,
save it from evil, guard it still,
perfect it in thy love, unite it,
cleansed and conformed unto thy will.

4

As grain, once scattered on the hillsides,
was in this broken bread made one,
so from all lands thy Church be gathered
into thy kingdom by thy Son.

From the *Didache*,
(1st or 2nd century)
tr. F. BLAND TUCKER (1895–1984)

58 (HHT 25)

Quem pastores 8 8 8.7. German Medieval Melody

Into the world

Father, who in Jesus found us,
God, whose love is all around us,
who to freedom new unbound us,
keep our hearts with joy aflame.

2

For the sacramental breaking,
for the honour of partaking,
for your life our lives remaking,
young and old, we praise your name.

3

From the service of this table
lead us to a life more stable;
for our witness make us able;
blessing on our work we claim.

4

Through our calling closely knitted,
daily to your praise committed,
for a life of service fitted,
let us now your love proclaim.

FRED KAAN (b. 1929)

359 (HHT **26**)

Farley Castle 10 10.10 10. Henry Lawes (1596–166

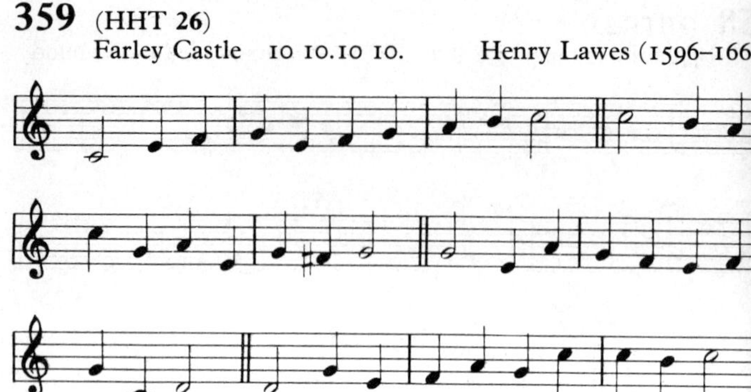

Fellowship in the Holy Spirit

Filled with the Spirit's power, with one accord
the infant Church confessed its risen Lord.
  O Holy Spirit, in the Church to-day
  no less your power of fellowship display.

2

Now with the mind of Christ set us on fire,
that unity may be our great desire.
  Give joy and peace; give faith to hear your call,
  and readiness in each to work for all.

3

Widen our love, good Spirit, to embrace
in your strong care the men of every race.
  Like wind and fire with life among us move,
  till we are known as Christ's, and Christians prove.

J. R. PEACEY (1896–1971)

360 (HHT 27)

St. Botolph C.M. Gordon Slater (1896–1979)

Mother of the Lord

For Mary, Mother of our Lord,
  God's holy name be praised,
who first the Son of God adored,
  as on her child she gazed.

2

Brave, holy Virgin, she believed,
  though hard the task assigned,
and by the Holy Ghost conceived‿
  the Saviour of mankind.

*3

God's handmaid, she at once obeyed,
  by her 'Thy will be done';
the second Eve love's answer made
  which our redemption won.

*4

The busy world had got no space‿
  or time for God on earth;
a cattle manger was the place‿
  where Mary gave him birth.

5

She gave her body as God's shrine,
  her heart to piercing pain;
she knew the cost of love divine,
  when Jesus Christ was slain.

6

Dear Mary, from your lowliness
  and home in Galilee
there comes a joy and holiness
  to every family.

7

Hail, Mary, you are full of grace,
  above all women blest;
and blest your Son, whom your embrace
  in birth and death confessed.

J. R. PEACEY (1896–1971)

361 (HHT 28)
Alleluia, dulce carmen 8 7.8 7.8 7. *Essay on t*
(Tantum ergo) *Church Plain Chant*, 17

Human Rights

For the healing of the nations,
  Lord, we pray with one accord;
for a just and equal sharing‿
  of the things that earth affords.
To a life of love in action
  help us rise and pledge our word.

2

Lead us, Father, into freedom,
  from despair your world release;
that, redeemed from war and hatred,
  men may come and go in peace.
Show us how through care and goodness
  fear will die and hope increase.

3

All that kills abundant living,
  let it from the earth be banned;
pride of status, race or schooling,
  dogmas keeping man from man.
In our common quest for justice
  may we hallow life's brief span.

4

You, creator-God, have written
  your great name on all mankind;
for our growing in your likeness
  bring the life of Christ to mind;
that by our response and service
  earth its destiny may find.

FRED KAAN (b. 1929)

362 (HHT 29)

Crowle C.M.

A Book of Psalmody
by James Green (c. 1690–1750)

Alternative Tune: *St. Bernard* (64)

The unforgiving heart

'Forgive our sins as we forgive'
you taught us, Lord, to pray;
but you alone can grant us grace
to live the words we say.

2

How can your pardon reach and bless‿
the unforgiving heart
that broods on wrongs, and will not let‿
old bitterness depart?

3

In blazing light your Cross reveals‿
the truth we dimly knew,
how small the debts men owe to us,
how great our debt to you.

4

Lord, cleanse the depths within our souls,
and bid resentment cease;
then, reconciled to God and man,
our lives will spread your peace.

ROSAMOND E. HERKLOTS (b. 1905)

63 (HHT **30**)
Love Unknown
6 6.6 6.4 4.4 4.

John Ireland (1879–1962)

All Saints

Glory to thee, O God,
for all thy saints in light,
who nobly strove and conquered in the well-fought fight.
Their praises sing,
who life outpoured
by fire and sword for Christ their King.

2

Thanks be to thee, O Lord,
for saints thy Spirit stirred
in humble paths to live thy life and speak thy word.
Unnumbered they,
whose candles shine
to lead our footsteps after thine.

3

Lord God of truth and love,
'thy kingdom come', we pray;
give us thy grace to know thy truth and walk thy way:
that here on earth‿
thy will be done,
till saints in earth and heaven are one.

H. C. A. Gaunt (1902–83)

364 (HHT **31**)
Lux Dei English Melody, 18th cent

Light, Love, and Life

God is Light,
away with blindness and unkindness;
all that's bright‿
is shining with his light.
Turn to him; if anything would dim‿
the light of happiness and praise
  and thankfulness to him.

2

God is Love,
and he rejoices in our voices,
God is Love,
around us and above.
Ask we him to fill our hearts with love,
to fill our thankful hearts with love‿
  and gladness to the brim.

3

God is Life,
his everlasting Son is giving‿
happy life
to those who trust in him.
Praises be, O risen Christ, to thee;
for thou hast set us free to live‿
  in thankfulness to thee.

J. M. C. Crum (1872–1958)

365 (HHT 32)
Alleluia 8 7.8 7.D. S. S. Wesley (1810–76

Alternative Tune: *Hyfrydol* (175, 262)

God is love

God is Love: let heav'n adore him;
God is Love: let earth rejoice;
let creation sing before him,
and exalt him with one voice.
He who laid the earth's foundation,
he who spread the heav'ns above,
he who breathes through all creation,
he is Love, eternal Love.

2

God is Love: and he enfoldeth‿
all the world in one embrace;
with unfailing grasp he holdeth‿
every child of every race.
And when human hearts are breaking
under sorrow's iron rod,
then they find that selfsame aching
deep within the heart of God.

3

God is Love: and though with blindness‿
sin afflicts the souls of men,
God's eternal loving-kindness
holds and guides them even then.
Sin and death and hell shall never‿
o'er us final triumph gain;
God is Love, so Love for ever
o'er the universe must reign.

TIMOTHY REES* (1874–1939)

366 (HHT 33)

Minterne 7 7·7 7·7 7· Cyril Taylor (b. 190

* *To these linked quavers two syllables are sung*

The earth is the Lord's

God of concrete, God of steel,
God of piston and of wheel,
God of pylon, God of steam,
God of girder and of beam,
God of atom, God of mine,
all the world of power is thine.

2

Lord of cable, Lord of rail,
Lord of motorway and mail,
Lord of rocket, Lord of flight,
Lord of soaring satellite,
Lord of lightning's livid line,
all the world of speed is thine.

3

Lord of science, Lord of art,
God of map and graph and chart,
Lord of physics and research,
Word of Bible, Faith of Church,
Lord of sequence and design,
all the world of truth is thine.

4

God whose glory fills the earth,
gave the universe its birth,
loosed the Christ with Easter's might,
saves the world from evil's blight,
claims mankind by grace divine,
all the world of love is thine.

RICHARD G. JONES (b. 1926)

367 (HHT **34**)

Regent Square 8 7.8 7.8 7. Henry Smart (1813–79

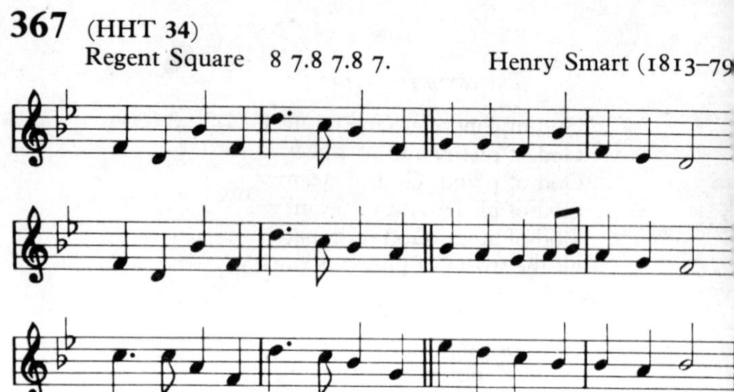

Faith for living

God of grace and God of glory,
on thy people pour thy power;
now fulfil thy Church's story;
bring her bud to glorious flower.
Grant us wisdom, grant us courage,
for the facing of this hour.

2

Lo, the hosts of evil round us‿
scorn thy Christ, assail his ways;
from the fears that long have bound us
free our hearts to faith and praise.
Grant us wisdom, grant us courage,
for the living of these days.

3

Cure thy children's warring madness,
bend our pride to thy control;
shame our wanton selfish gladness,
rich in goods and poor in soul.
Grant us wisdom, grant us courage,
lest we miss thy kingdom's goal.

4

Set our feet on lofty places,
gird our lives that they may be‿
armoured with all Christlike graces
in the fight to set men free.
Grant us wisdom, grant us courage,
that we fail not man nor thee.

H. E. Fosdick* (1878–1969)

368 (HHT 35)

Carolyn 8 5.8 5.8 8.8 5. Herbert Murrill (1909–5

Hallowed be thy name

God of love and truth and beauty,
  hallowed be thy name;
fount of order, law, and duty,
  hallowed be thy name.
As in heaven thy hosts adore thee,
and their faces veil before thee,
so on earth, Lord, we implore thee,
  hallowed be thy name.

2

Lord, remove our guilty blindness,
  hallowed be thy name;
show thy heart of loving kindness,
  hallowed be thy name.
By our heart's deep-felt contrition,
by our mind's enlightened vision,
by our will's complete submission,
  hallowed be thy name.

3

In our worship, Lord most holy,
  hallowed be thy name;
in our work, however lowly,
  hallowed be thy name.
In each heart's imagination,
in the Church's adoration,
in the conscience of the nation,
  hallowed be thy name.

TIMOTHY REES (1874–1939)

369 (HHT 36)

Quedlinburg 10 10.10 10. From a Chorale b
J. C. Kittel (1732–180

Adam

1 God who created this Eden of earth
giving to Adam and Eve their fresh birth,
what have we done with that wonderful tree?
Lord, forgive Adam,
for Adam is me.

2 Adam ambitious desires to be wise,
casts out obedience, then lusts with his eyes;
grasps his sweet fruit, 'As God I shall be'.
Lord, forgive Adam,
for Adam is me.

3 Thirst after pow'r is this sin of my shame,
pride's ruthless thrust after status and fame,
turning and stealing and cowering from thee.
Lord, forgive Adam,
for Adam is me.

4 Cursed is the earth through this cancerous crime,
symbol of man through all passage of time,
put it all right, Lord; let Adam be free;
do it for Adam,
for Adam is me.

5 Glory to God! what is this that I see?
Man made anew, second Adam is he,
bleeding his love on another fine tree;
dies second Adam,
young Adam, for me.

6 Rises that Adam the master of death,
pours out his Spirit in holy new breath;
sheer liberation! with him I am free!
lives second Adam
in mercy in me.

RICHARD G. JONES (b. 1926)

70 (HHT **37**)
Gott will's machen 8 7.8 7. J. L. Steiner (1688–1761)

God's farm

God, whose farm is all creation,
take the gratitude we give;
take the finest of our harvest,
crops we grow that men may live.

2

Take our ploughing, seeding, reaping,
hopes and fears of sun and rain,
all our thinking, planning, waiting,
ripened in this fruit and grain.

3

All our labour, all our watching,
all our calendar of care,
in these crops of your creation,
take, O God: they are our prayer.

JOHN ARLOTT (b. 1914)

371 (HHT **38**)

Hambleden 8 9.8 9.D. W. K. Stanton (1891–19

Offertory

Good is our God who made this place
whereon our race in plenty liveth.
Great is the praise to him we owe,
that we may show 'tis he that giveth.
Then let who would for daily food
give thanks to God who life preserveth;
offer this board to our good Lord,
and him applaud who praise deserveth.

2

Praise him again whose sovereign will
grants us the skill of daily labour;
whose blessèd Son to our great good
fashioned his wood to serve his neighbour.
Shall we who sing not also bring‿
of this world's wages to the table?
giving again of what we gain,
to make it plain God doth enable.

3

So let us our Creator praise,
who all our days our life sustaineth;
offer our work, renew our vow,
adore him now who rightly reigneth;
that we who break this bread, and take‿
this cup of Christ to our enjoyment,
may so believe, so well receive,
never to leave our Lord's employment.

J. K. Gregory (b. 1929)

372 (HHT 39)

Doncaster S.M. Samuel Wesley (1766–1837

Trusting God

Have faith in God, my heart,
trust and be unafraid;
God will fulfil in every part‿
each promise he has made.

2

Have faith in God, my mind,
though oft thy light burns low;
God's mercy holds a wiser plan
than thou canst fully know.

3

Have faith in God, my soul,
his Cross for ever stands;
and neither life nor death can pluck‿
his children from his hands.

4

Lord Jesus, make me whole;
grant me no resting place,
until I rest, heart, mind, and soul,
the captive of thy grace.

B. A. Rees (1911–83)

73 (HHT **40**)
Sandys S.M. W. Sandys' *Christmas Carols*, 1833

Living the faith

Help us, O Lord, to learn
the truths thy Word imparts:
to study that thy laws may be
inscribed upon our hearts.

2

Help us, O Lord, to live
the faith which we proclaim,
that all our thoughts and words and deeds
may glorify thy name.

3

Help us, O Lord, to teach
the beauty of thy ways,
that yearning souls may find the Christ,
and sing aloud his praise.

WILLIAM WATKINS REID (b. 1923)

374 (HHT **41**)
Dunfermline C.M. *Scottish Psalter*, 1

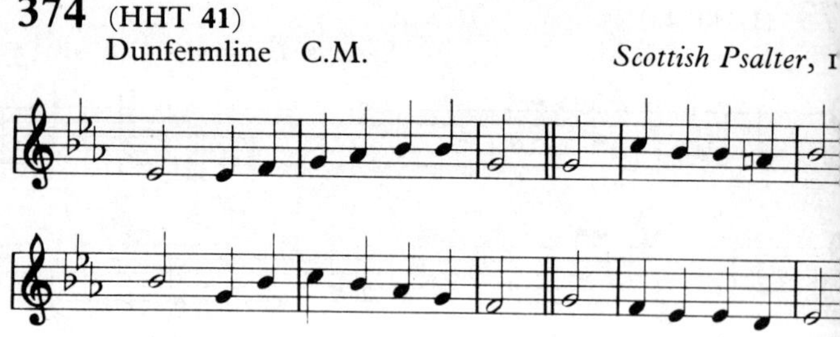

Charity

Help us to help each other, Lord,
each other's cross to bear;
let each his friendly aid afford,
and feel his brother's care.

2

Up into thee, our living head,
let us in all things grow,
and by thy sacrifice be led‿
the fruits of love to show.

3

Drawn by the magnet of thy love
let all our hearts agree;
and ever towards each other move,
and ever move towards thee.

4

This is the bond of perfectness,
thy spotless charity.
O let us still, we pray, possess‿
the mind that was in thee.

Cento from CHARLES WESLEY* (1707–88)

375 (HHT 42)

Shaker Tune — Adapted by Sydney Carter (b. 191

(Two bars organ introduction)

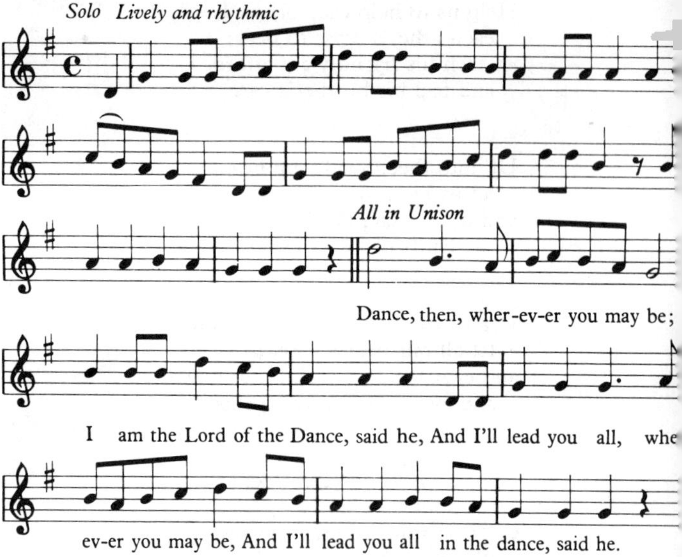

Solo *Lively and rhythmic*

All in Unison

Dance, then, wher-ev-er you may be;

I am the Lord of the Dance, said he, And I'll lead you all, whe

ev-er you may be, And I'll lead you all in the dance, said he.

Melody of last verse

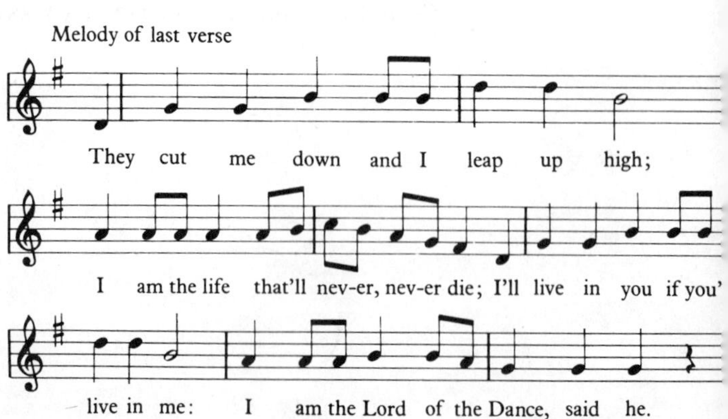
They cut me down and I leap up high;
I am the life that'll nev-er, nev-er die; I'll live in you if you'
live in me: I am the Lord of the Dance, said he.

Lord of the Dance

Solo
I danced in the morning
when the world was begun,
and I danced in the moon
and the stars and the sun,
and I came down from heaven
and I danced on the earth;
at Bethlehem
I had my birth:

All
Dance, then, wherever you may be;
I am the Lord of the Dance, said he,
and I'll lead you all, wherever you
may be,
and I'll lead you all in the dance,
said he.

2

danced for the scribe
and the pharisee,
ut they would not dance
and they wouldn't follow me;
danced for the fishermen,
for James and John;
hey came with me
and the dance went on:

3

danced on the Sabbath
and I cured the lame:
he holy people
said it was a shame.
Γhey whipped and they stripped
and they hung me high,
nd they left me there
on a cross to die:

4

I danced on a Friday
when the sky turned black;
it's hard to dance
with the devil on your back.
They buried my body
and they thought I'd gone;
but I am the dance
and I still go on:

5

They cut me down
and I leap up high;
I am the life
that'll never, never die;
I'll live in you
if you'll live in me:
I am the Lord
of the Dance, said he:

SYDNEY CARTER (b. 1915)

376 (HHT **43**)

Kilmarnock C.M. Neil Dougall (1776–186

Brotherhood

In Christ there is no east or west,
in him no south or north,
but one great fellowship of love
throughout the whole wide earth.

2

In him shall true hearts everywhere
their high communion find;
his service is the golden cord,
close binding all mankind.

3

Join hands, then, brothers of the faith,
whate'er your race may be;
who serves my Father as a son
is surely kin to me.

4

In Christ now meet both east and west,
in him meet south and north;
all Christlike souls are one in him,
throughout the whole wide earth.

JOHN OXENHAM* (1852–1941

77 (HHT 44)

Claudius D.C.M.

Adapted from a song by G. W. Fink (1783–1846)

Alternative Tune: *Ellacombe* (75)

The world's need

In humble gratitude, O God,
  we bring our best to thee,
to serve thy cause and share thy love
  with all humanity.
O thou who gavest us thyself
  in Jesus Christ thy Son,
teach us to give ourselves each day
  until life's work is done.

2

A world in need now summons us
  to labour, love, and give;
to make our life an offering‿
  to God, that man may live;
the Church of Christ is calling us
  to make the dream come true:
a world redeemed by Christlike love,
  all life in Christ made new.

Frank von Christierson* (b. 1900)

378 (HHT 45)

Quem pastores 8 8 8.7. German Medieval Melody

Son of Man

Jesus, good above all other,
gentle child of gentle mother,
in a stable born our brother,
give us grace to persevere.

2

Jesus, cradled in a manger,
for us facing every danger,
living as a homeless stranger,
make we thee our King most dear.

3

Jesus, for thy people dying,
risen Master, death defying,
Lord in heaven, thy grace supplying,
keep us to thy presence near.

4

Jesus, who our sorrows bearest,
all our thoughts and hopes thou sharest,
thou to man the truth declarest;
help us all thy truth to hear.

5

Lord, in all our doings guide us;
pride and hate shall ne'er divide us;
we'll go on with thee beside us,
and with joy we'll persevere.

PERCY DEARMER (1867–1936)
partly based on J. M. NEALE (1818–66)

79 (HHT **46**)
Buckland 7 7.7 7. L. G. Hayne (1836–83)

Christ in us

Jesus, humble was your birth,
when you came from heaven to earth;
  every day, in all we do,
  make us humble, Lord, like you.

2

Jesus, strong to help and heal,
showing that your love is real;
  every day in all we do,
  make us strong and kind like you.

3

Jesus, when you were betrayed,
still you trusted God and prayed;
  every day in all we do,
  help us trust and pray like you.

4

Jesus, risen from the dead,
with us always, as you said;
  every day in all we do,
  help us live and love like you.

PATRICK APPLEFORD* (b. 1924)

380 (HHT 47)

Vienna 7 7.7 7. J. H. Knecht (1752–181

Unity

Jesus, Lord, we look to thee,
let us in thy name agree:
show thyself the Prince of Peace;
bid all strife for ever cease.

2

Make us of one heart and mind,
courteous, pitiful, and kind,
lowly, meek in thought and word,
altogether like our Lord.

3

Let us for each other care,
each the other's burden bear;
to thy Church the pattern give,
show how true believers live.

4

Still our fellowship increase,
knit us in the bond of peace:
join our new-born spirits, join‿
each to each, and all to thine.

5

Free from anger and from pride,
let us thus in God abide;
all the depths of love express,
all the heights of holiness.

Cento from Charles Wesley* (1707–88

381 (HHT **48**)
St. Etheldreda C.M. Thomas Turton (1780–1864)

Our brother's need

Jesus, my Lord, how rich thy grace,
how fair thy bounties shine!
what can my poverty bestow,
when all the worlds are thine?

2

But thou hast needy brethren here,
the partners of thy grace,
and wilt confess their humble names
before thy Father's face.

3

In them thou may'st be clothed and fed,
and visited and cheered,
and in their accents of distress
the Saviour's voice is heard.

4

Thy face with reverence and with love
I in thy poor would see;
O let me rather beg my bread,
than hold it back from thee.

PHILIP DODDRIDGE* (1702–51)

382 (HHT **49**)
Henfield
Patrick Appleford (b. 1924)

(Two bars organ introduction before verse 1)

Following Christ

Jesus our Lord, our King and our God,
  ruling in might and love,
all power on earth is given to you,
  you are our King above;
    help us to use the power you give,
    humbly to order how men live.
Lord, we are called to follow you;
this we ask strength to do.

2

Jesus our Lord, and humblest of Priests,
  doing your Father's will;
suffering servant, working with men,
  your work continues still.
    Help us to offer in our prayer,
    all of our work and service here.
Lord, we are called to follow you;
this we ask strength to do.

3

Jesus our Lord, and Shepherd of men,
  caring for human needs;
feeding the hungry, healing the sick,
  showing your love in deeds;
    help us in your great work to share;
    people in want still need your care.
Lord, we are called to follow you;
this we ask strength to do.

4

Jesus our Lord, and Prophet of God,
  preaching his mighty plan,
you are the Way, the Truth and the Life,
  teaching the mind of man;
    help us in all our words to show
    you are the truth men need to know.
Lord, we are called to follow you;
this we ask strength to do.

5

Jesus our Lord, our God and our Priest,
  Prophet and Shepherd-King,
yours is the kingdom, glory and power,
  yours is the praise we sing.
    Leader of men, you show the way
    we are to follow day by day.
Glorious God, we follow you;
this you give strength to do.

PATRICK APPLEFORD (b. 1924)

383 (HHT 50)

Stracathro C.M. C. Hutcheson (1792–186[illegible]

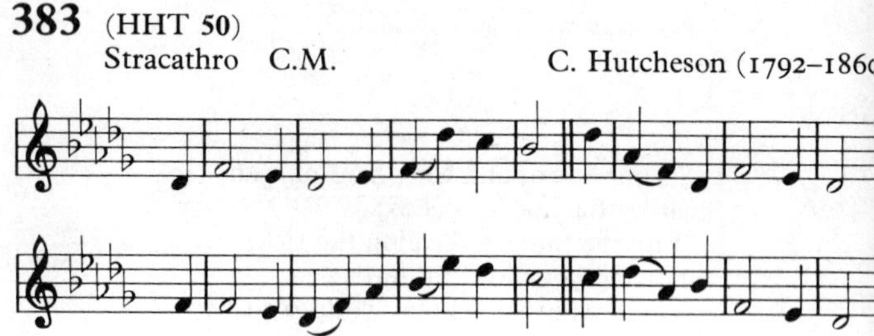

Sinners' Friend

Jesus, whose all-redeeming love
  no penitent did scorn,
who didst the stain of guilt remove,
  till hope anew was born;

2

to thee, physician of the soul,
  the lost, the outcast, came;
thou didst restore and make them whole,
  unburdened of their shame.

3

'Twas love, thy love, their bondage brake,
  whose fetters sin had bound;
for faith to love did answer make,
  and free forgiveness found.

4

Thou didst rebuke the scornful pride
  that called thee 'sinners' friend';
thy mercy as thy Father's wide,
  God's mercy without end.

5

Jesus, that pardoning grace to find,
  I too would come to thee;
O merciful to all mankind,
  be merciful to me.

G. W. Briggs* (1875–1959)

384 (HHT **51**)
Lindeman
8 7.8 7.8 8 7.

Ludwig Matthias Lindema
(1812–87

Alternative Tune: *Luther's Hymn* (193)

The Justice of God

Lo, in the wilderness a voice
  'Make straight the way' is crying:
when men are turning from the light,
  and hope and love seem dying,
the prophet comes to make us clean:
'There standeth one you have not seen,
  whose voice you are denying'.

2

God, give us grace to hearken now
  to those who come to warn us;
give sight and strength, that we may kill‿
  the vices that have torn us;
lest love professed should disappear
in creeds of hate, contempt, and fear,
  that crash and overturn us.

3

When from the vineyard cruel men‿
  cast out the heavenly powers,
and Christendom denies its Lord,
  the world in ruin cowers.
Now come, O God, in thy great might!
unchanged, unchanging is thy right,
  unswayed thy justice towers.

PERCY DEARMER (1867–1936)

385 (HHT 52)
Wansbeck 11.11.11.5. Erik Routley (1917–8

Alternative Tune: *Christe sanctorum* (440)

Into the world

Lord, as we rise to leave the shell of worship,
called to the risk of unprotected living,
willing to be at one with all your people,
we ask for courage.

2

For all the strain with living interwoven,
for the demands each day will make upon us,
and all the love we owe the world around us,
Lord, make us cheerful.

3

Give us an eye for openings to serve you,
make us alert when calm is interrupted,
ready and wise to use the unexpected;
sharpen our insight.

4

Lift from our life the blanket of convention,
give us the nerve to lose our life to others,
lead on your church through death to resurrection,
Lord of all ages.

FRED KAAN (b. 1929)

386 (HHT 53)

Hampton Poyle 8 8 5.8 6. Peter Cutts (b. 1937)

Make us one

Lord Christ, the Father's mighty Son,
whose work upon the cross was done‿
all men to receive,
make all our scattered churches one,
that the world may believe.

2

To make us one your prayers were said,
to make us one you broke the bread‿
for all to receive;
its pieces scatter us instead:
how can others believe?

3

Lord Christ, forgive us, make us new!
what our designs could never do
your love can achieve.
Our prayers, our work, we bring to you,
that the world may believe.

4

We will not question or refuse
the way you work, the means you choose,
the pattern you weave;
but reconcile our warring views,
that the world may believe.

BRIAN WREN (b. 1936)

87 (HHT 54)

Allein Gott
8 7.8 7.8 8 7.

Later form of melody adapted (1524) from an Easter *Gloria*

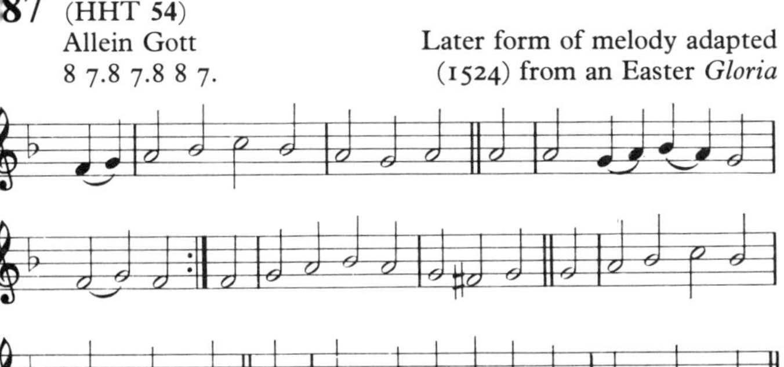

Alternative Tune: *Luther's Hymn* (193)

The reign of love

1 Lord Christ, when first thou cam'st to men,
upon a cross they bound thee,
and mocked thy saving kingship then
by thorns with which they crowned thee:
and still our wrongs may weave thee now
new thorns to pierce that steady brow,
and robe of sorrow round thee.

2 New advent of the love of Christ,
shall we again refuse thee,
till in the night of hate and war
we perish as we lose thee?
From old unfaith our souls release
to seek the kingdom of thy peace,
by which alone we choose thee.

3 O wounded hands of Jesus, build‿
in us thy new creation;
our pride is dust, our vaunt is stilled;
we wait thy revelation.
O Love that triumphs over loss,
we bring our hearts before thy cross,
to finish thy salvation.

W. Russell Bowie (1882–1969)

388 (HHT 55)

Gonfalon Royal L.M. P. C. Buck (1871–194

Caring

Lord Christ, who on thy heart didst bear‿
the burden of our shame and sin,
and now on high dost stoop to share‿
the fight without, the fear within;

2

thy patience cannot know defeat,
thy pity will not be denied,
thy loving-kindness still is great,
thy tender mercies still abide.

3

O brother Man, for this we pray,
thou brother Man and sovereign Lord,
that we thy brethren, day by day,
may follow thee and keep thy word;

4

that we may care, as thou hast cared,
for sick and lame, for deaf and blind,
and freely share, as thou hast shared,
in all the sorrows of mankind;

5

that ours may be the holy task‿
to help and bless, to heal and save;
this is the happiness we ask,
and this the service that we crave. Amen

ARNOLD THOMAS* (1848–1924)

389 (HHT 56)

Morestead 10 10.10 10. Sydney Watson (b. 1903)

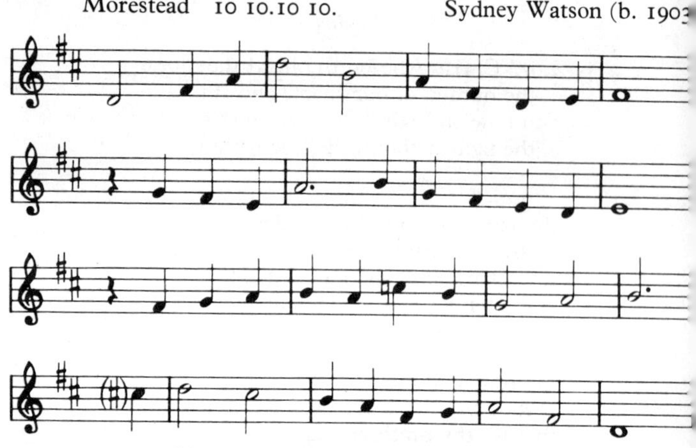

Alternative Tune: *Farley Castle* (359)

Our destiny

1 Lord God, thou art our maker and our end;
from thee we come and to thee we ascend;
we have no rest, nor are we ever free
until we find our joy and peace in thee.

2 We know we are thy sons, and heaven our home,
and yet with laggard steps to prayer we come;
and, since on others little love we spend,
we cannot know thy love which has no end.

3 Then to us, Lord, faith, hope, and courage give
to see thy face in Christ and in him live,
to learn thy love through him who for us died,
and find his faith by walking at his side.

4 In Christ, our hope and glory, give us light,
and, after life's last sacrifice, full sight;
in death a new beginning, then with thee
adoring service, glorious liberty.

J. R. Peacey (1896–1971)

90 (HHT 57)
Ach Herr 8 8 8.D. Michael Praetorius (1571–1621)

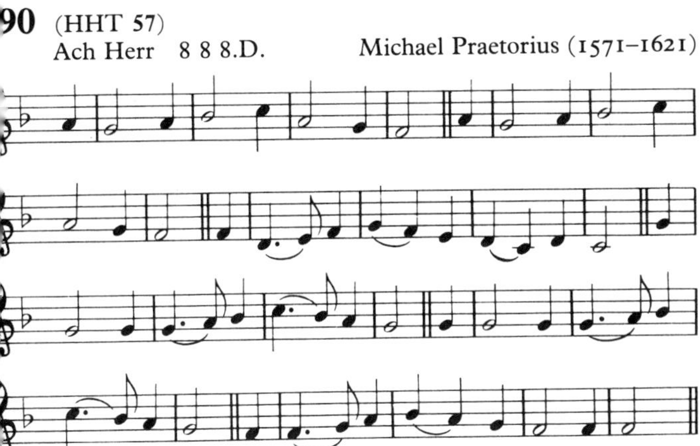

Alternative Tune: *Ascendit Deus* (449)

Humility

1 Lord God, we see thy power displayed
in all the marvels thou hast made
in earth around and sky above;
but nothing that the mind can know,
nor all creation has to show,
can tell the splendour of thy love.

2 When to thy people thou didst come
among the humble was thy home,
and with the poor and simple men;
nor wealth, nor power, nor majesty,
but wisdom found its way to thee,
and shepherds knelt around thee then.

3 The little fashions of our day
have turned in unbelief away,
and we are in the age of doubt;
yet still with humble men of heart
and all who know their need thou art,
for such thou never wilt cast out.

DONALD WYNN HUGHES* (1911–67)

391 (HHT 58)
Living Lord

Patrick Appleford (b. 192

Living Lord

Lord Jesus Christ,
you have come to us,
you are one with us,
    Mary's Son;
cleansing our souls from all their sin,
pouring your love and goodness in;
Jesus, our love for you we sing,
    living Lord.

*2

Lord Jesus Christ,
now and every day‿
teach us how to pray,
    Son of God.
You have commanded us to do‿
this in remembrance, Lord, of you:
into our lives your power breaks through,
    living Lord.

3

Lord Jesus Christ,
you have come to us,
born as one of us,
    Mary's Son.
Led out to die on Calvary,
risen from death to set us free,
living Lord Jesus, help us see‿
    you are Lord.

4

Lord Jesus Christ,
I would come to you,
live my life for you,
    Son of God.
All your commands I know are true,
your many gifts will make me new,
into my life your power breaks through,
    living Lord.

Patrick Appleford (b. 1924)

392 (HHT 59)

Cerne Abbas L.M. Cyril Taylor (b. 190

Alternative Tune: *Winchester New* (27)

The Gospel

Lord Jesus, once you spoke to men
upon the mountain, in the plain;
O help us listen now, as then,
and wonder at your words again.

2

We all have secret fears to face,
our minds and motives to amend;
we seek your truth, we need your grace,
our living Lord and present Friend.

3

The Gospel speaks; and we receive‿
your light, your love, your own command.
O help us live what we believe
in daily work of heart and hand.

H. C. A. Gaunt (1902–83

93 (HHT **60**)
Magda 10 10.10 10. R. Vaughan Williams (1872–1958)

Alternative Tune: *Woodlands* (422)

Self-giving

Lord of all good, our gifts we bring to thee;
use them thy holy purpose to fulfil:
tokens of love and pledges they shall be
that our whole life is offered to thy will.

2

We give our mind to understand thy ways,
hands, eyes, and voice to serve thy great design;
heart with the flame of thine own love ablaze,
till for thy glory all our powers combine.

3

Father, whose bounty all creation shows,
Christ, by whose willing sacrifice we live,
Spirit, from whom all life in fulness flows,
to thee with grateful hearts ourselves we give.

ALBERT F. BAYLY (1901–84)

394 (HHT 61)

Miniver 10 11.11 12. Cyril Taylor (b. 190

Alternative Tune: *Slane* (395)

Our life in his hands

Lord of all hopefulness, Lord of all joy,
whose trust, ever childlike, no cares
could destroy,
be there at our waking, and give us,
we pray,
your bliss in our hearts, Lord,
at the break of the day.

2

Lord of all eagerness, Lord of all faith,
whose strong hands were skilled at the
plane and the lathe,
be there at our labours, and give us,
we pray,
your strength in our hearts, Lord,
at the noon of the day.

3

Lord of all kindliness, Lord of all grace,
your hands swift to welcome, your arms to
embrace,
be there at our homing, and give us,
we pray,
your love in our hearts, Lord,
at the eve of the day.

4

Lord of all gentleness, Lord of all calm,
whose voice is contentment, whose presence
is balm,
be there at our sleeping, and give us,
we pray,
your peace in our hearts, Lord,
at the end of the day.

JAN STRUTHER (1901–1953)

395 (HHT **62**)

Slane 10 11.11 11. Irish Traditional Melod

Self-giving

Lord of all power, I give you my will,
in joyful obedience your tasks to fulfil.
  Your bondage is freedom, your service is song,
  and, held in your keeping, my weakness is strong.

2

Lord of all wisdom, I give you my mind,
rich truth that surpasses man's knowledge to find.
  What eye has not seen and what ear has not heard
  is taught by your Spirit and shines from your Word.

3

Lord of all bounty, I give you my heart;
I praise and adore you for all you impart:
  your love to inspire me, your counsel to guide,
  your presence to cheer me, whatever betide.

4

Lord of all being, I give you my all;
if e'er I disown you I stumble and fall;
  but, sworn in glad service your word to obey,
  I walk in your freedom to the end of the way.

JACK C. WINSLOW* (1882–1974)

396 (HHT **63**)

FIRST TUNE

Lingwood
8 7.8 7.8 7.

C. Armstrong Gibbs (1889–19

SECOND TUNE

Obiit 8 7.8 7.8 7.

Walter Parratt (1841–192

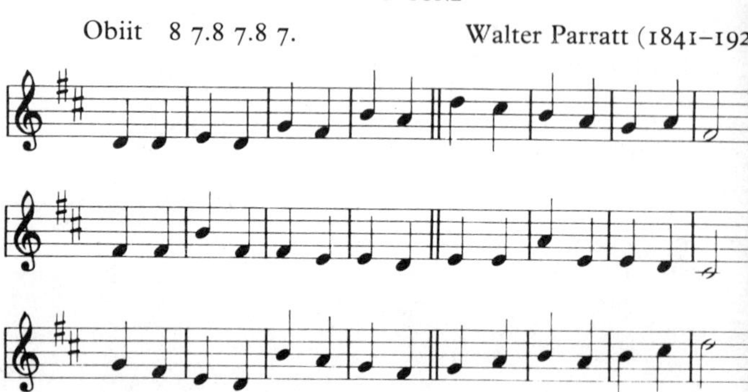

Alternative Tune: *Rhuddlan* (263)

For the Church and Nation

Lord of lords and King eternal,
  down the years in wondrous ways
you have blessed our land and guided,
  leading us through darkest days.
For your rich and faithful mercies,
  Lord, accept our thankful praise.

2

Speak to us and every nation,
  bid our jarring discords cease;
to the starving and the homeless
  bid us bring a full release;
and on all this earth's sore turmoil
  breathe the healing of your peace.

3

Love that binds us all together‿
  be upon the Church outpoured;
shame our pride and quell our factions,
  smite them with your Spirit's sword;
till the world, our love beholding,
  claims your power and calls you Lord.

4

Brace the wills of all your people
  who in every land and race
know the secrets of your kingdom,
  share the treasures of your grace;
till the summons of your Spirit
  wakes new life in every place.

5

Saviour, by your mighty Passion
  once you turned sheer loss to gain,
wrestling in your risen glory
  victory from your cross and pain;
now in us be dead and risen,
  in us triumph, live, and reign.

JACK C. WINSLOW* (1882–1974)

397 (HHT 64)

Breslau L.M. *As Hymnodus Sacer* (Leipzig, 162

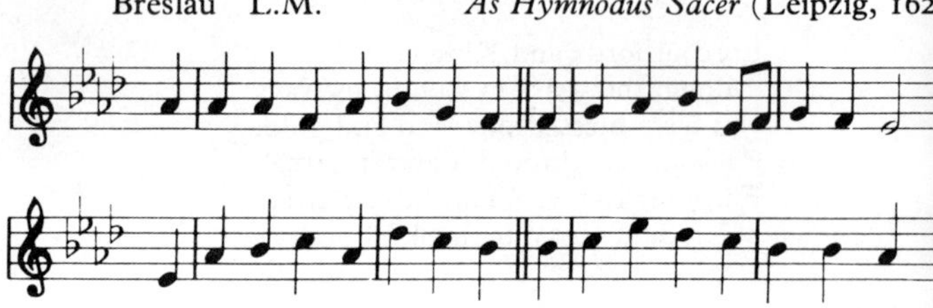

The world's need

Lord, save thy world; in bitter need‿
thy children lift their cry to thee;
we wait thy liberating deed
to signal hope and set us free.

2

Lord, save thy world; our souls are bound‿
in iron chains of fear and pride;
high walls of ignorance around
our faces from each other hide.

3

Lord, save thy world; we strive in vain‿
to save ourselves without thine aid;
what skill and science slowly gain,
is soon to evil ends betrayed.

4

Lord, save thy world; but thou hast sent‿
the Saviour whom we sorely need;
for us his tears and blood were spent,
that from our bonds we might be freed.

5

Then save us now, by Jesus' power,
and use the lives thy love sets free,
to bring at last the glorious hour
when all men find thy liberty.

ALBERT F. BAYLY (1901–84

98 (HHT **65**)

Lanteglos 8 8.4. John Dykes Bower (1905–81)

Adoration

Lord that descendedst, Holy Child,
dwelling amongst us, Word of God,
Thee we adore.

2

Jesus our Gospel, Way and Truth,
Master and Lover, Light and Life,
Thee we adore.

3

Saviour uplifted, Man for men,
shamèd and slaughtered, Lamb of God,
Thee we adore.

4

Christ the immortal Risen Lord,
Christ that ascended, King of kings,
Thee we adore.

5

Throned in the highest, Very Man,
Alpha, Omega, God of God,
Thee we adore.

6

Lord ever-blessèd, God most high,
Lord ever-blessèd, God with us,
Thee we adore.

ERIC MILNER-WHITE (1884–1963)

399 (HHT **66**) FIRST TUNE

Godmanstone 8 8 8.4. Cyril Taylor (b. 190

Men born blind

Lord, we are blind; the world of sight‿
is as a shadow in the dark.
Yet we have eyes; Lord, give us light
that we may see.

2

Lord, we are blind; the world around‿
confuses us, although we see.
In Christ the pattern is refound;
he sets us free.

3

Lord, we are blind; our sight, our life‿
by our own efforts cannot be.
Breathe on our clay and touch our eyes;
we would serve thee.

DAVID EDGE (b. 193

SECOND TUNE

Es ist kein Tag   8 8 8.4.   J. D. Meyer
(*Geistliche Seelen-Freud*, 1692)

Men born blind

Lord, we are blind; the world of sight
is as a shadow in the dark.
Yet we have eyes; Lord, give us light
that we may see.

2

Lord, we are blind; the world around
confuses us, although we see.
In Christ the pattern is refound;
he sets us free.

3

Lord, we are blind; our sight, our life
by our own efforts cannot be.
Breathe on our clay and touch our eyes;
we would serve thee.

DAVID EDGE (b. 1932)

400 (HHT 67)

Camden

Sydney Carter (b. 1915)

Solo. Free, in spoken time
Strict time
All
Stand-ing in the rain, Knock-ing on the wind-ow, Knock-ing on the wind-ow on a Christ-mas Day.
There he is a-gain, Knock-ing on the wind-ow, Knock-ing on the wind-ow in the same old way.
D.C.

House full

Solo
No use knocking on the window,
there is nothing we can do, sir;
all the beds are booked already,
there is nothing left for you, sir:

All *Standing in the rain,*
knocking on the window,
knocking on the window
on a Christmas Day.
There he is again,
knocking on the window,
knocking on the window
in the same old way.

2

No use knocking on the window,
some are lucky, some are not, sir.
We are Christian men and women,
but we're keeping what we've got, sir:

3

No, we haven't got a manger,
no, we haven't got a stable.
We are Christian men and women
always willing, never able:

4

Jesus Christ has gone to heaven;
one day he'll be coming back, sir.
In this house he will be welcome,
but we hope he won't be black, sir:

5

Wishing you a merry Christmas
we will now go back to bed, sir.
Till you woke us with your knocking
we were sleeping like the dead, sir:

Sydney Carter (b. 1915)

401 (HHT **68**)
Cornwall 8 8 6.8 8 6. S. S. Wesley (1810–76)

Truth and light

Not far beyond the sea, nor high
above the heavens, but very nigh
thy voice, O God, is heard.
For each new step of faith we take
thou hast more truth and light to break
forth from thy Holy Word.

2

Rooted and grounded in thy love,
with saints on earth and saints above
we join in full accord.
To grasp the breadth, length, depth, and height,
the crucified and risen might
of Christ, the Incarnate Word.

3

Help us to press toward that mark,
and, though our vision now is dark,
to live by what we see.
So, when we see thee face to face,
thy truth and light our dwelling-place
for evermore shall be.

George B. Caird (1917–84)

402 (HHT **69**)

Christchurch 6 6.6 6.8 8. C. Steggall (1826–1905)

The new life

1 Now is eternal life,
  if ris'n with Christ we stand,
in him to life reborn,
  and holden in his hand;
no more we fear death's ancient dread,
in Christ arisen from the dead.

2 Man long in bondage lay,
  brooding o'er life's brief span;
was it, O God, for naught,
  for naught, thou madest man?
Thou art our hope, our vital breath;
shall hope undying end in death?

3 And God, the living God,
  stooped down to man's estate;
by death destroying death,
  Christ opened wide life's gate.
He lives, who died; he reigns on high;
who lives in him shall never die.

4 Unfathomed love divine,
  reign thou within my heart;
from thee nor depth nor height,
  nor life nor death can part;
my life is hid in God with thee,
now and through all eternity.

G. W. Briggs (1875–1959)

403 (HHT 70)

Solothurn L.M. Swiss Traditional Melody

The sacrament of care

Now let us from this table rise,
  renewed in body, mind, and soul;
with Christ we die and live again,
  his selfless love has made us whole.

2

With minds alert, upheld by grace,
  to spread the Word in speech and deed,
we follow in the steps of Christ,
  at one with man in hope and need.

3

To fill each human house with love,
  it is the sacrament of care;
the work that Christ began to do
  we humbly pledge ourselves to share.

4

Then give us courage, Father God,
  to choose again the pilgrim way,
and help us to accept with joy‿
  the challenge of tomorrow's day.

FRED KAAN (b. 1929)

404 (HHT 71)

Llangloffan 7 6.8 6.D. Welsh Hymn Melod

100 Hymns for Today

Christ crucified today

O crucified Redeemer,
  whose life-blood we have spilt,
to thee we raise our guilty hands,
  and humbly own our guilt.
Today we see thy Passion
  spread open to our gaze;
the crowded street, the country lane,
  its Calvary displays.

2

Wherever love is outraged,
  wherever hope is killed,
where man still wrongs his brother man,
  thy Passion is fulfilled.
We see thy tortured body,
  we see the wounds that bleed,
where brotherhood hangs crucified,
  nailed to the cross of greed.

3

We hear thy cry of anguish,
  we see thy life outpoured,
where battlefield runs red with blood,
  our brothers' blood, O Lord.
And in that bloodless battle,
  the fight for daily bread,
where might is right and self is king,
  we see thy thorn-crowned head.

4

The groaning of creation,
  wrung out by pain and care,
the anguish of a million hearts
  that break in dumb despair;
O crucified Redeemer,
  these are thy cries of pain;
O may they break our selfish hearts,
  and love come in to reign.

TIMOTHY REES* (1874–1939)

405 (HHT 72)
St. Michael S.M.

Adapted from *Anglo-Genevan Psalms, 156*

The Day of God

O Day of God, draw nigh
in beauty and in power,
come with thy timeless judgment now
to match our present hour.

2

Bring to our troubled minds,
uncertain and afraid,
the quiet of a steadfast faith,
calm of a call obeyed.

3

Bring justice to our land,
that all may dwell secure,
and finely build for days to come
foundations that endure.

4

Bring to our world of strife
thy sovereign word of peace,
that war may haunt the earth no more
and desolation cease.

5

O Day of God, draw nigh;
as at creation's birth
let there be light again, and set‿
thy judgments in the earth.

R. B. Y. Scott (b. 1899)

06 (HHT 73)
St. Petersburg D. S. Bortnianski (1752–1825)
8 8.8 8.8 8.

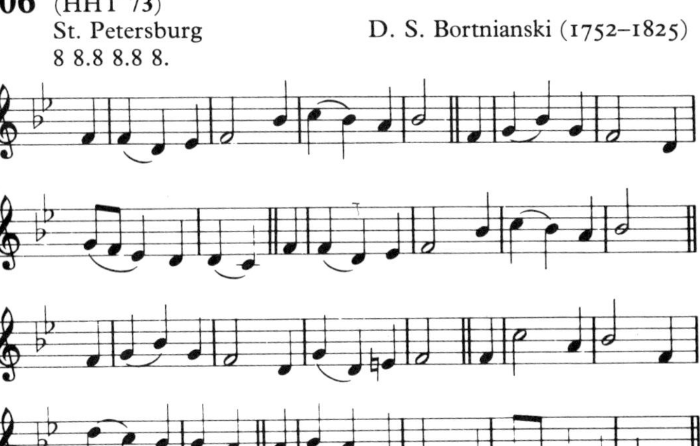

The healing God

1 O God, by whose almighty plan
first order out of chaos stirred,
and life, progressive at your word,
matured through nature up to man;
grant us in light and love to grow,
your sovereign truth to seek and know.

2 O Christ, whose touch unveiled the blind,
whose presence warmed the lonely soul;
your love made broken sinners whole,
your faith cast devils from the mind.
Grant us your faith, your love, your care
to bring to sufferers everywhere.

3 O Holy Spirit, by whose grace‿
our skills abide, our wisdom grows,
in every healing work disclose‿
new paths to probe, new thoughts to trace.
Grant us your wisest way to go
in all we think, or speak, or do.

H. C. A. Gaunt (1902–83)

407 (HHT 74)

Melita 8 8.8 8.8 8. J. B. Dykes (1823–

Our homes

1 O God in heaven, whose loving plan
ordained for us our parents' care,
and, from the time our life began,
the shelter of a home to share;
Our Father, on the homes we love
send down thy blessing from above.

2 May young and old together find‿
in Christ the Lord of every day,
that fellowship our homes may bind
in joy and sorrow, work and play.
Our Father, on the homes we love
send down thy blessing from above.

3 The sins that mar our homes forgive;
from all self-seeking set us free;
parents and children, may we live‿
in glad obedience to thee.
Our Father, on the homes we love
send down thy blessing from above.

4 O Father, in our homes preside,
their duties shared as in thy sight;
in kindly ways be thou our guide,
on mirth and trouble shed thy light.
Our Father, on the homes we love
send down thy blessing from above.

HUGH MARTIN* (1890–1964

408 (HHT 75)

Crucis victoria C.M. M. B. Foster (1851–1922)

For those who heal

O God, whose will is life and good
for all of mortal breath,
unite in bonds of brotherhood‿
all those who fight with death.

2

Make strong their hands and hearts and wills
to drive disease afar,
to battle with the body's ills,
and wage thy holy war.

3

Where'er they heal the sick and blind,
Christ's love may they proclaim;
make known the good Physician's mind,
and prove the Saviour's name.

4

Before them set thy holy will,
that they, with heart and soul,
to thee may consecrate their skill,
and make the sufferer whole.

H. D. Rawnsley* (1851–1920)

409 (HHT 76) FIRST TUNE

Sancta Civitas 8 6.8 6.8 6. Herbert Howells (1892–198

SECOND TUNE

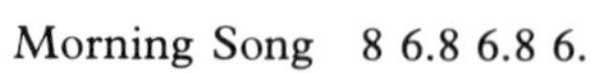
Morning Song 8 6.8 6.8 6. *The Union Harmon*
(Virginia, 1848

Alternative Tune: *Crediton* (502) *repeating lines 3 and 4*

The City of God

O holy City, seen of John,
  where Christ, the Lamb, doth reign,
within whose four-square walls shall come‿
  no night, nor need, nor pain,
and where the tears are wiped from eyes‿
  that shall not weep again.

2

O shame to us who rest content
  while lust and greed for gain
in street and shop and tenement
  wring gold from human pain,
and bitter lips in blind despair
  cry, 'Christ hath died in vain'.

3

Give us, O God, the strength to build‿
  the City that hath stood
too long a dream, whose laws are love,
  whose ways are brotherhood,
and where the sun that shineth is‿
  God's grace for human good.

4

Already in the mind of God
  that City riseth fair:
lo, how its splendour challenges‿
  the souls that greatly dare:
yea, bids us seize the whole of life
  and build its glory there.

W. Russell Bowie (1882–1969)
suggested by St. John's vision in Revelation 21

410 (HHT 77)

Sussex Carol 8 8.8 8.8 8. English Traditional Melod[y]

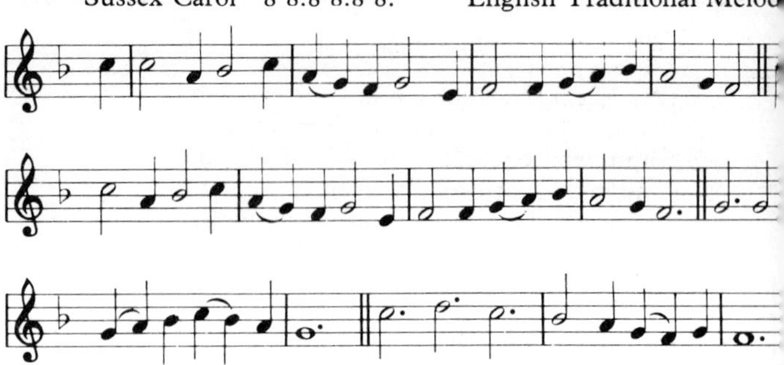

Offertory

O Holy Father, God most dear,
behold us round thy altar here,
accept for sacrifice, we pray,
the common food we here display.
For bread set forth, for wine outpoured
we bless thee, all-creating Lord.

2

O Christ, who at the supper-board
took bread and wine and spoke the word,
and in that solemn paschal meal
gave Flesh and Blood our wound to heal;
for man redeemed, for life restored,
we bless thee, all-creating Word.

3

O Holy Spirit, be thou nigh
this bread and cup to sanctify,
that, eating of the food unpriced,
we form one body, one in Christ.
Redeemed, restored in unity,
we bless thee, Holy Trinity.

G. A. TOMLINSON (b. 1906

411 (HHT 78)

St. Osyth 11 10.11 10. Thomas Wood (1892–1950)

Alternative Tune: *Stonegate* (486)

God's age-long plan

1 O Lord of every shining constellation
that wheels in splendour through the midnight sky,
grant us your Spirit's true illumination
to read the secrets of your work on high.

2 You, Lord, have made the atom's hidden forces,
your laws its mighty energies fulfil;
teach us, to whom you give such rich resources,
in all we use, to serve your holy will.

3 O Life, awaking life in cell and tissue,
from flower to bird, from beast to brain of man;
help us to trace, from birth to final issue,
the sure unfolding of your age-long plan.

4 You, Lord, have stamped your image on your creatures,
and, though they mar that image, love them still;
lift up our eyes to Christ, that in his features
we may discern the beauty of your will.

5 Great Lord of nature, shaping and renewing,
you made us more than nature's sons to be;
you help us tread, with grace our souls enduring,
the road to life and immortality.

Albert F. Bayly* (1901–84)

412 (HHT 79)
Surrey 8 8.8 8.8 8. Henry Carey (c. 1690–1743)

Walking by faith

O Lord, we long to see your face,
to know you risen from the grave,
but we have missed the joy and grace‿
of seeing you, as others have.
  Yet in your company we'll wait,
  and we shall see you, soon or late.

2

O Lord, we do not know the way,
nor clearly see the path ahead;
so often, therefore, we delay
and doubt your power to raise the dead.
  Yet with you we will firmly stay;
  you are the Truth, the Life, the Way.

3

We find it hard, Lord, to believe;
all habit makes us want to prove;
we would with eye and hand perceive‿
the truth and person whom we love.
  Yet, as in fellowship we meet,
  you come yourself each one to greet.

4

You come to us, our God, our Lord;
you do not show your hands and side;
but faith has its more blest reward;
in love's assurance we confide.
  Now we believe, that we may know,
  and in that knowledge daily grow.

J. R. Peacey (1896–1971)

413 (HHT **80**)
Kingsfold D.C.M. English Traditional Meloc

The name above every name

O sing a song of Bethlehem,
of shepherds watching there,
and of the news that came to them
from angels in the air:
the light that shone on Bethlehem
fills all the world today;
of Jesus' birth and peace on earth
the angels sing alway.

2

O sing a song of Nazareth,
of sunny days of joy,
O sing of fragrant flowers' breath
and of the sinless Boy:
for now the flowers of Nazareth
in every heart may grow;
now spreads the fame of his dear name
on all the winds that blow.

3

O sing a song of Galilee,
of lake and woods and hill,
of him who walked upon the sea
and bade its waves be still:
for though, like waves on Galilee,
dark seas of trouble roll,
when faith has heard the Master's word,
falls peace upon the soul.

4

O sing a song of Calvary,
its glory and dismay;
of him who hung upon the tree,
and took our sins away:
for he who died on Calvary
is risen from the grave,
and Christ our Lord, by heaven adored,
is mighty now to save.

LOUIS F. BENSON (1855–1930)

414 (HHT **81**)
Confession — Francis Westbrook (1903–7

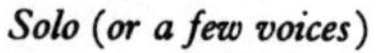

Lighten our darkness

Peter feared the Cross for himself and his Master;
Peter tempted Jesus to turn and go back.
O Lord, have mercy,
lighten our darkness.
We've all been tempters,
our light is black.

*2

Judas loved his pride and rejected his Master;
Judas turned a traitor and lost his way back.
O Lord, have mercy,
lighten our darkness.
We've all been traitors,
our light is black.

*3

Peter, James and John fell asleep when their Master
asked them to be praying a few paces back.
O Lord, have mercy,
lighten our darkness.
We've all been sleeping,
our light is black.

4

Peter, vexed and tired, thrice denied his own Master;
said he never knew him, to stop a girl's clack.
O Lord, have mercy,
lighten our darkness.
We've all denied you,
our light is black.

5

Twelve all ran away and forsook their dear Master;
left him lonely prisoner, a lamb in wolves' pack.
O Lord, have mercy,
lighten our darkness.
We've all been failures,
our light is black.

*6

Pilate asked the crowd to set free their good Master.
'Crucify', they shouted, 'we don't want him back!'
O Lord, have mercy,
lighten our darkness.
We crucified you,
our light is black.

7

We have watched the Cross and we've scoffed at the Master;
thought the safe way better and tried our own tack.
O Lord, have mercy,
lighten our darkness.
We've all reviled you,
our light is black.

EMILY CHISHOLM (b. 1910)

415 (HHT 82)

Bunessan 5 5.5 4.D. Old Gaelic Melo

Bread for the world

1

Praise and thanksgiving,
Father, we offer,
for all things living‿
thou madest good;
harvest of sown fields,
fruits of the orchard,
hay from the mown fields,
blossom and wood.

2

Bless thou the labour‿
we bring to serve thee,
that with our neighbour‿
we may be fed.
Sowing or tilling,
we would work with thee;
harvesting, milling,‿
for daily bread.

3

Father, providing‿
food for thy children,
thy wisdom guiding
teaches us share
one with another,
so that rejoicing
with us, our brother‿
may know thy care.

4

Then will thy blessing‿
reach every people;
all men confessing‿
thy gracious hand.
Where thy will reigneth
no man will hunger:
thy love sustaineth;
fruitful the land.

ALBERT F. BAYLY (1901–8

416 (HHT **83**)

Evangelists 8 8 7.D.
(Alles ist an Gottes Segen)

Adapted from J. S. Bach's version of a chorale by J. Löhner (1691) and others

Into the world

Praise the Lord, rise up rejoicing,
worship, thanks, devotion voicing:
glory be to God on high!
Christ, your Cross and Passion sharing,
by this Eucharist declaring
yours the eternal victory.

2

Scattered flock, one Shepherd sharing,
lost and lonely, one voice hearing,
ears are open to your word;
by your Blood new life receiving,
in your Body firm, believing,
we are yours, and you the Lord.

3

Send us forth alert and living,
sins forgiven, wrongs forgiving,
in your Spirit strong and free.
Finding love in all creation,
bringing peace in every nation,
may we faithful followers be.

H. C. A. Gaunt (1902–83)

417 (HHT 84)
Savannah 7 7.7 7. John Wesley's *Foundery Collection*
1742

The Gospel

Praise we now the Word of grace;
may our hearts its truth embrace:
from its pages may we hear‿
Christ our Teacher, speaking clear.

2

May the Gospel of the Lord‿
everywhere be spread abroad,
that the world around may own‿
Christ as King, and Christ alone.

S. N. SEDGWICK* (1872–1941)

18 (HHT **85**)
Falcon Street (Silver Street) S.M. Late form of melody by Isaac Smith (c. 1770)

Alternative Tune: *Carlisle* (318)

Service

Rise up, O men of God;
have done with lesser things;
  give heart and soul and mind and strength‿
to serve the King of kings.

2

Rise up, O men of God;
his kingdom tarries long;
  bring in the day of brotherhood,
and end the night of wrong.

3

Rise up, O men of God;
the Church for you doth wait:
  her strength unequal to her task;
rise up, and make her great.

4

Lift high the Cross of Christ;
tread where his feet have trod;
  as brothers of the Son of Man
rise up, O men of God.

W. P. MERRILL (1867–1954)

419 (HHT **86**)

Cannons L.M. G. F. Handel (1685–175

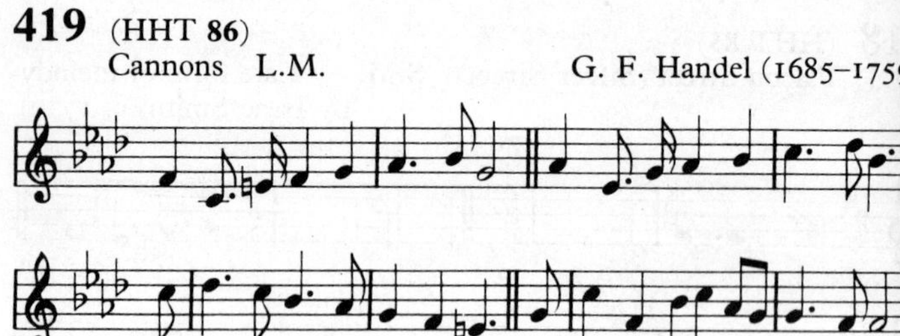

Alternative Tune: *Truro* (483)

Magnificat now

Sing we a song of high revolt;
make great the Lord, his name exalt:
  sing we the song that Mary sang
  of God at war with human wrong.

2

Sing we of him who deeply cares
and still with us our burden bears;
  he, who with strength the proud disowns,
  brings down the mighty from their thrones.

3

By him the poor are lifted up;
he satisfies with bread and cup‿
  the hungry men of many lands;
  the rich are left with empty hands.

4

He calls us to revolt and fight‿
with him for what is just and right,
  to sing and live Magnificat
  in crowded street and council flat.

FRED KAAN (b. 1929)

420 (HHT 87)

Lawes' Psalm 47 6 6.6 6.8 8. Henry Lawes (1596–16

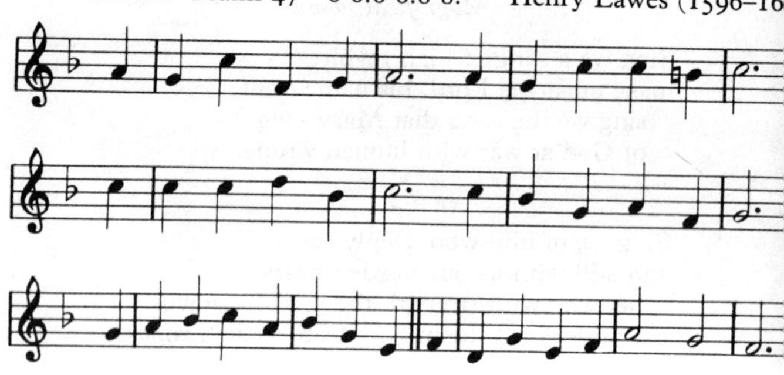

Son of Man

Son of the Lord Most High,
  who gave the worlds their birth,
he came to live and die
  the Son of Man on earth:
    in Bethlem's stable born was he,
    and humbly bred in Galilee.

2

Born in so low estate,
  schooled in a workman's trade,
not with the high and great‿
  his home the Highest made:
    but labouring by his brethren's side,
    life's common lot he glorified.

3

Then, when his hour was come,
  he heard his Father's call:
and leaving friends and home,
  he gave himself for all:
    glad news to bring, the lost to find;
    to heal the sick, the lame, the blind.

4

Toiling by night and day,
  himself oft burdened sore,
where hearts in bondage lay,
  himself their burden bore:
    till, scorned by them he died to save,
    himself in death, as life, he gave.

5

O lowly Majesty,
  lofty in lowliness.
Blest Saviour, who am I‿
  to share thy blessedness?
    Yet thou hast called me, even me,
    Servant divine, to follow thee.

G. W. Briggs (1875–1959)

421 (HHT 88)

Ach Gott und Herr *Neu-Leipziger Gesangbuch*, 16[illegible]
8 7.8 7.

Into the world

Strengthen for service, Lord, the hands‿
that holy things have taken;
let ears that now have heard thy songs
to clamour never waken.

2

Lord, may the tongues which 'Holy' sang
keep free from all deceiving;
the eyes which saw thy love be bright,
thy blessèd hope perceiving.

3

The feet that tread thy holy courts
from light do thou not banish;
the bodies by thy Body fed
with thy new life replenish.

Ascr. to EPHRAIM the Syrian (c. 306–73
tr. C. W. HUMPHREYS (1841–1921
and PERCY DEARMER (1867–1936

Another translation of these words is at 278

22 (HHT **89**)

Woodlands 10 10.10 10. Walter Greatorex (1877–1949)

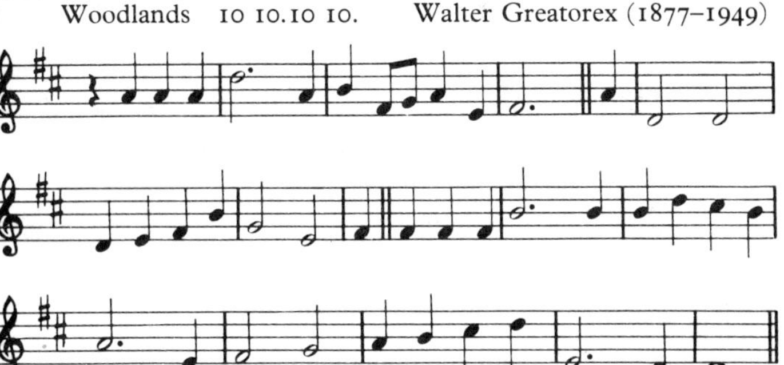

Magnificat

Tell out, my soul, the greatness of the Lord:
unnumbered blessings, give my spirit voice;
tender to me the promise of his word;
in God my Saviour shall my heart rejoice.

2

Tell out, my soul, the greatness of his name:
make known his might, the deeds his arm has done;
his mercy sure, from age to age the same;
his holy name, the Lord, the Mighty One.

3

Tell out, my soul, the greatness of his might:
powers and dominions lay their glory by;
proud hearts and stubborn wills are put to flight,
the hungry fed, the humble lifted high.

4

Tell out, my soul, the glories of his word:
firm is his promise, and his mercy sure.
Tell out, my soul, the greatness of the Lord
to children's children and for evermore.

TIMOTHY DUDLEY-SMITH (b. 1926)
based on Luke 1. 46–55
in *The New English Bible*

423 (HHT **90**)
Kingley Vale 8 7.8 7.4 7. H. P. Allen (1869–1946

Alternative Tune: *St. Helen* (263)

The Word of God

Thanks to God whose Word was spoken
in the deed that made the earth.
His the voice that called a nation,
his the fires that tried her worth.
God has spoken:
praise him for his open Word.

2

Thanks to God whose Word incarnate
glorified the flesh of man.
Deeds and words and death and rising
tell the grace in heaven's plan.
God has spoken:
praise him for his open Word.

3

Thanks to God whose Word was written
  in the Bible's sacred page,
record of the revelation
  showing God to every age.
    God has spoken:
praise him for his open Word.

4

Thanks to God whose Word is published
  in the tongues of every race.
See its glory undiminished
  by the change of time or place.
    God has spoken:
praise him for his open Word.

5

Thanks to God whose Word is answered
  by the Spirit's voice within.
Here we drink of joy unmeasured,
  life redeemed from death and sin.
    God is speaking:
praise him for his open Word.

R. T. Brooks (b. 1918)

424 (HHT **91**)
St. Thomas S.M. Aaron Williams (1731–7

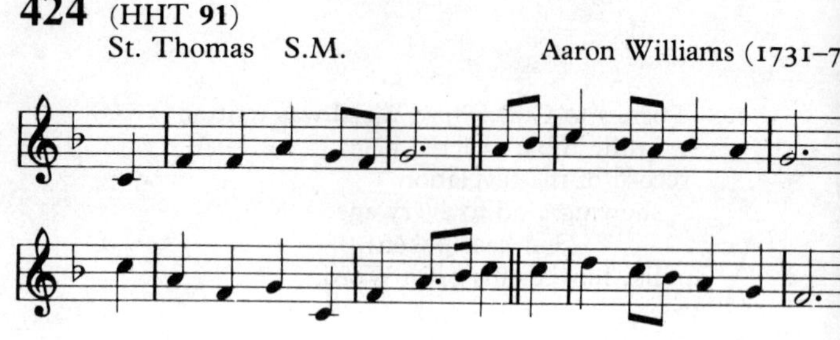

The Lord's day

The first day of the week,
his own, in sad despair,
could not believe for very joy
the risen Lord was there.

2

Now they obeyed his word,
now shared what Jesus gave,
and, one in him, in breaking bread
knew what it costs to save.

3

And each day of the week,
and on the Lord's own day,
they walked in Christian liberty
his new and living Way.

4

And on the Lord's own day,
from needless burdens freed,
they kept a Sabbath made for man,
to fit man's inmost need.

5

How soon men forge again
the fetters of their past!
as long as Jesus lives in us,
so long our freedoms last.

6

This day his people meet,
this day his word is sown.
Lord Jesus, show us how to use‿
this day we call your own.

F. PRATT GREEN (b. 1903)

425 (HHT **92**)

Harewood 6 6.6 6.8 8. S. S. Wesley (1810–76

Race Relations

The God who rules this earth
  gave life to every race;
he chose its day of birth,
  the colour of its face;
so none may claim superior grade
within the family he's made.

2

But sin infects us all,
  distorts the common good;
the universal fall‿
  corrupts all brotherhood;
so racial pride and colour strife
spread fear and hate throughout man's life.

3

Between the West and East,
yet neither black nor white
behold, God's Son released!
in whom all men unite.
He comes with unrestricted grace
to heal the hearts of every race.

4

That Man alone combines‿
all lives within his own;
that Man alone enshrines‿
all flesh, all blood, all bone;
that Man accepts all human pain,
that Man breaks death; that Man
shall reign.

5

To him we bring our praise,
on him all hopes depend;
sole Master of our days,
in him we see the End;
man's final Lord, God's perfect Son,
in Jesus Christ are all made one.

RICHARD G. JONES (b. 1926)

426 (HHT 93)

Crimond C.M. Jessie S. Irvine (1836–87

God's providence

1 The Lord's my Shepherd, I'll not want;
he makes me down to lie‿
in pastures green; he leadeth me‿
the quiet waters by.

2 My soul he doth restore again,
and me to walk doth make‿
within the paths of righteousness,
e'en for his own name's sake.

3 Yea, though I walk through death's dark vale,
yet will I fear none ill;
for thou art with me, and thy rod‿
and staff me comfort still.

4 My table thou hast furnishèd
in presence of my foes;
my head thou dost with oil anoint,
and my cup overflows.

5 Goodness and mercy all my life
shall surely follow me;
and in God's house for evermore
my dwelling-place shall be.

Psalm 23 in *Scottish Psalter*, 1650

27 (HHT **94**)
Mount Ephraim S.M. B. Milgrove (1731–1810)

Alternative Tune: *Carlisle* (318)

Lord of life and death

1 The Son of God proclaim,
the Lord of time and space;
the God who bade the light break forth
now shines in Jesus' face.

2 He, God's creative Word,
the Church's Lord and Head,
here bids us gather as his friends
and share his wine and bread.

3 The Lord of life and death
with wond'ring praise we sing;
we break the bread at his command
and name him God and King.

4 We take this cup in hope;
for he, who gladly bore‿
the shameful Cross, is risen again
and reigns for evermore.

Basil E. Bridge (b. 1927)

428 (HHT 95)

Maccabaeus G. F. Handel (1685–1759)

10 11.11 11. and refrain

Risen with Christ

1 Thine be the glory, risen, conquering Son,
endless is the victory thou o'er death hast won;
angels in bright raiment rolled the stone away,
kept the folded grave-clothes where thy body lay.

Thine be the glory, risen, conquering Son,
endless is the victory thou o'er death hast won.

2 Lo, Jesus meets us, risen from the tomb;
lovingly he greets us, scatters fear and gloom;
let the Church with gladness hymns of triumph sing,
for her Lord now liveth, death hath lost its sting:

3 No more we doubt thee, glorious Prince of Life;
life is nought without thee: aid us in our strife;
make us more than conquerors through thy deathless love;
bring us safe through Jordan to thy home above:

E. L. Budry (1854–1932)
tr. R. B. Hoyle (1875–1939)

429 (HHT **96**)
Brockham L.M. Jeremiah Clarke (c. 1659–1707)

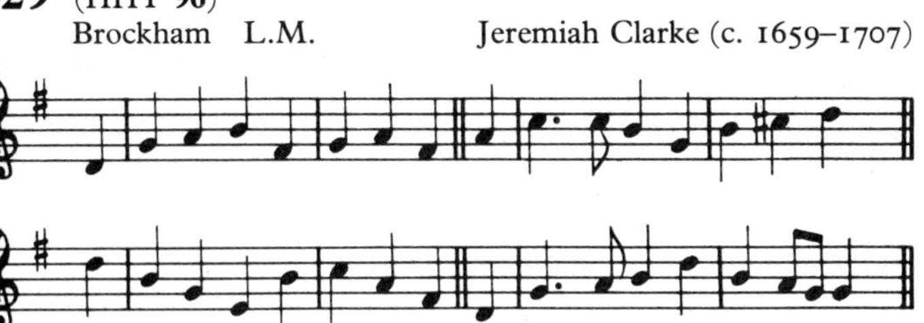

Offertory

Upon thy table, Lord, we place‿
these symbols of our work and thine,
life's food won only by thy grace,
who giv'st to all the bread and wine.

2

Within these simple things there lie‿
the height and depth of human life,
the thought of man, his tears and toil,
his hopes and fears, his joy and strife.

3

Accept them, Lord; from thee they come:
we take them humbly at thy hand.
These gifts of thine for higher use
we offer, as thou dost command.

M. F. C. Willson* (1884–1944)

430 (HHT **97**)
Wilford 8 7.8 7.

Adapted from a melody
George Gardner (1853–192

Incognito

We find thee, Lord, in others' need,
we see thee in our brothers;
by loving word and kindly deed
we serve the Man for Others.

2

We look around and see thy face‿
disfigured, marred, neglected;
we find thee Lord in every place,
sought for and unexpected.

3

We offer in simplicity‿
our loving gift and labour;
and what we do, we do to thee,
incarnate in our neighbour.

4

We love since we are loved by thee;
new strength from thee we gather;
and in thy service we shall be‿
made perfect with each other.

GILES AMBROSE (b. 1912

31 (HHT **98**)
Fulda L.M. William Gardiner, *Sacred Melodies, 1815*

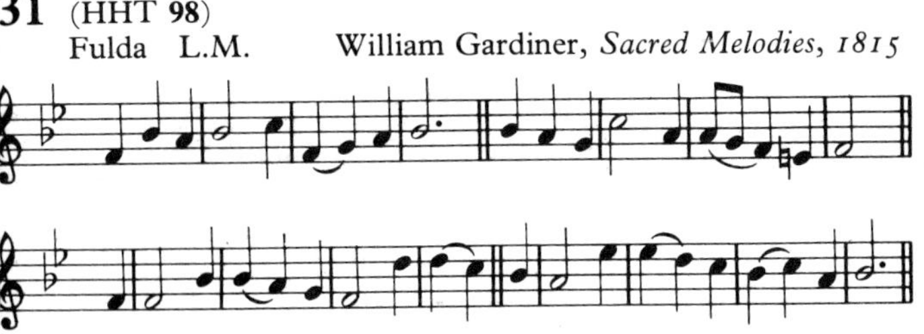

Good news

1 We have a gospel to proclaim,
good news for men in all the earth;
the gospel of a Saviour's name:
we sing his glory, tell his worth.

2 Tell of his birth at Bethlehem
not in a royal house or hall
but in a stable dark and dim,
the Word made flesh, a light for all.

3 Tell of his death at Calvary,
hated by those he came to save,
in lonely suffering on the Cross;
for all he loved his life he gave.

4 Tell of that glorious Easter morn:
empty the tomb, for he was free.
He broke the power of death and hell
that we might share his victory.

5 Tell of his reign at God's right hand,
by all creation glorified.
He sends his Spirit on his Church
to live for him, the Lamb who died.

6 Now we rejoice to name him King:
Jesus is Lord of all the earth.
This gospel-message we proclaim:
we sing his glory, tell his worth.

EDWARD J. BURNS (b. 1938)

432 (HHT **99**)
Sharpthorne 6 6.6 6.3 3.6. Erik Routley (1917–82

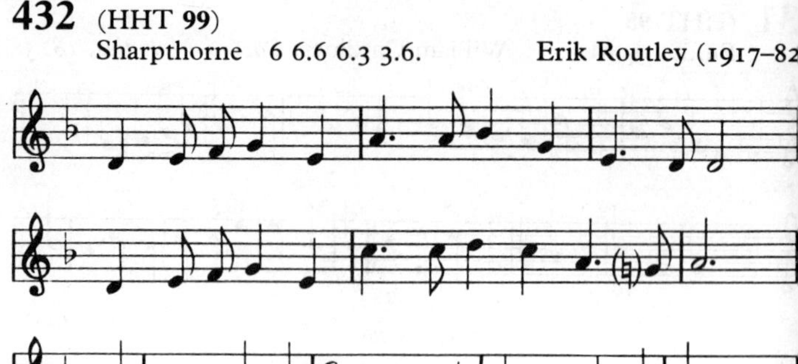

True religion

What does the Lord require‿
for praise and offering?
what sacrifice desire‿
or tribute bid you bring?
Do justly;
love mercy;
walk humbly with your God.

2

Rulers of men, give ear!
should you not justice know?
will God your pleading hear,
while crime and cruelty grow?
Do justly;
love mercy;
walk humbly with your God.

3

Masters of wealth and trade,
  all you for whom men toil,
think not to win God's aid,
  if lies your commerce soil.
    Do justly;
    love mercy;
walk humbly with your God.

4

Still down the ages ring‿
  the prophet's stern commands:
to merchant, worker, king,
  he brings God's high demands:
    do justly;
    love mercy;
walk humbly with your God.

5

How shall our life fulfil‿
  God's law so hard and high?
let Christ endue our will‿
  with grace to fortify.
    Then justly,
    in mercy,
we'll humbly walk with God.

ALBERT F. BAYLY* (1901–84)
based on Micah 6. 6–8

433 (HHT **100**)
Neighbour

Sydney Carter (b. 1915

Solo
All
And the creed and the col-our and th
vv. 1–5
last verse
name won't mat-ter, Were you there? 2 I was there.
(last verse) I'll be

Christian Aid

Solo When I needed a neighbour, were you there,
were you there?
When I needed a neighbour, were you there?

All *And the creed and the colour and the name*
won't matter,
were you there?

2

I was hungry and thirsty, were you there,
were you there?
I was hungry and thirsty, were you there?

3

I was cold, I was naked, were you there,
were you there?
I was cold, I was naked, were you there?

4

When I needed a shelter, were you there,
were you there?
When I needed a shelter, were you there?

5

When I needed a healer, were you there,
were you there?
When I needed a healer, were you there?

6

Wherever you travel, I'll be there,
I'll be there,
wherever you travel, I'll be there,

And the creed and the colour and the name
won't matter,
I'll be there.

SYDNEY CARTER (b. 1915)

434 (MHT 101)
Folksong 9 8.9 8.

English Traditional Melod[y]
arr. John Wilso[n]

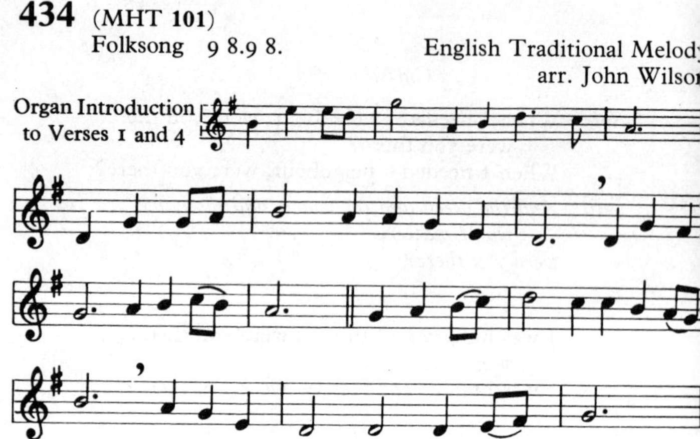

An upper room

Organ introduction

An upper room did our Lord prepare
  for those he loved until the end:
and his disciples still gather there,
  to celebrate their risen friend.

2

A lasting gift Jesus gave his own –
  to share his bread, his loving cup.
Whatever burdens may bow us down,
  he by his cross shall lift us up.

3

And after supper he washed their feet,
  for service, too, is sacrament.
In him our joy shall be made complete –
  sent out to serve, as he was sent.

Organ introduction

4

No end there is: we depart in peace.
  He loves beyond our uttermost:
in every room in our Father's house
  he will be there, as Lord and host.

F. PRATT GREEN (b. 1903)

The words were written for this tune

435 (MHT 102)

Jacob's Ladder 18th c. English Carol Meloc

11 11.11 11. and refrain

Jacob's ladder

1 As Ja - cob with tra - vel was wea - ry one day, at_
2 This lad - der is long, it is strong and well-made, has sto
3 Come let us a - scend! all may climb it who will; for th
4 And when we ar - rive at the ha - ven of rest we sh

night on a stone for a pil - low he lay; he__
hun-dreds of years and is not yet de-cayed; ma-ny
an - gels of Ja - cob are guard - ing it still: and re-
hear the glad words, 'Come up hi - ther, ye blest, here are

saw in a vi - sion a lad - der so high that its
mil - lions have climbed it and reached Si - on's hill, and_
mem - ber, each step that by faith we pass o'er, some
re - gions of light, here are man - sions of bliss'. O

Refrai

foot was on earth and its top in the sky:
thou - sands by faith are climb - ing it still: *Al - le -*
pro - phet or mar - tyr has trod it be-fore:
who would not climb such a lad - der as this?

-lu-ya to Je-sus who died on the tree, and has
raised up a lad-der of mer-cy for me, and has
raised up a lad-der of mer-cy for me.

18th cent.

436 (MHT **103**)

St. Petersburg L.M. D. S. Bortnianski (1752–1825

The Christian Race

Awake, our souls; away, our fears;
  let every trembling thought be gone;
awake and run the heavenly race,
  and put a cheerful courage on.

2

True, 'tis a strait and thorny road,
  and mortal spirits tire and faint;
but they forget the mighty God
  that feeds the strength of every saint:

3

the mighty God, whose matchless power
  is ever new and ever young,
and firm endures, while endless years
  their everlasting circles run.

4

From thee, the overflowing spring,
  our souls shall drink a fresh supply,
while such as trust their native strength
  shall melt away, and drop, and die.

5

Swift as an eagle cuts the air,
  we'll mount aloft to thine abode;
on wings of love our souls shall fly,
  nor tire amidst the heavenly road.

ISAAC WATTS (1674–1748)
Isaiah 40. 28–31

437 (MHT **104**)

Blairgowrie 8 8.8 6.8 6. R. G. Thompson (1862–1934

A new spring

1 Away with gloom, away with doubt,
with all the morning stars we sing;
with all the sons of God we shout‿
the praises of a King,
Alleluia, alleluia,
of our returning King.

2 Away with death, and welcome life;
in him we died and live again:
and welcome peace, away with strife,
for he returns to reign.
Alleluia, alleluia,
the Crucified shall reign.

3 Then welcome beauty, he is fair;
and welcome youth, for he is young;
and welcome spring; and everywhere‿
let merry songs be sung,
Alleluia, alleluia,
for such a King be sung.

EDWARD SHILLITO (1872–1948)

438 (MHT **105**)

Epworth C.M. Adapted from a melody by Charles Wesley the younger (1757–1834)

Alternative Tune: *St. Bernard* (64)

The light of Christ

1 Can man by searching find out God
or formulate his ways?
can numbers measure what he is
or words contain his praise?

2 Although his being is too bright
for human eyes to scan,
his meaning lights our shadowed world
through Christ, the Son of Man.

3 Our boastfulness is turned to shame,
our profit counts as loss,
when earthly values stand beside‿
the manger and the cross.

4 We there may recognise his light,
may kindle in its rays,
find there the source of penitence,
the starting-point for praise.

5 There God breaks in upon our search,
makes birth and death his own:
he speaks to us in human terms
to make his glory known.

Elizabeth Cosnett (b. 1936)

439 (MHT **106**)
Jackson C.M. Thomas Jackson (1715–81)

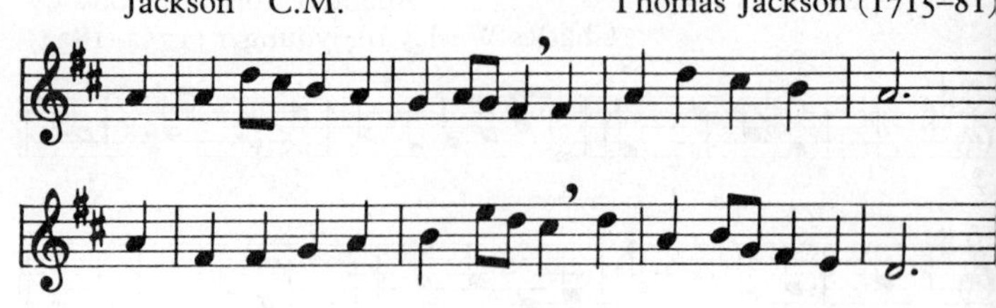

The Body of Christ

Christ is the heavenly food that gives‿
to every famished soul
new life and strength, new joy and hope,
and faith to make them whole.

2

We all are made for God alone,
without him we are dead;
no food suffices for the soul,
but Christ, the living bread.

3

Christ is the unity that binds‿
in one the near and far;
for we who share his life divine
his living body are.

4

On earth and in the realms beyond
one fellowship are we;
and at his altar we are knit
in mystic unity.

TIMOTHY REES (1874–1939)

440 (MHT **107**)

Christe sanctorum 10 11 11.6. *Paris Antiphoner, 1681*

No other name

1 Christ is the world's light, he and none other:
born in our darkness, he became our brother;
if we have seen him, we have seen the Father:
Glory to God on high.

2 Christ is the world's peace, he and none other:
no man can serve him and despise his brother;
who else unites us, one in God the Father?
Glory to God on high.

3 Christ is the world's life, he and none other;
sold once for silver, murdered here, our brother –
he, who redeems us, reigns with God the Father:
Glory to God on high.

4 Give God the glory, God and none other;
give God the glory, Spirit, Son and Father;
give God the glory, God in man my brother;
Glory to God on high.

F. Pratt Green (b. 1903)

441 (MHT **108**)
Feniton — Sydney H. Nicholson (1875–1947
7 8.7 8. and Alleluias

Al-le-lu-ia, Al-le-lu - ia, Al - le - lu - ia.

Transfiguration

Christ upon the mountain peak
  stands alone in glory blazing;
let us, if we dare to speak,
  with the saints and angels praise him:
        Alleluia.

2

Trembling at his feet we saw‿
  Moses and Elijah speaking;
all the prophets and the Law
  shout through them their joyful greeting:
        Alleluia.

3

Swift the cloud of glory came,
  God proclaiming in the thunder
Jesus as his Son by name;
  nations, cry aloud in wonder!
        Alleluia.

4

This is God's belovèd Son:
  Law and prophets fade before him;
First and Last, and only One,
  let creation now adore him.
        Alleluia.

BRIAN A. WREN (b. 1936)

442 (MHT 109)

Caithness C.M. *Scottish Psalter, 163*

The baptism of Jesus

Christ, when for us you were baptized
  God's Spirit on you came,
as peaceful as a dove, and yet‿
  as urgent as a flame.

2

God called you his belovèd Son,
  called you his servant too;
his kingdom you were called to preach,
  his holy will to do.

3

Straightway and steadfast until death
  you then obeyed his call,
freely as Son of Man to serve,
  and give your life for all.

4

Baptize us with your Spirit, Lord,
  your cross on us be signed,
that likewise in God's service we‿
  may perfect freedom find.

F. BLAND TUCKER (1895–1984)

43 (MHT **110**)

Ave virgo virginum 7 6.7 6.D. Melody as given by J. Horn (1544)

New life

Christian people, raise your song,
chase away all grieving;
sing your joy and be made strong,
our Lord's life receiving;
nature's gifts of wheat and vine
now are set before us:
as we offer bread and wine
Christ comes to restore us.

2

Come to welcome Christ today,
God's great revelation;
he has pioneered the way‿
of the new creation.
Greet him, Christ our risen King
gladly recognizing,
as with joy men greet the spring‿
out of winter rising.

COLIN P. THOMPSON (b. 1945)

444 (MHT **111**)
Salve festa dies R. Vaughan Williams (1872–1958

Praise for the Spirit

Irregular
Verse 1 (repeated as a refrain after verses 2 to 7)
Chris - tians, lift up your hearts, and
make this a day of re - joic - ing; God is our strength and
song: glo - ry and praise to his name!
Verses 2, 4, 6
2 Praise for the Spi - rit of God, who
*4 Praise that his love ov - er - flowed in the
6 Come, Ho - ly Spi - rit, to us, who
came to the wait - ing dis - ci - ples; there in the
hearts of all who re - ceived him, join - ing to -
live by your pre - sence with - in us, come to di -
wind and the fire God gave new life to his own:
geth - er in peace those once di - vid - ed by sin:
rect our course, give us your life and your power:
Repeat refrai

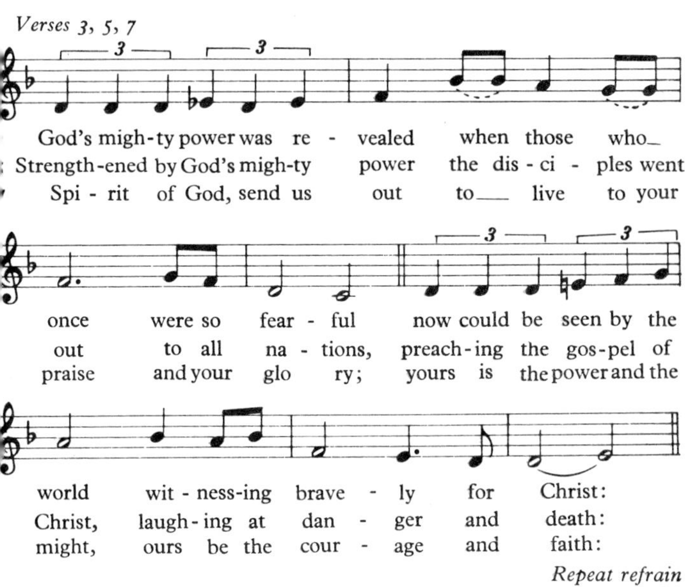
Verses 3, 5, 7
God's migh-ty power was re - vealed when those who once were so fear - ful now could be seen by the world wit - ness-ing brave - ly for Christ:
Strength-ened by God's migh-ty power the dis - ci - ples went out to all na - tions, preach-ing the gos-pel of Christ, laugh-ing at dan - ger and death:
Spi - rit of God, send us out to live to your praise and your glo ry; yours is the power and the might, ours be the cour - age and faith:
Repeat refrain

JOHN E. BOWERS (b. 1923)

445 (MHT **112**)
Salve festa dies — R. Vaughan Williams (1872–1958)

The House of God

Irregular

Verse 1 (repeated as a refrain after verses 2 to 7)
Chris-tians, lift up your hearts, and
make this a day of re-joic-ing; God is our strength and
song; glo-ry and praise to his name!
Verses 2, 4, 6
2 This is the house of the Lord, where
4 Here God's life-giv-ing word once
6 Sum-moned by Christ's com-mand his
seek-ers and find-ers are wel-come; en-ter its
more is pro-claimed to his peo-ple, up-lift-ing
peo-ple draw near to his ta-ble, glad-ly to
gates with your praise, fill all its courts with your song:
those who are down, chal-leng-ing all with its truth:
greet their Lord, known in the break-ing of bread:
Repeat refrain

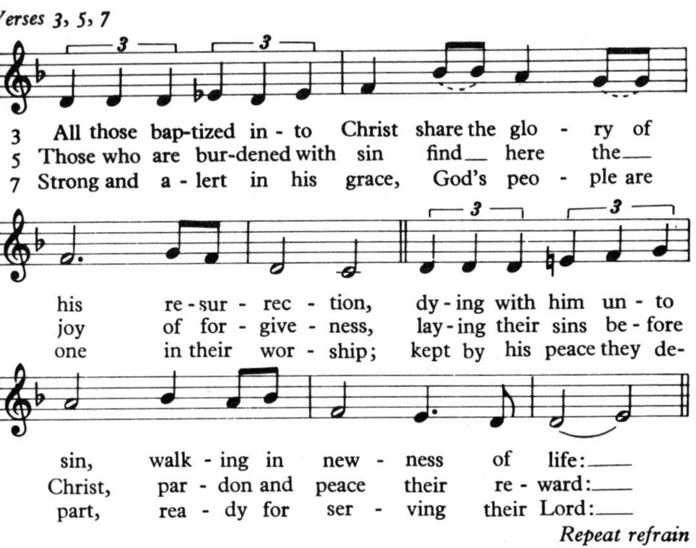
Verses 3, 5, 7
3 All those bap-tized in - to Christ share the glo - ry of
5 Those who are bur-dened with sin find here the
7 Strong and a - lert in his grace, God's peo - ple are
his re - sur - rec - tion, dy - ing with him un - to
joy of for - give - ness, lay - ing their sins be - fore
one in their wor - ship; kept by his peace they de-
sin, walk - ing in new - ness of life:
Christ, par - don and peace their re - ward:
part, rea - dy for ser - ving their Lord:
Repeat refrain

JOHN E. BOWERS (b. 1923)

446 (MHT **113**)
Salve festa dies R. Vaughan Williams (1872–195

Irregular
Verse 1 (repeated as a refrain after verses 2 and 3)
Chris-tians, lift up your hearts, and
make this a day of re - joic - ing; God is our strength a
song: glo - ry and praise to his name!
Verse 2
Here God's life - giv - ing word once
more is pro-claimed to his peo - ple, up - lift - ing
those who are down, chal-leng-ing all with its truth:
Repeat refrai

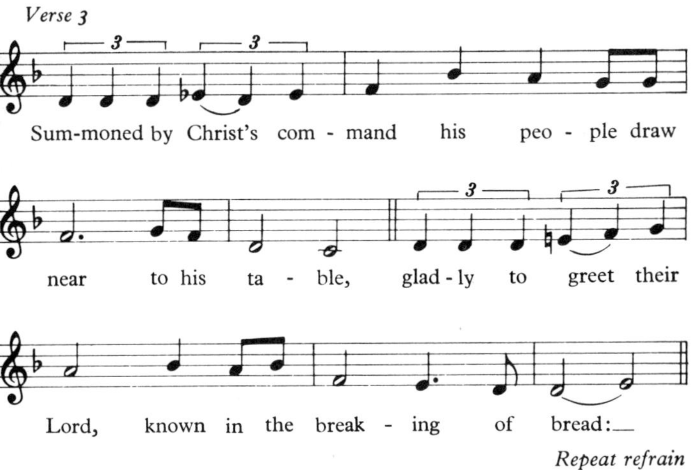
Verse 3
3
3
Sum-moned by Christ's com - mand his peo - ple draw
near to his ta - ble, glad - ly to greet their
3
3
Lord, known in the break - ing of bread:
Repeat refrain

Word and sacrament

1 *Christians, lift up your hearts,*
and make this a day of rejoicing;
God is our strength and song:
glory and praise to his name!

2 Here God's life-giving word
once more is proclaimed to his people,
uplifting those who are down,
challenging all with its truth:

3 Summoned by Christ's command
his people draw near to his table,
gladly to greet their Lord,
known in the breaking of bread:

Christians, lift up your hearts,
and make this a day of rejoicing;
God is our strength and song:
glory and praise to his name!

JOHN E. BOWERS (b. 1923)

447 (MHT **114**)

Alleluia, dulce carmen 8 7.8 7.8 7. *An Essay o*
(Tantum ergo) *the Church Plain Chant*, 178

Offertory

Christians, lift your hearts and voices,
let your praises be outpoured;
come with joy and exultation
to the table of the Lord;
come believing, come expectant,
in obedience to his word.

2

See, presiding at his table,
Jesus Christ our great high priest;
where he summons all his people,
none is greatest, none is least;
graciously he bids them welcome
to the eucharistic feast.

3

Lord, we offer in thanksgiving
life and work for you to bless;
yet unworthy is the offering,
marred by pride and carelessness;
so, Lord, pardon our transgressions,
plant in us true holiness.

4

On the evening of his passion
Jesus gave the wine and bread,
so that all who love and serve him
shall for evermore be fed.
Taste and see the Lord is gracious,
feed upon the living bread.

JOHN E. BOWERS (b. 1923)

448 (MHT **115**)

Nun danket all C.M. *Praxis pietatis melica*, 164

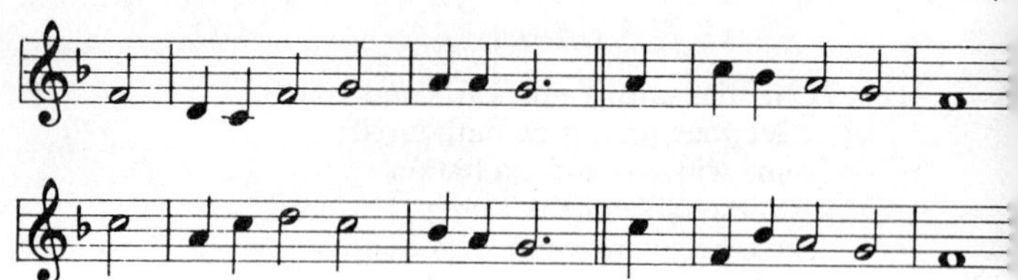

Before reading the Scriptures

Come, Holy Ghost, our hearts inspire,
let us thine influence prove;
source of the old prophetic fire,
fountain of life and love.

2

Come, Holy Ghost – for, moved by thee,
thy prophets wrote and spoke –
unlock the truth, thyself the key,
unseal the sacred book.

3

Expand thy wings, celestial Dove,
brood o'er our nature's night;
on our disordered spirits move,
and let there now be light.

4

God, through himself, we then shall know,
if thou within us shine;
and sound, with all thy saints below,
the depths of love divine.

CHARLES WESLEY (1707–88)

449 (MHT **116**)

Ascendit Deus 888.D. J. G. Schicht (1753–1823)

The Lord's day

Come, let us with our Lord arise,
our Lord who made both earth and skies,
and gave men gifts of life and peace;
he died to save the world he made,
he rose triumphant from the dead;
and stamped the day for ever his.

2

This is the day the Lord has made,
that all may see his power displayed,
be filled with all the life of God;
may feel his resurrection's power,
and rise again, to fall no more,
in perfect righteousness renewed.

3

Then let us render him his own,
with solemn prayer approach his throne,
our joyful hearts and voices raise;
with meekness hear the gospel word,
with thanks his dying love record,
and fill his courts with songs of praise.

CHARLES WESLEY* (1707–88)

450 (MHT **117**)
England's Lane
7 7·7 7·7 7·

Adapted from an English melody
by Geoffrey Shaw (1879–1943)

Alternative Tune: *Heathlands* (179)

At a wedding

Crown with love, Lord, this glad day,
  love to humble and delight,
love which until death will stay,
  testing all life's depth and height;
such a love as took our part,
spendthrift in its generous art.

2

Lord, give joy on this glad day,
  joy to face life's hurt and ill,
all that tests the wedded way,
  forging union deeper still;
joy like his who, for our gain,
lightly weighed the cross and pain.

3

Crown with peace, Lord, this glad day,
  peace the world may not invent,
nor misfortune strip away
  from two hearts in you content,
knowing love will never cease
from that source who is our peace.

IAN M. FRASER (b. 1917)

451 (MHT **118**)
St. Bavon 8 7.8 7. A. T. I. Jagger (b. 1911

Alternative Tune: *Omni die* (456)

With us always

Early morning. 'Come, prepare him,
to the tomb your spices bring;
death is cold and death decaying,
we must beautify our King.'

2

Early morning, women excited,
seeking Peter everywhere;
telling of a man who told them,
'He is risen: don't despair'.

3

Peter racing, early morning,
to the tomb and rushing in;
seeing shrouds of death dispensed with,
finding new-born faith begin.

4

Early morning, Mary weeping,
asking if the gardener knew;
knowing, as his voice says, 'Mary',
'Lord, Rabbuni, it is you'.

5

'Mary, you can live without me,
as I now to God ascend;
peace be with you; I am with you
early morning without end.'

6

Early morning, stay for ever,
early morning, never cease;
early morning, come to all men
for their good and power and peace.

JOHN GREGORY (b. 1929)

452 (MHT **119**)

St. Fulbert C.M. H. J. Gauntlett (1805–76

Baptized into Christ

Eternal God, we consecrate‿
these children to your care,
to you their talents dedicate,
for they your image bear.

2

To them our solemn pledge we give
their lives by prayer to shield.
May they in truth and honour live,
and to your guidance yield.

3

Your Spirit's power on them bestow,
from sin their hearts preserve;
in Christ their master may they grow,
and him for ever serve.

4

So may the waters of this rite
become a means of grace,
and these your children show the light
that shone in Jesus' face.

Robert Dobbie (b. 1901)

453 (MHT **120**)
Pastor pastorum 6 5.6 5. F. Silcher (1789–1860)

Nunc Dimittis

Faithful vigil ended,
 watching, waiting cease;
Master, grant thy servant‿
 his discharge in peace.

2

All thy Spirit promised,
 all the Father willed,
now these eyes behold it
 perfectly fulfilled.

3

This thy great deliverance‿
 sets thy people free;
Christ their light uplifted‿
 all the nations see.

4

Christ, thy people's glory!
 watching, doubting cease;
grant to us thy servants‿
 our discharge in peace.

TIMOTHY DUDLEY-SMITH (b. 1926)
Luke 2. 29–32 (*N.E.B.*)

454 (MHT 121)

All kinds of light 5.8 8.5 5. Caryl Micklem (b. 1925)

All kinds of light

1 Father, we thank you
for the light that shines all the day;
for the bright sky you have given,
most like your heaven;
Father, we thank you.

2 Father, we thank you
for the lamps that lighten the way;
for human skill's exploration‿
of your creation;
Father, we thank you.

3 Father, we thank you
for the friends who brighten our play;
for your command to call others‿
sisters and brothers;
Father, we thank you.

4 Father, we thank you
for your love in Jesus today,
giving us hope for tomorrow
through joy and sorrow;
Father, we thank you.

Caryl Micklem (b. 1925)

455 (MHT **122**)
Surrexit 8 8 8. and Alleluias — A. Gregory Murray (b. 1905)

Swallowed up in victory

Finished the strife of battle now,
gloriously crowned the victor's brow:
sing with gladness, hence with sadness:
Alleluia, alleluia!

2

After the death that him befell,
Jesus Christ has harrowed hell:
songs of praising we are raising:

3

On the third morning he arose,
shining with victory o'er his foes;
earth is singing, heaven is ringing:

4

Lord, by your wounds on you we call:
now that from death you've freed us all:
may our living be thanksgiving:
Alleluia, alleluia!

tr. J. M. Neale* (1818–66)

Another translation of these words is at 78

456 (MHT **123**) FIRST TUNE

Wraysbury 8 7.8 7. E. J. Hopkins (1818–1901)

After Communion

For the bread which you have broken,
  for the wine which you have poured,
for the words which you have spoken,
  now we give you thanks, O Lord.

2

By these pledges that you love us,
  by your gift of peace restored,
by your call to heaven above us,
  hallow all our lives, O Lord.

3

In your service, Lord, defend us,
  in our hearts keep watch and ward;
in the world to which you send us
  let your kingdom come, O Lord.

L. F. Benson (1855–1930)

SECOND TUNE

Omni die 8 7.8 7. Corner's *Gesangbuch*, 1631
arr. W. S. Rockstro (1823–95)

After Communion

For the bread which you have broken,
for the wine which you have poured,
for the words which you have spoken,
now we give you thanks, O Lord.

2

By these pledges that you love us,
by your gift of peace restored,
by your call to heaven above us,
hallow all our lives, O Lord.

3

In your service, Lord, defend us,
in our hearts keep watch and ward;
in the world to which you send us
let your kingdom come, O Lord.

L. F. Benson (1855–1930)

457 (MHT **124**)

East Acklam 8 4.8 4.8 8 8.4. Francis Jackson (b. 1917

Harvest

For the fruits of his creation,
  thanks be to God;
for his gifts to every nation,
  thanks be to God;
for the ploughing, sowing, reaping,
silent growth while men are sleeping,
future needs in earth's safe keeping,
  thanks be to God.

2

In the just reward of labour,
  God's will is done;
in the help we give our neighbour,
  God's will is done;
in our world-wide task of caring‿
for the hungry and despairing,
in the harvests men are sharing,
  God's will is done.

3

For the harvests of his Spirit,
  thanks be to God;
for the good all men inherit,
  thanks be to God;
for the wonders that astound us,
for the truths that still confound us,
most of all, that love has found us,
  thanks be to God.

F. Pratt Green (b. 1903)

458 (MHT 125)
Duke Street L.M.

Late 18th c. meloc
Attributed to J. Hatton (d. 179

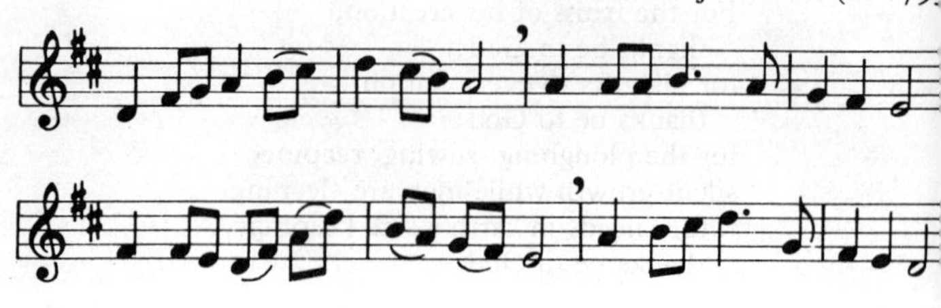

Prophets, priests, and kings

Forth in the peace of Christ we go;
  Christ to the world with joy we bring;
Christ in our minds, Christ on our lips,
  Christ in our hearts, the world's true King.

2

King of our hearts, Christ makes us kings;
  kingship with him his servants gain;
with Christ, the Servant-Lord of all,
  Christ's world we serve to share Christ's reign.

3

Priests of the world, Christ sends us forth
  this world of time to consecrate,
this world of sin by grace to heal,
  Christ's world in Christ to re-create.

4

Christ's are our lips, his word we speak;
  prophets are we whose deeds proclaim‿
Christ's truth in love, that we may be‿
  Christ in the world, to spread Christ's name.

5

We are the Church; Christ bids us show
  that in his Church all nations find‿
their hearth and home, where Christ restores‿
  true peace, true love, to all mankind.

JAMES QUINN (b. 1919)

459 (MHT 126)
Sing Hosanna
10 8.10 9. and refrain
Traditional Meloc
1 Give me joy
2 Give me peace
3 Give me love
in my heart, keep me
prai-sing,
lov-ing,
ser-ving,
give m
joy
peace
love
in my heart, I pray;
give me
joy
peace
love
in my heart, keep
prais-ing
lov-ing
serv-ing
keep me
prais-ing
lov-ing
serv-ing
till the break of day.
Refrain
Sing ho-san - na, sing ho-san - na, sing ho-san-na to the
King of kings! Sing ho-san - na, sing ho-san - na,
sing ho - san - na to the King!

Hosanna

Give me joy in my heart, keep me praising,
give me joy in my heart, I pray;
give me joy in my heart, keep me praising,
keep me praising till the break of day.

Sing hosanna, sing hosanna,
sing hosanna to the King of kings!
Sing hosanna, sing hosanna,
sing hosanna to the King!

2

Give me peace in my heart, keep me loving,
give me peace in my heart, I pray;
give me peace in my heart, keep me loving,
keep me loving till the break of day:

3

Give me love in my heart, keep me serving,
give me love in my heart, I pray;
give me love in my heart, keep me serving,
keep me serving till the break of day:

Sing hosanna, sing hosanna,
sing hosanna to the King of kings!
Sing hosanna, sing hosanna,
sing hosanna to the King!

Traditional

460 (MHT 127)

Dunedin L.M. Vernon Griffiths (b. 1894

Alternative Tune: *Warrington* (494)

The Salvation of God

1 Give to our God immortal praise;
mercy and truth are all his ways:
wonders of grace to God belong,
repeat his mercies in your song.

2 Give to the Lord of lords renown,
the King of kings with glory crown:
his mercies ever shall endure
when lords and kings are known no more.

3 He sent his Son with power to save
from guilt and darkness and the grave:
wonders of grace to God belong,
repeat his mercies in your song.

4 Through this vain world he guides our feet,
and leads us to his heavenly seat:
his mercies ever shall endure
when this vain world shall be no more.

ISAAC WATTS (1674–1748)
Psalm 136

461 (MHT **128**)
Benifold 8.3 3.6.D. Francis B. Westbrook (1903–75)

Our sacrifice of thanks and praise

Glory, love, and praise, and honour
for our food‿
now bestowed
render we the Donor.
Bounteous God, we now confess thee;
God, who thus‿
blessest us,
meet it is to bless thee.

2

Thankful for our every blessing,
let us sing‿
Christ the Spring,
never, never ceasing.
Source of all our gifts and graces‿
Christ we own;
Christ alone‿
calls for all our praises.

3

He dispels our sin and sadness,
life imparts,
cheers our hearts,
fills with food and gladness.
Who himself for all hath given,
us he feeds,
us he leads‿
to a feast in heaven.

Charles Wesley (1707–88)

462 (MHT 129)

Highwood 11 10.11 10. R. R. Terry (1865–193

Made flesh

1 'Glory to God!' all heav'n with joy is ringing;
angels proclaim the gospel of Christ's birth –
'Glory to God!', and still their song is bringing
good news of God incarnate here on earth.

2 Lowly in wonder shepherds kneel before him,
no gift to bring save love of heart and mind.
Come like those shepherds, sing his praise, adore him,
a babe so weak, yet Saviour of mankind.

3 Humble, yet regal, wise men kneel before him,
gold, incense, myrrh, their gifts to Christ they bring.
Come like those wise men, sing his praise, adore him,
a babe so poor and modest, yet a King.

4 Though now no crib or cradle is concealing
Jesus our Lord in that far-distant shrine,
Christ at each eucharist is still revealing
his very self in forms of bread and wine.

John E. Bowers (b. 1923

463 (MHT **130**)

Lobet den Herren 11 11 11.5. J. Crüger (1598–1662)

To the altar of God

1 God everlasting, wonderful and holy,
Father most gracious, we who stand before thee
here at thine altar, as thy Son has taught us,
come to adore thee.

2 Countless the mercies thou hast lavished on us,
source of all blessing to all creatures living,
to thee we render, for thy love o'erflowing,
humble thanksgiving.

3 Now in remembrance of our great Redeemer,
dying on Calvary, rising and ascending,
through him we offer what he ever offers,
sinners befriending.

4 Strength to the living, rest to the departed,
grant, Holy Father, through this pure oblation;
may the life-giving Bread for ever bring us‿
health and salvation.

Harold Riley (b. 1903)

464 (MHT **131**)

Blaenwern 8 7.8 7.D. William P. Rowlands (1860–1937

Worship and life

God is here; as we his people‿
meet to offer praise and prayer,
may we find in fuller measure
what it is in Christ we share.
Here, as in the world around us,
all our varied skills and arts
wait the coming of his Spirit
into open minds and hearts.

2

Here are symbols to remind us‿
of our lifelong need of grace;
here are table, font and pulpit,
here the cross has central place;
here in honesty of preaching,
here in silence as in speech,
here in newness and renewal
God the Spirit comes to each.

3

Here our children find a welcome
in the Shepherd's flock and fold,
here, as bread and wine are taken,
Christ sustains us, as of old.
Here the servants of the Servant
seek in worship to explore‿
what it means in daily living
to believe and to adore.

4

Lord of all, of Church and Kingdom,
in an age of change and doubt
keep us faithful to the gospel,
help us work your purpose out.
Here, in this day's dedication,
all we have to give, receive.
We, who cannot live without you,
we adore you, we believe.

F. PRATT GREEN (b. 1903)

465 (MHT 132)

Ubi caritas — A. Gregory Murray (b. 190

12 12 12 12 and refrain

Refrain

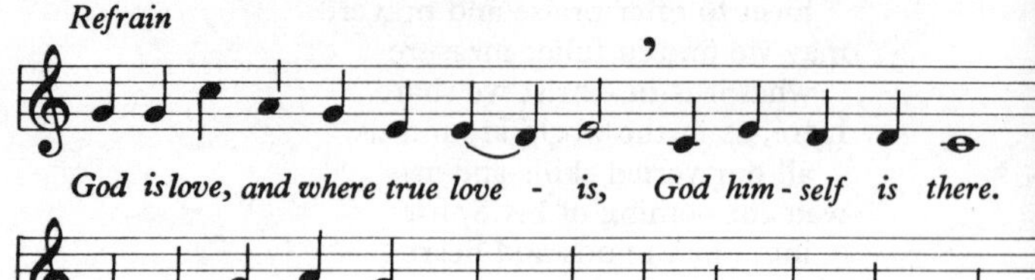

1. Here in Christ we ga - ther, love of Christ our call - ing.
2. When we Chris - tians ga - ther, mem - bers of one Bo - dy,
3. Grant us love's ful - fil - ment, joy with all the bles - sèd,

Christ, our love, is with us, glad - ness be his greet - ing.
let there be in us no dis - cord, but one spi - rit.
when we see your face, O Sa - viour, in its glo - ry.

Let us all re - vere and love him, God e - ter - nal.
Ban - ished now be an - ger, strife and ev' - ry quar - rel.
Shine on us, O pur - est Light of all cre - a - tion,

Lov - ing him, let each love Christ in all his bro - thers.
Christ, our God, be pre - sent al - ways here a - mong us.
be our bliss while end - less a - ges sing your prai - ses.

Refrain

Serving Christ in one another

God is love, and where true love is, God himself is there.

Here in Christ we gather, love of Christ our calling.
Christ, our love, is with us, gladness be his greeting.
Let us all revere and love him, God eternal.
Loving him, let each love Christ in all his brothers.

God is love, and where true love is, God himself is there.

2

When we Christians gather, members of one Body,
let there be in us no discord, but one spirit.
Banished now be anger, strife and every quarrel.
Christ, our God, be present always here among us.

God is love, and where true love is, God himself is there.

3

Grant us love's fulfilment, joy with all the blessèd,
when we see your face, O Saviour, in its glory.
Shine on us, O purest Light of all creation,
be our bliss while endless ages sing your praises.

God is love, and where true love is, God himself is there.

From the Latin Liturgy of Maundy Thursday
tr. JAMES QUINN (b. 1919)

For another translation see 528

466 (MHT **133**)
Oriel 8 7.8 7.8 7. C. Ett's *Cantica Sacra*, 1840

A descant to this tune is at 121

Baptism

God the Father, name we treasure,
  each new generation draws‿
from the past that you have given
  for the future that is yours;
may these children, in your keeping,
  love your ways, obey your laws.

2

Christ, the name that Christians carry,
  Christ, who from the Father came,
calling men to share your sonship,
  for these children grace we claim;
may they be your true disciples,
  yours in deed as well as name.

3

Holy Spirit, from the Father
  on the friends of Jesus poured,
may our children share those graces
  promised to them in the Word,
and their gifts find rich fulfilment,
  dedicated to our Lord.

Basil E. Bridge (b. 1927)

467 (MHT **134**)
Causa divina 14 14.4 7.8. Frederick R. C. Clarke (b. 1931)

'Read, mark, learn . . .'

God, who hast caused to be written thy word for our learning,
grant us that, hearing, our hearts may be inwardly burning.
Give to us grace,
that in thy Son we embrace‿
life, all its glory discerning.

2

Now may our God give us joy, and his peace in believing
all things were written in truth for our thankful receiving.
As Christ did preach
from man to man love must reach,
grant us each day love's achieving.

3

Lord, should the powers of the earth and the heavens be shaken,
grant us to see thee in all things, our vision awaken.
Help us to see,
though all the earth cease to be,
thy truth shall never be shaken.

T. HERBERT O'DRISCOLL (b. 1928)

468 (MHT 135)

New Malden 8 7.8 7.8 7. David McCarthy (b. 193

Alternative Tune: *Rhuddlan* (263)

The first and final word

God who spoke in the beginning,
forming rock and shaping spar,
set all life and growth in motion,
earthly world and distant star;
he who calls the earth to order
is the ground of what we are.

2

God who spoke through men and nations,
through events long past and gone,
showing still today his purpose,
speaks supremely through his Son;
he who calls the earth to order
gives his word and it is done.

3

God whose speech becomes incarnate –
Christ is servant, Christ is Lord –
calls us to a life of service,
heart and will to action stirred;
he who uses man's obedience
has the first and final word.

FRED KAAN (b. 1929)

469 (MHT **136**)
Bangor C.M W. Tans'ur's *Compleat Melody*, 1735

Science

God, you have giv'n us power to sound‿
depths hitherto unknown:
to probe earth's hidden mysteries,
and make their might our own.

2

Great are your gifts: yet greater far‿
this gift, O God, bestow,
that as to knowledge we attain
we may in wisdom grow.

3

Let wisdom's godly fear dispel‿
all fears that hate impart;
give understanding to the mind,
and with new mind new heart.

4

So for your glory and our good‿
may we your gifts employ,
lest, maddened by the lust of power,
we shall ourselves destroy.

G. W. Briggs* (1875–1959)

470 (MHT **137**)

Little Cornard 66.66.88. Martin Shaw (1875–1958

Hope of the world

Hills of the North, rejoice,
   echoing songs arise,
hail with united voice‿
   him who made earth and skies:
he comes in righteousness and love,
he brings salvation from above.

2

Isles of the Southern seas,
   sing to the listening earth,
carry on every breeze‿
   hope of a world's new birth:
in Christ shall all be made anew,
his word is sure, his promise true.

3

Lands of the East, arise,
  he is your brightest morn,
greet him with joyous eyes,
  praise shall his path adorn:
the God whom you have longed to know‿
in Christ draws near, and calls you now.

4

Shores of the utmost West,
  lands of the setting sun,
welcome the heavenly guest
  in whom the dawn has come:
he brings a never-ending light
who triumphed o'er our darkest night.

5

Shout, as you journey on,
  songs be in every mouth,
lo, from the North they come,
  from East and West and South:
in Jesus all shall find their rest,
in him the sons of earth be blest.

Editors of *English Praise*
based on C. E. OAKLEY (1832–65)

471 (MHT **138**)

All for Jesus 8 7.8 7. John Stainer (1840–1901

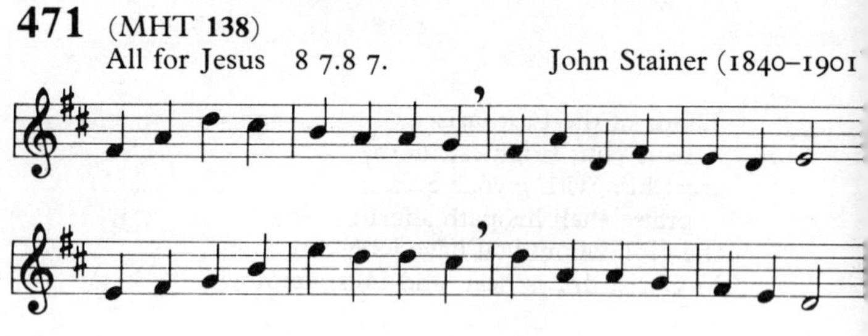

Life in the Spirit

Holy Spirit, come, confirm us‿
 in the truth that Christ makes known;
we have faith and understanding
 through your helping gifts alone.

2

Holy Spirit, come, console us,
 come as Advocate to plead,
loving Spirit from the Father,
 grant in Christ the help we need.

3

Holy Spirit, come, renew us,
 come yourself to make us live,
holy through your loving presence,
 holy through the gifts you give.

4

Holy Spirit, come, possess us,
 you the love of Three in One,
Holy Spirit of the Father,
 Holy Spirit of the Son.

BRIAN FOLEY (b. 1919)

472 (MHT **139**)

Soll's sein D.C.M. Corner's *Geistliche Nachtigal*, 1649

Alternative Tune: *Kingsfold* (413)

The majesty of God

1 How shall I sing that majesty
  which angels do admire?
let dust in dust and silence lie;
  sing, sing, ye heavenly choir.
Thousands of thousands stand around
  thy throne, O God most high;
ten thousand times ten thousand sound
  thy praise; but who am I?

2 Thy brightness unto them appears,
  whilst I thy footsteps trace;
a sound of God comes to my ears,
  but they behold thy face.
They sing because thou art their Sun;
  Lord, send a beam on me;
for where heav'n is but once begun
  there alleluias be.

3 How great a being, Lord, is thine,
  which doth all beings keep!
Thy knowledge is the only line
  to sound so vast a deep.
Thou art a sea without a shore,
  a sun without a sphere;
thy time is now and evermore,
  thy place is everywhere.

John Mason (c. 1645–1694)

473 (MHT **140**)

St. Botolph C.M. Gordon Slater (1896–1979)

Christ making friends

I come with joy to meet my Lord,
  forgiven, loved, and free,
in awe and wonder to recall‿
  his life laid down for me.

2

I come with Christians far and near‿
  to find, as all are fed,
man's true community of love
  in Christ's communion bread.

3

As Christ breaks bread for men to share,
  each proud division ends.
The love that made us, makes us one,
  and strangers now are friends.

4

And thus with joy we meet our Lord.
  His presence, always near,
is in such friendship better known:
  we see, and praise him here.

5

Together met, together bound,
  we'll go our different ways,
and as his people in the world,
  we'll live and speak his praise.

BRIAN A. WREN (b. 1936)

474 (MHT **141**)

St. Nicholas
C.M.

Holdroyd'
The Spiritual Man's Companion, 1753
as adapted in *Scottish Psalmody*, 185

Alternative Tune: *St. Mary* (517)

Lost and found

1 In Adam we have all been one,
one huge rebellious man;
we all have fled that evening voice
that sought us as we ran.

2 We fled thee and, in losing thee,
we lost our brother too;
each singly sought and claimed his own,
each man his brother slew.

3 But thy strong love, it sought us still,
and sent thine only Son
that we might hear his shepherd's voice
and, hearing him, be one.

4 O thou who, when we loved thee not,
didst love and save us all,
thou great Good Shepherd of mankind,
O hear us when we call.

5 Send us thy Spirit, teach us truth;
thou Son, O set us free
from fancied wisdom, self-sought ways,
to make us one in thee.

Martin Franzmann (1907–1976)

475 (MHT 142)

FIRST TUNE

Seelenbräutigam 5 5.8 8.5 5. A. Drese (1620–1701)

SECOND TUNE

Westron Wynde 5 5.8 8.5 5. William Llewellyn (b. 1925)

At a wedding

1

Jesus, Lord, we pray,
be our guest today;
gospel story has recorded
how your glory was afforded
to a wedding day;
be our guest, we pray.

2

Lord of love and life,
blessing man and wife,
as they stand, their need confessing,
may your hand take theirs in blessing;
you will share their life;
bless this man and wife.

3

Lord of hope and faith,
faithful unto death,
let the ring serve as a token
of a love sincere, unbroken,
love more strong than death;
Lord of hope and faith.

Basil E. Bridge (b. 1927)

476 (MHT **143**) FIRST TUNE

Buriton 4 5.4 5.D. Cyril V. Taylor (b. 1907

SECOND TUNE

Little Venice 4 5.4 5.D. Gerald H. Knight (1908–79)

Best of all friends

Jesus, my Lord,
 let me be near you;
by your own word
 help me to hear you.
Jesus, my Lord,
 lead me to love you,
nothing more dear,
 no one above you.

2

All through the day,
sisters and brothers,
yours we will be,
caring for others,
hearing your words,
learning your story,
bearing your cross,
sharing your glory.

3

Teach us to know
seeing from blindness,
help us to show‿
everywhere kindness.
Jesus, our Lord,
lead us and guide us,
best of all friends,
always beside us.

H. C. A. Gaunt (1902–83)

477 (MHT **144**)
Windermere S.M. Arthur Somervell (1863–1937)

The supper of the Lamb

1

Jesus, we thus obey‿
thy last and kindest word;
here in thine own appointed way
we come to meet thee, Lord.

2

Our hearts we open wide‿
to make the Saviour room;
and lo, the Lamb, the Crucified,
the sinner's friend, is come.

3

Thy presence makes the feast;
now let our spirits feel‿
the glory not to be expressed,
the joy unspeakable.

4

With high and heavenly bliss‿
thou dost our spirits cheer;
thy house of banqueting is this
and thou hast brought us here.

5

Now let our souls be fed‿
with manna from above,
and over us thy banner spread‿
of everlasting love.

Charles Wesley* (1707–88)

478 (MHT **145**)
Ludgate 6 6 6.D. John Dykes Bower (1905–1981

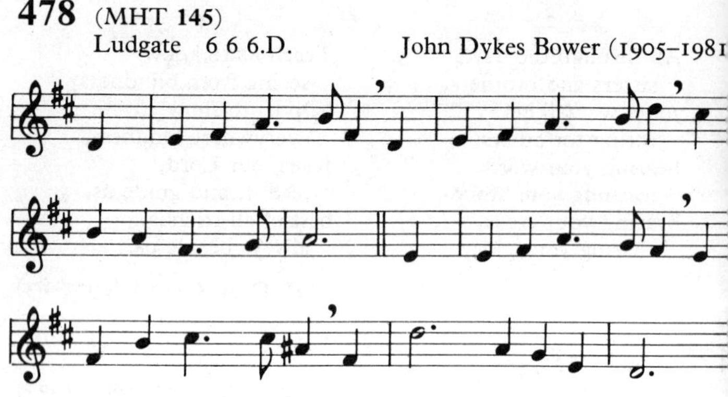

The Holy Spirit and the Church

Let every Christian pray,
this day, and every day,
  come, Holy Spirit, come.
Was not the Church we love‿
commissioned from above?
  come, Holy Spirit, come.

2

The Spirit brought to birth‿
the Church of Christ on earth
  to seek and save the lost:
never has he withdrawn,
since that tremendous dawn,
  his gifts at Pentecost.

3

Age after age, he strove‿
to teach her how to love:
  come, Holy Spirit, come;
age after age, anew‿
she proved the gospel true:
  come, Holy Spirit, come.

4

Only the Spirit's power‿
can fit us for this hour:
  come, Holy Spirit, come;
instruct, inspire, unite;
and make us see the light:
  come, Holy Spirit, come.

F. Pratt Green (b. 1903)

479 (MHT 146)

Chartres (Angers) 11 11 11.5. *Chartres Antiphoner, 1784*

The Lord's own

Let the Lord's People, heart and voice uniting,
praise him who calls them out of sin and darkness
into his own light, that he may create them
his holy priesthood.

2

This is the Lord's House, home of all his people,
school for the faithful, refuge for the sinner,
rest for the pilgrim, haven for the weary;
all find a welcome.

3

This is the Lord's Day, day of God's own making,
day of creation, day of resurrection,
day of the Spirit, Pentecost repeated,
day for rejoicing.

4

In the Lord's Service bread and wine are offered,
that Christ may take them, bless them, break and give them
to all his people, his own life imparting,
food everlasting.

JOHN E. BOWERS (b. 1923)

480 (MHT 147)

Let us break bread *Irregular* American Folk Melody

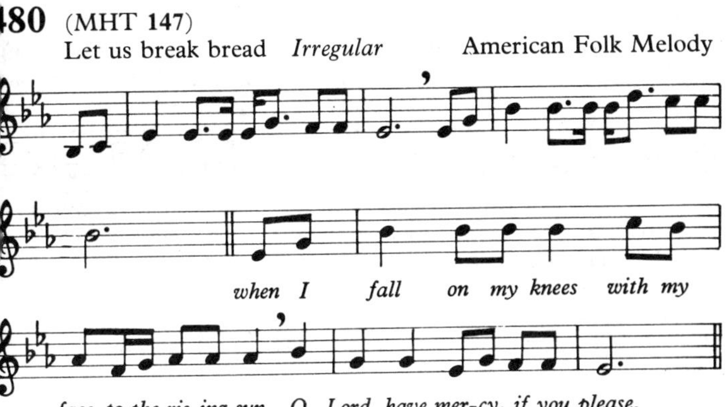

when I fall on my knees with my
face to the ris-ing sun, O Lord, have mer-cy, if you please.

Have mercy

Let us break bread together on our knees;
let us break bread together on our knees:

when I fall on my knees
with my face to the rising sun,
O Lord, have mercy, if you please.

2

Let us drink wine together on our knees;
let us drink wine together on our knees:

when I fall on my knees
with my face to the rising sun,
O Lord, have mercy, if you please.

3

Let us praise God together on our knees;
let us praise God together on our knees:

when I fall on my knees
with my face to the rising sun,
O Lord, have mercy, if you please.

American Folk Hymn

481 (MHT 148)

Linstead L.M. and refrain — Jamaican Folk Song
Adapted by Doreen Potter (1925–8c

1 Let us tal-ents and tongues em-ploy, reach-ing out with a
2 Christ is ab - le to make us one, at his ta - ble he
3 Je - sus calls us in, sends us out bear-ing fruit in a

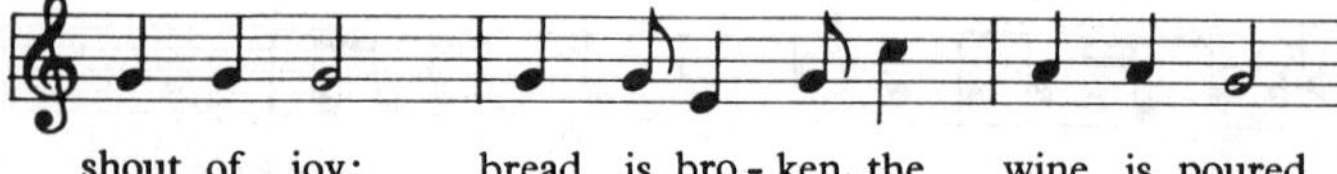

shout of joy: bread is bro - ken, the wine is poured,
sets the tone, teach-ing peo - ple to live to bless,
world of doubt, gives us love to tell, bread to share:

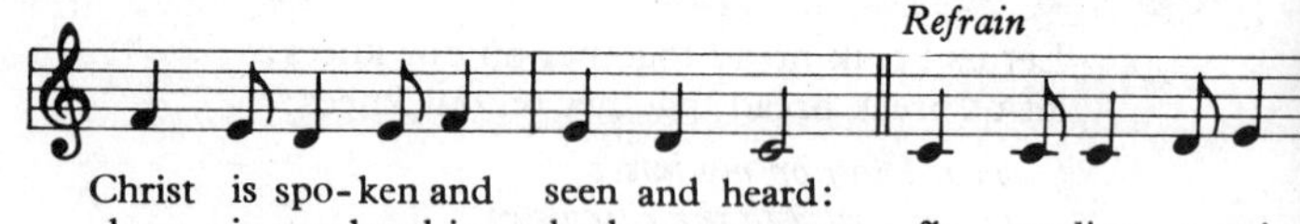

Refrain

Christ is spo-ken and seen and heard:
love in word and in deed ex - press: *Je - sus lives a-gain,*
God Im-man-u-el ev' - ry-where:

earth can breathe a-gain, pass the Word a-round: loaves a - bound.

Communion calypso

Let us talents and tongues employ,
reaching out with a shout of joy:
bread is broken, the wine is poured,
Christ is spoken and seen and heard:

Jesus lives again, earth can breathe again,
pass the Word around: loaves abound.

2

Christ is able to make us one,
at his table he sets the tone,
teaching people to live to bless,
love in word and in deed express:

Jesus lives again, earth can breathe again,
pass the Word around: loaves abound.

3

Jesus calls us in, sends us out
bearing fruit in a world of doubt,
gives us love to tell, bread to share:
God-Immanuel everywhere:

Jesus lives again, earth can breathe again,
pass the Word around: loaves abound.

FRED KAAN (b. 1929)

482 (MHT **149**)

Litherop 8 7.8 7.8 7. Peter Cutts (b. 193

A song of love and living

1 Life is great! So sing about it,
as we can and as we should –
shops and buses, towns and people,
village, farmland, field and wood.
Life is great and life is given;
life is lovely, free and good.

2 Life is great! – whatever happens,
snow or sunshine, joy or pain,
hardship, grief or disillusion,
suffering that I can't explain –
life is great if someone loves me,
holds my hand and calls my name.

3 Love is great! – the love of lovers,
whispered words and longing eyes;
love that gazes at the cradle
where a child of loving lies;
love that lasts when youth has faded,
bends with age, but never dies.

4 Love is giving and receiving –
boy and girl, or friend with friend;
love is bearing and forgiving‿
all the hurts that hate can send;
love's the greatest way of living,
hoping, trusting to the end.

5 God is great! In Christ he loved us,
as we should, but never can –
love that suffered, hoped and trusted
when disciples turned and ran,
love that broke through death for ever.
Praise that loving, living Man!

BRIAN A. WREN (b. 1936)

483 (MHT **150**)

Truro L.M.

Melody from T. Williams's *Psalmodia Evangelica*, 1789

The coming of Christ

1 Lift up your heads, you mighty gates,
behold, the King of Glory waits,
the King of kings is drawing near,
the Saviour of the world is here.

2 O blest the land, the city blest
where Christ the ruler is confessed.
O happy hearts and happy homes
to whom this King in triumph comes.

3 Fling wide the portals of your heart,
make it a temple set apart
from earthly use for heaven's employ,
adorned with prayer and love and joy.

4 Come, Saviour, come, with us abide;
our hearts to thee we open wide:
thy Holy Spirit guide us on,
until our glorious goal is won.

GEORG WEISSEL (1590–1635)
tr. CATHERINE WINKWORTH* (1827–78)

484 (MHT **151**)
Personent hodie *Piae Cantiones*, 15
6 6.6 6 6. and refrain

Jesus comes

Long ago, prophets knew
Christ would come, born a Jew,
come to make all things new,
bear his people's burden,
freely love and pardon.

Ring, bells, ring, ring, ring!
Sing, choirs, sing, sing, sing!
When he comes,
when he comes,
who will make him welcome?

2

God in time, God in man,
this is God's timeless plan:
he will come, as a man,
born himself of woman,
God divinely human:

3

Mary, hail! Though afraid,
she believed, she obeyed.
In her womb God is laid,
till the time expected,
nurtured and protected:

4

Journey ends: where afar‿
Bethlem shines, like a star,
stable door stands ajar.
Unborn Son of Mary,
Saviour, do not tarry.

Ring, bells, ring, ring, ring!
Sing, choirs, sing, sing, sing!
Jesus comes,
Jesus comes:
we will make him welcome.

F. Pratt Green (b. 1903)

485 (MHT 152)

Ainsdale L.M. John M. Etherton (b. 1939

Our wills are ours, to make them thine

Lord, as I wake I turn to you,
  yourself the first thought of my day:
my King, my God, whose help is sure,
  yourself the help for which I pray.

2

There is no blessing, Lord, from you‿
  for those who make their will their way;
no praise for those who will not praise,
  no peace for those who will not pray.

3

Your loving gifts of grace to me,
  those favours I could never earn,
call for my thanks in praise and prayer,
  call me to love you in return.

4

Lord, make my life a life of love,
  keep me from sin in all I do;
Lord, make your law my only law,
  your will my will, for love of you.

BRIAN FOLEY (b. 1919)
Psalm 5

86 (MHT **153**)

Stonegate 11 10.11 10. Cyril V. Taylor (b. 1907)

Harvest

Lord, by whose breath all souls and seeds are living
with life that is and life that is to be,
fruits of the earth we offer with thanksgiving
for fields in flood with summer's golden sea.

2

Lord of the earth, accept these gifts in token
thou in thy works art to be all-adored,
from whom the light as daily bread is broken,
sunset and dawn as wine and milk are poured.

3

Poor is our praise, but these shall be our psalter;
lo, like thyself they rose up from the dead;
Lord, give them back when at thy holy altar
we feed on thee, who art our living bread.

Andrew Young* (1885–1971)

487 (MHT **154**)

Abingdon 8 8.8 8.8 8. Erik Routley (1917–8

Through Christ . . . a living sacrifice

Lord Christ, we praise your sacrifice,
your life in love so freely given:
for those who took your life away
you prayed, that they might be forgiven;
and there, in helplessness arrayed,
God's power was perfectly displayed.

2

Once helpless in your mother's arms,
dependent on her mercy then,
you made yourself again, by choice,
as helpless in the hands of men;
and, at their mercy crucified,
you claimed your victory and died.

3

Though helpless and rejected then,
you're now as reigning Lord acclaimed;
for ever by your victory
is God's eternal love proclaimed –
the love which goes through death to find
new life and hope for all mankind.

4

So, living Lord, prepare us now
your willing helplessness to share;
to give ourselves in sacrifice
to overcome the world's despair;
in love to give our lives away
and claim your victory today.

ALAN GAUNT (b. 1935)

488 (MHT 155)

Cliff Town 10 10.10 10. Erik Routley (1917–82)

God's saints

Lord God, we give you thanks for all your saints
who sought the trackless footprints of your feet,
who took into their own a hand unseen
and heard a voice whose silence was complete.

2

In every word and deed they spoke of Christ,
and in their life gave glory to his name;
their love was unconsumed, a burning bush
of which the Holy Spirit was the flame.

3

Blest Trinity, may yours be endless praise
for all who lived so humbly in your sight;
your holy ones who walked dark ways in faith
now share the joy of your unfailing light.

MARCELLA MARTIN (b. 1908)

489 (MHT **156**)

Ryburn 8 8.8 8.8 8. Norman Cocker (1889–1953)

By grace alone

Lord God, your love has called us here,
as we, by love, for love were made.
Your living likeness still we bear,
though marred, dishonoured, disobeyed.
We come, with all our heart and mind
your call to hear, your love to find.

*2

We come with self-inflicted pains
of broken trust and chosen wrong,
half-free, half-bound by inner chains,
by social forces swept along,
by powers and systems close confined,
yet seeking hope for humankind.

3

Lord God, in Christ you call our name,
  and then receive us as your own,
not through some merit, right or claim,
  but by your gracious love alone.
We strain to glimpse your mercy-seat,
and find you kneeling at our feet.

4

Then take the towel, and break the bread,
  and humble us, and call us friends.
Suffer and serve till all are fed,
  and show how grandly love intends
to work till all creation sings,
to fill all worlds, to crown all things.

*5

Lord God, in Christ you set us free
  your life to live, your joy to share.
Give us your Spirit's liberty
  to turn from guilt and dull despair
and offer all that faith can do,
while love is making all things new.

BRIAN A. WREN (b. 1936)

490 (MHT 157)
Billing C.M. R. R. Terry (1865–1938

The excellency and variety of Scripture

Lord, I have made thy word my choice,
my lasting heritage:
there shall my noblest powers rejoice,
my warmest thoughts engage.

2

I'll read the histories of thy love,
and keep thy laws in sight,
while through thy promises I rove
with ever-fresh delight.

3

'Tis a broad land of wealth unknown,
where springs of life arise,
seeds of immortal bliss are sown,
and hidden glory lies.

ISAAC WATTS* (1674–1748
from Psalm 11

491 (MHT 158)
Niagara L.M. Robert Jackson (1840–1914)

Before reading the Scriptures

Lord Jesus Christ, be present now,
and let your Holy Spirit bow‿
all hearts in love and fear today
to hear the truth and keep your way.

2

Open our lips to sing your praise,
our hearts in true devotion raise,
strengthen our faith, increase our light,
that we may know your name aright.

Anon, German
tr. CATHERINE WINKWORTH* (1827–78)

492 (MHT **159**) FIRST TUNE

Guarda 7 7 7.5. Sydney Watson (b. 1903

SECOND TUNE

Huddersfield 7 7 7.5. Walter Parratt (1841–1924

Hear and save

Lord of all, to whom alone
all our hearts' desires are known,
when we stand before thy throne,
Jesu, hear and save.

2

Son of Man, before whose eyes
every secret open lies,
at thy great and last assize,
Jesu, hear and save.

3

Son of God, whose angel host
(thou hast said) rejoiceth most
o'er the sinner who was lost,
Jesu, hear and save.

4

Saviour, who didst not condemn
those who touched thy garments' hem,
mercy show to us and them:
Jesu, hear and save.

5

Lord, the Way to sinners shown,
Lord, the Truth by sinners known,
Love Incarnate on the throne,
Jesu, hear and save.

C. A. ALINGTON (1872–1955)

493 (MHT **160**) FIRST TUNE

San Rocco C.M. Derek Williams (b. 194

Original key D♭ (324)

SECOND TUNE

London New C.M. *Scottish Psalter*, 163
As adapted in Playford's *Psalms*, 167

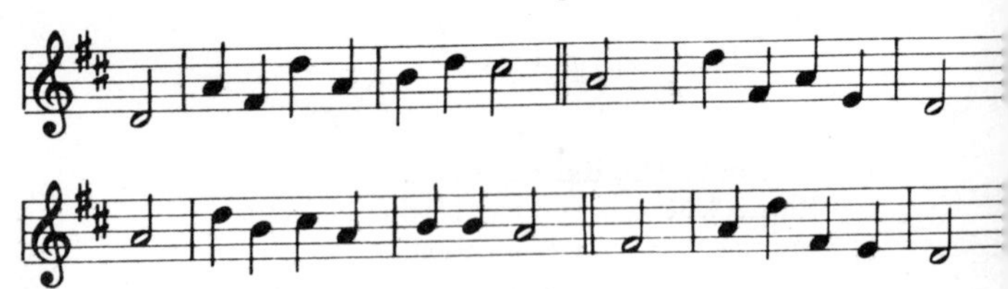

Creator and Redeemer

Lord of the boundless curves of space
  and time's deep mystery,
to your creative might we trace‿
  all nature's energy.

2

Your mind conceived the galaxy,
  each atom's secret planned,
and every age of history
  your purpose, Lord, has spanned.

3

Your Spirit gave the living cell‿
its hidden, vital force:
the instincts which all life impel
derive from you, their source.

4

Yours is the image stamped on man,
though marred by man's own sin;
and yours the liberating plan
again his soul to win.

5

Science explores your reason's ways,
and faith can this impart
that in the face of Christ our gaze‿
looks deep within your heart.

6

Christ is your wisdom's perfect word,
your mercy's crowning deed:
in him the sons of earth have heard‿
your strong compassion plead.

7

Give us to know your truth; but more,
the strength to do your will;
until the love our souls adore
shall all our being fill.

ALBERT F. BAYLY (1901–84)

494 (MHT **161**)
Warrington L.M. R. Harrison (1748–1810)

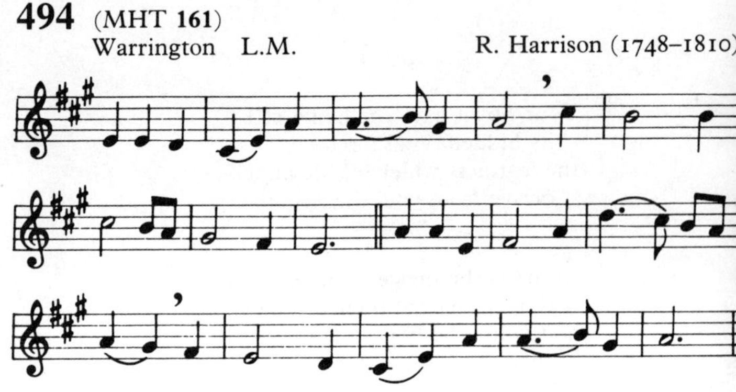

Our homes

Lord of the home, your only Son‿
  received a mother's tender love,
and from an earthly father won‿
  his vision of your home above.

2

Help us, O Lord, our homes to make‿
  your Holy Spirit's dwelling place;
our hands' and hearts' devotion take
  to be the servants of your grace.

3

Teach us to keep our homes so fair
  that, were our Lord a child once more,
he might be glad our hearth to share,
  and find a welcome at our door.

4

Lord, may your Spirit sanctify‿
  each household duty we fulfil;
may we our Master glorify
  in glad obedience to your will.

ALBERT F. BAYLY (1901–84)

495 (MHT **162**)

Rex gloriae 8 7.8 7.D. H. Smart (1813–79

Offerings

Lord, to you we bring our treasure,
  wealth of mind and hand and heart,
fruit of toil and joy of leisure,
  music, word, and craftsman's art,
truths of prophets, saints, and sages,
  patient skills of hearth and home;
Father, giver down the ages,
  these are yours; to you we come.

2

Jesus, Servant, in your Passion
  offering all for all mankind,
teach us in ourselves to fashion
  day by day your will, your mind,
live for truth, for justice striving,
  heal the sick, the hungry feed,
by your work, your words, your giving
  set to help all human need.

3

In your sacrament now sharing
  round your table, risen Lord,
each for every other caring,
  wrongs forgiven, faith restored,
bread and wine of life receiving,
  yours the Body, yours the Blood,
may we be your Church believing,
  one in worldwide brotherhood.

H. C. A. Gaunt (1902–83)

496 (MHT **163**)

Song 13 7 7.7 7. Orlando Gibbons (1583–1625)

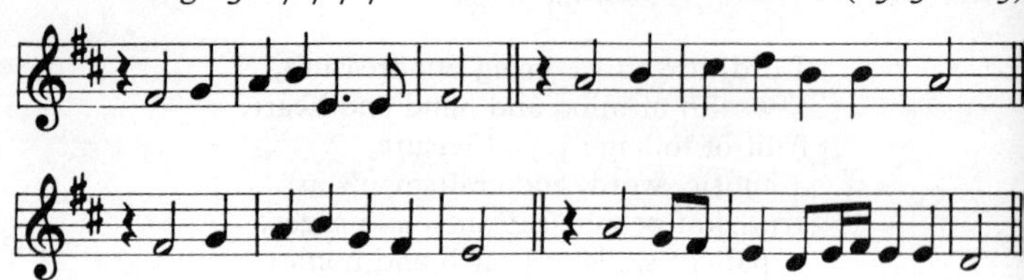

Alternative Tune: *Vienna* (380)

Love's endeavour, love's expense

Morning glory, starlit sky,
  soaring music, scholars' truth,
flight of swallows, autumn leaves,
  memory's treasure, grace of youth:

2

open are the gifts of God,
  gifts of love to mind and sense;
hidden is love's agony,
  love's endeavour, love's expense.

3

Love that gives, gives ever more,
gives with zeal, with eager hands,
spares not, keeps not, all outpours,
ventures all, its all expends.

4

Drained is love in making full,
bound in setting others free,
poor in making many rich,
weak in giving power to be.

5

Therefore he who shows us God
helpless hangs upon the tree;
and the nails and crown of thorns
tell of what God's love must be.

6

Here is God: no monarch he,
throned in easy state to reign;
here is God, whose arms of love
aching, spent, the world sustain.

W. H. Vanstone (b. 1923)

497 (MHT **164**)
Nürnberg L.M.

From an original hymn-tu
by J. S. Bach (1685–175
adapted by John Wils

Christ crucified, the wisdom and power of God

Nature with open volume stands
  to spread her maker's praise abroad,
and every labour of his hands
  shows something worthy of our God.

2

But in the grace that rescued man
  his brightest form of glory shines;
here on the Cross 'tis fairest drawn
  in precious blood and crimson lines.

3

Here his whole name appears complete;
  nor wit can guess, nor reason prove
which of the letters best is writ,
  the power, the wisdom, or the love.

4

O the sweet wonders of that Cross
  where God the Saviour loved and died;
her noblest life my spirit draws
  from his dear wounds and bleeding side.

5

I would for ever speak his name
  in sounds to mortal ears unknown,
with angels join to praise the Lamb,
  and worship at his Father's throne.

Isaac Watts* (1674–1748)

498 (MHT **165**)

Rendez à Dieu — *La Forme des Prières*, Strasbourg, 1545

9 8.9 8.D. — (2nd line as in *Genevan Psalter* of 1551)

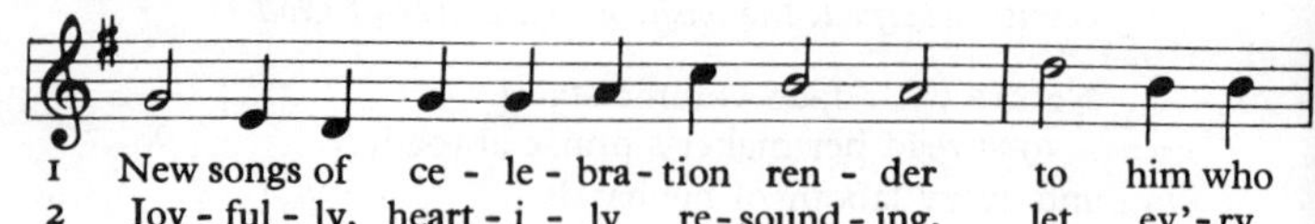

1 New songs of ce - le - bra - tion ren - der to him who
2 Joy - ful - ly, heart - i - ly re - sound - ing, let ev' - ry
3 Riv - ers and seas and tor - rents roar - ing, hon - our the

has great won-ders done. Love sits en-throned in age-less splen-dour:
in-stru-ment and voice peal out the praise of grace a-bound-ing,
Lord with wild ac-claim; moun-tains and stones look up a - dor - ing

come and a-dore the migh-ty one. He has made known his great sal-
call-ing the whole world to re-joice. Trum-pets and or-gans, set in
and find a voice to praise his name. Right-eous, com-mand-ing, ev-er

va - tion which all his friends with joy con-fess: he has re-
mo - tion such sounds as make the hea - vens ring; all things that
glo-rious, prai - ses be his that ne - ver cease: just is our

vealed to ev' - ry na - tion his ev - er - last-ing right-eous-ness.
live in earth and o - cean, make mu-sic for your migh-ty King.
God, whose truth vic-tor - ious es - tab-lish-es the world in peace.

A joyful noise

New songs of celebration render
  to him who has great wonders done.
Love sits enthroned in ageless splendour:
  come and adore the mighty one.
He has made known his great salvation
  which all his friends with joy confess:
he has revealed to every nation
  his everlasting righteousness.

2

Joyfully, heartily resounding,
  let every instrument and voice
peal out the praise of grace abounding,
  calling the whole world to rejoice.
Trumpets and organs, set in motion‿
  such sounds as make the heavens ring;
all things that live in earth and ocean,
  make music for your mighty King.

3

Rivers and seas and torrents roaring,
  honour the Lord with wild acclaim;
mountains and stones look up adoring
  and find a voice to praise his name.
Righteous, commanding, ever glorious,
  praises be his that never cease:
just is our God, whose truth victorious
  establishes the world in peace.

ERIK ROUTLEY (1917–82)
Psalm 98

499 (MHT **166**)
Glasgow C.M.

Moore's *Psalm-Singer Pocket Companion*, 175

Alternative Tune: *University* (169)

A new day

1 Now from the altar of our hearts
let incense flames arise;
assist us, Lord, to offer up‿
our morning sacrifice.

2 Awake, my love; awake, my joy;
awake, my heart and tongue.
Sleep not: when mercies loudly call,
break forth into a song.

3 This day be God our sun and shield,
our keeper and our guide;
his care be on our frailty shown,
his mercies multiplied.

4 New time, new favour, and new joys
a new song all require;
till we shall praise thee as we would,
accept our hearts' desire.

JOHN MASON* (c. 1645–1694)

500 (MHT **167**)
Harvest 9 8.9 8. Geoffrey Laycock (b. 1927)

Harvest

1 Now join we, to praise the Creator,
our voices in worship and song;
we stand to recall with thanksgiving
that to him all seasons belong.

2 We thank you, O God, for your goodness,
for the joy and abundance of crops,
for food that is stored in our larders,
for all we can buy in the shops.

3 But also of need and starvation
we sing with concern and despair,
of skills that are used for destruction,
of land that is burnt and laid bare.

4 We cry for the plight of the hungry
while harvests are left on the field,
for orchards neglected and wasting,
for produce from markets withheld.

5 The song grows in depth and in wideness:
the earth and its people are one.
There can be no thanks without giving,
no words without deeds that are done.

6 Then teach us, O Lord of the harvest,
to be humble in all that we claim:
to share what we have with the nations,
to care for the world in your name.

Fred Kaan (b. 1929)

501 (MHT **168**) FIRST TUNE

Noel nouvelet 11 10.10 11. Old French Melody

SECOND TUNE

Green Blade 11 10.10 11. Greville Cooke (b. 1894)

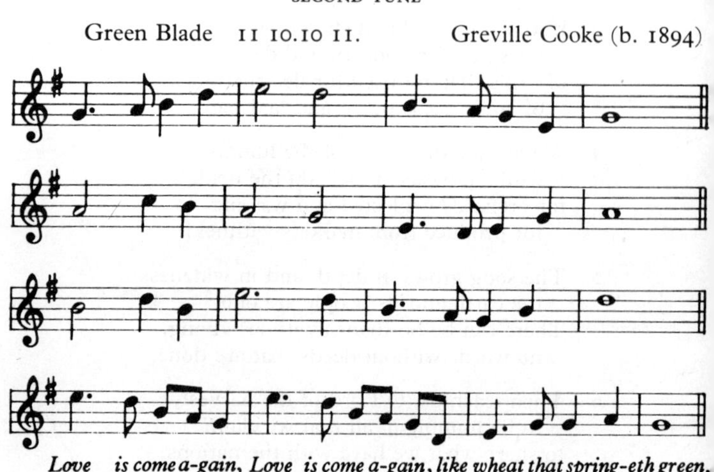
Love is come a-gain, Love is come a-gain, like wheat that spring-eth green.

Life through death

Now the green blade riseth from the buried grain,
wheat that in dark earth many days has lain;
Love lives again, that with the dead has been:

Love is come again,
like wheat that springeth green.

2

In the grave they laid him, Love whom men had slain,
thinking that never he would wake again,
laid in the earth like grain that sleeps unseen:

3

Forth he came at Easter, like the risen grain,
he that for three days in the grave had lain,
quick from the dead my risen Lord is seen:

4

When our hearts are wintry, grieving, or in pain,
thy touch can call us back to life again,
fields of our hearts that dead and bare have been:

Love is come again,
like wheat that springeth green.

J. M. C. CRUM (1872–1958)

502 (MHT **169**)
Crediton C.M. Thomas Clark (1775–1859

Transfiguration

O raise your eyes on high and see,
there stands our sovereign Lord;
his glory is this day revealed,
his Word a two-edged sword.

2

We glimpse the splendour and the power‿
of him who conquered death,
the Christ in whom the universe‿
knows God's creating breath.

3

Of every creed and nation King
in him all strife is stilled;
the promise made to Abraham
in him has been fulfilled.

4

The prophets stand and with great joy‿
give witness as they gaze;
the Father with a sign has sealed‿
our trust, our hope, our praise.

Ralph Wright (b. 1938)

503 (MHT 170)
Ripponden 8 8 8.4. Norman Cocker (1889–1953)

Fruit of the Spirit

Of all the Spirit's gifts to me,
I pray that I may never cease‿
to take and treasure most these three:
love, joy, and peace.

2

He shows me love is at the root‿
of every gift sent from above,
of every flower, of every fruit,
that God is love.

3

He shows me that if I possess‿
a love no evil can destroy,
however great is my distress,
that this is joy.

4

Though what's ahead is mystery,
and life itself is ours on lease,
each day the Spirit says to me,
'Go forth in peace'.

5

We go in peace, but made aware
that in a needy world like this
our clearest purpose is to share‿
love, joy, and peace.

F. Pratt Green (b. 1903)

504 (MHT 171)
Whitsun Carol 7 6.7 7. Erik Routley (1917–82)

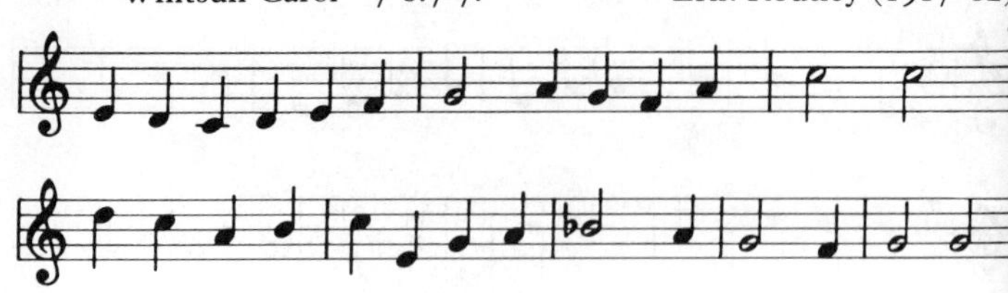

Pentecost

1 On the day of Pentecost,
when the twelve assembled,
came on them the Holy Ghost
in fire that tongues resembled.

2 In the power of God he came,
as the Lord had told them,
in his blessèd, holy name‿
with wisdom to uphold them.

3 In the Spirit then they stood
to proclaim Christ dying,
and that he for all men's good
doth live, true strength supplying.

4 Still the might by which we live‿
from our God descendeth;
still his Spirit Christ doth give,
who guideth and defendeth.

5 Praise, O praise our heavenly King
for his grace toward us;
gladly now his glory sing,
who doth his power afford us.

T. C. Hunter Clare (1910–84)

05 (MHT 172)

Rhosymedre 6 6.6 6.8 8 8. J. D. Edwards (1805–85)

The family

1 Our Father, by whose name
  all fatherhood is known,
who in your love proclaim‿
  each family your own,
direct all parents, guarding well,
with constant love as sentinel,
the homes in which your people dwell.

2 Lord Christ, yourself a child
  within an earthly home,
with heart still undefiled
  you did to manhood come;
our children bless in every place,
that they may all behold your face,
and knowing you may grow in grace.

3 Blest Spirit, who can bind‿
  our hearts in unity,
and teach us so to find‿
  the love from self set free,
in all our hearts such love increase
that every home, by this release,
may be the dwelling place of peace.

F. Bland Tucker (1895–1984)

506 (MHT 173)

Coelites plaudant 11 11 11.5. (Rouen) *Rou* *Antiphoner*, 17

Baptism

Praise and thanksgiving be to our Creator,
source of this blessing: Father, Mediator,
baptize and make your own those who come before you,
while we adore you.

2

Not our own holiness, nor that we have striven,
brings us the peace which you, O Christ, have given.
Baptize and set apart: come, O risen Saviour,
with grace and favour.

3

Come, Holy Spirit, come in visitation:
you are the truth, our hope and our salvation.
Baptize with joy and power: give, O Dove descending,
life never ending.

HAROLD FRANCIS YARDLEY (b. 191
FRANK J. WHITELEY (b. 191

507 (MHT 174)
Worlebury 10 7.10 7. and refrain John Ainslie (b. 1942)

Refrain

Offertory

1 Reap me the earth as a harvest to God,
gather and bring it again,
all that is his, to the maker of all;
lift it and offer it high.

Bring bread, bring wine,
give glory to the Lord;
whose is the earth but God's,
whose is the praise but his?

2 Go with your song and your music, with joy,
go to the altar of God;
carry your offerings, fruits of the earth,
work of your labouring hands:

Bring bread, bring wine, ...

3 Gladness and pity and passion and pain,
all that is mortal in man,
lay all before him, return him his gift,
God, to whom all shall go home.

Bring bread, bring wine, ...

'Peter Icarus'

508 (MHT 175)

Old 104th 10 10.11 11.

Adapted from T. Ravenscroft's *Psalmes*, 162

A descant to this tune is at 298

God's saints

Rejoice in God's saints, today and all days:
a world without saints forgets how to praise.
  Their faith in acquiring the habit of prayer,
  their depth of adoring, Lord, help us to share.

2

Some march with events to turn them God's way;
some need to withdraw, the better to pray;
  some carry the gospel through fire and through flood:
  our world is their parish; their purpose is God.

3

Rejoice in those saints, unpraised and unknown,
who bear someone's cross or shoulder their own;
  they shame our complaining, our comforts, our cares:
  what patience in caring, what courage, is theirs!

4

Rejoice in God's saints, today and all days:
a world without saints forgets how to praise.
  In loving, in living, they prove it is true –
  the way of self-giving, Lord, leads us to you.

F. PRATT GREEN (b. 1903)

509 (MHT **176**) FIRST TUNE

Sussex 8 7.8 7. English Traditional Melody

The word of the Lord

Rise and hear! The Lord is speaking,
as the gospel words unfold;
man, in all his agelong seeking,
finds no firmer truth to hold.

2

Word of goodness, truth, and beauty,
heard by simple folk and wise,
word of freedom, word of duty,
word of life beyond our eyes.

3

Word of God's forgiveness granted‿
to the wild or guilty soul,
word of love that works undaunted,
changes, heals, and makes us whole.

4

Speak to us, O Lord, believing,
as we hear, the sower sows;
may our hearts, your word receiving,
be the good ground where it grows.

H. C. A. Gaunt (1902–83)

SECOND TUNE

Great Wilkins 8 7.8 7. Ian A. Copley (b. 1926)

The word of the Lord

Rise and hear! The Lord is speaking,
as the gospel words unfold;
man, in all his agelong seeking,
finds no firmer truth to hold.

2

Word of goodness, truth, and beauty,
heard by simple folk and wise,
word of freedom, word of duty,
word of life beyond our eyes.

3

Word of God's forgiveness granted‿
to the wild or guilty soul,
word of love that works undaunted,
changes, heals, and makes us whole.

4

Speak to us, O Lord, believing,
as we hear, the sower sows;
may our hearts, your word receiving,
be the good ground where it grows.

H. C. A. Gaunt (1902–83)

510 (MHT 177)

The Ash Grove 12 11.12 11.D. Welsh Traditional Melody

After Communion

Sent forth by God's blessing, our true faith confessing,
the People of God from his dwelling take leave.
The supper is ended: O now be extended
the fruits of his service in all who believe.
The seed of his teaching, our hungry souls reaching,
shall blossom in action for God and for man.
His grace shall incite us, his love shall unite us
to work for his kingdom and further his plan.

2

With praise and thanksgiving to God everliving,
the task of our everyday life we will face,
our faith ever sharing, in love ever caring,
embracing as brothers all men of each race.
One feast that has fed us, one light that has led us,
unite us as one in his life that we share.
Then may all the living, with praise and thanksgiving,
give honour to Christ and his name that we bear.

OMER WESTENDORF (b. 1916)

511 (MHT **178**)

Haresfield C.M. John Dykes Bower (1905–1981

Alternative Tune: *Westminster* (Turle) (102)

The Saviour

The great Creator of the worlds,
the sovereign God of heaven,
his holy and immortal truth
to men on earth has given.

2

He sent no angel of his host
to bear his mighty word,
but him through whom the worlds were made,
the everlasting Lord.

3

He sent him not in wrath and power,
  but grace and peace to bring;
in kindness, as a king might send‿
  his son, himself a king.

4

He sent him down as sending God;
  as man he came to men;
as one with us he dwelt with us,
  and died and lives again.

5

He came as Saviour to his own,
  the way of love he trod;
he came to win men by good will,
  for force is not of God.

6

Not to oppress, but summon men‿
  their truest life to find,
in love God sent his Son to save,
  not to condemn mankind.

From *Epistle to Diognetus* (2nd cent.)
tr. F. BLAND TUCKER (1895–1984)

512 (MHT 179)

Wolvercote 7 6.7 6.D. W. H. Ferguson (1874–1950)

The kingdom of God

'The kingdom is upon you!'
the voice of Jesus cries,
fulfilling with its message‿
the wisdom of the wise;
it lightens with fresh insight
the striving human mind,
creating new dimensions‿
of purpose for mankind.

2

'God's kingdom is upon you!'
the message sounds today,
it summons every pilgrim
to take the questing way,
with eyes intent on Jesus,
our leader and our friend,
who trod faith's road before us,
and trod it to the end.

3

The kingdom is upon us!
Stirred by the Spirit's breath,
we glory in its freedom‿
from emptiness and death;
we celebrate its purpose,
its mission and its goal,
alive with the conviction
that Christ can make us whole.

ROBERT WILLIS (b. 1947)

613 (MHT **180**)
Forgive our sins C.M. American Folk Hymn Melody in
A Supplement to the Kentucky Harmony, 1820

Alternative Tune: *St. Stephen* (29)

The Gospel

The prophets spoke in days of old
to men of stubborn will.
Their message lives and is retold
where hearts are stubborn still.

2

And Jesus spoke to sinful men
of love, of joy, of peace.
His message lives, he speaks again,
and sinners find release.

3

Shall we not hear that message, Lord,
to lead us on the way?
Come, Christ, make plain your saving word,
and speak to us today.

JOHN E. BOWERS (b. 1923)

514 (MHT **181**)

Diva servatrix 11 11 11.5. *Bayeux Antiphoner*, 1739

The tree of life

There in God's garden stands the tree of wisdom
whose leaves hold forth the healing of the nations:
tree of all knowledge, tree of all compassion,
tree of all beauty.

2

Its name is Jesus, name that says 'Our Saviour':
there on its branches see the scars of suffering:
see where the tendrils of our human selfhood
feed on its lifeblood.

3

Thorns not its own are tangled in its foliage;
our greed has starved it, our despite has choked it;
yet, look, it lives! its grief has not destroyed it,
nor fire consumed it.

4

See how its branches reach to us in welcome;
hear what the voice says, 'Come to me, ye weary:
give me your sickness, give me all your sorrow:
I will give blessing'.

5

All heaven is singing, 'Thanks to Christ whose Passion
offers in mercy healing, strength and pardon:
peoples and nations, take it, take it freely'.
Amen, my Master.

ERIK ROUTLEY (1917–82)
based on the Hungarian of
KIRÀLY IMRE VON PÉCSELY
(c. 1590–c. 1641)

515 (MHT **182**)

Lauds 7 7.7 7. John Wilson (b. 1905)

Praise the Holy Spirit

1 There's a spirit in the air,
telling Christians everywhere:
'Praise the love that Christ revealed,
living, working, in our world'.

2 Lose your shyness, find your tongue,
tell the world what God has done:
God in Christ has come to stay;
we can see his power today.

3 When believers break the bread,
when a hungry child is fed,
praise the love that Christ revealed,
living, working, in our world.

4 Still his Spirit leads the fight,
seeing wrong and setting right:
God in Christ has come to stay;
we can see his power today.

5 When a stranger's not alone,
where the homeless find a home,
praise the love that Christ revealed,
living, working, in our world.

6 May his Spirit fill our praise,
guide our thoughts and change our ways.
God in Christ has come to stay;
we can see his power today.

7 There's a Spirit in the air,
calling people everywhere:
Praise the love that Christ revealed,
living, working, in our world.

BRIAN A. WREN (b. 1936)

516 (MHT **183**)
Addington 5 5.5 4.D. Cyril V. Taylor (b. 1907)

St Patrick's breastplate

1 This day God gives me‿
strength of high heaven,
sun and moon shining,
flame in my hearth;
flashing of lightning,
wind in its swiftness,
deeps of the ocean,
firmness of earth.

2 This day God sends me‿
strength as my steersman,
might to uphold me,
wisdom as guide.
Your eyes are watchful,
your ears are listening,
your lips are speaking,
friend at my side.

3 God's way is my way,
God's shield is round me,
God's host defends me,
saving from ill;
angels of heaven,
drive from me always
all that would harm me,
stand by me still.

4 Rising, I thank you,
mighty and strong one,
King of creation,
giver of rest,
firmly confessing‿
threeness of Persons,
oneness of Godhead,
Trinity blest.

JAMES QUINN (b. 1919)
from 8th century Irish

517 (MHT 184)

FIRST TUNE

St. Mary C.M. E. Prys's *Llyfr y Psalmau*, 162

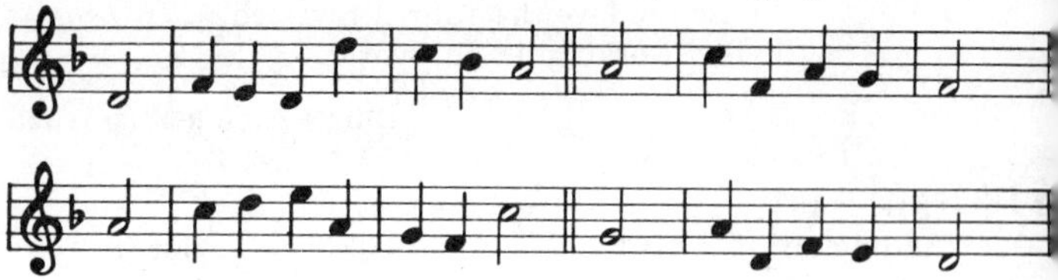

Wigtown C.M. *Scottish Psalter*, 163

It is intended that the first half of each verse shall be sung to *St. Mary* and the second half to *Wigtown*

SECOND TUNE

Third Mode Melody D.C.M

Thomas Tallis (c. 1515–85) edited by John Wilson

Royal insignia

To mock your reign, O dearest Lord,
  they made a crown of thorns;
set you with taunts along that road
  from which no man returns.
They could not know, as we do now,
  how glorious is that crown:
that thorns would flower upon your brow,
  your sorrows heal our own.

2

In mock acclaim, O gracious Lord,
  they snatched a purple cloak,
your passion turned, for all they cared,
  into a soldier's joke.
They could not know, as we do now,
  that, though we merit blame,
you will your robe of mercy throw
  around our naked shame.

3

A sceptred reed, O patient Lord,
  they thrust into your hand,
and acted out their grim charade
  to its appointed end.
They could not know, as we do now,
  though empires rise and fall,
your kingdom shall not cease to grow
  till love embraces all.

F. PRATT GREEN (b. 1903)

The words were written for the second tune

518 (MHT **185**)

Au clair de la lune

6 5 6 5.6 5 7 5.

French Traditional Melody

Gardens

Walking in a garden‿
at the close of day,
Adam tried to hide him
when he heard God say:
'Why are you so frightened,
why are you afraid?
You have brought the winter in,
made the flowers fade.'

2

Walking in a garden‿
where the Lord had gone,
three of the disciples,
Peter, James, and John;
they were very weary,
could not keep awake,
while the Lord was kneeling there,
praying for their sake.

3

Walking in a garden‿
at the break of day,
Mary asked the gardener‿
where the body lay;
but he turned towards her,
smiled at her and said:
'Mary, spring is here to stay,
only death is dead.'

HILARY GREENWOOD (b. 1929)

519 (MHT **186**)

Whitfield 5 4·5 5·7· John Wilson (b. 1905)

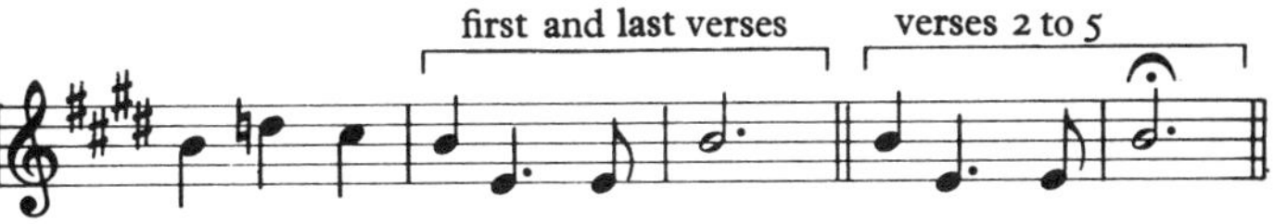

Ministers of Christ

1

/e are your people:
.ord, by your grace,
you dare to make us
Christ to our neighbours
f every nation and race.

2

Iow can we demonstrate
our love and care?
speaking or listening?
battling or serving?
.elp us to know when and where.

3

:alled to portray you,
elp us to live
closer than neighbours
open to strangers,
ble to clash and forgive.

4

Glad of tradition,
help us to see
in all life's changing
where you are leading,
where our best efforts should be.

5

Joined in community,
breaking your bread,
may we discover
gifts in each other,
willing to lead and be led.

6

Lord, as we minister
in different ways,
may all we're doing
show that you're living,
meeting your love with our praise.

Brian A. Wren (b. 1936)

520 (MHT **187**)
Croft's 136th 6 6.6 6.4 4.4 4.

William Croft
(1678–1727)

A song of praise to the Blessed Trinity

1

We give immortal praise
to God the Father's love
for all our comforts here,
and better hopes above:
  he sent his own
  eternal Son,
  to die for sins
  that man had done.

2

To God the Son belongs‿
immortal glory too,
who bought us with his blood
from everlasting woe:
  and now he lives,
  and now he reigns,
  and sees the fruit
  of all his pains.

3

To God the Spirit's name
immortal worship give,
whose new-creating power
makes the dead sinner live:
  his work completes‿
  the great design,
  and fills the soul‿
  with joy divine.

4

Almighty God, to thee‿
be endless honours done,
the undivided Three,
and the mysterious One:
  where reason fails
  with all her powers,
  there faith prevails,
  and love adores.

ISAAC WATTS* (1674–1748)

521 (MHT **188**)
Crucis victoria C.M. M. B. Foster (1851–1922)

Baptized into Christ

We praise you, Lord, for Jesus Christ
who died and rose again;
he lives to break the power of sin,
and over death to reign.

2

We praise you that this child now shares‿
the freedom Christ can give,
has died to sin with Christ, and now‿
with Christ is raised to live.

3

We praise you, Lord, that now this child‿
is grafted to the vine,
is made a member of your house
and bears the cross as sign.

4

We praise you, Lord, for Jesus Christ;
he loves this child we bring:
he frees, forgives, and heals us all,
he lives and reigns as King.

JUDITH BEATRICE O'NEILL (b. 1930)

522 (MHT **189**) FIRST TUNE

Intercessor 11 10.11 10. C. Hubert H. Parry (1848–1918)

SECOND TUNE

Harding 11 10.11 10. Cyril V. Taylor (b. 1907)

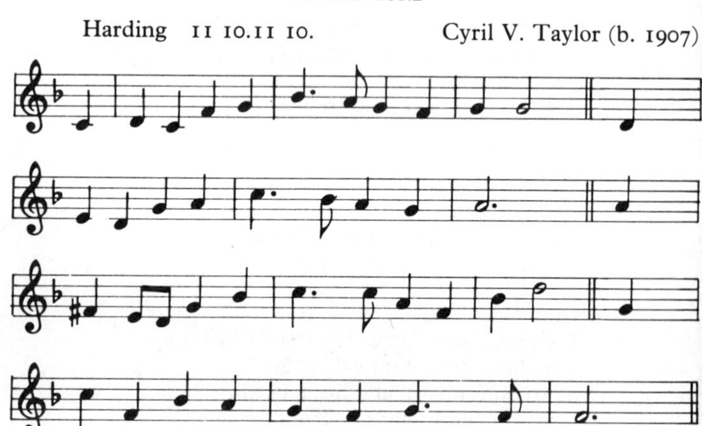

The family of nations

We turn to you, O God of every nation,
giver of life and origin of good;
your love is at the heart of all creation,
your hurt is people's broken brotherhood.

2

We turn to you, that we may be forgiven
for crucifying Christ on earth again.
We know that we have never wholly striven,
forgetting self, to love the other man.

3

Free every heart from pride and self-reliance,
our ways of thought inspire with simple grace;
break down among us barriers of defiance,
speak to the soul of all the human race.

4

On men who fight on earth for right relations
we pray the light of love from hour to hour.
Grant wisdom to the leaders of the nations,
the gift of carefulness to those in power.

5

Teach us, good Lord, to serve the need of others,
help us to give and not to count the cost.
Unite us all, for we are born as brothers:
defeat our Babel with your Pentecost.

FRED KAAN (b. 1929)

523 (MHT **190**)
Were you there? — American Folk Hymn Melody
Irregular

Were you there?

Were you there when they crucified my Lord?
Were you there when they crucified my Lord?
Oh, sometimes it causes me to tremble, tremble, tremble;
were you there when they crucified my Lord?

2

Were you there when they nailed him to the tree?
Were you there when they nailed him to the tree?
Oh, sometimes it causes me to tremble, tremble, tremble;
were you there when they nailed him to the tree?

3

Were you there when they laid him in the tomb?
Were you there when they laid him in the tomb?
Oh, sometimes it causes me to tremble, tremble, tremble;
were you there when they laid him in the tomb?

American Folk Hymn

524 (MHT **191**)
Hermon 8 6.8 6 6. Jeremiah Clarke (1673–1707)

Adam and Christ

1

What Adam's disobedience cost,
  let holy scripture say:
mankind estranged, an Eden lost,
  and then a judgement day:
  each day a judgement day.

2

An ark of mercy rode the flood;
  but man, where waters swirled,
rebuilt, impatient of the good,
  another fallen world:
  an unrepentant world.

3

A little child is Adam's heir,
  is Adam's hope and Lord.
Sing joyful carols everywhere
  that Eden is restored:
  in Jesus is restored.

4

Regained is Adam's blessedness:
  the angels sheathe their swords.
In joyful carols all confess‿
  the kingdom is the Lord's;
  the glory is the Lord's.

F. Pratt Green (b. 1903)

The words were written for this tune

525 (MHT **192**)

Rodmell C.M. English Traditional Melody

Accept one another as Christ accepted us

When Christ was lifted from the earth
his hands out-stretched above‿
to every culture, every birth,
to draw an answering love.

2

Still east and west his love extends,
and always, near or far,
he calls and claims us as his friends
and loves us as we are.

3

Thus freely loved, though fully known,
may I in Christ be free
to welcome and accept his own
as Christ accepted me.

Brian A. Wren (b. 1936)
Romans 15.7

26 (MHT **193**)

Offertorium 7 6.7 6.D.

Adapted from Michael Haydn (1737–1806)

Alternative Tune: *Crüger* (142)

The baptism of Jesus

When Jesus came to Jordan
to be baptized by John,
he did not come for pardon,
but as his Father's Son.
He came to share repentance
with all who mourn their sins,
to speak the vital sentence
with which good news begins.

2

He came to share temptation,
our utmost woe and loss;
for us and our salvation
to die upon the cross.
So when the Dove descended‿
on him, the Son of Man,
the hidden years had ended,
the age of grace began.

3

Come, Holy Spirit, aid us
to keep the vows we make;
this very day invade us,
and every bondage break;
come, give our lives direction,
the gift we covet most –
to share the resurrection
that leads to Pentecost.

F. Pratt Green (b. 1903)

527 (MHT **194**) FIRST TUNE

Sheet 8 7.8 7. Cyril V. Taylor (b. 1907)

The nativity of our Lord

Where is this stupendous stranger?
prophets, shepherds, kings, advise:
lead me to my Master's manger,
show me where my Saviour lies.

2

O most mighty, O most holy,
far beyond the seraph's thought,
art thou then so mean and lowly
as unheeded prophets taught?

3

O the magnitude of meekness,
worth from worth immortal sprung,
O the strength of infant weakness,
if eternal is so young.

4

Good all-bounteous, all-creative,
whom no ills from good dissuade,
is incarnate, and a native‿
of the very world he made.

CHRISTOPHER SMART (1722–71)

SECOND TUNE

Halton Holgate 8 7.8 7. Later form of melody by William Boyce (1710–79)

The nativity of our Lord

Where is this stupendous stranger?
prophets, shepherds, kings, advise:
lead me to my Master's manger,
show me where my Saviour lies.

2

O most mighty, O most holy,
far beyond the seraph's thought,
art thou then so mean and lowly
as unheeded prophets taught?

3

O the magnitude of meekness,
worth from worth immortal sprung,
O the strength of infant weakness,
if eternal is so young.

4

Good all-bounteous, all-creative,
whom no ills from good dissuade,
is incarnate, and a native‿
of the very world he made.

CHRISTOPHER SMART (1722–71)

528 (MHT 195)

Maisemore C.M. John Dykes Bower (1905–1981)

Alternative Tune: *St. Etheldreda* (228)

Serving Christ in one another

Where love and loving-kindness dwell,
there God will ever be:
One Father, Son, and Holy Ghost
in perfect charity.

2

Brought here together into one
by Christ our Shepherd-king,
now let us in his love rejoice,
and of his goodness sing.

3

Here too let God, the living God,
  both loved and honoured be;
and let us each the other love
  with true sincerity.

4

Brought here together by Christ's love,
  let no ill-will divide,
nor quarrels break the unity
  of those for whom he died.

5

Let envy, jealousy and strife
  and all contention cease,
for in our midst serves Christ the Lord,
  our sacrament of peace.

6

Together may we with the saints
  thy face in glory see,
and ever in thy kingdom feast,
  O Christ our God, with thee.

From the Latin Liturgy of Maundy Thursday
tr. GEOFFREY PRESTON (1936–77)

For another translation see 465

529 (MHT **196**)

People of God 7 5.7 5.6 6.6 5. Patrick Wedd (b. 1948

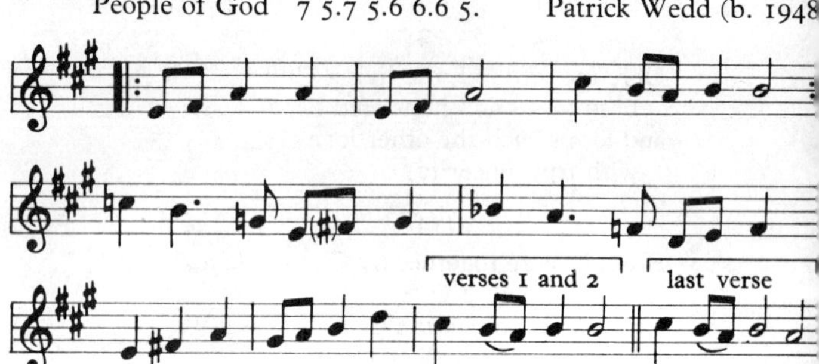

Alternative Tune: *Monks Gate* (212 (1))

The people of God

Who are we who stand and sing?
  We are his people.
What this bread and wine we bring?
  Food for his people.
As once with twelve he spake,
poured wine, and bread did break,
  he now will of us make‿
  a faithful people.

2

What command does he impart‿
  to us his people?
With your mind and strength and heart
  serve me, my people.
As God in Christ came low,
man's world and work to know,
  to life he bids us go‿
  to be his people.

3

Who are we who say one creed?
  We are his people.
What the word we hear and read?
  Word for his people.
Through time, in every race,
from earth to farthest space,
  we through our God's good grace‿
  will be his people.

T. HERBERT O'DRISCOLL (b. 1928)

530 (MHT **197**)
Salzburg C.M.

Adapted from Michael Haydn (1737–1806)

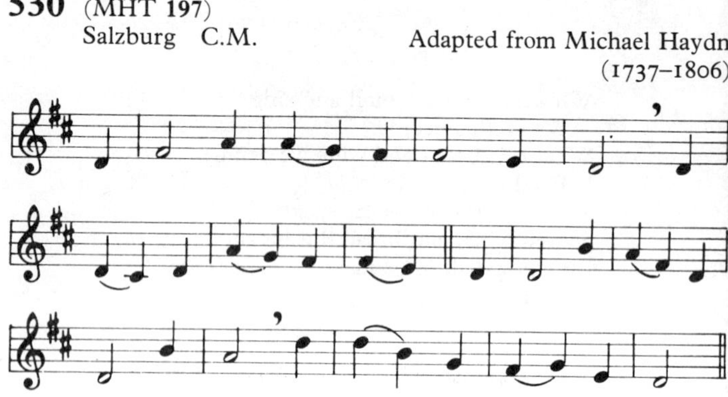

Christ's compassion
to the weak and tempted

With joy we meditate the grace‿
  of our High Priest above;
his heart is made of tenderness,
  and ever yearns with love.

2

Touched with a sympathy within,
  he knows our feeble frame;
he knows what sore temptations mean
  for he has felt the same.

3

He in the days of feeble flesh
  poured out his cries and tears;
and, in his measure, feels afresh‿
  what every member bears.

4

He'll never quench the smoking flax,
  but raise it to a flame;
the bruisèd reed he never breaks,
  nor scorns the meanest name.

5

Then let our humble faith address‿
  his mercy and his power:
we shall obtain delivering grace
  in every needful hour.

Isaac Watts* (1674–1748)
Hebrews 4. 15–16, and 5. 7

531 (MHT **198**)

Wadham College 8 8 8.4. Watkins Shaw (b. 1911)

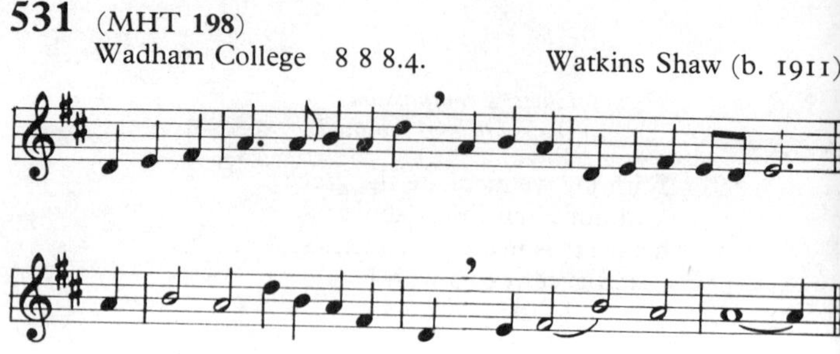

Alternative Tune: *Ripponden* (503)

The Creator

With wonder, Lord, we see your works,
  we see the beauty you have made,
this earth, the skies, all things that are
  in beauty made.

2

With wonder, Lord, we see your works,
  and childlike in our joy we sing
to praise you, bless you, Maker, Lord‿
  of everything.

3

The stars that fill the skies above,
  the sun and moon which give our light,
are your designing for our use
  and our delight.

4

We praise your works, yet we ourselves
  are works of wonder made by you,
not far from you in all we are
  and all we do.

5

All you have made is ours to rule,
  the birds and beasts at will to tame,
all things to order for the glory‿
  of your name.

BRIAN FOLEY (b. 1919)
Psalm 8

532 (MHT **199**)
Lasst uns erfreuen
8 8.4 4.8 8. and Alleluias

Geistliche Kirchengesang
(Cologne, 1623)
arr. R. Vaughan Williams (1872–1958)

Al - le - lu - ia.
Al - le - lu - ia, Al - le - lu - ia, Al - le -
- lu - ia, Al - le - lu - ia, Al - le - lu - ia.

The AMR version of this tune is at 98

With angels and archangels

Ye watchers and ye holy ones,
bright Seraphs, Cherubim and Thrones,
raise the glad strain, Alleluia.
Cry out, Dominions, Princedoms, Powers,
Virtues, Archangels, Angels' choirs,
Alleluia.

2

O higher than the Cherubim,
more glorious than the Seraphim,
lead their praises, Alleluia.
Thou Bearer of the eternal Word,
most gracious, magnify the Lord.
Alleluia.

3

Respond, ye souls in endless rest,
ye Patriarchs and Prophets blest,
Alleluia, alleluia.
Ye holy Twelve, ye Martyrs strong,
all Saints triumphant, raise the song
Alleluia.

4

O friends, in gladness let us sing,
supernal anthems echoing,
Alleluia, alleluia.
To God the Father, God the Son,
and God the Spirit, Three in One,
Alleluia.

ATHELSTAN RILEY (1858–1945)

533 (MHT 200)

Palace Green 8 7.8 7.8 8 7. Michael Fleming (b. 1928

Alternative Tune: *Luther's Hymn* (193)

Christ in glory

You, living Christ, our eyes behold,
  amid your Church appearing,
all girt about your breast with gold
  and bright apparel wearing;
your countenance is burning bright,
a sun resplendent in its might:
  Lord Christ, we see your glory.

2

Your glorious feet have sought and found
  your sons of every nation;
with everlasting voice you sound‿
  the call of our salvation;
your eyes of flame still search and scan‿
the whole outspreading realm of man:
  Lord Christ, we see your glory.

3

O risen Christ, today alive,
  amid your Church abiding,
who now your blood and body give,
  new life and strength providing,
we join in heavenly company
to sing your praise triumphantly,
  for we have seen your glory.

E. R. MORGAN (1888–1979)
Revelation 1. 12–16

INDEXES

HYMNS FOR SUNDAY THEMES IN THE NEW LECTIONARY

9 BEFORE CHRISTMAS

The Creation

All creatures of our God and King 105
All things bright and beautiful 116
Eternal Ruler 353
For the beauty of the earth 104
For the fruits of his creation 457
God of concrete 366
God who spoke in the beginning 468
God, you have given us power 469
Let us with a gladsome mind 204
Lord of the boundless curves of space 493
Nature with open volume lies 497
O Lord of every shining constellation 411
O worship the King 101
Praise the Lord! Ye heavens adore him 195
Songs of praise the angels sang 196
The spacious firmament on high 103
Thou whose almighty word 180
With wonder, Lord, we see your works 531

8 BEFORE CHRISTMAS

The Fall

Creator of the earth and skies 351
Father of heaven, whose love profound 97
Glory be to Jesus 66
God who created this Eden of earth 369
In Adam we have all been one 474
Just as I am 246
Lord God, your love has called us here 489
Nature with open volume stands 497
O God of truth, whose living word 222
Praise to the Holiest 117
Sing, my tongue, the glorious battle 59
The God who rules this earth 425
Walking in a garden 518
We turn to you, O God of every nation 522
What Adam's disobedience cost 524

7 BEFORE CHRISTMAS

The Election of God's People: Abraham

Awake, our souls 436
Be thou my vision 343
Children of the heavenly King 213
Father, hear the prayer we offer 113
Forth in the peace of Christ we go 458
Guide me, O thou great Redeemer 214
Have faith in God, my heart 372
Let every Christian pray 478
Lord God, thou art our maker 389
O God of Bethel 216

O raise your eyes on high 502
O thou who camest from above 233
Put thou thy trust in God 223
Rise up, O men of God 418
The God of Abraham praise 331
This day God gives me 516
Through the night of doubt and sorrow 211
We are your people 519
Who are we who stand and sing? 529
Who would true valour see 212

6 BEFORE CHRISTMAS

The Promise of Redemption: Moses

All my hope on God is founded 336
Bread of heaven 271
Come, ye faithful, raise the strain 76
Eternal Ruler 353
Father, we thank thee who hast planted 357
Guide me, O thou great Redeemer 214
Lord, enthroned in heavenly splendour 263
O God of Bethel 216
There is a land of pure delight 190
Through all the changing scenes of life 209
Through the night of doubt and sorrow 211

5 BEFORE CHRISTMAS

The Remnant of Israel

A safe stronghold 114
City of God 173
Dear Lord and Father of mankind 115
Guide me, O thou great Redeemer 214
Jesus, where'er thy people meet 162
Lead us, heavenly Father 224
O thou not made with hands 174
Oft in danger, oft in woe 210
Praise the Lord, rise up rejoicing 416
The Church's one foundation 170
Through the night of doubt and sorrow 211
Thy hand, O God, has guided 171
Who would true valour see 212

ADVENT 1

The Advent Hope

Awake, awake, fling off the night 342
Christ is the world's true light 346
Come, thou long-expected Jesus 31
Hail to the Lord's Anointed 142
Hark! a thrilling voice is sounding 24
Hark the glad sound 30
Hills of the north 470
Jesus shall reign 143
Lift up your heads, you mighty gates 483
Lo, he comes with clouds descending 28
Lord, save thy world 397
O Day of God, draw nigh 405
Sleepers, wake! 32
Soldiers of Christ, arise 219
The advent of our King 25
The Lord will come, and not be slow 29
Thy kingdom come, O God 177
Thy kingdom come; on bended knee 178
When I needed a neighbour 433

ADVENT 2

The Word of God in the Old Testament

Christians, lift up your hearts 446
Come, Holy Ghost, our hearts inspire 448
Father of mercies, in thy word 167
God who hast caused thy word to be written 467
God, who spoke in the beginning 468
Hark the glad sound 30
Help us, O Lord, to learn 373
How beauteous are their feet 301
Long ago prophets knew 484
Lord, be thy word my rule 232
Lord, I have made thy word my choice 490
Lord Jesus Christ, be present now 491
Lord, thy word abideth 166
Not far beyond the sea 401
O Day of God, draw nigh 405
Rise and hear, the Lord is speaking 509
Thanks to God whose word was spoken 423
The prophets spoke in days of old 513
Thou whose almighty word 180

ADVENT 3

The Forerunner

Awake, awake, fling off the night 342
Christ is the world's true light 346
Hark! a thrilling voice is sounding 24
Help us, O Lord, to learn 373
Lo, from the desert homes 316
Lo, in the wilderness a voice 384
On Jordan's bank 27
Rejoice! the Lord is King 139
Sing we the praises of the great forerunner 315
The advent of our King 25

ADVENT 4

The Annunciation

Come, thou long-expected Jesus 31
For Mary, Mother of our Lord 360
Hark the glad sound 30
Her Virgin eyes saw God incarnate born 310
Jerusalem the golden 184
Long ago prophets knew 484
Love divine, all loves excelling 131
O come, O come, Emmanuel 26
O Holy City, seen of John 409
O what their joy 186
Sing we a song of high revolt 419
Tell out, my soul 422
The God whom earth and sea and sky 309
Thy kingdom come; on bended knee 178
To the name of our salvation 121
Virgin-born, we bow before thee 311
Ye watchers and ye holy ones 532

CHRISTMAS 1

Year 1: The Incarnation

A great and mighty wonder 43
Angels, from the realms of glory 39
Behold, the great Creator makes 44
'Glory to God': all heaven with joy is ringing 462
God from on high hath heard 38
God who spoke in the beginning 468
Hills of the North 470

In humble gratitude, O God 377
Long ago prophets knew 484
Lord Jesus Christ, you have come to us 391
Lord that descendedst, Holy Child 398
Of the Father's love begotten 33
Son of God, eternal Saviour 132
The great Creator of the worlds 511
To us a Child of royal birth 45
Where is this stupendous stranger? 527

Year 2: The Presentation

Faithful vigil ended 453
Hail to the Lord who comes 314
Take my life 249
For Year Two see also Pentecost 18 (The Offering of Life)

CHRISTMAS 2

Year 1: The Holy Family

Filled with the Spirit's power 359
I come with joy 473
Life is great 482
Lift up your heads, you mighty gates 483
Lord of all hopefulness 394
Lord of the home, your only Son 494
O God in heaven, whose loving plan 407
Once in royal David's city 46
Our Father, by whose name 505
The heavenly Child in stature grows 50

Year 2: Light of the World

As with gladness 51
Awake, awake, fling off the night 342
Brightest and best 47
Can man by searching 438
Christ is the world's light 440
Christ is the world's true light 346
Earth has many a noble city 48
From the eastern mountains 327
Glorious things 172
Hail to the Lord's Anointed 142
Lord, we are blind 399
O worship the Lord 49
The people that in darkness sat 52
Thou whose almighty word 180

EPIPHANY 1

Revelation: The Baptism of Jesus

Awake, awake, fling off the night 342
Be thou my vision 343
Christ, when for us you were baptized 442
Christians, lift up your hearts 444, 445, 446
Come, Lord, to our souls 348
Hail to the Lord's Anointed 142
In Christ there is no east or west 376
Now is eternal life 402
O love, how deep 119
Praise and thanksgiving 506
Songs of thankfulness 53
When Jesus came to Jordan 526

EPIPHANY 2

Revelation: The First Disciples

Dear Lord and Father of mankind 115
Disposer supreme 298
Firmly I believe and truly 118
Jesus calls us 312
Jesus our Lord, our King and our God 382
Jesus, where'er thy people meet 162
Lord, as I wake I turn to you 485

Lord Jesus, once you spoke to men 392
Lead us, heavenly Father 224
O Jesus, I have promised 235
O thou who camest from above 233
Take my life 249
Take up thy cross 237
The eternal gifts of Christ the King 297
We are your people 519
Who are we who stand and sing? 529

EPIPHANY 3

Revelation: Signs of Glory

Author of life divine 258
Awake, awake, fling off the night 342
Bread of heaven 271
Can man by searching 438
Christians, lift up your hearts 444, 445, 446
Christ is the heavenly food 439
Christ is the world's light 440
Christ upon the mountain peak 441
God of concrete 366
Guide me, O thou great Redeemer 214
Holy, holy, holy 95
Lord, enthroned in heavenly splendour 263
May the grace of Christ our Saviour 181
Songs of thankfulness and praise 53
Tell out, my soul 422

EPIPHANY 4

Revelation: The New Temple

All my hope on God is founded 336
Blessed City, heavenly Salem 283, 332
Blest are the pure in heart 238
Christ is our corner-stone 161
Christians, lift up your hearts 444, 445, 446
Glorious things 172
Good is our God 371
Jerusalem, my happy home 187
Jesus, where'er thy people meet 162
Lord of the worlds above 165
Love divine, all loves excelling 131
O thou not made with hands 174
The Church's one foundation 170
Where high the heavenly temple stands 130

EPIPHANY 5

Revelation: The Wisdom of God

Be thou my vision 343
Can man by searching 438
God moves in a mysterious way 112
God, you have given us power 469
Immortal, invisible God 199
Lord of the boundless curves 493
Nature with open volume stands 497
O Lord of every shining constellation 411
Praise to the Holiest 117
Put thou thy trust in God 223
'The Kingdom is upon you!' 512
The spacious firmament 103
This day God gives me 516
Thou whose almighty word 180
With wonder, Lord, we see your works 531

EPIPHANY 6

Revelation: Parables

Christians, lift up your hearts 444, 445, 446
Come, Lord, to our souls 348
Happy are they 176
Help us, O Lord, to learn 373
Lord Jesus, once you spoke 392
Not far beyond the sea 401
O God of truth, whose living word 222
Rise and hear, the Lord is speaking 509
The prophets spoke in days of old 513

9 BEFORE EASTER

Christ the Teacher

Blest are the pure in heart 238
Can man by searching 438
Father of mercies, in thy word 167
Fight the good fight 220
Help us, O Lord, to learn 373
Lord, I have made thy word my choice 490
Lord Jesus, once you spoke 392
Lord, thy word abideth 166
Praise we now the word of grace 417
'The Kingdom is upon you!' 512
The prophets spoke in days of old 513
Thou art the way 128
Through all the changing scenes 209
Who would true valour see 212

8 BEFORE EASTER

Christ the Healer

A man there lived in Galilee 334
A stranger once did bless the earth 335
And didst thou travel light 339
As pants the hart 226
At even, ere the sun was set 9
Dear Lord and Father of mankind 115
For the healing of the nations 361
From thee all skill and science flow 286
How sweet the name of Jesus sounds 122
Immortal love 133
Just as I am 246
Lord Christ, who on thy heart didst bear 388
Lord of all, to whom alone 492
Morning glory, starlit sky 496
O for a thousand tongues 125
O God, by whose almighty plan 406
O God, whose will is life 408
Praise, my soul, the King of heaven 192
Sing praise to God 193
There in God's garden 514
Thine arm, O Lord 285
When I needed a neighbour 433
With joy we meditate the grace 530

7 BEFORE EASTER

Jesus, Friend of Sinners

All ye who seek for sure relief 64
Forgive our sins as we forgive 362
God is love: let heaven adore him 365
How sweet the name of Jesus sounds 122
I come with joy to meet my Lord 473
I heard the voice of Jesus say 247
Jesu, lover of my soul 123
Jesus, whose all-redeeming love 383
Just as I am 246

LENT 1 (Ash Wednesday)

The King and the Kingdom: Temptation

LENT 2

The King and the Kingdom: Conflict

LENT 3

The King and the Kingdom: Suffering

Lord Christ, who on thy heart didst bear 388
Now join we, to praise our Creator 500
O happy band of pilgrims 208
O God of Bethel 216
Praise to the Holiest 117
Rock of Ages 135
Sometimes a light surprises 108
Souls of men! why will ye scatter 251
Take up thy cross 237
The head that once was crowned 141
Through all the changing scenes 209
When I needed a neighbour 433

LENT 4

The King and the Kingdom: Transfiguration

Christ is the world's true light 346
Christ upon the mountain peak 441
Christ whose glory fills the skies 4
From glory to glory advancing 276
Light's abode 185
Lord, as we rise 385
Love divine, all loves excelling 131
O raise your eyes on high 502
'Tis good, Lord, to be here 318

Mothering Sunday

For Mary, Mother of the Lord 360
For the beauty of the earth 104
Happy are they 176
Her virgin eyes saw God incarnate born 310
I come with joy to meet my Lord 473
Jesus, where'er thy people meet 162
Life is great 482
Lift up your heads, you mighty gates 483
Lord of all hopefulness 394
Lord of the home 494
O God in heaven, whose loving plan 407
Our Father, by whose name 505

LENT 5

The King and the Kingdom: The Victory of the Cross

A man there lived in Galilee 334
All ye who seek 64
As Jacob with travel was weary 435
Glory be to Jesus 66
It is a thing most wonderful 70
Lift high the Cross 72
My song is love unknown 63
O sacred head 68
Once, only once 261
Praise to the Holiest 117
Sing, my tongue, the glorious battle 59
Take up thy cross 237
The head that once 141
The royal banners forward go 58
We sing the praise 138
When I survey 67

PALM SUNDAY

The Way of the Cross

All glory, laud and honour 60, 328
All praise to thee 337
At the name of Jesus 148
Glory be to Jesus 66
Just as I am 246
Lord Christ, we praise your sacrifice 487
My God, I love thee, not because 65
My song is love unknown 63
Nature with open volume lies 497
O sacred head 68
Peter feared the Cross 414
Praise to the Holiest 117

Ride on, ride on in majesty 61
Ride on triumphantly 62
Sing, my tongue, the glorious battle 59
The heavenly Word, proceeding forth 253
Thee we adore, O hidden Saviour 254
The royal banners forward go 58
There is a green hill 137
To mock your reign, O dearest Lord 517
We sing the praise 138
Were you there 523
When I survey 67

EASTER DAY

At the Lamb's high feast 81
Away with gloom 437
Christ the Lord is risen again 79
Christian people, raise your song 443
Come, let us with our Lord arise 449
Early morning. 'Come, prepare him' 451
Finished the strife 455
Good Christian men, rejoice and sing 85
Jesus Christ is risen today 77
Light's glittering morn 329
Now is eternal life 402
Now the green blade riseth 501
The day of resurrection 75
The first day of the week 424
The Lord is risen indeed 84
The strife is o'er 78
Thine be the glory 428
Walking in a garden 518
Ye choirs of new Jerusalem 73

EASTER 1

Year 1: The Upper Room

Breathe on me, Breath of God 157
Christ the Lord is risen again 79
Come, risen Lord, and deign to be our guest 349
Come, ye faithful, raise the anthem 145
Come, ye faithful, raise the strain 76
Jesus lives! 82
Jesus, these eyes have never seen 245
Light's glittering morn 329
Love's redeeming work is done 83
O holy Father, God most dear 410
O Lord, we long to see your face 412
O sons and daughters, let us sing 74
The day of resurrection 75
The first day of the week 424
The Lord is risen indeed 84
The strife is o'er 78
Thee we adore 254

Year 2: The Bread of Life

Alleluia, hearts to heaven 80
As the disciples, when thy Son had left them 341
At the Lamb's high feast 81
Bread of heaven 271
Bread of the world 270
Christ is the heavenly food 439
Christian people, raise your song 443
Father, we thank thee who hast planted 357
God everlasting, wonderful and holy 463
Guide me, O thou great Redeemer 214
Jesus lives! 82
Jesus, we thus obey 477
Let us break bread together 480
Lord, enthroned in heavenly splendour 263
O holy Father, God most dear 410

EASTER 2

Year 1: The Emmaus Road

Abide with me 13
Come, risen Lord, and deign to be our guest 349
I come with joy to meet my Lord 473
Lord, enthroned in heavenly splendour 263
The Lord is risen indeed 84
This is the day the Lord hath made 22
We have a gospel 431
Ye choirs of new Jerusalem 73

Year 2: The Good Shepherd

Christ who knows all his sheep 347
In Adam we have all been one 474
Jesus our Lord, our king and our God 382
Jesus, where'er thy people meet 162
Praise the Lord, rise up rejoicing 416
The God of love 110
The King of love 126
The Lord my pasture shall prepare 111
Thine for ever 234

EASTER 3

Year 1: The Lakeside

Alleluia, hearts to heaven 80
Alleluia, sing to Jesus 262
Come, let us with our Lord arise 449
Dear Lord and Father of mankind 115
Light's glittering morn 329
Love's redeeming work is done 83
Now the green blade riseth 501
The Son of God proclaim 427
Thine be the glory 428
We have a gospel 431
You, living Christ, our eyes behold 533

Year 2: The Resurrection and the Life

Awake, awake, fling off the night 342
Away with gloom 437
Come, let us with our Lord arise 449
Good Christian men, rejoice and sing 85
Jesus lives! 82
Jesus, my Lord, let me be near you 476
Let saints on earth in concert sing 182
Now is eternal life 402
There in God's garden 514
Thou art the Way 128

EASTER 4

Year 1: The Charge to Peter

Christ is the King 345
Forth in the peace of Christ 458
Hark, my soul: it is the Lord 244
O Jesus, I have promised 235
Rise and hear, the Lord is speaking 509

Year 2: The Way, the Truth, and the Life

Jerusalem the golden 184
Light's abode 185
My soul, there is a country 191
O what their joy 186
Sing Alleluia forth 188
There is a land of pure delight 190
Thine for ever 234
Thou art the Way 128

EASTER 5

Going to the Father

Alleluia, hearts to heaven 80
Give to our God immortal praise 460
Have faith in God 372
Immortal, invisible 199
Jesus lives! 82
Now is eternal life 402

ASCENSION

A man there lived in Galilee 334
All hail the power 140
Alleluia, sing to Jesus 262
At the name of Jesus 148
Come let us join our cheerful songs 144
Come, ye faithful, raise the anthem 145
Crown him with many crowns 147
Give to our God immortal praise 460
Hail to the Lord's Anointed 142
Hail the day that sees him rise 87
Immortal, invisible God 199
Jesu, our hope 86
Jesus shall reign 143
King of glory 194
Lift high the Cross 72
'Lift up your hearts!' We lift them 241
New songs of celebration render 498
Rejoice, the Lord is King 139
See the Conqueror mounts 88
The head that once was crowned 141
We have a gospel 431
Where high the heavenly temple 130
With joy we meditate 530
Ye servants of God 149
You, living Christ 533

PENTECOST

Breathe on me, Breath of God 157
Christians, lift up your hearts 444, 445, 446
Come down, O Love divine 156
Come, gracious Spirit 153
Come, Holy Ghost, our hearts inspire 448
Come, Holy Ghost, our souls inspire 93
Come, thou Holy Spirit, come 92
Eternal Ruler 353
Father, Lord of all creation 356
Filled with the Spirit's power 359
Gracious Spirit, Holy Ghost 154
Holy Spirit, come, confirm us 471
Let every Christian pray 478
Love of the Father 159
O Holy Ghost, thy people bless 155
O Holy Spirit, Lord of grace 152
O King enthroned on high 158
Of all the Spirit's gifts to me 503
On the day of Pentecost 504
Our blest Redeemer 151
Our Lord, his Passion ended 91
Spirit of mercy 89
There's a spirit in the air 515
When God of old 90
When Jesus came to Jordan 526

PENTECOST 1

Trinity Sunday

All my hope 336
Angel-voices ever singing 163
Eternal Ruler 353
Father all-loving 355 (2)
Father all-powerful 355 (1)
Father, Lord of all creation 356
Father most holy 94
Father of heaven 97
Holy, holy, holy 95
How shall I sing that majesty 472

Lord of the boundless curves 493
May the grace of Christ 181
My God, how wonderful thou art 102
O God, by whose almighty plan 406
O worship the King 101
Stand up and bless the Lord 201
This day God gives me 516
We give immortal praise 520
Ye watchers and ye holy ones 532

PENTECOST 2

Year 1: The People of God
Year 2: The Church's Unity and Fellowship
(*Many of the hymns suggested are interchangeable*)

Christ is our corner-stone 161
Christ is the heavenly food 439
Christ is the King 345
Christ is the world's true light 346
Christians, lift up your hearts 444, 445, 446
City of God 173
Come, risen Lord 349
Eternal Ruler 353
Father, Lord of all creation 356
Father, we thank thee who hast planted 357
Filled with the Spirit's power 359
Forth in the peace of Christ 458
God is here; as we his people 464
God is love, and where true love is 465
He wants not friends 183
Help us to help each other 374
I come with joy 473
In Christ there is no east 376
Jesus, Lord, we look to thee 380
Let every Christian pray 478
Let saints on earth 182
Let us talents and tongues employ 481
Lord Christ, the Father's mighty Son 386
Lord of lords and King eternal 396
May the grace of Christ 181
O thou who at thy Eucharist 265
The Church of God a Kingdom is 169
The Church's one foundation 170
Through the night of doubt 211
Thy hand, O God 171
We are your people 519
Where love and loving-kindness dwell 528
Who are we who stand and sing? 529
Ye that know the Lord is gracious 175

PENTECOST 3

Year 1: The Life of the Baptized

Alleluia, hearts to heaven 80
Awake, awake, fling off the night 342
Be thou my vision 343
Breathe on me, Breath of God 157
Christ, when for us you were baptized 442
Christians, lift up your hearts 444, 445, 446
Help us to help each other 374
Holy Spirit, come, confirm us 471
In Christ there is no east 376
Jesus, my Lord, let me be with you 476
Love divine 131
My God, accept my heart 279
Now is eternal life 402
O Jesus, I have promised 235
'The Kingdom is upon you'! 512
This day God gives me 516
We are your people 519
When Jesus came to Jordan 526

Year 2: The Church's Confidence in Christ

A Man there lived in Galilee 334
All my hope in God is founded 336
At the name of Jesus 148
Christ is our corner-stone 161
Christ is the world's light 440
Christian, dost thou see them 55
Christians, lift up your hearts 444, 445, 446
Fierce raged the tempest 225
How sweet the name 122
Let all the world 202
Lift high the Cross 72
Lord, be thy word my rule 232
O for a thousand tongues 125
Onward, Christian soldiers 333
Soldiers of Christ, arise 219
Tell out, my soul 422
The head that once was crowned 141
To the name of our salvation 121
We have a gospel 431
Where high the heavenly temple stands 130
Ye servants of God 149

PENTECOST 4

Year 1: The Freedom of the Sons of God

All my hope on God is founded 336
Christ is the world's true light 346
Christ who knows all his sheep 347
In Christ there is no east 376
Jesus, Lord, we look to thee 380
Lead us, heavenly Father 224
Lord God, your love has called us 489
Lord of all hopefulness 394
O for a heart to praise 230
O for a thousand tongues 125
The God who rules this earth 425
Thine for ever 234
When Christ was lifted 525
Ye that know the Lord is gracious 175

Year 2: The Church's Mission to the Individual

All ye who seek for sure relief 64
Come, O thou Traveller 243
Hark, my soul, it is the Lord 244
Help us to help each other 374
I heard the voice of Jesus 247
Jesus, my Lord, let me be with you 476
Just as I am 246
Lord, as I wake 485
Loving Shepherd 134
Take my life 249
The God of love 110
The King of love 126
The Lord my pasture 111
Thou didst leave thy throne 250

PENTECOST 5

Year 1: The New Law

Awake, awake, fling off the night 342
Awake, my soul 1
Blest are the pure in heart 238
Christ, when for us you were baptized 442
Eternal Ruler 353
God, who hast caused to be written 467
Gracious Spirit, Holy Ghost 154
O God of truth, whose living word 222
Of all the Spirit's gifts to me 503
Rise and hear, the Lord is speaking 509
Thou art the Way 128

Year 2: The Church's Mission to all Men

Christ for the world 344
Christ is the world's true light 346
Father all-loving 355(ii)
Father all-powerful 355(i)
Filled with the Spirit's power 359
Forth in the peace of Christ 458
In Christ there is no east 376
Let every Christian pray 478
Let us talents and tongues employ 481
Lord of lords 396
We are your people 519
We have a gospel 431
When Christ was lifted 525
Who are we 529

PENTECOST 6

The New Man

Awake, awake, fling off the night 342
Breathe on me, Breath of God 157
Christ is the world's light 440
Christian people, raise your song 443
Come down, O Love divine 156
Come, let us with our Lord arise 449
Eternal Ruler 353
Forth in the peace of Christ 458
Give me joy in my heart 459
I heard the voice of Jesus 247
Immortal love 133
Jesus, my Lord, let me be with you 476
Jesus, Lord, we look to thee 380
Just as I am 246
Lord God, your love has called us 489
Lord, we are blind 399
Now is eternal life 402
O for a closer walk 231
O for a heart to praise 230
O Holy Spirit, Lord of grace 152
Praise, my soul, the King of heaven 192
There in God's garden 514
You, living Christ 533

PENTECOST 7

The More Excellent Way

Almighty Father, who for us 338
Come down, O Love divine 156
Filled with the Spirit's power 359
For the healing of the nations 361
Forgive our sins 362
God is love, and where true love is 465
Gracious Spirit, Holy Ghost 154
Happy are they 176
Help us to help each other 374
In humble gratitude 377
Jesus, my Lord, how rich 381
Lord Christ, who on thy heart 388
Lord, to you we bring our treasure 495
Love divine 131
O for a heart 230
O Holy Ghost, thy people bless 155
O Holy Spirit, Lord of grace 152
O Love divine, how sweet 124
Of all the Spirit's gifts 503
Strengthen for service 421
What does the Lord require 432
When I needed a neighbour 433
Where love and loving-kindness dwell 528

PENTECOST 8

The Fruit of the Spirit

Breathe on me, Breath of God 157
Christians, lift up your hearts 444, 445, 446
Come down, O Love divine 156
Come, gracious Spirit 153

Come, thou Holy Spirit 92
Eternal Ruler 353
Filled with the Spirit's power 359
Give me joy in my heart 459
Gracious Spirit, Holy Ghost 154
Holy Spirit, come, confirm us 471
Let every Christian pray 478
Love divine 131
O Holy Ghost, thy people bless 155
O Holy Spirit, Lord of grace 152
Of all the Spirit's gifts 503
On the day of Pentecost 504
Our blest Redeemer 151
There's a spirit in the air 515
When Jesus came to Jordan 526

PENTECOST 9

The Whole Armour of God

Be thou my vision 343
Christian, dost thou see them 55
Eternal Ruler 353
Father, hear the prayer 113
Fight the good fight 220
God of grace and God of glory 367
Oft in danger, oft in woe 210
O God of truth, whose living word 222
Onward, Christian soldiers 333
Put thou thy trust 223
Soldiers of Christ, arise 219
Soldiers who are Christ's below 302
Stand up, stand up for Jesus 221
This day God gives me 516
Who would true valour see 212

PENTECOST 10

The Mind of Christ

All praise to thee 337
Blest are the pure in heart 238
Come down, O Love divine 156
Filled with the Spirit's power 359
Forgive our sins 362
Help us to help each other 374
Jesus, Lord, we look to thee 380
Lord God, your love has called us 489
O for a heart 230
Son of God, eternal Saviour 132
We are your people 519

PENTECOST 11

The Serving Community

Almighty Father, who for us 338
An upper room 434
For the healing of the nations 361
Forth in the peace of Christ 458
Help us to help each other 374
Jesus, my Lord, how rich thy grace 381
Lord, as we rise 385
Lord Christ, who on thy heart 388
Lord, to you we bring our treasure 495
Now let us from this table 403
Praise and thanksgiving be to our Creator 506
Rise up, O men of God 418
Son of God, eternal Saviour 132
Strengthen for service 421
When I needed a neighbour 433
Where love and loving-kindness dwell 528

PENTECOST 12

The Witnessing Community

Captains of the saintly band 299
Christ is the King 345
Christ is the world's true light 346
For all the saints 305
Forth in the peace of Christ 458
Give me joy in my heart 459
God of mercy, God of grace 179
I come with joy 473
Let every Christian pray 478
Let us talents and tongues employ 481

Lift high the Cross 72
Lord Christ, the Father's mighty Son 386
O thou who camest 233
Tell out, my soul 422
We are your people 519
We have a gospel 431
Who are we 529
Ye servants of God 149

PENTECOST 13

The Suffering Community

A safe stronghold 114
All ye who seek 64
Be thou my guardian 217
Fight the good fight 220
God moves in a mysterious way 112
Happy are they 176
Jesu, grant me this 136
Lead us, heavenly Father 224
Now thank we all our God 205
O God of Bethel 216
Oft in danger, oft in woe 210
Sing praise to God 193
Sometimes a light surprises 108
The Church's one foundation 170
The Lord is King 107
Through all the changing scenes 209
Thy Kingdom come, O God 177

PENTECOST 14

The Family

For the beauty of the earth 104
God of love and truth 368
I come with joy 473
Jesus, where'er thy people meet 162
Lead us, heavenly Father 224
Life is great 482
Lift up your heads, you mighty gates 483
Lord of all hopefulness 394
Lord of the home 494
May the grace of Christ 181
Now thank we all our God 205
O God in heaven 407
O Holy Spirit, Lord of grace 152
O Lord of heaven and earth 287
O love, how deep 119
Our Father, by whose name 505
Praise, my soul 192
Through all the changing scenes 209

PENTECOST 15

Those in Authority

And did those feet 294
Christ is the world's true light 346
Eternal Ruler 353
Father all-loving 355 (2)
For the healing of the nations 361
God of love and truth 368
I vow to thee, my country 295
Lift up your heads, you mighty gates 483
Lord of lords 396
O Day of God, draw nigh 405
Rejoice, O land 296
Rise up, O men of God 418
The Lord will come 29
To thee, our God, we fly 330
We turn to you, O God 522
What does the Lord require 432
Ye servants of the Lord 150
Ye that know the Lord is gracious 175

PENTECOST 16

The Neighbour

Almighty Father, who for us 338
For the fruits of his creation 457
For the healing of the nations 361
God is love, and where true love is 465
Gracious Spirit, Holy Ghost 154
Help us to help each other 374

I come with joy 473
In humble gratitude, O God 377
Jesus, Lord, we look to thee 380
Jesus, my Lord, how rich thy grace 381
Lord, as we rise 385
Lord Christ, who on thy heart 388
Lord, save thy world 397
Lord, to you we bring 495
Now join we 500
Sing we a song of high revolt 419
Son of God, eternal Saviour 132
The God who rules this earth 425
We find thee, Lord, in others' need 430
What does the Lord require 432
When I needed a neighbour 433
Where love and loving-kindness dwell 528

PENTECOST 17

The Proof of Faith

A safe stronghold 114
As Jacob with travel 435
Awake, our souls 436
Be thou my vision 343
Fill thou my life 200
Firmly I believe and truly 118
God of grace 367
Happy are they 176
Have faith in God 372
Jesu, thou joy 255
New every morning 2
Now let us from this table rise 403
O Lord, we long to see 412
Put thou thy trust in God 223
Sent forth by God's blessing 510
Son of God, eternal Saviour 132
This day God gives me 516

PENTECOST 18

The Offering of Life

Almighty Father, Lord most high 267
Fill thou my life 200
For the bread which you have broken 456
Forth in thy name 239
Give me joy in my heart 459
God is here; as we his people 464
Lord, as I wake 485
My Father, for another night 3
My God, accept my heart 279
Now from the altar of our hearts 499
Now let us from this table rise 403
O Jesus, I have promised 235
Sent forth by God's blessing 510
Son of God, eternal Saviour 132
Take my life 249
Take up thy cross 237
Teach me, my God and King 240
We are your people 519
When I survey 67
Who are we 529
In Subject Index to Supplements see DEDICATION, HOLY COMMUNION (*At the Offertory* and *After Communion*) and WORSHIP AND LIFE

PENTECOST 19

The Life of Faith

As Jacob with travel 435
Awake, our souls 436
Be thou my vision 343
Give us the wings of faith 324
God be in my head 236
Help us, O Lord, to learn 373
How sweet the name 122
Jesu, lover of my soul 123
Jesu, thou joy 255
Just as I am 246
Lord, teach us how to pray 227
O for a closer walk 231
O for a thousand tongues 125
O God of Bethel 216
O Lord of every shining constellation 411

O Love divine 124
Put thou thy trust in God 223
Rock of Ages 135
Sent forth by God's blessing 510
Stand up and bless 201
The God of Abraham praise 331
This day God gives me 516
Through all the changing scenes 209

PENTECOST 20

Endurance

A safe stronghold 114
Awake, our souls 436
Be thou my guardian 217
Children of the heavenly King 213
Come, O thou Traveller 243
Father, hear the prayer 113
Fight the good fight 220
God of grace and God of glory 367
Guide me, O thou great Redeemer 214
Have faith in God 372
Jesus, good above all other 378
Lead, kindly Light 215
Lord, teach us how to pray 227
O God of Bethel 216
O God of truth 222
O happy band of pilgrims 208
O thou who camest 233
Oft in danger, oft in woe 210
Soldiers of Christ, arise 219
Take up thy cross 237
Through all the changing scenes 209
Who would true valour see 212

PENTECOST 21

The Christian Hope

All my hope on God is founded 336
As Jacob with travel 435
As pants the hart 226
Christ is the world's light 440
Christ who knows 347
Come, let us with our Lord arise 449
Faithful vigil ended 453
Father, we thank you 454
Finished the strife 455
Give to our God 460
Hail to the Lord's Anointed 142
Jesu, the very thought 120
Jesus lives! 82
Lord God, thou art our maker 389
Love's redeeming work 83
Not far beyond the sea 401
Now is eternal life 402
O God, our help 99
Praise the Lord! ye heavens 195
Put thou thy trust 223
Sometimes a light surprises 108
The King of love 126
The Lord my pasture 111
Thine be the glory 428
Through the night of doubt 211
Ye that know the Lord is gracious 175

PENTECOST 22

The Two Ways

Be thou my guardian 217
Be thou my vision 343
Christ, whose glory 4
Christian, dost thou see them 55
Eternal Ruler 353
God of grace and God of glory 367
God of love and truth 368
Lead, kindly Light 215
Lord, be thy word my rule 232
Lord, I have made thy word 490
Lord of all power 395
My God, accept my heart 279
O for a closer walk 231
O Jesus, I have promised 235
O King enthroned on high 158
O thou who camest 233
Stand up for Jesus 221
Take my life 249

The Lord is King 107
Who would true valour see 212

LAST SUNDAY AFTER PENTECOST

Citizens of Heaven

As Jacob with travel 435
Bright the vision 96
Children of the heavenly King 213
Christ is our corner-stone 161
Come, let us join our cheerful songs 144
Give us the wings of faith 324
Holy, holy, holy 95
How bright these glorious spirits shine 306
How shall I sing 472
Jerusalem, my happy home 187
Jerusalem the golden 184
Light's abode 185
Lo, round the throne 303
Lord God, we give you thanks 48
My God, how wonderful 102
Now is eternal life 402
O heavenly Jerusalem 322
O what their joy 186
Palms of glory 307
Sing Alleluia forth 188
Ten thousand times 189
There is a land 190
Through the night of doubt 211
Ye holy angels bright 198
Ye servants of God 149
Ye servants of the Lord 150
Ye watchers and ye holy ones 53

SUBJECT INDEX TO THE SUPPLEMENTS (HYMNS 334–533)

(*These hymns are arranged alphabetically*)

BAPTISM

CHURCH OF GOD, THE

Its Mission

Its Unity

CREATION

DEDICATION

Subject Index to the Supplements

Subject Index to the Supplements

Subject Index to the Supplements

RACE RELATIONS

SAINTS

SCIENCE

SERVICE OF OTHERS

SUNDAY

THANKSGIVING

TRINITY, THE HOLY

WHOLENESS

WORLD PEACE

WORSHIP AND LIFE

ADDITIONAL HYMNS FOR VARIOUS TIMES AND SEASONS

(These hymns are arranged under Subjects: this Index gives additional classification. For Subject Index to the Supplements see page xxxvii)

Additional Hymns for Various Times and Seasons

EASTER

Come, ye faithful, raise the anthem 145
Light's abode, celestial Salem 185
Light's glittering morn 329
In Subject Index to Supplements see
JESUS CHRIST, *Crucified and risen, King, His life, death, and glory, New life in him, His shame and glory*
PRAISE
SUNDAY

ROGATION

God of mercy, God of grace 179
Lord, teach us how to pray aright 227
O God of Bethel, by whose hand 216
Rejoice, O land 296
To thee, our God we fly 330
In Subject Index to Supplements see
CREATION
GOD, *Creator*
NATIONAL
WORSHIP AND LIFE

ASCENSION

Where high the heavenly temple stands 130
JESUS: HIS POWER AND GLORY 139–149
In Subject Index to Supplements see
JESUS CHRIST, *Following him, Hope of the world, His shame and glory*

WHITSUN

THE HOLY SPIRIT 151–159
In Subject Index to Supplements see
CHURCH OF GOD
HOLY SPIRIT

THE ETERNAL GOD

The God of Abraham praise 331
In Subject Index to Supplements see
GOD, *His glory, His majesty*
PRAISE
TRINITY, THE HOLY

HOLY COMMUNION

To us a Child of royal birth 45
In Subject Index to Supplements see
HOLY COMMUNION

HOLY BAPTISM

Alleluia, Alleluia, hearts to heaven 80
Come, ye faithful, raise the strain 76
Fill thou my life 200
Love divine, all loves excelling 131
Loving Shepherd of thy sheep 134
THE HOLY SPIRIT 151–159
THE CHURCH AND THE KINGDOM 169–181
PILGRIMAGE 208–218
In Subject Index to Supplements see
BAPTISM
CHURCH OF GOD
DEDICATION
HOLY SPIRIT
HOME LIFE AND FAMILY
JESUS CHRIST, *His baptism*

CONFIRMATION

WHITSUN 89–93
PILGRIMAGE 208–218
WARFARE 219–222
DEDICATION 230–241
In Subject Index to Supplements see
CHURCH OF GOD
DEDICATION
FAITH IN GOD

MARRIAGE

FUNERAL AND COMMEMORATION

ORDINATION

DEDICATION FESTIVAL

THE SICK

STEWARDSHIP

HARVEST

NATIONAL

THE PRESENTATION

THE ANNUNCIATION

ST. JOHN THE BAPTIST

MICHAELMAS

ALL SAINTS

INDEX OF FIRST LINES AND TUNES

Index of First Lines and Tunes

Index of First Lines and Tunes